Cognitive Behavioral Group Therapy

Cognitive Behavioral Group Therapy

Challenges and Opportunities

Ingrid Söchting

WILEY Blackwell

This edition first published 2014

Registered Office
John Wiley & Sons, Ltd, The Atrium, Southern Gate, Chichester, West Sussex, PO19 8SQ, UK

Editorial Offices
350 Main Street, Malden, MA 02148-5020, USA
9600 Garsington Road, Oxford, OX4 2DQ, UK
The Atrium, Southern Gate, Chichester, West Sussex, PO19 8SQ, UK

For details of our global editorial offices, for customer services, and for information about how to apply for permission to reuse the copyright material in this book please see our website at www.wiley.com/wiley-blackwell.

Library of Congress Cataloging-in-Publication Data

Söchting, Ingrid.
Cognitive behavioral group therapy : challenges and opportunities / Ingrid Söchting.
pages cm
Includes bibliographical references and index.
ISBN 978-1-118-51035-3 (cloth) – ISBN 978-1-118-51034-6 (pbk.) 1. Cognitive therapy.
2. Group psychotherapy. I. Title.
RC489.C63S63 2014
616.89′1425–dc23

2014005687

A catalogue record for this book is available from the British Library.

Cover image: Diana Ong, Masked emotion, 2006. © Diana Ong / SuperStock

Set in 10.5/13pt Minion by SPi Publisher Services, Pondicherry, India
Printed and bound in Malaysia by Vivar Printing Sdn Bhd

1 2014

Dedication

For my group therapy colleagues

Contents

About the Author

Ingrid Söchting is chief clinical psychologist in an outpatient mental health program and clinical assistant professor in the Department of Psychiatry at the University of British Columbia. Over the past 20 years, she has been instrumental in developing cognitive behavioral group therapy (CBGT) programs for depression, obsessive-compulsive disorder, generalized anxiety disorder, panic disorder, social anxiety disorder, and posttraumatic stress disorder, as well as interpersonal therapy (IPT) groups for later life depression. She supervises and teaches CBGT and IPT to psychology and psychiatry residents and is the codirector of the Richmond Psychotherapy Training Program. She has received several teaching excellence awards. She lectures and consults nationally and internationally. She is involved in group psychotherapy research and has published over 25 peer-reviewed journal articles and book chapters. She received her PhD in clinical psychology at Simon Fraser University, Vancouver, Canada, and trained at the University of British Columbia as an intern and postdoctoral fellow from 1994 to 1997 to become a CBT therapist. She is a Canadian certified CBT therapist and a Certified Group Therapist of the American Group Psychotherapy Association.

Acknowledgments

This book is the sum of many people's work. I have benefited from their teaching, supervision, consultation, group cofacilitation, research collaboration, and collegial inspiration.

This book is also written in gratitude to the hundreds, if not thousands, of group members in our program who trusted their facilitators and were therefore able to engage in challenging exposures and revisions of their previously held self-denigrating beliefs.

First and foremost, thanks to my team of exceptionally skilled and supportive outpatient mental health group program colleagues. They are, in alphabetical order: Ellen Abrams, clinical counselor; psychiatrist Jaswant Bhopal; Veronica Clifton, social worker; Lorna Clutterham, psychiatric nurse; Denise Coles, clinical counselor; Abi Dahi, psychiatrist; Heather Donaldson, psychiatrist; Maureen Edgar, counseling psychologist; Rosemary Messmer, clinical counselor; Jamal Mirmiran, psychiatrist; Erica O'Neal, psychiatrist; Sue Paul, rehabilitation assistant; Nicola Piggott, nurse; Dan Ring, recreational therapist; Petra Rutten, recreational therapist; Shelagh Smith, occupational therapist; Betty Third, occupational therapist; Darren Thompson, psychiatrist; and Tova Wolinsky, social worker. I also extend my appreciation to psychiatrists Harry Karlinsky, Raj Katta, Carolyn Steinberg, David Cohen and psychologists Timothy Crowell, Ingrid Fedoroff, and Suja Srikameswaran for their collegiality and cheerful support for this book.

Going back to an earlier era, I offer thanks to my graduate school supervisors and mentors James Marcia and Robert Ley, who provided rich teachings in psychodynamic theory, Erik Erikson's psychosocial developmental stages, and Carl Rogers's psychotherapy principles. Thanks to my first cognitive behavioral therapy (CBT) practicum supervisor, Georgia Nemetz, who continues to be a role model, and to my internship and postdoctoral CBT supervisors for their commitment to excellent supervision, teaching, and thoughtful applications of CBT: William Koch, the late Peter McLean, Randy Paterson, Charles Brasfield, and Lynn Alden.

Several people have kindly donated their time and mental energy to read some or all chapters. I am deeply thankful to psychiatry residents Margaret Wong,

John Tavares, and Alan Bates, who offered valuable feedback from their novice CBGT perspectives, as well as to experienced group therapists who read chapters related to their expertise. A profound thank you to psychologist Colleen Allison, who read the entire manuscript, for her keen attention to where the reader "stumbles," for alerting me to new research findings, and for her insightful and sharp perspective; to psychiatrist George Hadjipavlou, who read several chapters and offered substantial comments on content and style; to psychologist Rosalind Catchpole for sharing in enthusiasm and research updates on groups for children; to doctoral students in clinical psychology Alison Welsted and Kirstie Kellman-McFarlane for their clinical and research experience with compulsive hoarding; to psychologist Heather Fulton for her ability to effectively teach and disseminate CBT for addictions; and to psychologist Mahesh Menon for his encouraging and helpful comments on the psychosis chapter.

A special thanks to Shannon Long, the librarian who for years has helped with literature searches and supplied articles for various group programming needs, to formatting wizard Suzanne Daigle for help with the appendices, and to Kjartan Jaccard for his careful attention and diligence in producing the author index.

A number of other colleagues—too many to name—have played a large role in supporting and influencing my CBT work over the years. Some have played a more direct role in this book. Thanks to psychologists Theo De Gagné and Christopher Wilson for our collaboration on a chapter in the *Oxford Guide to Low Intensity CBT* (2010), which provided some of the "bare bones" for this book; to psychologist Mark Lau for the Oxford Guide chapter opportunity and other collaborations as well as his detailed comments on the mindfulness section; and to professor John Ogrodniczuk for his mentoring in my development as a clinician-researcher.

Thanks to my manager Jo-Anne Kirk for granting me a leave of absence to complete this book.

A huge thank you to the Wiley Blackwell team: senior editors Darren Reed and Karen Shield, editorial assistants Olivia Wells and Amy Minshull, copyeditor Kumudhavalli Narasiman, account manager Revathy Kaliyamoorthy and production project manager Radjan Lourde Selvanadin. Your encouragement, reasonableness, and excellent communication have made this project more enjoyable. Also a heartfelt thank you to the four reviewers of the initial proposal for this book. They were not only enthusiastic about the need for it, but also offered constructive feedback and suggestions.

Thanks to my family without whom my stamina would quickly have been depleted. I am especially grateful to my patient partner, journalist Douglas Todd, who read the entire manuscript more than once and offered excellent suggestions for giving this book a livelier tone. I particularly value and learn from Douglas's genuine interest in psychology and psychotherapy. A hearty thank you to my adult children—Ingram, Kjartan, Torsten, and Sigbrit—your expressions of support, each in your own way, make a big and meaningful difference. I treasure your sibling group cohesion.

"Tak" to my Danish family for their moral support from afar: my mother Karin Michelsen, her partner Martin Daugaard-Hansen, my sister, psychiatrist Astrid Söchting, and last, but not least, my loving and bookish late father, Robert Söchting.

Thank you to all who have directly or indirectly shaped this book. Any mistakes, unclear writing, misunderstandings, or misrepresentations are solely my responsibility.

Introduction: The Depth and Breadth of Cognitive Behavior Group Therapy

As a graduate student in the 1980s in a psychology department known for its focus on individual psychodynamic therapy, I did not imagine eventually writing a book in which I shared my enthusiasm for cognitive behavioral group therapy (CBGT).

While I'm grateful for my psychodynamic training, I have come to appreciate the many benefits of cognitive behavioral therapy (CBT) including its shorter term duration making it more affordable, if individuals are paying themselves. Individual CBT and group CBT (CBGT) both offer specific interventions for specific problems, especially problems with mood and anxiety. Clinicians typically present CBT as a symptom or problem-focused psychological treatment with an emphasis on personal change in behaviors and patterns of thinking about oneself, other people, and one's day to day living environment. CBT clinicians focus more on what maintains problems or disorders than on what causes them, and they help clients understand and problem solve barriers to living their lives more fully. CBT always conveys deep respect and empathy for clients' goals, needs, and unique personal histories. Indeed, CBT is credited with coining terms such as *client-centred* and *client collaboration*.

CBGT at its finest has much to offer. Not only are clients offered effective help for their fear of, let's say, becoming contaminated and seriously ill by taking public transit. They also get to experience that they are not alone in their fears and, perhaps most importantly, that they are perceived by others as a wholesome human being and not just as an "OCD patient." To witness clients undergo this transformation is one of the many benefits of CBGT for clients and therapists alike. Unlike individual CBT, CBGT gives clients an opportunity to connect meaningfully with society, however small the slice. It is an undisputed psychological fact that human beings benefit—they feel and

Cognitive Behavioral Group Therapy: Challenges and Opportunities, First Edition. Ingrid Söchting.

do better—when connected to a larger community. With increased levels of social isolation in many Western societies, in-person group CBT may indeed offer individuals far more than symptom relief.

Across mental health training in the Western world, we are seeing a renewed interest in promoting individuals' well-being, resilience, and sense of purpose and meaning—the so-called *positive psychology* approach. Positive psychology proponents led by psychologist Martin Seligman and psychiatrist George Vailliant, among others, argue that psychology and psychiatry have for too long been too confined to working with all the negatives that come with pejorative diagnostic labels and debilitating symptoms, instead of taking a more holistic, strength-based view of our clients. I argue throughout this book that CBGT offers *both* effective symptom relief *and* promotion of positive individual resources, which are harder to bring about in individual therapy. CBGT also moves therapy from a concern with the individual to the societal and even global arena. CBGT embodies a democratic and communitarian feel given its vast opportunities for people struggling with mental health problems to break the isolation and stigma as they interact with and feel supported by peers in addition to mental health professionals.

In the earlier text, I deliberately used the phrase "group CBT at its finest" to imply that those moments are not the norm. The rewarding times are of course what keep us going as group therapists, but they also challenge us to ask why we do not experience them more often. As with any craft, some solid basic skills are imperative for the CBGT therapist, but equally important is openness to revisions and trying new ways without losing one's foothold in and fidelity to CBT theory and principles. A helpful analogy may be a musical one where practicing scales is tedious but necessary for later improvising and playing with others in the same key—and in tune, including with one's group cofacilitator!

I have written this book to help CBGT facilitators become more confident in leading their groups and more appreciative of the many ways groups can be strengthened and become even more effective. My own journey as a CBT group therapist has come a long way since conducting a first panic disorder group as an intern in 1994. Thinking back on this group, I feel embarrassed when remembering how we did the homework review go-round in the traditional CBT fashion dealing with one person at the time: "Thanks, next!" It's sad to think of how much was lost by not tapping into the collective experience of the group on the difficulty of completing home practice and ways to overcome this common problem. I believe this introduction to group therapy installed some inflated self-confidence because, for some baffling reason, we did not have any dropouts. (I hasten to say that panic disorder may be a problem that requires the least process attention, thus it is a good "starter" group for CBGT novice therapists.) Our success made it seem so obvious that trapping eight people with anxiety in the same room for 2 hours during 8 weeks was the way to go in terms of human and financial efficiency. I was "converted" and have co-conducted four to six CBT groups weekly since.

This guide is meant as a conversation with both beginner and experienced CBGT therapists. I find it helpful to think of myself as a conduit. I aim to share much of what we already know about CBGT based on academic and clinical research in addition to my experience over the past 20 years with developing, running, training, and evaluating CBT groups—and always talking to and learning from other group therapists. Unlike individual therapy, there is usually at least one other professional being a witness—and critic—to our work, something that took me a little while to get used to given how intensely private the individual therapy room feels. But CBGT presents a wonderful opportunity for peer feedback and consultation, something many individual therapists often miss after their training is completed. The term "we" thus refers to my colleagues and trainees, primarily psychology and psychiatry students, but also students from occupational therapy, counseling, social work, and nursing. This book is similar to other books on this topic in that it covers most of the disorders for which CBGT has been shown to be especially helpful, namely the so-called *common mental health problems* of mood and anxiety disorders. It is different in that it also offers more discussion on how to troubleshoot problems in implementing and running CBT groups. In addition, it shows how to apply CBGT to problems and populations where the clinical research is limited but promising.

Readers will notice my bias for emphasizing the "B" in CBT when it comes to CBGT. In individual therapy, I tend to be more balanced in including both cognitive and behavioral interventions. My experience has unequivocally been that the more *doing*, in form of exposures and group activities, the better the cohesion in CBT groups becomes, which in turn positively influences motivation and outcomes for everyone. In addition to underlining behavioral interventions, three other themes recur throughout this book.

The first theme I emphasize is that CBGT offers a unique opportunity to promote the *common good* by offering access to high-quality, cost-attractive mental health care for the most prevalent mental ailments. Second, CBGT must take group process variables more seriously in order to become even more effective. Third, while it does not necessarily require several university degrees to be a CBGT leader, it does necessitate a thoughtful approach to training, to the nature of cofacilitation, and to ongoing professional development in order to achieve and maintain basic and advanced skills.

The book is organized into three parts. Part 1 offers an introduction to basic principles, research, and theory related to CBGT. This part ends with two highly practical chapters on how to implement CBGT for depression, the most common mental health problem. In reading Part 1 experienced clinicians may enjoy having their CBGT skills validated and getting a new perspective or idea for consideration in their practice.

Part 2 tackles practical, or how-to, questions facing clinicians and mental health program managers interested in developing and conducting viable CBGT programs. We will look at questions such as *How much training is necessary in order to take the lead in a CBT group? How homogeneous do groups need to be in order to be effective? How to prepare people for CBGT? How to prevent dropouts?* And *How to develop individual exposure hierarchies in a group?* Part 2 discusses several challenges for successful implementation of CBGT as well as suggestions for solutions. In addition to drawing on my own experience, I refer to the literature when relevant. This is especially the case for Chapter 7 where I present a literature review of transdiagnostic approaches to CBGT before offering practical examples.

Part 3 explores opportunities for CBGT in populations that have received less attention in the group therapy literature. These populations are included because they are likely to be new health care priorities, certainly within the public system. CBT, whether individual or in group, has traditionally been limited to a fairly narrow age range and presenting problems, usually anxiety and depression for people between the ages of 18 and 65. Part 3 shows how CBGT is an effective intervention for older adults, children, and cultural and language minorities, as well as for people with compulsive hoarding, addictions, and psychosis. Each chapter in this section will describe the population presented, including diagnostic criteria following the *American Psychiatric Association's Diagnostic and Statistical Manual of Mental Disorders*, fifth edition (DSM-5) approach, review the existing literature, as well as present an example of a CBGT protocol. I seek to strike a balance between literature reviews and practical examples. The reviews are meant to aid busy clinicians with getting a sense of the latest developments within the CBGT areas chosen for this book.

This guide is for clinicians running groups for people whose stress and symptoms have already reached a threshold of clinical significance—or just below, but who do not require hospitalization or day treatment. The CBGT programs described could be considered a secondary level of care. Typical clients will be referred by primary care level family physicians or community mental health clinic case managers, who recognize that more specialized treatment is needed. Clients referred to CBGT may have tried less intensive treatment such as self-help books, DVDs, or interactive mental health web sites, but found these insufficient. The focus of the book may seem mostly on groups run in outpatient community mental health settings, but the information applies equally to groups in private mental health care.

All clinical examples and dialogues presented in this book have been modified to protect client privacy and confidentiality. Therefore, illustrations are disguised to eliminate identifying information, or they represent composite descriptions, combining aspects and material from several clients. I use the terms group therapist and group facilitator entirely interchangeably. References in the chapters are listed at the end of each chapter with some listed under the heading "Recommended Readings for Clinicians."

I hope this book will inspire everyone interested in group CBT to go further with this powerful intervention for common mental health problems.

Part 1

The Basics of Cognitive Behavioral Group Therapy

The first three chapters in Part 1 explain basic principles, research, and theory related to cognitive behavioral group therapy (CBGT). These opening chapters are sprinkled with clinical examples to illustrate how the principles of CBGT work in practice. Chapter 1 makes a case for extending individual cognitive behavioral therapy (CBT) to groups. Chapter 2 discusses why group CBT becomes more effective when clinicians are familiar with and actively engage with group process factors. Chapter 3 reviews research findings on CBGT for all the disorders covered in this book. This background information will provide a context for the last two more practical chapters of Part 1, which detail how to implement CBGT for depression.

Cognitive Behavioral Group Therapy: Challenges and Opportunities, First Edition. Ingrid Söchting.

1

Extending CBT to Groups

Cognitive behavioral group therapy (CBGT) can play an important role in making effective therapy for mental health problems more accessible and less costly—whether paid for by individual clients or governments. Within governmental mental health systems, CBGT offers significant cost savings and efficiencies without compromising effectiveness (Bennett-Levy, Richards, & Farrand, 2010). Groups run out of private offices or agencies are less expensive for clients because private group therapists do not charge the equivalent of an individual fee when they treat more than one person at the same time. This chapter provides an overview of how individual cognitive behavioral therapy (CBT) has gained momentum and why a group format is a logical extension of this success. Adapting an individual CBT protocol to a group setting is, however, not straightforward. A panic disorder group example illustrates some of these challenges. The chapter closes with a discussion of the unique therapeutic benefits offered by CBGT compared to individual CBT and how to be off to a good start with a CBT group.

Why CBT Is Increasingly Used for Common Mental Health Problems

The number of individuals who suffer from mental health problems is steadily increasing. Depression and anxiety disorders account for the majority of these mental health problems, with North American lifetime prevalence rates estimated at 16% for adult depression and 28% for anxiety disorders (Kessler, Chiu, Demler, & Walters, 2005). There are several reasons for this upward trend. Some likely reflect increased awareness of mental health problems and treatment options. However,

Cognitive Behavioral Group Therapy: Challenges and Opportunities, First Edition. Ingrid Söchting.

even after taking better public education into consideration, rates of anxiety and depression are still on the rise. Larger socioeconomic trends may be operating, leading some health researchers to argue convincingly for a strong association between higher rates of mental illness and socioeconomic inequality. Rates for almost all mental health problems, but especially anxiety disorders, increase as socioeconomic status decreases, making poor mental health both a cause and consequence of poverty and inequality (White, 2010). Interestingly, inequality may also hurt the more affluent. In countries where the gap between rich and poor is large and widening, such as the United States (US), we see higher rates of depression and anxiety even among the financially comfortable members. Conversely, Japan has a relatively narrow income gap, and rates of mental illness across socioeconomic status are lower (Wilkinson & Pickett, 2010). Over and above socioeconomic factors, having a well-integrated family, friendship, and community network may be even more critical than previously thought for the psychological well-being of both men and women (Cable, Bartley, Chandola, & Sacker, 2013); conversely, any breakdown of family and community structure and support has been linked to increases in mental health problems (Alexander, 2010).

Medication can be helpful for many kinds of anxiety and depression and is usually the first treatment offered when a person talks to their family doctor about feeling anxious or depressed. For depression, the advent of the selective serotonin reuptake inhibitors (SSRIs) antidepressant medication in the 1980s was welcomed by family physicians because of their milder side effects compared to the "older" types of antidepressants, the tricyclics, such as imipramine. SSRIs are also routinely prescribed for anxiety. Research suggests that CBT and medication may be roughly equally effective for treating the acute phase of depression (DeRubeis, Siegle, & Hollon, 2008) but that CBT is more likely to help people stay free of depression after discontinuing treatment, whereas ceasing medication has a higher likelihood of relapse (Hollon, Stewart, & Strunk, 2006). A combination of medication and CBT may be especially helpful for depression. A recent randomized controlled trial involving 469 United Kingdom (UK) patients treated for depression with medication by their family physicians showed that only when CBT was added to their usual care did patients begin to improve. At 6 months follow-up, 46% in the CBT group had responded well to treatment compared to only 22% in the care as usual. The treatment gains were maintained at 12 months follow-up (Wiles et al., 2013). It is our experience that people with more severe depression, who respond to antidepressant treatment, are in a better position to commit to regular group attendance. In particular, we notice that those group members benefit from better sleep regulation and increased levels of energy after starting medication and are therefore less likely to miss group sessions due to inertia and low motivation.

Still, regardless of effectiveness, many people prefer not to take medications for various reasons. For depressed people, antidepressants often include side effects such as weight gain and diminished sexual interest, which can lead to a further decrease in social and interpersonal confidence and well-being. For older people with depression, lower rates of metabolism create a necessity for lower dosages which may not even be therapeutic. Others simply prefer to learn sustainable self-help skills rather than relying on external agents such as medication, which can also be costly (Cooper et al., 2007; Dwight-Johnson, Sherbourne, Liao, & Wells, 2000). For people who prefer to take a more active role in their own health, CBT is an attractive option. Clinicians present CBT as a symptom- or problem-focused psychological treatment with an emphasis on personal change in behaviors and patterns of thinking about oneself, other people, and one's day-to-day living environment. Clients are informed that CBT is a shorter-term treatment, typically 8–16 weeks, and that a commitment to practice new skills between sessions is necessary if treatment gains are to be sustained over time.

CBT is available in most Western countries and increasingly also in other parts of the world such as China. Indeed, clinical guidelines in Canada, outlined by the Canadian Network for Mood and Anxiety Treatments (CANMAT), recommend CBT as a first-line treatment for both depression (Ravindran et al., 2009) and anxiety (Swinson et al., 2006) due to the steadily growing body of evidence supporting the effectiveness of CBT. In the United Kingdom the National Institute for Health and Clinical Excellence (NICE, 2009) also recommends CBT for anxiety and depression, including for people who may not meet all diagnostic criteria, that is, minor or sub threshold depression. Not only is CBT helping individuals enjoy a better quality of life, but it is also cost-effective. Before highlighting the cost-effectiveness of CBT, I briefly summarize what CBT is.

Principles of CBT

CBT as we know it today has evolved from the original behavioral therapies developed in the 1960s as a result of the experiments by B.F. Skinner, Joseph Wolpe, Hans Eysenck, and I.P. Pavlov among several other physiologists and medical scientists. These early behaviorists conceptualized psychopathology as simple learning processes either involving *classical* or *operant* conditioning (Hawton, Salkovskis, Kirk, & Clark, 1989). They reacted to the notion in psychodynamic theory, as formulated by Sigmund Freud and his followers, of psychopathology being the result of unresolved intrapsychic conflict caused during the first 5 years of life. Instead of focusing on mind phenomena such as dreams, memories, and free associations, the early behavioral therapists focused exclusively on environmental determinants of behavior. They demonstrated that environmental factors lead to two basic forms of learning, classical conditioning and operant conditioning. We are all familiar with the classical conditioning of Pavlov's dogs.

Initially, the dogs exhibited an unconditioned response of salivation to the smell of food (unconditioned stimulus). However, over time, the presentation of food was systematically paired with a bell. Simply hearing the sound of the bell therefore led the dogs to salivate even though no food was present. The bell (conditioned stimulus) had thus produced a conditioned response. We see other versions of classical conditioning in the modern CBT office. A woman may show a strong anxiety reaction to, and avoidance of, cats. She is puzzled because she is not afraid of cats per se. It becomes apparent that she had a first panic attack in a friend's home where there were several cats around. Seeing a cat becomes a conditioned stimulus because of its association with the extreme unpleasantness of a panic attack. Avoiding cats as much as possible becomes the conditioned response. Treatment would in part involve exposure to cats and other places associated with panic attacks. Operant conditioning involves manipulation of environmental factors in order to shape a person's behavior. For example, as will be reviewed in Chapter 17, people who receive treatment for an addiction may agree to receive vouchers that can be used to purchase goods as rewards for decreased engagement with their addictions. The presence of a reward thus serves to positively reinforce the desired behavior.

By the 1970s, behavioral therapy working within the paradigm of classical and operant conditioning was widely used for treating a number of problems, mostly anxiety and specific phobias. However, observations from the cognitive sciences challenged the strict behavioral models of learning. CBT psychotherapist pioneers such as Albert Ellis (psychologist) and Aaron Beck (psychiatrist) emphasized the role of mediating cognitive factors. They found that specific thoughts or interpretations of a stimulus influenced the person's behavioral response (Hawton et al., 1989). For example, the woman who avoids cats fearing she will have a panic attack in their presence will likely have powerful thoughts increasing her fear, thoughts such as "I cannot cope with a panic attack" or "having a panic attack means I'm going crazy." For people with depression, the importance of self-critical and exaggerated thoughts in maintaining symptoms of depression (e.g., "everyone else is so smart, and I have nothing to say") became a major focus for Beck. His groundbreaking cognitive theory of depression continues to inform CBT for depression (Beck, Rush, Shaw, & Emery, 1979).

Most CBT practitioners vary their relative focus between environmental and cognitive determinants of behaviors. As we will see throughout this book, some mental health problems call for more behavioral interventions, others for more cognitive, and most for a mix of both. The key treatment principle in behavioral therapy is *exposure* (facing one's fears), which always aims to extinguish the conditioned fear response through *systematic desensitization*. Central to cognitive therapy is *cognitive restructuring* (changing one's thoughts and interpretations). Cognitive restructuring involves gently helping clients become more flexible in their thinking and not lock in to "the first" interpretation or understanding of what is happening around them (e.g., "I'm convinced my boss wants to fire me") or within their bodies (e.g., "my racing heart means I'm having a heart attack").

More recently, CBT has undergone another transformation often referred to as the *third wave* after the initial behavioral wave and, secondly, the cognitive. Mindfulness training and acceptance and commitment therapy (ACT) characterize this newest branch on the CBT tree. Mindfulness training can be described as a continual practice of *awakening* to the present-moment experience (Bishop et al., 2004). Mindfulness-based cognitive therapy (MBCT) differs from traditional CBT in that it is less concerned with the kinds of thoughts people have but more with the *acceptance* of the thought and the way the person *relates* to their thought. Chapter 5 shows how MBCT was developed in response to a need for better maintenance therapy to prevent relapse after successful CBT for depression (Lau, 2010).

Today, CBT is a broad term including a wide array of distinct yet often overlapping approaches to the optimal treatment of a range of mental health problems. After six decades of empirical validation, CBT has proven to be a highly effective treatment for numerous psychiatric disorders (e.g., depression, panic disorder, obsessive–compulsive disorder (OCD), generalized anxiety disorder (GAD), social anxiety disorder (SAD), phobias, posttraumatic stress disorder (PTSD), addiction, and psychosis), medical disorders (e.g., disorders related to sleep, sexual functioning, diabetes, chronic pain, and heart disease), and nondiagnosable problems in living (e.g., lack of assertiveness, low self-esteem, and anger). CBT is also helpful for personality disorders (Beck, Freeman, & Davis, 2004), although particularly challenging to administer in a group format (Bieling, McCabe, & Antony, 2006).

Cost-Effectiveness of CBT

The benefits of CBT as a cost-saving measure may be especially well understood and recognized in the United Kingdom. In 2007, the then Labour government led by Prime Minister Tony Blair made improving public access to CBT a government priority based on a major study, The Depression Report, from the London School of Economics (2006) showing that the societal cost of lost productivity was estimated at approximately US$ 19 billion per year, about 1% of the total national income. In 2006, according to The Depression Report, a million people in the United Kingdom received *Incapacity Benefits* because of mental disorders, at a cost of US$ 1,200 a month per person. A Canadian report estimated that employers saved US$ 4,000–$9,000 a month in average wage replacement, sick leave, and prescription drug costs for every employee with a mental health problem—including drug and alcohol addiction—who received effective treatment (Mood Disorders Society of Canada, 2009). The Depression Report in Britain further showed that less than 5% of the population had access to effective psychotherapy. Informed by this economic report, the Tony Blair government dedicated US$ 280 million per year to train therapists in CBT in order to improve access to effective psychotherapy—at no cost to the individuals receiving the therapy. This project is referred to as the British Improving Access to Psychological Therapy (IAPT). The present UK coalition government led by David Cameron has continued the funding by committing another US$ 652 million for 2011–2015. This continuation is based on evidence of improved outcomes and accountability for how funds are spent (Clark, 2011; Clark et al., 2009).

Although it is heartwarming to think of the UK government placing such high value on citizens receiving government-funded therapy, its reasons are highly pragmatic. This government realized that it could not afford to avoid improving the function of its citizens, especially when lack of treatment results in missed work days and extended leaves of absences. Australia is another example of a jurisdiction that has taken steps to increase access to effective psychological treatment such as CBT. The Australian *Better Access* initiative allows physicians to refer a person to a psychologist for up to 10 government-paid therapy sessions (Australian Department of Health and Aging, 2009).

If offered in a group setting, CBT is even more cost-effective given that, compared to individual therapy, a single therapist or two cotherapists can treat up to four times as many clients within the same number of hours. The group format also optimizes use of costly psychotherapy. If a client fails to attend an individual hour of psychotherapy, the therapist's time is wasted, whereas if someone fails to show for a group, it does not impact the therapist's ability to provide services for those who attend. Furthermore, in a real cost analysis, Otto, Pollack, and Maki (2000) estimated absolute costs for the treatment of panic disorder using CBT and arrived at US$ 523 for CBGT, US$ 1,357 for individual CBT, and US$ 2,305 for pharmacotherapy (medication). With CBGT being the least costly, it is easy to see why CBGT is becoming increasingly popular in publicly funded outpatient community mental health settings. At the same time, it is also puzzling why CBGT is not even more popular to the point of being mandated by health-care departments and authorities. Some of the reasons for the relative lack of public access to CBGT may have to do with insufficient number of trained therapists and the challenges this can lead to in terms of developing and maintaining CBT groups. Getting enough people with the same problem to form a group in a timely manner is another problem in smaller communities. These and other reasons for lack of access to and engagement with CBGT are discussed in Chapters 6, 7, and 10.

Transporting Individual CBT to a Group Setting

Even for the well-trained CBT therapist, transporting individual CBT to a group setting requires careful planning and attention. Not only are there practical challenges regarding how to take the content from an individual CBT protocol and turn it into a group protocol but also with how to manage the group dynamic. In the following text, I address first the content challenge—using a panic disorder group as a specific example—and then the group process challenge from a general CBGT perspective.

CBT protocols delivered in an individual context have successfully been translated into group CBT. Clinical research provides "good-to-excellent" evidence for the effectiveness of CBGT for a number of disorders including OCD, depression, SAD, eating disorders, psychosis, and substance abuse (Burlingame, Strauss, & Joyce, 2013). Despite these good results, protocol translations are not straightforward. The proliferation of available individual CBT protocols, and the fact that most are highly disorder specific, means that specialized training is needed for at least one of the group leaders if the implementation is to be effective. Even for anxiety, there is a distinct protocol for each of the roughly 10 different anxiety disorders. Because protocols used in CBT groups tend to be adaptations of individual CBT protocols, some reorganizing of treatment components may be needed given the fixed number of sessions in CBGT. This panic protocol is just one example. Individual CBT protocols for other disorder such as OCD and depression will similarly require various adaptions to a group setting.

Adapting CBT to CBGT: panic disorder illustration

Panic disorder with or without agoraphobia is a common anxiety problem often rendering otherwise high-functioning people unable to drive or take public transit outside of their immediate neighborhood. According to the *Diagnostic and Statistical Manual of Mental Disorders, Fifth Edition* (DSM-5) (American Psychiatric Association [APA], 2013),[1] panic disorder is characterized by recurrent unexpected panic attacks. A panic attack is an abrupt surge of intense fear or intense discomfort that reaches a peak within minutes and during which time four (or more) symptoms occur: pounding heart, sweating, trembling or shaking, sensations of shortness of breath or smothering, feelings of choking, chest pain or discomfort, nausea or abdominal distress, feeling dizzy, light-headed or faint, tingling sensations, derealization (feelings of unreality) or depersonalization (being detached from oneself), fear of losing control or "going crazy," or fear of dying. At least one attack must be followed by 1 month or more of one or both of the following: (1) persistent concern or worry about having another attack and/or (2) a significant maladaptive behavior related to the attacks (e.g., behaviors designed to avoid having panic attacks, such as avoidance of exercise or unfamiliar situations). Panic disorder may or may not involve agoraphobia. *Agoraphobia*, according to the DSM-5 (APA, 2013), involves marked fear or anxiety about two (or more) of the following five situations: (1) using public transportation (e.g., automobiles, buses, planes), (2) being in open spaces (e.g., parking lots, marketplaces), (3) being in enclosed places (e.g., shops, theaters, cinemas), (4) standing in line or being in a crowd, and (5) being outside of one's home alone.

In more extreme cases, people with panic disorder avoid leaving their homes and become nearly housebound. In public treatment settings where there is pressure to prioritize more serious mental illness, panic disorder is often considered less severe. The loss, however, of human and societal potential in regard to untreated panic disorder is profound. It is costly to society to have educated, high-functioning employees on sick leave for a disorder that is highly treatable with CBT.

A panic disorder CBT group typically meets for 1.5–2 hours per week for 10 weeks. In a homogeneous panic disorder group, up to 12 people can be accommodated, even though the usually recommended optimal number for a CBT group is eight people. A panic group usually involves both people with agoraphobia and those without. A panic disorder group is the most structured and "classroom"-like of all the CBT groups. Clients tend to be highly motivated and relatively free of other problems, including significant family of origin issues. This allows the facilitators to take more of a teaching role as they go through the standard protocol. A panic group is generally considered to be the easiest to run. Treatment manuals do not differ that much, and the one by Barlow and Craske, *Mastery of Your Anxiety and Panic*, Fourth Edition (2007), is excellent. It offers a 12-session CBT program for treating panic disorder. Similar to many other CBT manuals, it requires adaptation to a group setting. Mainly, certain treatment components need to be introduced earlier in the group compared to the outline in the Barlow and Craske manual.

A typical panic disorder group session starts with a *go-round* where all members in turn report back on how many panic attacks they had, or how many times they came close to panicking in the past week, and how they used their coping skills. This go-round is followed by a didactic component such as information about the physiology of breathing and the importance of the CO_2/oxygen balance. Or the didactic component could be instruction on how to build a personal exposure hierarchy (more about this in Chapter 9) or how to challenge misinterpretations of bodily sensations. All these different treatment components for panic disorder are outlined in the Barlow and Craske therapist guide. The session concludes with another go-round where facilitators ensure that all clients have set realistic and appropriate tasks for homework. The main task for facilitators of a panic group is to manage time, which can be a challenge when the group is large, and ensure that all the material is covered. We have found it to be especially challenging to have enough time for people to work through their *exposure* to both internal body sensations and actual feared situations, in vivo (real life) exposure. The practice of these exposure exercises does not begin until around sessions 6–8 in the Barlow and Craske client manual (and even later in earlier versions of this manual). Unlike individual CBT for panic, for which the Barlow and Craske manual was developed, the group has a finite number of sessions—usually 10—and extension to complete exposure work is usually not possible.

Deliberately bringing on the feared bodily sensations—such as a sense of restricted air intake by breathing through a straw—is a key CBT principle in treating panic disorder. By actually producing the feared body sensations, clients begin to realize that while the sensations are certainly uncomfortable, they are not life-threatening. This challenge is also called interoceptive exposure. It is critical in treating people with panic attacks whose sensitivity to body sensations is extremely heightened. It is not fear of, for example, a shopping mall in and of itself but fear of the body sensations such as accelerated heart rate that keeps people away from the shopping mall. We recommend group therapists work flexibly with manuals and introduce this practice in session 4 and then support clients in setting weekly exposure goals. The Barlow and Craske manual recommends about eight interoceptive exposures (e.g., over breathing, running on the spot, restricted breathing through a straw, spinning), and they can all—and ought to—be practiced together in the group with the therapists leading. If therapists start this practice earlier, such as in session 4, they can introduce two or three interoceptive exposures over 3–4 weeks.

Similarly, in vivo exposure can also be started around session 4 for those members who have agoraphobia. The therapists need to be aware of who these members are and ensure they get homework related to facing places and situations they avoid. For example, a client Amir, who had a fear of panicking in crowded places, had a top exposure hierarchy item of "go on a 4-hour airplane flight" to his favorite vacation place. Knowing that he was not likely to meet this goal and report back to the group within the 10-week duration, we attempted to get Amir—and other group members with agoraphobia—started on exposure goals earlier in the group. Starting in session 4, Amir set weekly goals to drive to the local airport and hang out in it and to discuss travel plans with his wife and a travel agent. As for interoceptive exposure, Amir was guided through restricted breathing using straws during the group sessions. His fear of panic attacks in the plane was to a large extent driven by his oversensitivity to a feeling of not getting enough air and thus dying of lack of oxygen. Similar to many people with panic disorder, Amir was not particularly afraid of the airplane crashing. His continued practice of tolerating restricted air intake helped Amir become more confident about tolerating being in an enclosed space such as an airplane for a prolonged period of time. In vivo exposures to being in a crowded room and on buses also helped him prepare for going on an airplane.

The cognitive components of *overestimation* and *decatastrophizing* in the Barlow and Craske protocol are introduced according to the outline in the manual. Group discussions on how to challenge overestimations of the likelihood of dying of a heart attack or decatastrophizing fears of, for example, other people noticing one has symptoms of anxiety, are rich and productive. Group facilitators will use the board to work through individual member's examples. As I point out later in this chapter, any group discussion or exercise requires that the facilitators engage the whole group as much as possible. They do this by not providing the answers themselves, but instead by deferring to the group. They also encourage more quiet members by gently including them without putting them on the spot. For example, a therapist may say: "We now have three pieces of evidence suggesting it is extremely unlikely, if not impossible, for Jennifer's heart to reach a dangerous level of beating (no evidence of heart disease, accelerated heart rate is safe for the heart, a faster heart rate eventually slows down). Linda, do these reasons make sense to you too, or is there something you'd like to add?." Linda, an extremely quiet member, may simply say "yes it makes sense to me, I get it" and thus enjoy the experience of being included and practicing speaking up. Or Linda may add an additional piece of evidence such as "for me, I've learned to notice that my heart rate changes quite a bit all the time for no particular reason." Jennifer may reply: "Thanks for that, Linda, I guess our hearts are not these perfect little machines and the more we try to just let them 'do their thing,' the calmer we are."

Managing the group process across CBGT

Clinicians trained in psychodynamic therapy understand the many complicated manifestations of the emotional connection between an individual patient and therapist. It is dizzying to try to map out the multiple connections in a group of eight clients plus two facilitators. Not only are group members reacting to the group therapists and vice versa but also to each other. The group therapists themselves also have their own dynamic, which in turn is projected onto the rest of the group. The sum and quality of all these interactions is usually referred to as the *group dynamic*, the *group climate*, or the *group process* and is the equivalent to the nonspecific factors referred to as the *therapeutic bond or alliance* in individual therapy. The term group process will be used throughout the rest of this book. The group process involves a number of separate factors, which I will describe in Chapter 2.

The complexity of the group process places additional demands on therapists' expertise. They wrestle not only with implementation of specific CBT techniques but also with all the interpersonal interactions and processes taking place in any group. It is not uncommon to hear CBGT cotherapists agree to divide their roles with one delivering the material and the other keeping an eye on how individual members are doing, that is, the process. Although this makes some practical sense, my experience is that the nature of CBGT work does not lend itself well to such a division of labor. The unexpected always happens, as the following examples illustrate.

The credibility of the group leadership is easily undermined if one cotherapist answers that he is "not really here to explain how *exposure and response prevention* (ERP) works [in case of OCD], but to make sure everyone is OK." This may be interpreted by some group members to mean that the therapist who presumably knows about ERP may not keep everyone safe.

Here is another situation where the therapists could be perceived as less competent and engaging. In this example, one cotherapist was intensely focused on working with a group member, Susan, who was asked to produce evidence countering her self-denigrating *negative automatic thought*: "I am a disorganized scatterbrain." The therapist working with Susan got carried away in asking her for examples of when she may not be disorganized, and this became more of a mini one-to-one therapy encounter, which is inevitable in group CBT and certainly permitted to some extent. But, in this case, the "group process" facilitator was trying to monitor another group member, Tom, who was crying and making attempts to leave the room. The rest of the group began to feel disconnected, drifting into their own moods and thoughts. This loss of group cohesion could have been prevented if the "content delivery" therapist had taken steps to engage the rest of the group by asking their perceptions of Susan as a group member. Someone might have said that Susan always arrives on time with her folder, a good piece of evidence against the idea that "I am disorganized."

While there is much that can be effectively imported from individual therapy into CBGT, protocols for disorder-specific group CBT that explicitly address how to pay attention to the group process are essentially nonexistent; I have come across one, *Group Cognitive Therapy for Addictions* (Wenzel, Liese, Beck, & Friedman-Wheeler, 2012). Chapter 2 will continue this discussion on the distinction between, and integration of, process and content.

Before I review how to start a CBT group and the importance of the first session, I present some of the unique benefits of CBGT compared to individual CBT.

Unique Benefits of the Group Format

Any kind of therapy becomes more effective when three conditions are met. The *bond* between the client and therapist, or the group *process*, must be strong. The *goals* for therapy must be clear and agreed upon by both client and therapist, and the client must have a good understanding of which *tasks* will be the focus of therapy in order to meet the goals. CBGT offers a unique opportunity to create a strong group bond or group dynamic, to develop skills, and even to strengthen the standard CBT procedural aspects *because* of the group format (Coon et al., 2005). These procedures include review of homework, in-session tasks such as exposure and thought challenging, and setting new homework.

Groups have the potential for providing participants with a sense of belonging, which counters social isolation and the common feeling of being stigmatized or marginalized in society. Sometimes, a remarkable improvement in social confidence develops even though most CBT groups do not explicitly address self-esteem. We are often aware of clients continuing to meet over coffee, walks, or even day trips after the group has ended. I continue to be struck—but not surprised—by how much it means to human beings to have a sense of being in "the same boat." One of the rewarding aspects of group therapy is to walk into a first session—for example, with a group for people with OCD—and be witness to how quickly the initial atmosphere of anxiety and shame changes to one of relaxed openness, acceptance of oneself and others, and lots of hope. During only 2 hours, some not readily explicable group magic has taken place.

Agreeing on goals for therapy is less of a problem in CBGT because each group usually has a name that clearly indicates what the group is about, for example, panic disorder group, depression group, or traumatic stress group. Pregroup assessment and group orientation sessions further help to ensure clients have a good understanding of whether their chosen group can help them achieve their goals. The first session offers a kind of additional check when each member states what they hope to get from the group. Members may say they seek to understand their problems better and develop skills to manage their anxiety or depression more effectively. Hearing other people desiring similar outcomes strengthens the overall goal of the group and increases motivation for everyone.

A principal component in CBT is the emphasis on learning adaptive coping skills by engaging with various behavioral and cognitive tasks. This focus on learning new skills and replacing less helpful ones (avoidance is an example of a common maladaptive coping skill for people seeking CBT) may be the most important rationale for conducting CBT in groups as much as possible. The group format allows clients to learn together from the facilitators but also to learn from each other. CBGT therapists teach that it is possible to have more control over one's thinking—and therefore over one's emotions and behaviors. In many cases, CBGT may provide the first opportunity for clients to obtain feedback on their behaviors from peers. A group offers a unique opportunity for both receiving and giving constructive feedback. The CBT concept of *Socratic dialogue*[2] or *guided discovery* takes on a new meaning in the group setting.

Guided discovery in CBT means that therapists do not offer quick answers or solutions but rather engage the client in a series of questions to uncover relevant information outside the client's current awareness (Padesky & Greenberger, 1995). The therapist listens, reflects, and summarizes. Through this process, clients come up with a new way of understanding their problems. Because they arrived at an alternative view through their own reasoning, their new understanding seems more believable. In CBGT, group therapists encourage group members to offer this kind of supportive questioning to one another. Here is an example of how the group therapists defer to the group to support Mandeep, who has panic disorder, in increasing his ability to understand and cope with his fear of certain body sensations.

MANDEEP: I'm not going to go the retirement party for my boss because it would be ridiculous and embarrassing if I fainted.

THERAPIST: Sounds like your fear of fainting is a key factor in why you prefer to stay home and avoid social events?

MANDEEP: It is. I know someone in our last session said something about how it is almost impossible to faint during a panic attack, but that does not seem true for me.

THERAPIST: Does anyone have some suggestions for how Mandeep can address his fear of fainting?

NADIA: I'm curious about how many times you have fainted when feeling panicky?

MANDEEP: Well, I haven't actually fainted if you mean loss of consciousness, but I've come really close.

LEE: How do you know when you're really close?

MANDEEP: Well, my legs feel like jelly, my mind goes blank, and I sometimes have blurred vision, so I know I'm close to fainting.

LARRY: Remember when we talked in our first two sessions about all the symptoms that can happen in a panic attack? Seems to me you're experiencing some of them, especially the wobbly legs. I get that too and I used to be terrified of fainting

LEE: I can't quite remember how it goes, but something about blood pressure being either high or low when we panic

MANDEEP: I think we learned that our blood pressure tends to go up a bit when we panic.

NADIA: Yes, and when we faint, our blood pressure is actually down. It has to do with the different impact of our sympathetic and parasympathetic nervous systems. The sympathetic gets activated when we panic, right? [Looks at the facilitators]

MANDEEP: Oh, so it feels similar to fainting but it is actually very different from real fainting?

LARRY: I just want to say, that I really hear you, Mandeep, but it seems to me that both you and I mistakenly think that our anxiety symptoms mean we're about to faint, when physiologically that is not really possible.

MANDEEP: I'm going to remind myself that all the scary feelings of light-headedness and wobbly legs are uncomfortable but not dangerous. They have to do with the adrenaline rush in the fight-flight-freeze reaction we talked about in the first sessions.

LARRY: Yeah, and even if you or I were to faint, that's not really dangerous either. But the chance of that is so low, so I'm not going to worry about it anymore.

NADIA: I wonder if our therapists would mind just reviewing again the fight-flight-freeze response when we panic?

THERAPIST: Sure we can do a review. Is there perhaps someone in the group who would like to start this review?

With the help of questioning and summary statements from the group, Mandeep was supported in developing an alternative perspective or interpretation of his panic symptoms that made sense to him. Going through this group process of questioning and exploring usually makes the answers more credible compared to the therapists simply telling the group members what to think or do.

Lastly, the CBGT setting can also strengthen the standard CBT procedural aspects of running a group. These include review and setting of homework as well as in-session tasks. The Mandeep example showed how the therapists let the group support a member in challenging his overestimation of fainting. Individual group members who struggle with homework can benefit from learning how other group members succeed at their chosen homework. As the group develops, therapists are often impressed with how group members help each other set new and relevant homework. Members may even gently tease each other to set more challenging homework. Therapists encourage humor whenever possible and appropriate to strengthen the procedural aspects of CBGT. Even depression groups are known for outbursts of laughter when the group process is strong. We find that group members collaborate with both the group leaders, and each other, to maximize their individual treatment plans including planning their homework.

In the following sections, I go into some detail about how to start a CBT group. The important issues of the bond (group process), goals, and tasks are addressed right from the beginning of the group.

How to Start a CBT Group

CBT is a time-limited, goal-focused, and highly structured form of therapy. CBGT does not differ from this general description. CBT groups tend to be closed groups, meaning that everyone starts and finishes together. However, open groups in which one or two new clients enter each week can be effective too, and I review some examples in Chapters 5 and 17. Toward the shorter time end of the spectrum are groups for anxiety, such as panic disorder (typically 8–10 sessions). At the longer end are groups for moderate to severe depression, PTSD, problems with hoarding, and addictions (typically 16–20 sessions).

Setting up the group room

Prior to the first session of a new group, facilitators ensure that the room is set up. It is important that this is done ahead of time so that clients feel welcomed—and not imposing themselves on therapists who they would see busily running around moving tables and chairs. Typically, a CBT group involves clients sitting around a square- or horseshoe-shaped table. The facilitators can sit next to each other, but do not have to. Sitting together reinforces the fact that CBGT facilitators do function in large part as teachers and it thus seems helpful to have all group members turn their head toward the leaders as opposed to constantly moving their head depending on which leader is talking. Other therapists prefer to sit across from each other and develop nonverbal gestures for communication about process issues, such as a light tap on the table as code for "you're talking too much—let me help out." On the other hand, sitting next to each other allows for nonverbal communication variants of "kicking under the table." I will keep referring to *the therapists* with the assumption of their being two. It is, however, not uncommon that a CBT group is run by only one therapist. Some groups lend themselves better to a solo therapist than others. Groups with intense in-session exposures such as social anxiety and OCD are best conducted with a pair of therapists. Most CBGT programs agree that two cotherapists are preferred but that at times this is not possible due to insufficient staff resources.

The room usually also has a whiteboard with markers, or a flip chart, or a projector for Power Point slides. It is important not to forget to have some boxes of Kleenex on the tables. Sharpened pencils should also be available. In busy work settings, it is a good idea to put a notice on the door stating: "Group in process—please do not disturb." We made such a sign even more visible after a large man who was part of the engineering team for the hospital flung the door open and loudly asked about the location of the fan. The timing was unfortunate in that a female group member was just in the middle of offering a verbal account of her sexual assault as part of her exposure in *a cognitive processing therapy* (*CPT*) group (Chapter 7 discusses this approach to trauma).

The first session

The first session is critical. It sets the framework by explaining the structure of the group, the ground rules, the CBT treatment rationale, and the creation of hope and positive expectations. The therapists also set a tone of transparency, warmth, and collaboration. We rarely allow clients to miss the first session (acceptable reasons would be family or home emergencies) and, if they do, we ask that they go on the wait list for the next group.

In the first group session for all CBT groups, clients are given a folder, which has the outline of the group sessions including dates and topics (see Appendix A for an example of a depression group). This is followed by handouts pertaining to the first four sessions. Clients are instructed to insert new handouts as the group progresses. Clients are told to bring the folder, which can also be called the client's self-help manual, to each session. If budgets allow, some programs give each client a copy of a published manual, such as *Mastery of Your Anxiety and Panic*, Fourth Edition (Barlow & Craske, 2007).

Everyone is given a name tag with his or her first name, including the facilitators. The facilitators first offer their welcome plus a few words intended to validate nervousness about coming to a group of strangers with only a vague idea of what to expect. The facilitators state the agenda for today's session, as they do at the beginning of every subsequent group session. They may say: "For our first session today, we have a lot to accomplish. First, we facilitators will introduce ourselves. We will then review some ground rules and expectations for this group before hearing about your hopes for this group. This will be followed by a discussion of what panic disorder (or other disorder depending on the type of group) is. We will discuss a model showing why it is difficult to break free of panic attacks. We will end our session by describing what this group treatment involves, and get you started with your first homework. How does that sound? Anything you would like to add to this agenda?"

After the agenda has been set, the facilitators introduce themselves, emphasizing their area of specialty and experience. Students should be honest about their lack of training, and for some, it may be their first group. The manner in which the facilitators introduce themselves matters as they model respect, honesty, and openness. Sometimes, clients will ask if the facilitators have personal experience with a particular problem or disorder. It is best to avoid therapist self-disclosure of this nature. There are a number of ways in which to genuinely respond to such a question. Group therapists may say that they understand human struggles as falling on a continuum and do not believe anyone is immune to mental health problems.

We then review ground rules as well as expectations for attendance, how to handle absences and arriving late to the group, confidentiality, socializing outside of the group, and, lastly, a general introduction to CBT, including its focus on active participation and homework. As for ground rules, programs will develop their own, and there are no strict guidelines within the CBGT practice community. Some programs allow clients to bring food or even offer tea and refreshments. Others only allow clients to bring a beverage into the group room. Generally, CBT groups are more permissive compared to non-CBT groups in terms of what can be brought into the group room. My suggestions for how to handle a number of issues pertaining to the organization and structure of the group reflect my preference and may be somewhat different from other experienced CBGT therapists. By being quite specific, I hope to help more junior CBGT therapists with getting groups off to a good start.

Absences and being late

Absences in a CBT group are a problem because the groups tend to be shorter term and each session includes new didactic information. We ask that clients make a commitment to not miss more than two sessions. Clients are made aware that if they miss more than that, we may ask them to leave the group and start over again in a next group. Clients are usually cooperative with this and see it as being in their own best interest. Arriving late to group is another issue that should be addressed from the start. CBT groups, just like other kinds of psychotherapy groups, work best if they start and end on time as this reinforces the importance of keeping a structure and respecting everyone's time. Group facilitators are free to develop their own lateness "rules" so long as they state them clearly. There are of course many reasons for why group members might not arrive on time, with avoidance being a common one. Symptoms can get in the way too, as they did with a school teacher whose washing compulsions necessitated she spend 30 minutes in the school washroom and therefore often arrived late for group with hands and lower arms red and swollen.

It is understandable that people may feel ambivalent about coming to a program where they are asked to confront some of their strongest fears or emotions. We speak about this using exactly those terms. While we validate group members' fears and ambivalence, we also make it clear that the group room door will be closed 5 minutes after we start and that those who come late should quietly enter and take their seat. (If somebody will be more than 30 minutes late, we ask they call the program in advance if at all possible.) If members miss the go-round (the first part of the group where each member in turn reports on their previous week and homework), we may not give them an opportunity to review their week. With the risk of coming across as slightly punitive, we also attempt to extinguish this problematic behavior by not rewarding late coming with positive attention. Brushing up on CBT learning principles is highly recommended for the CBGT therapist!

Confidentiality and socializing outside the group

Confidentiality is universally a rule in any mental health therapy group. While clients usually nod and say they get it, they often indicate confusion about what confidentiality does not mean. To lessen this anxiety, we tell clients that they are free to talk about their own experience in the group as much as they want to whomever but that they simply do not mention by name or describe any other person in the group. Similarly, there is sometimes confusion about why the group facilitators ask people not to meet outside of the group when we also encourage people to make strong connections. When we explain about the possibility of some people feeling left out if they hear others are meeting outside of the group, everyone usually gets it. Interestingly, it can take repeated reminders and therapists need to pay attention throughout the group. In a group for older adults, one woman had a hard time understanding why she could not invite another group member for Christmas dinner when he was otherwise going to be alone. Not wanting to appear inhuman, the facilitators decided in their debriefing to have the whole group discuss this issue and come to a group decision about this, including agreed-upon limits to the invitation. This example shows how rules are not inflexibly imposed by the therapists but can be negotiated by participation of all group members.

There is another wrinkle to confidentiality. Occasionally, in smaller communities, two people in the same first group session realize they know each other. Their children may be on the same sports team; they may attend the same church or live in the same apartment building. There is no way to prevent this as the identity of group members obviously cannot be shared before the group or at any time. When this happens, the facilitators express their concern, saying that it does happen. We explain that the two people can stay in the group so long as they are both absolutely comfortable with this, or one can choose to withdraw and go on the list for the next group. It usually gets sorted out but may require some individual discussion with the group facilitators. In one case, two people working as volunteers for the same organization clearly had a strong negative reaction upon recognizing each other. One said: "I don't want to leave, but she definitely needs therapy!" It is awkward and frustrating to lose a group member who cannot easily be replaced but also something facilitators learn to deal with in a matter-of-fact way.

Member introductions

Group members are then asked to introduce themselves. Empathizing with how terrifying this can be even for people who do not have social anxiety, we lessen this by structuring the introductions. We ask clients to answer three questions written on the board: (1) What is your favorite food? (2) What brought you to this group? and (3) What is one thing you hope to get from this group? The first question is obviously meant to break the ice and strengthen the group process by creating a more personal, light atmosphere. The second question is a sort of double check on whether the group matches each member's goal for their improvement. If a group member in an OCD group says she is hoping to overcome abuse from her childhood, this goal is not likely to be met. In response to the third question, members tend to say "to learn how to handle my anxiety better" or "to understand why I keep falling into the same patterns." These answers offer an opportunity for the therapists to reinforce what tasks and skills will be presented in the group.

It is important that the facilitators not engage in lengthy one-to-one dialogues during these introductions. Some members are eager to "tell their stories." The facilitators firmly but gently connect what the members say to the purpose of the group and to what other members have said. For example, if Sam is going on about how unfair his many bosses have been, the facilitator will say: "You will have many opportunities to address your concerns in this group over the next several weeks, Sam, and we're glad you came to this group. Similar to Mary, your challenges at work seem to have contributed to your depression. In this group, we hope to offer you a number of skills to help you cope better." If facilitators are not sure how to keep introductions fairly short, they will be unable to accomplish what they stated in their agenda. This undermines confidence in the group and especially in the facilitators.

Expectations for CBGT commitment

It is imperative that all clients leave the first session with a strong sense of what to expect from the CBT group, how the treatment will proceed, their commitment to daily homework, and, just as importantly, an experience of the group as safe and led by competent facilitators whom they can trust to guide them through the difficulties of facing their challenges. While the facilitators acknowledge their expertise, they also remind the group that all sessions will be a combination of presentation of new material as well as working together as a group on helping one another. Facilitators explain that they do most of the talking in the first sessions but increasingly expect group members to support each other by asking questions, offering suggestions and feedback, as well as being able to receive feedback. They further explain that feedback must be respectful. They may comment on how some group members will find it easier to talk than others, and they encourage those who are more comfortable with talking to attempt to bring out the more quiet members. It is worth emphasizing that gains from a CBGT group do not depend on how much a member talks. Some very quiet people gain a lot from CBGT.

The second-to-last part of the first session is dedicated to education about the particular problem or disorder, often augmented by a video. The very last part involves handing out a set of outcome measures relevant to the particular CBT group. The therapists explain the benefits of tracking individual progress and also overall comparisons for program evaluation purposes. Group members are asked to complete the measures at home and bring them to the next session. Chapter 6 includes more information on various outcome measurements.

Note-taking by CBGT therapists

CBGT therapists tend to have a notepad or clipboard with note paper in front of them in the group. This allows them to make brief written notes during the go-round where group members report back on their homework. They also make notes during the checkout go-round where new homework is assigned. CBGT groups include various work sheets and forms for tracking anxiety or creating behavioral experiments. Group therapists can make copies of these work sheets at the end of the session so that clients can keep them in their folders. After the session, group therapists use their notes for making formal progress notes in their clients' charts. Having careful documentation from each session is mandatory in most mental health programs and also helps therapists summarize clients' progress in treatment in their final discharge notes. Although note-taking during CBGT sessions is permissible, it is important that it does not interfere with the group process. If a therapist writes extensively, seems absorbed, and is not looking up and around that much, this obviously sends a message of disengaging from the group. It may also make group members suspicious of what the therapist is writing down about them. My practice is to explain why I take a few notes and how I use them and add that clients are welcome to see what I note about their work in the group.

Subsequent sessions

After the first session, all subsequent sessions follow the same structure of (1) welcome and go-round with review of each member's week and their homework, (2) presentation by the facilitators of new material or review of previously introduced material, (3) in-session practice of tasks such as exposures or cognitive restructuring and (4) go-round where new homework is set for each member based on what they worked on in the session.

At the beginning of each session, the facilitators welcome everyone, announce who may have called in to say they are unable to attend or will be late, and set the agenda by stating what new material will be introduced or what will be practiced in the session. They ask if there is any addition to the agenda, and if there is, this is added. For example, a member may say that she had a bad week because of being fired from her job and would like some support from the group. The facilitators may suggest that the go-round ends with this member and that the group takes some time to support her before moving to other tasks.

Summary

This chapter reviews the historical development, principles, and common applications of CBT. CBT is the treatment of choice for a number of mental health problems across the world. CBT is cost-effective, and if delivered in a group format, even more so. Some of the challenges with transporting individual CBT protocols to a group setting are discussed and illustrated with a panic disorder protocol example. This is followed by a review of the basic common components in the first group session no matter what kind of problem. Despite the limitation to group CBT of less individualized treatment plans, the group format has the potential for offering clients a sense of belonging and validation above and beyond symptom relief. The very format of the group, with its rich possibilities for support and connection, is a critical strength of CBGT. In the next chapter, we take a closer look at how to work with the uniqueness of the group format and especially at how to infuse process factors into basic CBGT.

Notes

1. The diagnostic criteria for panic disorder have not changed from the *Diagnostic and Statistical Manual of Mental Disorders, Fourth Edition* (DSM-IV) (APA, 2000) to the DSM-5 (APA, 2013).
2. The CBT term Socratic dialogue credits the Greek philosopher Socrates (470-399 BC) with his ability to help people understand they already have the insight or solution to their problems within them; it is more a matter of drawing this out by asking good quetions.

Recommended Readings for Clinicians

Barlow, D. H., & Craske, M. G. (2007). *Mastery of your anxiety and panic* (4th ed.). New York: Oxford University Press.

Burlingame, G. M., Strauss, B., & Joyce, A. S. (2013). Change mechanisms and effectiveness of small group treatments. In M. J. Lambert, A. E. Bergin, & S. L. Garfield (Eds.), *Bergin and Garfield's handbook of psychotherapy and behavior change* (6th ed., pp. 640–689). Hoboken, NJ: Wiley-Blackwell.

Coon, D., Shurgot, G. R., Roninson, G., Gillispie, Z., Cardenas, V., & Gallagher-Thompson, D. (2005). Cognitive-behavioral group interventions. In G. O. Gabbard, J. S. Beck, & J. Holmes (Eds.), *Oxford textbook of psychotherapy* (pp. 45–56). New York: Oxford University Press.

References

Alexander, B. (2010). *The globalization of addiction: A study in poverty of the spirit.* Oxford, UK: Oxford University Press.

American Psychiatric Association (APA). (2000). *Diagnostic and statistical manual of mental disorders, DSM* (4th ed.). Washington, DC: Author.

APA. (2013). *Diagnostic and statistical manual of mental disorders, DSM* (5th ed.). Washington, DC: Author.

Australian Department of Health and Aging. (2009). *Primary health care reform in Australia.* Canberra, Australia: Commonwealth of Australia.

Beck, A. T., Freeman, A., & Davis, D. D. (2004). *Cognitive therapy of personality disorders.* New York: Guilford Press.

Beck, A. T., Rush, A. J., Shaw, B. F., & Emery, G. (1979). *Cognitive therapy of depression.* New York: Guilford Press.

Bennett-Levy, J., Richard, D. A., & Farrand, P. (2010). Low intensity CBT interventions: A revolution in mental health care. In J. Bennett-Levy, D. A. Richards, P. Farrand, H. Christensen, K. M. Griffiths, D. J. Kavanagh, B. Klein, M. A. Lau, J. Proudfoot, L. Ritterband, J. White, & C. Williams (Eds.), *Oxford guide to low intensity CBT interventions* (pp. 3–18). Oxford, UK: Oxford University Press.

Bieling, P. J., McCabe, R. E., & Antony, M. A. (2006). *Cognitive-behavioral therapy in groups.* New York: Guilford Press.

Bishop, S. R., Lau, M. A., Shapiro, S., Carlson, L., Anderson, N. D., Carmody, J., et al. (2004). Mindfulness: A proposed operational definition. *Clinical Psychology, 1,* 230–241.

Cable, N., Bartley, M., Chandola, T., & Sacker, A. (2013). Friends are equally important to men and women, but family matters more for men's well-being. *Journal of Epidemiology & Community Health, 67(2)*, 166–171.

Clark, D. M. (2011) *Improving Access to Effective Psychotherapy*. Key note address Presented at the European Association of Behavioural and Cognitive Therapy (EABCT), September 1–3, Reykjavik, Iceland.

Clark, D. M., Layard, R., Smithies, R., Richards, D.A., Suckling, R., & Wright, B. (2009). Improving access to psychological therapy: Initial evaluation of two UK demonstration sites. *Behaviour Research and Therapy, 47*, 910–920.

Cooper, C., Bebbington, P., King, M., Brugha, T., Meltzer, H., Bhugra, D., et al. (2007). Why people do not take their psychotropic drugs as prescribed: Results of the 2000 National Psychiatric Morbidity Survey. *Acta Psychiatrica Scandinavica, 116(1)*, 47–53.

DeRubeis, R. J., Siegle, G. J., & Hollon, S. D. (2008). Cognitive therapy versus medication for depression: Treatment outcomes and neural mechanisms. *Nature Reviews in Neuroscience, 9*, 788–796.

Dwight-Johnson, M., Sherbourne, C. D., Liao, D., & Wells, K. B. (2000). Treatment preferences among depressed primary care patients. *Journal of General Internal Medicine, 15(8)*, 527–534.

Hawton, K., Salkovskis, P. M., Kirk, J., & Clark, D. M. (Eds.) (1989). The development and principles of cognitive-behavioural treatments. In *Cognitive behaviour therapy for psychiatric problems: A practical guide* (pp. 1–12). New York: Oxford University Press.

Hollon, S. D., Stewart, M. O., & Strunk, D. (2006). Cognitive behavior therapy has enduring effects in the treatment of depression and anxiety. *Annual Review of Psychology, 57*, 285–315.

Kessler, R. C., Chiu, W. T., Demler, O., & Walters, E. E. (2005). Prevalence, severity, and comorbidity of twelve-month DSM-IV disorder in the National Comorbidity Survey Replication (NCS-R). *Archives of General Psychiatry, 62*, 617–627.

Lau, M. A. (2010). Mindfulness-based cognitive therapy: A low intensity group program to prevent depressive relapse. In J. Bennett-Levy, D. A. Richards, P. Farrand, H. Christensen, K. M. Griffiths, D. J. Kavanagh, B. Klein, M. A. Lau, J. Proudfoot, L. Ritterband, J. White, & C. Williams (Eds.), *Oxford guide to low intensity CBT interventions* (pp. 407–414). Oxford, UK: Oxford University Press.

London School of Economics and Political Science; Centre for Economic Performance; & Mental Health Policy Group. (2006). *The depression report: A new deal for depression and anxiety disorders*. London: Centre for Economic Performance.

Mood Disorders Society of Canada. (2009). *Quick facts: Mental illness & addiction in Canada*. Retrieved March 4, 2013, from http://www.mooddisorderscanada.ca [accessed on February 20, 2014].

National Institute for Health and Clinical Excellence. (2009). *Depression in adults: NICE updated guideline*. London: Author.

Otto, M., Pollack, K., & Maki, K. (2000). Empirically supported treatments of panic disorder. *Journal of Consulting and Clinical Psychology, 68(4)*, 556–563.

Padesky, C. A., & Greenberger, D. (1995). *Clinician's guide to mind over mood*. New York: Guilford Press.

Ravindran, A., Lam, R., Filteau, M., Lespérance, F., Kennedy, S., Parikh, S., et al. (2009). Canadian Network for Mood and Anxiety Treatments (CANMAT) clinical guidelines for the management of major depressive disorders in adults II. Psychotherapy alone or in combination with antidepressant medication. *Journal of Affective Disorders, 117(1)*, S15–S25.

Swinson, R. P., Antony, M. M., Bleau, P., Chokka, P., Craven, M., Fallu, A., et al. (2006). Clinical practice guidelines: Management of anxiety disorders. *Canadian Journal of Psychiatry, 51(suppl. 2)*, 1S–92S.

Wenzel, A., Liese, B. S., Beck, A. T., & Friedman-Wheeler, D. G. (2012). *Group cognitive therapy for addictions*. New York: Guilford Press.

White, J. (2010). The STEPS model: A high volume, multi-level, multi-purpose approach to address common mental health problems. In J. Bennett-Levy, D. A. Richards, P. Farrand, H. Christensen, K. M. Griffiths, D. J. Kavanagh, B. Klein, M. A. Lau, J. Proudfoot, L. Ritterband, J. White, & C. Williams (Eds.), *Oxford guide to low intensity CBT interventions* (pp. 35–52). Oxford, UK: Oxford University Press.

Wiles, N., Thomas, L., Abel, A., Ridgway, N., Turner, N., Campbell, J., et al. (2013). Cognitive behavioural therapy as an adjunct to pharmacotherapy for primary care based patients with treatment resistant depression: Results of the CoBalT randomised controlled trial. *The Lancet, 381*, 375–384.

Wilkinson, R., & Pickett, K. (2010). *The spirit level: Why greater equality makes societies stronger*. London: Bloomsbury Press.

2

Working with Process and Content

The previous chapter showed how CBGT, despite its advantages and promises, is challenging to implement. This chapter continues the discussion of how therapists can make their groups stronger by paying careful attention to both delivering content and the group process. Although the main message from research comparing group CBT to individual CBT is that the formats are equally effective (to be reviewed in detail in Chapter 3), the lingering notion of group therapy being inferior is out there, even among CBT clinicians. I understand this skeptical attitude. It is indeed a tall order to adhere to a highly structured didactic program where each session must deliver a preset amount of educational material within a strict time period *and* at the same time not have the group look and sound like a classroom. When I do interpersonal therapy (IPT) groups, I admit to often relaxing into my chair because I don't have to worry about presenting anything in particular, but can rather work with what transpires and how it may further individual and group development. I am not minimizing the therapeutic skills required of more dynamically trained group therapists, but rather validating the experience of the conscientious and ambitious CBGT therapist: it is hard to combine two distinct therapeutic traditions, group therapy and CBT, into one seamless, elegantly flowing effective intervention! This chapter begins with a largely theoretical discussion of the distinction between the process and the content of a CBT group before offering concrete clinical examples illustrating how process factors support the delivery of the content in CBGT.

Cognitive Behavioral Group Therapy: Challenges and Opportunities, First Edition. Ingrid Söchting.

Process and Content in Group Therapy

A few words about the history of group therapy. Group psychotherapy was a movement that began in the 1950s. Many people with or without any particular mental health problems participated in these groups, often called T groups, with T standing for training (sensitivity training was the full name). These groups did not follow a certain format or structure but allowed members to freely interact and support one another. Today, these supportive groups are referred to as process groups. Process groups continue to be popular and available in public and academic mental health clinics. For many mental health professionals, especially more senior therapists, group therapy is still primarily equated with process groups. Professional group therapy organizations, such as those in the United States and Canada, also emphasize process groups, and it is rare to find them offering workshops on CBT groups. At the same time as process groups gained momentum, CBT arrived as the new kid on the therapy block, emphasizing a more structured, problem-focused, here and now therapy approach. CBT was originally developed as an individual form of therapy, and although CBT lends itself well to a group format, this adaptation is not straightforward. CBT groups are filled with content and structure as therapists educate group members about their problems and teach them coping skills. But the moment a group of people come together, a number of interpersonal dynamics take place, which can both undermine and enhance the way the group works.

The two key trends in group therapy literature provide a helpful background for understanding the challenges facing the group CBT therapist (Burlingame, Strauss, & Joyce, 2013). The first looks at the **process**—the ways group members relate and experience the group, with the assumption that these dynamics and interactions primarily contribute to positive change. Group process has been defined by Burlingame and colleagues (2013) as the theoretical mechanisms of change within the group, including group development, therapeutic factors, degree and timing of group structure, and interpersonal feedback. Within this group process, overall treatment outcome is also influenced by therapist factors (e.g., leader characteristics such as warmth, ability to understand and work with the group as a vehicle for change in addition to didactic presentation, perceived credibility, and multicultural competence), patient factors (e.g., interpersonal skills, empathy, and more recently language fluency), and structural factors (e.g., length, frequency, quality of setting). This process approach is exemplified in the seminal work by Irvin Yalom in *The Theory and Practice of Group Psychotherapy* (Yalom, 1970, 1995; Yalom & Leszcz, 2005). In a process group, people presumably get better because of the work done BY the group, that is, the process by which group members relate and experience the group.

In contrast, the **content** (also called **structured**) approach, which includes CBT focuses on adherence to specific treatment protocols in creating change. People are assumed to get better because of the work done IN the group, not by it. Clinicians and researchers have adapted individual CBT protocols to group settings for a number of disorders including depression, social and generalized anxiety, obsessive–compulsive, psychotic, and addiction-related disorders as classified in the DSM-IV (American Psychiatric Association [APA], 2000) and DSM-5 (APA, 2013). A few CBGT protocols have been published and provide step-by-step guidelines for treatment. Although research generally supports the efficacy of these adapted individual CBT protocols the clinical reality of running CBT groups in community settings is often less successful than described in the literature. CBGT therapists find themselves struggling with how to best deliver many treatment components in a tight time frame, how to give sufficient individual attention, and how to manage process-oriented interactional issues with little help from a given CBT protocol on how to do this.

Although useful in understanding larger trends, the dichotomy between content and process is not so clear-cut. To say that CBGT is all content and Yalom-style interpersonal groups are all process is an oversimplification. Experienced group therapists of all stripes know it is impossible to not have both elements in both kinds of groups. Interpersonal group therapists find themselves giving mini psychoeducational lectures in their groups, and CBT therapists often bring out tremendous support between group members as they themselves step back and let the group take over. Burlingame and colleagues (2013) offer a helpful conceptualization of how clinicians can better understand the many factors contributing to therapeutic outcomes in any group. They emphasize the importance of understanding both the adherence to a *formal theory of change*, such as CBT, and the *small group processes* operating independently of what therapists formally present in their group sessions.

Group Process in Theory

In an ideal CBT group, therapeutic outcome would be a result of (a) the ability of the facilitators to deliver the formal content presentations and (b) the way the same facilitators capitalize on the group process factors. Bieling, McCabe, and Antony (2006) compiled a list of factors they considered to be involved in the process of CBT groups. One can put these factors into the following categories: (a) group member factors (e.g., the effects of group members' symptoms and personality style on one another), (b) therapeutic relations (e.g., trust between the group and the therapists, between group members, between the cotherapists), (c) effects of individual variables (e.g., client expectations, client satisfaction, variables that may predict outcome or dropout), and (d) group mechanisms of change (e.g., the group processes of inspiration, inclusion, cohesiveness, and hope, among others).

The primary focus in this chapter is the fourth category, group mechanisms of change. (The other factors are, however, also relevant and will be addressed throughout the book.) Yalom's group process model is critical in any discussion of group mechanisms of change, an approach also taken by Bieling and colleagues (2006). The Yalom *group therapeutic factors lens* invigorates CBT groups. The positive benefits include, among many, increases in motivation for engaging with anxiety-provoking behavioral or cognitive challenges. It is, unfortunately, still a rare clinical psychology student in a doctoral CBT program who is familiar with the work of Yalom. Again, the opportunities for enriching existing therapeutic traditions with thoughtful integration are plenty.

In their *Theory and Practice of Group Psychotherapy*, Fourth Edition (2005), Yalom and Leszcz list 11 group therapeutic factors all hypothesized to bring about relief from suffering. For people unfamiliar with Yalom and Leszcz's therapy groups, it is important to know that they are typically for people who suffer from interpersonal problems or a sense of being stuck in their life. Group members may or may not suffer from a diagnosable mood or anxiety disorder, and the Yalom-style groups are not homogeneous in terms of being primarily for depression or anxiety. Thus, the idea of mapping these factors onto highly specific diagnostic CBT groups is perhaps a stretch but also a testament to the truly universal processes of human interactions identified by Yalom. Although 11 distinct factors have been identified and hypothesized to be present in all kinds of psychotherapy groups, readers will likely not be surprised to hear that there is a high correlation among the factors and they neither occur nor function separately (MacNair-Semands, Ogrodniczuk, & Joyce, 2010). The 11 factors are as follows: (1) instillation of hope, (2) universality, (3) imitative behavior, (4) imparting of information, (5) altruism, (6) group cohesiveness, (7) existential factors, (8) catharsis, (9) interpersonal learning, (10) development of socializing techniques, and (11) the corrective recapitulation of the primary family group.

The remainder of this chapter illustrates—using sample dialogue—how some of these group process factors operate. I use an OCD group as an example. The choice of OCD is somewhat arbitrary, and one could pick any group for purposes of illustration of specific process factors. But we have found that process factors seem especially relevant in OCD groups, in part because it can be a challenge to engage group members with OCD in exposure exercises. Chapter 13 offers a detailed description of how to implement CBGT for adolescents with OCD.

Group Process in Practice: Obsessive–Compulsive Disorder Illustration

In what follows, each of the Yalom therapeutic factors is discussed in the context of what typically happens in a group for OCD. I have listed the factors in order of importance, according to the perspective of therapists routinely offering CBT groups for OCD.

Instillation of hope

People with OCD are reluctant to go for group treatment. This is understandable given how they often feel guilty and ashamed. They worry about being judged as "crazy" or "disgusting." Their obsessions may involve fears of molesting children or demanding one's husband remove all of his clothes in the driveway upon returning home from work because he may "contaminate" the family home. It takes people with OCD an average of 10 years to seek help, which is much longer than for other anxiety problems. People with OCD often try to help themselves, and if family members are aware of their illness, they too try to help. Unfortunately, this help is often countertherapeutic and makes the symptoms worse. This happens because family members tend to comply with the request for compulsions or reassurance. It is, understandably, easier to agree to wash the same load of laundry a third time than put up with a temper tantrum. It is also fairly easy to quickly repeat to a loved one, even for the 15th time, as it literally takes only 2 seconds each time: "No, I don't think you touched that girl inappropriately." Thus, it is not surprising that when someone finally presents for treatment, hope is dwindling. Here is an example of how hope can be installed in the therapy group when members meet each other and realize they are not alone in wanting to face their fears.

THERAPIST: So, we're now nearing the end of our first session and we hope you all have a fairly good sense of how this group for OCD may help you. We know we have only spoken generally about the treatment components, and you probably have many unanswered questions about how this will work for you specifically, but it will all make more and more sense as we move on each week. Are there any further questions or comments before we let you go?

JIM: I just want to say I have never met another person with OCD and I can't believe that Jenny also turns her car around and drives home on her way to work so that she can check she locked the front door. Her saying she is ready to face this fear makes me feel I can do it too.

JULIA: Yes, I also feel ready to face my fears. Although it sounds scary to have to actually face what we fear and not give in to our compulsions, knowing that we'll do it together and support each other makes me so glad I came to this group.

SUN-MING: I really appreciate how you facilitators said that although it's going to be difficult, really difficult at times, you promise that whatever you ask us to do will be safe and that we're always in charge. I just feel so hopeful to have come to this group which I had no idea had been running in my city for so many years.

Therapists take steps to reinforce the sense of hope by concluding with words to the effect of: "We are glad you each found your way to this group, and the courage to give it a try. We know how hard it is for any person to confront something we would rather avoid. We can tell there is already tremendous support and this will make the hard work easier—and even fun at times. We really look forward to working with you all." Almost invariably, the first OCD group ends with people chatting, even laughing, and exchanging "good to meet you" and "see you next week, man."

Universality

Learning—often for the first time—that one is not the only person doing "weird" things or having "bad" thoughts is tremendously encouraging for an OCD sufferer. As therapists, we go out of our way to highlight universality—even to the point of making people realize their obsessions are quite common. Here is an example of how to work with universality to strengthen the commitment to treatment.

GERTRUDE: I know I'm the only person who hasn't shared what my obsessions are and I appreciate the therapists telling me during my assessment that I didn't have to. The treatment could still be effective as a big part of the group focuses on people's individual fears.

THOMPSON: That's OK by me, but I sure found it helpful to hear that Peter also stops to get out of his car when driving over speed bumps [a harm obsession often involves believing that a speed bump could have been a pedestrian or an animal struck by the OCD sufferer].

GERTRUDE: It's just that my obsessions are so unusual and I don't think anyone else has ever heard of them, probably not even you because I didn't say everything when I first met with you [looks at the facilitators]. OK, I'll say it then: I can't pick up my baby without someone else around because I fear I may strangle her [Gertrude starts crying—and someone pushes the Kleenex box across the table].

THERAPIST: We appreciate how hard it is to share this and imagine you fearing you may be judged by the group about what kind of mother you are, but you need to know that we have seen many mothers with exactly that same obsession. So, in some ways your fears are not unique. They're called "harm obsessions." It's a pretty common form of obsession. Remember, these obsessions you all have come in different forms but they have nothing to do with what you're really like as a person.

THOMPSON: Does that mean that I should not think of myself as a dangerous driver? [Group discussion ensues on how obsessions are clinical phenomena and do not reflect on the character of a person]

Imitative behavior and peer modeling

A great opportunity for assuaging anxiety about facing one's fears is to do it with someone who shares that fear. The main treatment component of any CBT protocol for OCD is *exposure and response prevention* (ERP) (Chapter 13 covers this in detail). ERP involves facing the feared or avoided stimulus (exposure) and refraining from performing the compulsive activity (response prevention). In all OCD groups, the first four sessions are devoted to education about OCD and developing a list of situations or triggers for the obsessions. Thereafter and until the last session, group members begin to do their individual exposures and response prevention in the session. The opportunity to have peers rather than the therapist model exposure and desensitization is a helpful part of group CBT, to the point where I can hardly imagine treating an OCD person individually again (unless of course there are legitimate reasons for not recommending a group).

In every session involving ERP, the therapists and the group members negotiate an exposure challenge in a go-round fashion. Therapists look for opportunities to implement imitative behaviors, that is, peer-assisted exposure, and may say something like:

THERAPIST: It's now our 6th session and what we wondered about for you, Joe, is whether you feel up for going with Boris to the men's washroom. Touching walls in a public washroom is rated 50/100 on your fear hierarchy, Joe, so now that you're halfway through your treatment, we thought you may feel ready for that. [Boris has already overcome many of his fears of public washrooms and is now working on obsessions related to contamination from household cleaning products.] Does this sound like something you would like to challenge yourself on today, or do you have something else in mind for an exposure?

JOE: I'm up for that, and I think it's time that I touch all the walls, the toilet seat, and flush a couple of times.

JOE, AFTER HAVING COMPLETED HIS IN-SESSION EXPOSURE: Wow—that was gross but seeing Boris being so cool about it, made it easier for me. He even made me keep my hands on the seat while he asked me about the hockey game last night. I almost forgot where my hands were—but not really, that's for sure! Pretty clever, Boris! [both men laugh].

Imparting of information

Imparting of information refers to how group members share what has helped them cope with their OCD. To illustrate how group members can learn from each other, we will continue with the example of Joe and Boris.

BORIS: Yeah, I've found that trying not to obsess [ha-ha] about what my hands are touching but instead think of something I care about really helps to keep my hands longer on what I think—or used to think—is really dirty. I'm crazy about hockey, so I often try to review a game or a great play in my mind.

JOE: I'm definitely going to try that, but given how our local team sucks this season, I'll try to bring my favorite American football team to mind when I do my exposure homework.

Altruism

The aforementioned example of Boris and Joe also showed how altruism can operate in CBT groups when members support each other through difficult exposures. Altruism usually develops spontaneously as most people readily empathize with others even though their concerns and problems are different. Group facilitators can promote altruism by reinforcing the benefits of learning from and helping each other. In the beginning of a group, group members are often unsure about how much they are allowed to help each other—knowing they're not permitted to socialize outside of the group. Usually, as the group develops, many acts of spontaneous altruism arise in addition to those fostered by the facilitators. Staying with Boris and Joe, we see such an example.

JOE: Although I'm proud of how I did my exposure, I don't think I can make it to my car without washing my hands.

THERAPIST: You know, Joe, nobody can prevent you from doing what you feel you must do. We encourage you to remind yourself that your obsession about your hands being contaminated is strong, but it is just an obsession. You can make choices on how you deal with it. You can wash now, you can delay until you get home, or until you eat your next meal.

JOE: I know, I know. The feeling is just so intense and to tell you the truth, after last session I washed my hands in another washroom in this building, not the one in this area but the one just by the main exit door.

BORIS: Hey Joe, let me accompany you to your car, if that's OK?

Group cohesiveness

This sense of belonging tends to build as the group develops and people feel more and more safe and comfortable talking about their obsessions and their difficulties adhering to the exposure exercises. Although therapists constantly look for opportunities to strengthen the sense of belonging and acceptance, some groups are clearly more cohesive than others. Not surprisingly, groups with the highest cohesion are also those where attendance and motivation are high—and expectations for improvement realistic. A couple of dropouts in earlier sessions is manageable as the group shakes into its final form, but dropouts in the middle and near the end can be detrimental to cohesion. Remaining group members may wonder if they caused someone to leave. OCD clients tend to be high in conscientiousness; thus, this is an issue that can interfere with cohesion.

When cohesion is strong, it is common for group members to fear the end of the group, especially for those OCD sufferers who felt understood and accepted perhaps for the first time. Therapists can help by offering a notion of the group lasting even after it is officially over.

MARGO: I am scared I'll not be able to keep up my home practice exposure when I will not be reporting back to you guys.

BEN: I too will miss my weekly injection of support as I always feel better about myself when I leave here.

THERAPIST: How could you still feel connected to this group even after it's over?

BEN: I will try to keep a mental image of all of you and I'll sure never forget you. When I feel stressed, I'll bring you all to mind and remember all the support you gave me.

MARGO: That's a great idea, and I'll do that too. If it's OK, I'll also pass a piece of paper around in our last session, and if any of you want to put your phone number on it, maybe we could agree to offer some support to each other as we continue with our exposures.

Existential factors

Existential factors refers to how group members face the human condition, become more fully engaged with their lives and less caught up in trivialities. At first glance, issues of existentialism may not seem relevant to the more symptom-oriented work of a CBT OCD group. We have, however, found that living with OCD has a profound and life-altering negative impact, trapping a person in a dark place where they question the meaning and value of their life. For those for whom treatment progresses well, existential issues often come up without prompting, as illustrated in this dialogue.

KAREN: I can't believe how much time I've wasted on senseless reordering of my kitchen, creating a hellish atmosphere for my husband and children. I wouldn't even allow my husband to cook with me because he would "mess up my counters and cupboards." I feel so free now that I care so much less about how I organize my kitchen. I'm almost ready to laugh at how I had my spices organized according to color [cries]. Here I am laughing and crying again.

TOR: But just think how many more years you have to make up for this lost time, and all the fun cooking times you can have with your family now that your OCD is no longer controlling you and turning your passions into prisons.

KAREN: Thanks, Tor, and I do feel so lucky that my son and daughter are still young enough to have many good memories of all of us having fun cooking and making messes. My husband gave me this wonderful Italian cookbook as recognition for how far I've come; he's so proud of me and our relationship feels stronger than ever.

Catharsis

Although traditional CBT groups do not explicitly focus on, or encourage catharsis—the purging of pent-up distress in the form of expressing negative (or positive) feelings—it naturally happens. In the first couple of sessions, the group therapists can invite members to express what their OCD feels, or even looks, like. Personifying OCD is a common intervention for children, and we find it works well for adults too.

Figure 2.1 Man chained to desk.

We ask members to draw a picture of their OCD. As is apparent from the depiction of a man chained to his desk, this group member experiences his OCD as a freedom-robbing torturer demanding that notes are rewritten for what feels like endless hours until they are absolutely perfect (Figure 2.1).

When group members share their graphic depictions in the go-round, this is often accompanied by tears or attempts to not choke up—and facilitators too become moved at the sense of imprisonment this disorder brings.

Interpersonal learning and new ways of socializing

An effective CBT OCD group must remain focused on symptoms and not derail into an interpersonal supportive therapy group. If the structure becomes loose, most members will not make any significant gains in overcoming their symptoms. Too much "talking" and not enough "doing" can encourage avoidance of facing the work that is necessary in breaking compulsive behaviors. Therapists, however, can encourage group members to experiment with new ways of relating to others while still keeping the focus on the OCD symptoms. The mutual support offered is one way of creating interpersonal opportunities and especially to offer difficult feedback. It is not uncommon for group members to surprise themselves by developing a new level of assertiveness, as shown in the way Brit expresses herself in the following dialogue.

BRIT: Jonathan, I find it interesting that you now for the third week in a row say you realize you don't mind your obsessions, which tell you to keep all aspects of your appearance absolutely symmetrical. While the rest of us struggle with exposures, you say yours don't cause you much anxiety—and you refused my offer of painting a few dots on your forehead during our group time last week. You don't seem to practice much at home either.

JONATHAN: I'm just not sure this therapy works for me.

BRIT: I hope I don't offend you, but I recall you saying how terrified you are of losing your good looks by caring less about your appearance. That suggests you may be avoiding the exposure work, and we are already past the halfway mark of our group.

JONATHAN: You're right. I needed to hear someone say that. My girlfriend is so afraid I'll leave therapy but also of upsetting me by asking how it's going. I'm very scared of messing up my appearance but will make a new commitment to therapy.

BRIT: I don't think I've ever talked so directly and frankly to someone before, but I really care about all of us here and enjoy being more honest also with myself.

Experiencing the group as similar to one's family of origin

This process factor is also referred to as the *corrective recapitulation of the primary family group* (Yalom & Leszcz, 2005). Symptom-focused groups deliberately do not attempt to create a sense of a second family with the opportunity to rework large or small childhood traumas. That of course does not mean these healing opportunities do not take place. Therapists can easily be experienced as benign and understanding parents, and the group members as caring siblings. The opposite can also take place, and it happens that a member in an OCD group has more family of origin issues than the therapists initially understood. This may be the case when, for example, OCD symptoms seem to serve the function of controlling intense internal conflicts related to childhood sexual or physical abuse. If there has not been any therapeutic disclosure or attempt to address some of the prior abuse, there is a risk of the group becoming a retraumatizing experience. Another group member or one of the facilitators may remind the client of an abusive family member. The intensity of exposures can also be experienced as attempts by the therapists and the group to disarm the client from using their compulsive defenses, such as spending 3 hours a day soaking in a bathtub to stay "clean." In such cases, the group member may agree to leave the group and accept a referral for trauma therapy or for a type of CBT specific to contamination obsessions stemming from interpersonal violations including sexual, physical, or psychological abuse (Coughtrey, Shafran, Lee, & Rachman, 2013). CBT for this kind of metaphorical or *mental contamination* recognizes that traditional exposure therapy does not work well for people whose obsessions are not triggered by an external tangible source of contamination—such as a doorknob in a public washroom—but rather by internal memories of their abuse or their self-loathing thoughts. Beliefs such as "I'm a dirty and disgusting person" reflect how people may internalize the abuse they suffered.

Group process research and CBGT application

Therapists conducting CBGT for OCD will hopefully feel an increase in confidence as they recognize, from their own groups, some of the scenarios sketched using the Yalom therapeutic factors lens. Keeping track, however, of 11 factors may seem overwhelming. They are not meant to be followed too literally. The main point of this chapter is to remind the therapist to *engage* the group as fully as possible, as this leads to better therapeutic outcomes. Work by group psychotherapy researchers suggests that the 11 factors may in fact be reduced to four main overarching factors: (1) *instillation of hope*, (2) *secure emotional expression*, (3) *awareness of relational impact*, and (4) *social learning*. These four factors were derived from a factor analysis study using items pertaining to all 11 therapeutic factors, the *Therapeutic Factors Inventory* (Lese & MacNair-Semands, 2000). This successful factor analysis created a shorter version, the *Therapeutic Factors Inventory-Short Form* (TFI-S; Joyce, MacNair-Semands, Tasca, & Ogrodniczuk, 2011; MacNair-Semands et al., 2010).

Keeping the aforementioned OCD group in mind, we see how Brit's more assertive feedback to Jonathan, and his taking her seriously, may have been brought about because both group members trusted and respected the group to be a place where they could express themselves honestly. Thus, the *secure emotional expression* and *awareness of relational impact* factors were operating. The support between Joe and Boris was an example of the group facilitators promoting *social learning*.

In addition to the work of MacNair-Semands, Joyce, and colleagues, other researchers have also attempted to identify *essential* therapeutic factors that operate in group therapy. Factors such as emotional awareness–insight, problem-definition change, relationship climate, and other-focus versus self-focus have been proposed (Kivlighan, Multon, & Brossart, 1996). Working with fewer, more global, group therapeutic factors makes the process aspects of CBGT seem more manageable. Future clinical research will likely uncover new group therapeutic factors.

CBGT therapists may realize how much they are already incorporating several process factors, or they may begin to see missed opportunities. It is fair to say that we are seeing a general trend to move away from strict didactic presentations in CBT groups to include a much more active encouragement of members to relate to one another. This change of energy in the CBT group brings numerous new opportunities for enhanced therapeutic outcomes. For example, in Chapters 16 and 17 on psychosis and addiction, respectively, I discuss two new recent CBGT manuals—both of which list the Yalom group therapeutic factors reviewed in this chapter (Strauss & Hayward, 2013; Wenzel, Liese, Beck, & Friedman-Wheeler, 2012). These may be the first CBGT manuals for a specific problem to explicitly offer instructions for how to work with group process factors in addition to structured CBT interventions. Throughout this book, I discuss how to integrate group process factors into standard CBGT approaches to specific problems.

Another practical way to work with group process factors is for therapists to evaluate how well they incorporate them in their CBT groups.

Scott's General Group Therapeutic Skills Rating Scale

In his group CBT book (limited to five homogeneous anxiety disorders and one mood disorder), Michael Scott (2011) offers a useful appendix, *General Group Therapeutic Skills Rating Scale*. It is a set of general guidelines that allow group therapists to work better in and with their CBT groups. The rating scale is designed to measure how well a therapist delivers the content in a CBT group and manages the *process*, defined by Scott—and many others—as the sum of the interactions in the group. The scale can be used as a self-assessment tool for group therapists including therapists in training. There are nine areas: (1) *Review of Homework/Agenda*, (2) *Relevance*, (3) *Adaptation*, (4) *Inclusion*, (5) *Additional Disorders*, (6) *Magnifying Support and Minimising Criticism*, (7) *Utilising Group Members as Role Models*, (8) *Therapist Presentation Skills, and* (9) *Addressing Group Issues*. Each area is rated with a score of either 0, 2, 4, or 6. Ratings of 6, the highest, would indicate maximal adeptness and competence in a given area. For example, the first area *Review of Homework/Agenda* is a basic structural part of individual and group CBT. The lowest score of 0 would be a therapist who "did not set an agenda/did not review homework." Other areas of Scott's group rating scale address more specifically the group format.

For example, the area of *Utilising Group Members as Role Models* allows one to rate whether the *therapist focused entirely on himself/herself as the source of persuasion* (rated 0, the lowest) or *therapist adeptly tuned into the assumptive world of each group member and was able to draw on it to reinforce alliances between members and ensure application of material taught outside the session* (rated 6, the highest). Another area is *Inclusion*, where the lowest level would be a *Therapist allowed the most vociferous group members to dominate the group* and the second highest level with a rating of 4 is *Therapist ensured all group members had reasonable air time but had some difficulties with some of the less vocal group members.*

Working with Scott's scale helps cotherapists to self-reflect and realize where they may want to pay more attention. During a debriefing after a depression group, therapists may decide to give themselves a score of 4 on the *Inclusion* scale, acknowledging that a few group members dominated today's session and that they "ran out of time" and did not get to review new homework with the two most quiet members. Cotherapists may use Scott's scale as a springboard for offering feedback to each other and show that they can openly hear this. After a panic group, a cotherapist may say to his colleague: "I was impressed with how you presented the rationale for exposure to internal body sensations—nice Power Point slides and some good links to useful self-help resources. I also like how you made the two of us first demonstrate the exercises. It was pretty funny when I broke the straw in straw breathing. I think it put everyone more at ease as they got into the exercises.[1] I think a high rating of 6 is appropriate for *Therapist Presentation Skills* in today's session."

Summary

This chapter reviews theory and practical approaches to combining process and content in CBGT for a range of mental health problems. In particular, the work of Irvin Yalom is highlighted, and a specific example of an OCD CBT group is used to offer clinical illustrations of 11 group therapeutic factors. The chapter also reviews group psychotherapy research aimed at reducing these 11 therapeutic factors to a smaller number while still capturing overarching and essential group processes. Lastly, the chapter presents a group process evaluation tool for CBGT therapists. The next chapter is less clinically focused as it reviews the literature to date on CBGT for the disorders covered in this book.

Note

1. Breathing through a straw, especially a small one like the stir sticks from Starbucks, restricts air intake and thus presents a challenge for people who become panicky at the sensation of "not getting enough air."

Recommended Readings for Clinicians

Bieling, P. J., McCabe, R. E., & Antony M. A. (2006). *Cognitive-behavioral therapy in groups*. New York: Guilford.

Burlingame, G. M., Strauss, B., & Joyce, A. S. (2013). Change mechanisms and effectiveness of small group treatments. In M. J. Lambert, A. E. Bergin, & S. L. Garfield (Eds.), *Bergin and Garfield's handbook of psychotherapy and behavior change* (6th ed., pp. 640–689). New York: Wiley-Blackwell.

Scott, M. J. (2011). *Simply effective group cognitive behaviour therapy: A practitioner's guide*. London: Routledge.

Yalom, I. D., & Leszcz, M. (2005). *The theory and practice of group psychotherapy* (5th ed.). New York: Basic Books.

References

American Psychiatric Association (APA). (2000). *Diagnostic and statistical manual of mental disorders, DSM* (4th ed.). Washington, DC: Author.

APA. (2013). *Diagnostic and statistical manual of mental disorders, DSM* (5th ed.). Washington, DC: Author.

Coughtrey, A. E., Shafran, R., Lee, M., & Rachman, S. (2013). The treatment of mental contamination: A case series. *Cognitive and Behavioral Practice, 20*, 221–231.

Joyce, A. S., MacNair-Semands, R. R., Tasca, G. A., & Ogrodniczuk, J. S. (2011). Factor structure and validity of the Therapeutic Factors Inventory-Short Form. *Group Dynamics: Theory, Research and Practice, 15(3)*, 201–219.

Kivlighan, D. M., Multon, K. S., & Brossart, D. F. (1996). Helpful impacts in group counselling: Development of a multidimensional rating system. *Journal of Counseling Psychology, 43*, 347–355.

Lese, K. P., & MacNair-Semands, R. R. (2000). The Therapeutic Factors Inventory: Development of a scale. *Group, 24*, 303–317.

MacNair, R. R., Ogrodniczuk, J. S., & Joyce, A. S. (2010). Structure and initial validation of a short form of the Therapeutic Factors Inventory. *International Journal of Group Psychotherapy, 60(2)*, 245–281.

Strauss, C., & Hayward, M. (2013). Group person-based cognitive therapy for distressing psychosis. In E. M. J. Morris, L. C. Johns, & J. E. Oliver (Eds.), *Acceptance and commitment therapy and mindfulness for psychosis* (pp. 240–255). West Sussex, UK: Wiley-Blackwell.

Wenzel, A., Liese, B. S., Beck, A. T., & Friedman-Wheeler, D. G. (2012). *Group cognitive therapy for addictions*. New York: Guilford Press.

Yalom, I. D. (1970). *The theory and practice of group psychotherapy*. New York: Basic Books.

Yalom, I. D. (1995). *The theory and practice of group psychotherapy* (4th ed.). New York: Basic Books.

3

Effectiveness of CBGT Compared to Individual CBT: Research Review

CBT clinicians can rightly feel pleased to be part of a therapy tradition where clinicians do not just "believe" we do good work. Instead, CBT clinicians are expected to remain open and nondefensively interested in reflecting and revising our interventions as informed by research and immediate client or group feedback. This stance is not unique to CBT clinicians but does tend to especially define them. Research shows that therapists have grossly inflated self-assessments about their personal effectiveness (Walfish, McAlister, O'Donnell, & Lambert, 2012), including findings showing that the least effective therapists rated themselves as being on par with the most effective therapists (Hiatt & Hargrave, 1995).

This praise for CBT does of course not mean that all CBT therapists are equally effective in delivering an empirically supported CBT intervention. Research has identified a number of therapist factors that enhance outcomes for all kinds of psychotherapy including CBT (e.g., ability to make clients feel understood, ability to adjust our interpersonal behavior to the needs of our clients, as well as ability to encourage our clients to attempt new solutions to their problems and abandon maladaptive patterns; Lambert, 2013). For CBT, technical interventions are not likely to be successful unless the therapeutic relationship, or group process, is characterized by trust, acceptance, empathy, and warmth. The empirically supported psychotherapist is as important as the empirically supported intervention (Lambert, 2013).

CBT is a comfortable professional home for many clinicians because of our willingness to subject clinical questions and hunches to further scrutiny, whether we become involved in conducting clinical research or consume research by

Cognitive Behavioral Group Therapy: Challenges and Opportunities, First Edition. Ingrid Söchting.

doing literature reviews. Either way, we become prepared to make practice changes based on new evidence. Evidence-based practice is thus a guiding principle for CBT therapists and means that we turn to the literature when choosing a treatment program for a particular disorder or problem. We are aware that research evidence does not imply absolute truths as the science of psychology and psychotherapy slowly evolves and new findings become translated into new guidelines for clinical practice. CBT therapists whose training involved courses on research methods are aware that research findings are only as good as the particular research method used—including the chosen statistical analyses. An ability to critically evaluate any research design and method is important. However, this skill is not consistently taught in mental health therapy training programs.

A problem with many treatment outcome studies, for which CBT has especially been famous, is that they tell us a lot about how people did *on average*, in other words which treatment approach "won" in the horse race comparing different treatments. But they hardly tell us anything about for whom this treatment did not work well and why. This group is sometimes referred to as the *alternative minority*. Instead of the horse race-type outcome studies, this minority would benefit from a "true horses for courses" approach (White, 2010). It is thus important to not interpret evidence-informed practice in a narrow sense—to mean only treatment outcome studies of the randomized controlled kind. CBT clinicians benefit from being informed by additional kinds of evidence. Evidence comes in many forms including case studies on individuals or groups in community clinic settings without control groups, pre- and posttreatment outcome evaluations, simple wait-list control designs, and research as well as theory on the importance of the therapeutic relationship and group cohesion as a necessary condition for more technical interventions. Indeed, with extensive research showing CBT produces positive long-term outcomes for between 50% and 80% of people receiving it (highest success for panic disorder and lowest for GAD), CBT research is turning more to questions pertaining to the *alternative minority* (Lambert, 2013).

This chapter will look at key literature findings on the effectiveness of CBGT for the mental health problems covered in this book. Of special interest are studies directly evaluating group CBT against individual CBT for the same disorder. Each subsequent chapter contains more detailed literature reviews for the various topics covered. When clinicians and program managers seek to become familiar with the CBGT research, they are naturally interested in both evidence of cost-effectiveness and improved client functioning. As will become clear, the majority of studies for all the reviewed disorders support the *equivalence hypothesis*. In other words, research ranging from randomized controlled trials to nonrandomized community clinic effectiveness studies has not found significant differences between individual and group CBT.

One important caveat to keep in mind when reviewing group treatment outcome studies is that not all aspects of improved well-being are measured. There may be other benefits not captured in traditional measurements of CBGT, such as increased self-esteem, decreased social isolation, and improved quality of life. For example, some members in a group for panic disorder became encouraged to sign up for a community class on yoga because a member spoke about how she enjoyed it. The benefits to her were apparent to the other members. On the other hand, although the literature indicates that for some problems a group format is highly promising or even superior to individual, this may not fully match clinicians' experiences. Our groups often feel less successful than what the outcome literature shows. This is due to the fact that group clients in research studies are carefully selected and screened, a luxury group therapists in community clinics do not enjoy to the same extent.

Lastly, treatment outcome evaluations naturally only reflect the kind of treatment offered. CBGT is a relatively new approach for a number of disorders. Many group therapists continue to feel they are experimenting to some degree with how to best tailor individual protocols to a group setting. Any evaluation of CBGT is thus limited to its present mode of delivery and is just one step in a continuous dynamic cycle of evaluating revised forms of interventions based on feedback from both research and frontline group therapists. The chapter closes with suggestions for research-informed improvements in CBGT practice.

Depression

Depression was the first disorder for which a group CBT format was created (Beck, Rush, Shaw, & Emery, 1979). The past three decades has seen an increase in research support for CBGT for depression. The steadily better outcomes are likely a reflection of CBT clinicians becoming more familiar and better trained with this format. As we see below, clinician researchers predict that CBGT for depression will become even more successful as clinicians begin to work consistently with the group process factors.

In their review, Tucker and Oei (2007) concluded that group CBT is as effective as individual and certainly less costly in terms of the ratio of paid clinician hours per client. Several other researchers draw a similar conclusion, stating that group CBT is effective and performs at roughly the same level as individual treatment (Burlingame, Strauss, & Joyce, 2013; Craigie & Nathan, 2009; Cramer, Salisbury, Conrad, Eldred, & Araya, 2011; DeRubeis & Crits-Cristoph, 1998; Oei & Dingle, 2008; Scott & Stradling, 1990). Most recently, a meta-analysis of 34 effectiveness studies on outpatient individual and group CBT for depression concluded that CBGT for depression was equally as effective as individual CBT (Hans & Hiller, 2013a). The most encouraging aspect of this is that CBGT required fewer sessions (about 11) to achieve the same improvement in depression compared to individual CBT (about 21 sessions). And CBGT resulted in fewer dropouts. Although the average individual CBT dropout rate is not reported, the overall dropout rate for both group and individual was 24.6%, compared to 21.4% for CBGT. These dropout rates are, however, considered unacceptably high by the authors (Hans & Hiller, 2013a). I agree and offer suggestions for how to improve dropouts from CBGT for depression in Chapter 6.

The aforementioned research was done on mid-age adults, usually from ages 18 to 65, but the same conclusions seem to hold for both older and younger depressed people. For older people, the few studies to date show that group CBT can be considered just as helpful as individual. Group CBT can in some ways even be viewed as superior, when one considers that social isolation is a greater risk factor for depression in elderly people compared to other age groups (Kennedy & Tanenbaum, 2000; Krishna et al., 2010). Krishna and colleagues dampen enthusiasm, however, when they point out that although they found a statistically significant effect (six qualifying trials) favoring CBGT for depression in the elderly, these differences between CBGT and other forms of treatment were "at best modest," suggesting that CBGT for the elderly could be improved (Chapter 11 discusses CBGT for depressed elderly people). For children and adolescents, we see the same picture of CBGT gaining in popularity as clinicians increasingly recognize it as at least equal to individual (Clarke, Rohde, Lewinsohn, Hops, & Seeley, 1999; Chapter 12 resumes this topic of CBGT for depressed children).

From the aforementioned summary, group therapists will hopefully feel supported in their commitment to preferring a group CBT format for depression. But they may also feel some frustration that, when subjected to quantitative scrutiny, this format does not look as effective as we would like to believe. Bieling and colleagues (Bieling, McCabe, & Antony, 2006) are convincing when they, in their discussion of the literature on CBGT for depression, point out that group process factors do not appear to have been formally taken into account, which may explain why many outcomes are not better. This speculation is consistent with the spirit of this book, namely, that we CBGT clinicians can capitalize even more on the group processes. Oei and Dingle (2008) echo this sentiment when they challenge clinicians to an "urgent need to develop and evaluate a coherent group CBT theory, in particular the roles of group processes, before further major advancement in this area can be made."

Social Anxiety Disorder (SAD)

The research is mixed on whether an individual or a group CBT approach is better, but, overall, it is reasonable to assume equivalence. Despite a couple of trials pointing to the superiority of a group format, the majority of studies—including meta-analyses (Fedoroff & Taylor, 2001; Gould, Buckminster, Pollack, Otto, & Yap, 1997)—have failed to find significant differences between formats. It makes clinical intuitive sense that a problem so clearly rooted in social situations may be best addressed in a group setting. As we will see, however, this is not always the case, and there is room for improvement in how we design and deliver CBGT for social anxiety.

While Hope, Heimberg, and Bruch (1995) found socially anxious people benefited from being in a group compared to those who were on a list waiting to go into a group, Stangier and colleagues (Stangier, Heidenreich, Peitz, Lauterbach, & Clark,

2003) did not find a group format especially effective. When Stangier and colleagues did a direct comparison of individual and group cognitive therapy over 15 weekly sessions, they found that individual outperformed group (50% no longer met criteria after individual treatment compared to only 13.6% after group). The protocol included the full range of standard treatment components, such as shifting attention to external cues, stopping safety behaviors, video feedback to correct distorted self-imagery, behavioral experiments, and cognitive restructuring. Although the treatment protocol seems comprehensive, Scott (2011) offers a helpful observation by pointing out that only half of the treatment sessions included actual in-session behavioral exposures. A further argument for the importance of exposure can be advanced from the Hope et al. (1995) study, where the exposure alone was more effective than the overall CBGT package, at least in the shorter term.

According to Scott's analysis of the Stangier study, with which I concur, it is possible that the clients involved were deprived of some unique opportunities provided by a group setting to "test out" and overcome their social fears. Those opportunities include creating more in-session exposures—such as role-playing and speaking in front of a "mock" audience, not to mention exposure to internal feared sensations, such as feeling hot and sensing sweaty palms and a dry mouth. Interestingly, one other study has found that a group format was superior to an individual when the key treatment ingredient was precisely *in vivo* exposures that rehearsed real-life social interactions (Wlazlo, Schroeder-Hartwig, Hand, Kaiser, & Münchau, 1990).

Despite studies showing CBGT to be effective, especially if exposure is included, many CBGT therapists admit with some frustration that their social anxiety groups do not seem to help their clients as much as the research claims. A recent study comparing four potential mediators in CBT for social anxiety (avoidance, self-focused attention, cognitive processing related to anticipation of social encounters, and postevent processing) found that individual CBT had larger positive effects on each of the four mediators (Hedman et al., 2013). But most interestingly, and contrary to expectations, the individual format resulted in larger improvements in avoidance behavior, despite exposure exercises being more emphasized both implicitly and explicitly in the group format. Hedman and colleagues offer various speculations on this somewhat puzzling finding. They wonder about the possibility that individual CBT allows for more idiosyncratically tailored designs of exposure exercises. They also suggest that the behavioral experiments used in individual CBT aimed at testing specific negative assumption have a more generalizable effect across feared situations compared to in-session exposure limited to the group room. Lastly, a recent meta-analysis on CBT for anxiety disorders shows no difference in dropout rates between individual CBT and CBGT for social anxiety (Hans & Hiller, 2013b).

These research findings on CBGT for social anxiety can help clinicians consider possible improvements to our groups. It appears that including behavioral exposures within the group is critical but that persistent practice of individual exposure between group sessions is equally important. There is no doubt that other creative solutions to better CBGT for social anxiety are needed. It is our experience—similar to other clinicians including Scott (2011)—that mixing panic disorder clients with socially anxious ones in the same group is one possible step toward making the group format more effective. All group members have in common an intense fear of unexpected panic attacks. But the mix of people with panic disorder and social anxiety creates a lighter atmosphere. The socially anxious people often enjoy the more forward and easy interactions that are typical of people with panic disorder. Even though it is not explicitly encouraged by the facilitators, group members with panic disorder become helpful models for social interactions. Chapter 7 offers more information on this transdiagnostic option.

Obsessive–Compulsive Disorder (OCD)

OCD may have received more group research attention than the other disorders discussed in this chapter, but only a handful of studies have directly compared group to individual. A number of studies have found that OCD can be treated effectively in a group format (Whittal & McLean, 2002; McLean et al., 2001; VanNoppen, Steketee, McCorkle, & Pato, 1997). When compared directly to individual, group CBT for OCD does well and is generally just as effective as individual CBT, including in regard to relapse prevention rates (Whittal, Robichaud, Thordarson, & McLean, 2008). Jaurrieta et al. (2008) not only found that group and individual are equally effective at 6 and 12 months follow-up but also equivalent regarding the number of dropouts. Similar results were obtained by Fals-Stewart, Marks, and Shafer (1993) who found no differences between group and individual in terms of symptom reduction. It is noteworthy that this latter outcome evaluation included an unusual high number of sessions, 24 for each modality. The most recent direct comparison of CBGT to individual CBT confirmed that the two formats are equivalent (Jónsson, Hougaard, & Bennedsen, 2011).

Some types of OCD may be especially challenging to treat in a pure CBGT format and may require additional individual CBT. O'Connor et al. (2005) did a treatment outcome study involving a subtype of OCD generally considered harder to treat, that is, primary obsessions without overt compulsions. An example would be a person who has intense worries about blurting out an obscenity in church, for example, "God sucks," and as a result has stopped going and feels the loss of a spiritual community. The O'Connor group treatment condition was not purely group CBT but also included four initial individual sessions before the 12 group sessions. The individual treatment condition consisted of 16 sessions (14 lasting an hour and 2 lasting an hour and a half). Both formats were effective, but the individual produced greater changes in anxiety and depression in addition to OCD symptoms. Also, as pointed out by Bieling (Bieling et al., 2006), the O'Connor groups were large—with 13 clients in each. This may have contributed to the weaker effect of the group format. OCD groups in community clinics do not usually exceed eight members.

Similar to other client presentations, it can be hard to "sell" a group format to people with OCD. O'Connor et al. (2005) found that 38% of OCD clients refused treatment in a group format. They stated several pregroup fears about having to share their problems with others, fearing they would not get sufficient attention, and possibly acquiring new obsessions from others in the group. Similar to the O'Connor clients, these fears are expressed in our OCD clients as well. The shame at divulging sexual, religious, or aggressive obsessive content is understandable. However, a recent meta-analysis of CBT for anxiety disorders shows no difference in dropout rates between individual CBT and CBGT for OCD. The average dropout rate was 15.06% (Hans & Hiller, 2013b). Some ways to address these specific OCD group fears are discussed in Chapter 6.

Generalized Anxiety Disorder (GAD)

Lead protocol developer and researcher Michel Dugas concluded that group CBT is as effective as individual CBT (Dugas et al., 2003) for GAD. An individual GAD protocol with focus on positive beliefs about worry, problem-solving training, and exposure to uncertainty was adapted to a group setting. Despite higher dropout rates in the group (10%) compared to none for those receiving individual CBT, these clinician researchers noted that many persons found the group helped them feel less socially isolated and provided opportunities to learn from others. Compared to other anxiety disorders, there is a somewhat puzzling lack of studies comparing individual CBT to CBGT for GAD, and GAD is thus omitted from a recent meta-analysis (Hans & Hiller, 2013b) and a literature review attempting to make such comparisons (Burlingame et al., 2013). Some researchers conclude that individual CBT is likely more effective than group (Covin, Ouimet, Seeds, & Dozois, 2008), but the absence of actual comparisons makes one less confident in this conclusion.

Clinicians are keen to run CBGT for GAD and many report success, although they also recognize that outcomes could be better. This may in part have to do with how the CBT protocol is delivered in a group setting. It is challenging for therapists to do problem solving, and especially worry exposure, in a group. Some clinicians sense that these traditional CBT interventions may not suffice, and they seek to augment CBGT for GAD with a mindfulness training component (Orsillo, Roemer, & Barlow, 2003). Chapter 8 will discuss how to administer problem solving and worry exposure interventions, while augmenting with mindfulness.

Panic Disorder

Panic disorder is no exception to the equivalence hypothesis (Evans, Holt, & Oei, 1991; Roberge, Marchand, Reinharz, & Savard, 2008; Sánchez-Meca, Rosa-Alcácar, Marín-Martínez, & Gómez-Conesa, 2010)—as long as depression is not also a significant issue (Néron, Lacroix, & Chaput, 1995; Rief, Trenkamp, Auer, & Fichter, 2000). Although people with panic attacks are less embarrassed about their symptoms compared to, for example, people with OCD, the majority (up to 95%, according to some studies) will opt for individual treatment if given the choice (Sharp, Power, & Swenson, 2004). Our clinical experience certainly does not match this high percentage. In contrast, people with panic disorder seem more open to group than those with other kinds of anxiety. Consistent with our experience, a recent meta-analysis on CBT for anxiety disorders (Hans & Hiller, 2013b) shows a statistically significant higher dropout rate from individual CBT for panic disorder compared to CBGT. The description of the panic group as highly didactic and structured may in part explain why it is easier to "sell."

Research on childhood anxiety disorders, including panic disorder, OCD, social anxiety, and GAD, has also found that CBGT is generally equivalent to individual CBT (Liber et al., 2008). Chapter 12 will review the benefits and challenges of CBGT for children.

Posttraumatic Stress Disorder (PTSD)

The most frequent traumas include traffic accidents, natural disasters and physical and sexual assaults. No meta-analysis specifically compares individual CBT to CBGT for PTSD except for one showing no difference in dropout rates between the two types of treatment formats (Hans & Hiller, 2013b). A few studies—limited to PTSD following motor vehicle accidents—point to the effectiveness of a group format. Gayle Beck and colleagues (Beck, Coffey, Foy, Keane, & Blanchard, 2009) found that a 14-session group CBT for motor vehicle accident-related PTSD was superior to a minimal contact individual treatment condition (consisting of four supportive telephone calls to assess PTSD symptoms, but no therapeutic intervention), with 88.3% versus 31.3% no longer meeting criteria. This minimal contact is of course not a fair comparison to a course of individual CBT. Taylor and colleagues (2001) achieved significant reductions in motor vehicle accident-related PTSD symptoms following a 12-session CBGT intervention; these results were slightly better than previous studies offering individual CBT for PTSD. The group protocol in the Taylor study included standard CBT components: education, relaxation, cognitive restructuring, and imaginal and *in vivo* exposure. The impressive results from the Taylor CBGT PTSD outcome study may be related to the homogeneity of the trauma, that is, all had experienced some form of road traffic collision either as drivers, pedestrians, or motorcyclists or vicariously by learning of an accident of a loved one.

A recent meta-analysis on the use of exposure in group therapy for trauma (disclosing details of the trauma through imaginal exposure) found that this approach is just as effective as group treatment without the exposure component. This review concludes that concerns about any negative impact of group exposure may be unwarranted. The selected studies included trauma related to motor vehicle accidents, sexual abuse and assault, and combat (Barrera, Mott, Hofstein, & Teng, 2013).

Not surprisingly, it can be especially hard to "sell" a group format to trauma survivors. Thompson, Wilde, and Boon (2009) found that half of the people invited to consider attending a PTSD group chose not to enroll. But many clinicians report success with running CBGT for PTSD despite the unique challenges in community settings of getting sufficient numbers of the same kind of trauma or mixing different kinds of trauma into the same CBT group. Some ways to deal with these challenges will be presented in Chapter 7.

Addictions

There is growing support for a group format when treating substance abuse and addiction. The two most recent comparisons for substance use revealed equal rates of effectiveness between group and individual CBT (Nyamathis et al., 2011; Sobell, Sobell, & Agrawal, 2009). Authors of both studies conclude that a group format is preferable to an individual. Not only does the group offer advantages for individual members but also a cost reduction in clinician time. These research findings are encouraging given the long tradition of various group approaches to substance use. A number of specific CBT-informed group protocols for addictions are reviewed in Chapter 17.

Psychosis

Based on the success of offering individual CBT to people with thought disorders, clinical researchers have examined its effectiveness in a group setting. Although far from superior to individual CBT, a group format for psychosis is empirically supported (Johns & Wykes, 2010). As with other disorders, the rationale for extending CBT to a group follows the same reasoning. In addition to cost effectiveness, group formats decrease social isolation, use positive peer pressure to encourage the practice of new skills, and in general offer new coping strategies through the examples set by other group members. The last 5 years has produced CBGT research for psychosis challenging the notion that individual CBT is, as a rule, superior to group CBT for psychosis (Chung, Yoon, Park, Yang, & Oh, 2013; Saksa, Cohen, Srihari, & Woods, 2009).

Although the literature endorses a group format, clinicians running groups for people with psychosis have much to say about the often substantial challenges. Chapter 17 offers a menu of brand new therapy approaches that promise to augment CBGT for psychosis.

Hoarding

There is much impressive high-quality treatment outcome research on group CBT for people who have problems with compulsive hoarding (Muroff et al., 2009; Steketee, Frost, Wincze, Greene, & Douglass, 2000). Hoarding-specific CBGT seems just as effective as individual and may not even need to involve additional individual home coaching. According to a study by Gilliam and colleagues (Gilliam et al., 2011), individual home coaching sessions, in addition to the group, do not seem to add much value above and beyond the active group treatment.

The Gilliam study is a good example of how research can inform our clinical practices. I imagine most clinicians share my counterintuitive clinical reaction but appreciate how eliminating home visits clearly reduces the clinician burden while retaining cost-effectiveness. These researchers—along with many other hoarding investigators—note that group treatment may be especially attractive in that it reduces the often extreme social isolation of people with compulsive hoarding. I will share more important research and its clinical implications for CBGT for hoarding in Chapter 15.

Language and Culture

Lastly, a few comments on the research for group CBT for clients with language and culture barriers. Although the number of studies is small, the outcomes are sufficient to stimulate creative clinical program thinking on how to adapt CBT protocols developed in Western cultures to a more global community arena. Despite an absence of direct comparisons of individual and group CBT, language and culture adaptations of English-based CBGT protocols for depression are producing good results with Chinese-speaking immigrants (Wong, 2011), Spanish-speaking immigrants (Miranda, Azocar, Organista, Dwyer, & Areane, 2003), and African American women (Kohn, Oden, Muñoz, Robinson, & Leavitt, 2002). These adaptations primarily involve additional components to the CBT protocol focusing on interpersonal and family relationships but also issues related to homework. These and other clinical issues related to successful implementation are discussed in Chapter 14.

What to Take Away from the Research Findings

Where does this research review leave the group CBT clinician in terms of strengthening the argument for groups instead of individual CBT? Obviously, if the two formats are equivalent, but the group option less expensive, it would not be a hard sell to any manager or program director.

As clinicians, however, we may also feel challenged by the research to date and motivated to respond by improving our groups. We may especially seek to understand and work more effectively with the group process and the many group therapeutic factors. Such improvements in CBGT may then become reflected in future outcome studies measuring both symptom reduction and benefits from the unique group experience. Considering that the majority of the investigators conducting clinical outcome studies on CBT and CBGT for various disorders tend not to consider themselves *group therapists* from the perspective of being keenly interested in the full range of issues pertaining to the nature of group development and processes, the potential benefits of CBGT may be underestimated and underreported in the literature. Many fellow CBT therapists share a desire to improve CBT groups, and there are a number of places we can start. The following points will be further fleshed out in all coming chapters, but especially Chapters 6 (how to "sell" group therapy), 7 (how to improve groups for SAD), and 13 (how to improve exposure therapy for youth with OCD).

First, groups probably work best when people in them really want to be there and do not feel disappointed about not getting their first choice of individual therapy. Improving the way we "sell" groups and orient clients is an obvious way to ensure people feel motivated—and even lucky—to be seeking help in a place where group CBT is offered. Second, deliberately expanding any behavioral components of CBT manuals—especially for OCD and SAD—may allow the group format to work better as clients get "to do" more with each other in their therapeutic and social interactions. Encouraging more exposures in trauma groups also widens the potential for working with the group process. All this requires skilled group therapists, who not only must be comfortable with implementing individual exposure tasks but also with *keeping the group together*. Third, we need to capitalize as much as possible on the group process across all types of groups to create opportunities for peer support, interactions, and meaningful human connections. Lastly, an improved group process requires cofacilitators to work well together as they are not just two separate presenters but model many important aspects of respectful cofacilitation (Chapter 10 discusses the art and skill of cofacilitation). Including outcome measures that directly invite group members to comment on the group experience—in addition to symptom improvement—will help clinicians revise the way we run our CBT groups in order to make them more attractive and effective.

Summary

This chapter reviews key research findings in the literature comparing individual CBT to CBGT for the mental health problems covered in this book. On balance, the literature suggests that CBGT is as effective as individual CBT. Clinicians are encouraged to make regular literature updates on CBGT a priority in their practice. Other ways of staying current include monthly journal clubs with colleagues where discussion of journal articles or book chapters helps everyone keep up a best practice approach. Regular group program reviews are also advisable. During those, new treatment manuals and clinicians' experiences with particular approaches are discussed and used to revise CBGT interventions.

The next two chapters build on the principles and research findings of CBT and CBGT. They show clinicians how to develop and implement effective CBGT for depression.

References

Barrera, T. L., Mott, J. M., Hofstein, R. F., & Teng, E. J. (2013). A meta-analytic review of exposure in group cognitive behavioral therapy for posttraumatic stress disorder. *Clinical Psychology Review*, *33*, 24–32.

Beck, A. T., Rush, A. J., Shaw, B. F., & Emery, G. (1979). *Cognitive therapy of depression*. New York: Guilford Press.

Beck, J. G., Coffey, S. F., Foy, D. W., Keane, T. M., & Blanchard, E. B. (2009). Group cognitive behavior therapy for chronic posttraumatic stress disorder: An initial randomized pilot study. *Behavior Therapy*, *40*, 82–92.

Bieling, P. J., McCabe, R. E., & Antony M. A. (2006). *Cognitive-behavioral therapy in groups.* New York: Guilford Press.

Burlingame, G. M., Strauss, B., & Joyce, A. S. (2013). Change mechanisms and effectiveness of small group treatments. In M. J. Lambert, A. E. Bergin, & S. L. Garfield (Eds.), *Bergin and Garfield's handbook of psychotherapy and behavior change* (6th ed., pp. 640–689). New York: Wiley-Blackwell.

Chung, Y.-C., Yoon, K.-S., Park, T.-W., Yang, J.-C., & Oh, K.-Y. (2013). Group cognitive-behavioral therapy for early psychosis. *Cognitive Therapy and Research, 37,* 403–411.

Clarke, G. N., Rohde, P., Lewinsohn, P. M., Hops, H., & Seeley, J. R. (1999). Cognitive-behavioral treatment of adolescent depression: Efficacy of acute group treatment and booster sessions. *Journal of the American Academy of Child and Adolescent Psychiatry, 38(3),* 272–279.

Covin, R., Ouimet, A. M., Seeds, P. M., & Dozois, D. J. (2008). A meta-analysis of CBT for pathological worry among clients with GAD. *Journal of Anxiety Disorders, 22(1),* 108–116.

Craigie, M. A., & Nathan, P. (2009). A nonrandomized effectiveness comparison of broad-spectrum group CBT to individual CBT for depressed outpatients in a community mental health setting. *Behavior Therapy, 40(3),* 302–314.

Cramer, H., Salisbury, C., Conrad, J., Eldred, J., & Araya, R. (2011). Group cognitive behavioural therapy for women with depression: Pilot and feasibility study for a randomized controlled trial using mixed methods. *BMC Psychiatry, 11(82),* 1–11.

DeRubeis, R. J., & Crits-Cristoph, P. (1998). Empirically supported individual and group cognitive behavior therapy for severely depressed outpatients: Meta-analysis of four randomized comparisons. *American Journal of Psychiatry, 156,* 1007–1013.

Dugas, M. J., Ladouceur, R., Leger, E., Freeston, M. H., Langolis, F., Provencher, M. D., et al. (2003). Group cognitive-behavioral therapy for generalized anxiety disorder: Treatment outcomes and long-term follow-up. *Journal of Consulting and Clinical Psychology, 71(4),* 821–825.

Evans, L., Holt, C., & Oei, T. P. (1991). Long term follow-up of agoraphobics treated by brief intensive group cognitive behavioural therapy. *Australian and New Zealand Journal of Psychiatry, 25,* 343–349.

Fals-Stewart, W., Marks, A. P., & Shafer, J. (1993). A comparison of behavioral group therapy and individual behavior therapy in treating obsessive-compulsive disorder. *Journal of Nervous and Mental Disease, 181,* 189–193.

Fedoroff, I. C., & Taylor, S. (2001). Psychological and pharmacological treatments of social phobia: A meta-analysis. *Journal of Clinical Pharmacology, 21,* 311–324.

Gilliam C. M., Norbert, M. M., Villavicencio, A., Morrison, S., Hannan, S. E., & Tolin, D. F. (2011). Group cognitive-behavioral therapy for hoarding disorder: An open trial. *Behaviour Research and Therapy, 49(11),* 802–807.

Gould, R. A., Buckminster, S., Pollack, M. H., Otto, M. W., & Yap, L. (1997). Cognitive-behavioral and pharmacological treatment for social phobia: A meta-analysis. *Clinical Psychology: Science and Practice, 4,* 291–306.

Hans, E., & Hiller, W. (2013a). Effectiveness of and dropout from outpatient cognitive behavioral therapy for adult unipolar depression: A meta-analysis of nonrandomized effectiveness studies. *Journal of Consulting and Clinical Psychology, 81(1),* 75–88.

Hans, E., & Hiller, W. (2013b). A meta-analysis of nonrandomized effectiveness studies on outpatient cognitive behavioral therapy for adult anxiety disorders. *Clinical Psychology Review, 33(8),* 954–964.

Hedman, E., Mörtberg, E., Hesser, H., Clark, D., Lekander, M., Andersson, E., et al. (2013). Mediators in psychological treatment of social anxiety disorder: Individual cognitive therapy compared to cognitive behavioral group therapy. *Behaviour Research and Therapy, 51(10)*, 696–705.

Hiatt, D., & Hargrave, G. E. (1995). The characteristics of highly effective therapists in managed behavioral provider networks. *Behavioral Healthcare Tomorrow, 4*, 19–22.

Hope, D. A., Heimberg, R. G., & Bruch, M. A. (1995). Dismantling cognitive-behavioral group therapy for social phobia. *Behaviour Research and Therapy, 33*, 637–650.

Jaurrieta, N., Jimenez-Murcia, S., Alonso, P., Granero, R., Segalas, C., Labad, J., et al. (2008). Individual versus group cognitive behavioral treatment for obsessive-compulsive disorder: Follow up. *Psychiatry and Clinical Neurosciences, 62*, 697–704.

Johns, L., & Wykes, T. (2010). Group cognitive behaviour therapy for psychosis. In F. Larø & A. Aleman (Eds.), *Hallucinations: A guide to treatment and management* (pp. 61–80). New York: Oxford University Press.

Jónsson, H., Hougaard, E., & Bennedsen, B. E. (2011). Randomized comparative study of group versus individual cognitive behavioural therapy for obsessive compulsive disorder. *Acta Psychiatrica Scandinavica, 123(5)*, 387–397.

Kennedy, G. J., & Tanenbaum, S. (2000). Psychotherapy with older adults. *American Journal of Psychotherapy, 54(3)*, 386–407.

Krishna, M., Jauhari, A., Lepping, P., Turner, J., Crossley, D., & Krishnamoorthy, A. (2010). Is group psychotherapy effective in older adults with depression? A systematic review. *International Journal of Geriatric Psychiatry, 26*, 331–340.

Kohn, L. P., Oden, T., Muñoz, R. F., Robinson, A., & Leavitt, D. (2002). Adapted cognitive behavioral group therapy for depressed low-income African American women. *Community Mental Health Journal, 38(6)*, 497–504.

Lambert, M. J. (2013). The efficacy and effectiveness of psychotherapy. In M. J. Lambert, A. E. Bergin, & S. L. Garfield (Eds.), *Bergin and Garfield's handbook of psychotherapy and behavior change* (6th ed., pp. 169–218). New York: Wiley-Blackwell.

Liber, J. M., Van Widenfelt, B. M., Utens, E. M. W. J., Ferdinand, R. F., Van der Leeden, A. J. M., Van Gastel, W., et al. (2008). No differences between group versus individual treatment of childhood anxiety disorders in a randomized clinical trial. *Journal of Child Psychology and Psychiatry, 49(8)*, 886–893.

McLean, P. D., Whittal, M. L., Thordarson, D., Taylor, S., Söchting, I., Koch, W. J., et al., (2001). Cognitive versus behavior therapy in the group treatment of obsessive-compulsive disorder. *Journal of Consulting and Clinical Psychology, 69*, 205–214.

Miranda, J., Azocar, F., Organista, K. C., Dwyer, E., & Areane, P. (2003). Treatment of depression among impoverished primary care patients from ethnic minority groups. *Psychiatric Services, 54*, 219–225.

Muroff, J., Steketee, G., Rasmussen, J., Gibson, A., Bratiotis, C., & Sorrentino, C. (2009). Group cognitive and behavioral treatment for compulsive hoarding: A preliminary trial. *Depression and Anxiety, 26*, 634–640.

Néron, S., Lacroix, D., & Chaput, Y. (1995). Group vs. individual cognitive behavior therapy in panic disorder: An open clinical trial with a six month follow up. *Canadian Journal of Behavioural Science, 27*, 379–392.

Nyamathis, A., Nandy, K., Greengold, B., Marfisee, M., Khalilifard, F., Cohen, A., et al. (2011). Effectiveness of intervention on improvement of drug use among methadone maintained adults. *Journal of Addictive Diseases, 30*, 6–16.

O'Connor, K., Freeston, M. H., Gareau, D., Careau, Y., Dufour, M. J., Aardema, F. et al. (2005). Group versus individual treatment in obsessions without compulsions. *Clinical Psychology and Psychotherapy, 12*, 87–96.

Oei, T. P. S., & Dingle, G. (2008). The effectiveness of group cognitive behavior therapy for unipolar depressive disorders. *Journal of Affective Disorders, 107(1–3)*, 5–21.

Orsillo, S. M., Roemer, L., & Barlow, D. H. (2003). Integrating acceptance and mindfulness into existing cognitive-behavioral treatment for GAD: A case study. *Cognitive and Behavioral Practice, 10(3)*, 222–230.

Rief, W., Trenkamp, S., Auer, C., & Fichter, M. M. (2000). Cognitive behavior therapy in panic disorder and comorbid major depression. *Psychotherapy and Psychosomatics, 69(2)*, 70–78.

Roberge, P., Marchand, A., Reinharz, D., & Savard, P. (2008). Cognitive-behavioral treatment for panic disorder with agoraphobia: A randomized controlled trial and cost effectiveness analysis. *Behavior Modification, 32*, 333–351.

Saksa, J. R., Cohen, S., Srihari, V. H., & Woods, S. W. (2009). Cognitive behavior therapy for early psychosis: A comprehensive review of individual vs. group treatment studies. *International Journal of Group Psychotherapy, 59(3)*, 357–383.

Sánchez-Meca, J., Rosa-Alcácar, A. I., Marín-Martínez, F., & Gómez-Conesa, A. (2010). Psychological treatment of panic disorder with or without agoraphobia: A meta-analysis. *Clinical Psychology Review, 30(1)*, 37–50.

Scott, M. J. (2011). *Simply effective group cognitive behaviour therapy: A practitioner's guide.* London: Routledge.

Scott, M. J., & Stradling, S. G. (1990). Group cognitive therapy for depression produces clinically significant reliable change in community-based settings. *Behavioural Psychotherapy, 18*, 1–19.

Sharp, D. M., Power, K. G., & Swenson, V. (2004). A comparison of the efficacy and acceptability of group versus individual cognitive behavior therapy in the treatment of panic disorder and agoraphobia in primary care. *Clinical Psychology and Psychotherapy, 11*, 73–82.

Sobell, L. C. Sobell, M. B., & Agrawal, S. (2009). Randomized controlled trial of a cognitive-behavioral motivational intervention in a group versus individual format for substance use disorders. *Psychology of Addictive Behaviors, 23*, 672–683.

Stangier, U., Heidenreich, T., Peitz, M., Lauterbach, W., & Clark, D. M. (2003). Cognitive therapy for social phobia: individual versus group treatment. *Behaviour Research and Therapy, 41*, 991–1007.

Steketee, G., Frost, R. O., Wincze, J., Greene, K., & Douglass, H. (2000). Group and individual treatment of compulsive hoarding: A pilot study. *Behavioural and Cognitive Psychotherapy, 28*, 259–268.

Taylor, S., Fedoroff, I., Koch, W., Thordarson, D., Fectau, G., & Nicki, R. (2001). Posttraumatic stress disorder arising after road traffic collisions: Patterns of responses to cognitive-behavior therapy. *Journal of Consulting and Clinical Psychology, 69(3)*, 541–551.

Thompson, A. R., Wilde, E., & Boon, K. (2009). The development of group CBT for the treatment of road-traffic-accident-related post-traumatic stress disorder. *The Cognitive Behaviour Therapist, 2*, 32–42.

Tucker, M., & Oei, T. P. S. (2007). Is group more cost effective than individual cognitive behaviour therapy? The evidence is not solid yet. *Behavioural and Cognitive Psychotherapy, 35*, 77–91.

VanNoppen, B., Steketee, G., McCorkle, B. H., & Pato, M. (1997). Group and multi-family behavioral treatment for obsessive compulsive disorder: A pilot study. *Journal of Anxiety Disorders, 11*, 431–446.

Walfish, S., McAlister, B., O'Donnell, P., & Lambert, M. J. (2012). An investigation of self-assessment bias in mental health providers. *Psychological Reports, 110(2)*, 1–6.

White, J. (2010). The STEPS model: A high volume, multi-level, multi-purpose approach to address common mental health problems. In J. Bennett-Levy, D. A. Richards, P. Farrand, H. Christensen, K. M. Griffiths, D. J. Kavanagh, et al. (Eds)., *Oxford guide to low intensity CBT interventions*. Oxford, UK: Oxford University Press.

Whittal, M. L., & McLean, P. D. (2002). Group cognitive behavioral therapy for obsessive compulsive disorder. In R. O. Frost & G. Steketee (Eds)., *Cognitive approaches to obsessions and compulsions; Theory, assessment, and treatment* (pp. 417–433). Oxford, UK: Elsevier.

Whittal, M. L., Robichaud, M., Thordarson, D. S., & McLean, P. D. (2008). Group and individual treatment of obsessive-compulsive disorder using cognitive therapy and exposure plus response prevention: A 2-year follow-up of two randomized trials. *Journal of Consulting and Clinical Psychology, 76*, 1003–1014.

Wlazlo, Z., Schroeder-Hartwig, K., Hand, I., Kaiser, G., & Münchau, N. (1990). Exposure in vivo vs. social skills training for social phobia: Long term outcome and differential effects. *Behaviour Research and Therapy, 28*, 181–193.

Wong, D. F. K. (2011). Cognitive behavioral group treatment for Chinese people with depressive symptoms in Hong Kong: Participants' perspectives. *International Journal of Group Psychotherapy, 61(3)*, 439–459.

4

CBGT for Depression: Psychoeducation and Behavioral Interventions

Depression is a major public health issue with significant personal and societal costs. By 2020, depression is predicted to become the second most costly and debilitating disorder, with heart disease first (Murray & Lopez, 1996). As reviewed in Chapter 1, about 16% of the United States population suffers at any given time from a mood disorder. In the United Kingdom, nearly one in six adults will experience a type of depression at some point in their lifetime (National Institute for Health and Clinical Excellence, 2009). These numbers are exacerbated by the fact that depression is a chronic illness. Many people experience several episodes throughout their lives. Helpful and cost-effective treatments for this serious illness are needed. CBT has proved effective across the severity spectrum and may be as helpful for more severe depression as it is for less (DeRubeis et al., 2005; Fournier et al., 2009). CBT clinicians should not be shy about sharing these research findings with the public and policymakers.

The high prevalence of depression and relapse has created an increased demand for improved public access to effective psychotherapy. CBGT for depression is thus a priority in community mental health settings. Because of this, I devote two chapters, 4 and 5, to a comprehensive CBGT program for depression. Other disorders in this book are limited to one chapter or a section of a chapter.

The Diagnoses of Depression

CBT groups are effective for two main types of depression: major depressive disorder (MDD) and dysthymia. MDD affects about 5–9% of the population at any given time and is characterized by (a) at least 2 weeks of depressed mood most of

Cognitive Behavioral Group Therapy: Challenges and Opportunities, First Edition. Ingrid Söchting.

the day, nearly every day, or (b) loss of interests or pleasure in most daily activities. According to the DSM-5 (American Psychiatric Association [APA], 2013),[1] one or both of the two main symptoms must be followed by three or four of the following symptoms, amounting to a total of at least five symptoms present nearly every day: significant appetite/weight loss or increase, insomnia or hypersomnia, agitated/restless behavior or slowing in movements that is observable to others, fatigue or loss of energy, feelings of worthlessness or excessive or inappropriate guilt, diminished ability to think or concentrate, indecisiveness, recurrent thoughts of death and suicide with or without a specific plan, or a suicide attempt. Depressive episodes can be categorized by severity as mild, moderate, severe, or severe with psychotic features (i.e., presence of delusions such as a belief that one is being conspired against, or hallucinations such as hearing a voice telling one to commit suicide). A major depressive episode lasting for at least 2 weeks can also be a component of other mental health disorders such as bipolar disorder or schizoaffective disorder.

Dysthymia, also referred to as chronic, milder depression, affects about 3% of a population at any given time and is characterized by at least 2 years of depressed mood nearly all the time, accompanied by at least two other symptoms (similar to the ones in a major depressive episode): poor appetite, insomnia or hypersomnia, low energy or fatigue, low self-esteem, poor concentration or difficulty making decisions, or feelings of hopelessness (APA, 2000). In the DSM-5 (APA, 2013), dysthymia is referred to as *persistent depressive disorder*. People with persistent depressive disorder must not have had symptom-free periods for more than 2 months at a time. It is noteworthy that passive suicidal ideation (e.g., believing it would not make much of a difference if one were dead) is often part of the presentation but not part of the actual diagnosis for persistent depressive disorder. It is entirely possible for a person to have had many years of dysthymia and then enter into one or more major depressive episodes. The person will then be diagnosed with persistent depressive disorder with intermittent major depressive episodes. This is sometimes referred to as "double depression." Depression is also often accompanied by anxiety. This led the DSM-5 (APA, 2013) to include the option of adding *with anxious distress* to a diagnosis of MDD or persistent depressive disorder.

An additional type of client is present in most CBT groups: those who do not meet criteria for either MDD or persistent depressive disorder. Some will have diagnoses of bipolar disorder (cycling between episodes of depression and mania) with mostly episodes of depression, whereas others may—or may not—have had any past episodes of depression. Although some programs will not accept people without a DSM diagnosis, the argument for prevention ought to be advanced if a history reveals significant vulnerability factors such as a pronounced, negative thinking style coupled with psychosocial stressors including divorce, loss of employment, serious financial setback, or major life transition such as retirement. People who acknowledge proneness to setting unreasonably high personal standards and castigation of themselves when falling short are good candidates for CBGT for depression.

Conversely, if a depressed client in an intake assessment shows no interest in their own thinking style, denies any self-denigration, and shows no curiosity about it, another form of psychotherapy, such as IPT (briefly reviewed in Chapter 8), may be a better treatment option. It can be problematic for CBT group cohesion if one or more members of a group continue to resist the notion of dysfunctional beliefs, the pivotal part of the cognitive strategies, which takes up at least half of a standard depression group. It is thus in everyone's best interest to screen out those clients and offer alternatives.

For severely depressed clients, cognitive work in the form of addressing dysfunctional beliefs is not recommended, at least not initially (Hollon, 2011). Instead, treatment needs to first focus on behavioral activation. Although behavioral activation is a core component of the CBGT protocol outlined here, some clients with severe depression may need exclusive behavioral activation treatment before being recommended for standard CBGT with its major emphasis on cognitive interventions.

Treatment Protocols Informed by Beck's Cognitive Model of Depression

All CBT protocols for depression are more or less based on Aaron Beck's cognitive theory. Beck maintains that a particular negative and self-critical thinking style stems from a mental filter through which perceptions of oneself, one's surroundings, and one's future become distorted (Beck, Rush, Shaw, & Emery, 1979). One can think of this filter as a deeper cognitive structure, a schema, giving rise to daily negative commentary. Consider the mind-set of a woman wondering why her friend is not phoning her: "Why did Lisa not call me back? She's probably trying to get out of having lunch with me, or she just wants to do it because she feels sorry for me. I think I saw her rolling her eyes to Barbara when we talked about going out for lunch." These "thought-locks," which cause a person to jump to a conclusion without first "checking the facts," are the norm for depressed people entering therapy.

In Beck's model, schemas develop over time, usually beginning in early childhood, and interact with critical life events resulting in symptoms of depression. Here is how Beck describes this process:

> In childhood and adolescence, the depression-prone individual becomes sensitized to certain types of life situations. The traumatic situations initially responsible for embedding or reinforcing the negative attitude that comprise the depressive constellation are the prototypes of the specific stresses that may later activate these constellations. When a person is subjected to situations reminiscent of the original traumatic experiences,

> s/he may then become depressed. The process may be likened to conditioning in which a particular response is linked to a specific stimulus, once the chain has been formed, stimuli similar to the original stimulus may evoke the conditioned response. (Beck, 1967/1972, p. 278)

Staying with the aforementioned case, the woman wondering why Lisa has not called her back may have had a painful experience of being excluded in junior high school by a group of girls she wanted to be part of. Even though she has had a positive university experience including some solid friendships with like-minded people, the original trauma is more easily activated than in someone who has not had such an experience of feeling ostracized.

From Beck's theory, we learn what a huge role is played by our thinking or what we say to ourselves. So, it is important to ensure that depressed people interested in a CBT group for depression are prepared for addressing their thinking style. We also see that any critique of CBT as a "superficial therapy lacking tradition" is unfounded. Even Shakespeare anticipated the coming of CBT when his Hamlet, caught in a chilling family drama, proclaimed: "For there is nothing either good or bad, but thinking makes it so" (Hamlet, Act 2, Scene 2). The Greek Stoic philosopher Epictetus (AD 55–135) also contributed to the philosophical underpinning of CBT with his famous saying: "We are not disturbed by what happens to us, but by our thoughts about what happens to us."

These quotes are inspiring but are not meant to place absolute value on thinking over the events themselves. Imagine how that could be manipulated to minimize real tragedies such as abuse, natural disasters, loss of loved ones, and social injustice. CBT takes very seriously what happened to a person throughout their childhood and adolescence and especially their perceptions and interpretations of events. Connecting present struggles back to their possible origins is a significant part of the work in a CBT group. Not only is this tremendously helpful for the individual, it also promotes a more empathic stance toward fellow group members.

Clinicians who routinely work with depressed clients, whether individually or in group, are aware of how "self-absorbed" such clients can come across. People with depression are usually aware of this too, which intensifies the vicious cycle of self-punishing thoughts: "I can understand why my girlfriend left me. She's right about my self-absorption. Some days I barely have the energy to ask about her day, let alone suggest we do something she enjoys on the weekend." Part of the psychoeducation in CBT for depression involves helping people understand that their character is not one of intense self-absorption (as it is in some personality disorders) but that the clinical manifestation of depression involves a lack of ability to get "out of one's own bubble" and engage more empathically with others. The opportunity for this more other-focused way of relating is naturally one of the many benefits of a group format for depression. It is indeed rewarding to notice the positive increase in feelings and self-evaluations when group members slowly show more care and interest in each other. It is not uncommon to hear people voice the relief they feel from breaking out of their self-preoccupation.

An Example of a CBGT Depression Protocol

Similar to individual CBT, there are four main components of a comprehensive CBGT protocol for depression: (a) education about depression and the cognitive model; (b) behavioral strategies, including self-monitoring of daily activities and goal setting; (c) cognitive strategies, including identifying, challenging, and replacing negative thinking; and (d) relapse prevention strategies.

Appendix A offers a sample outline of a 12-session, 2-hour weekly treatment protocol for group CBT. It is adapted from two key sources on individual CBT for depression: the depression chapter from *Cognitive Behaviour Therapy for Psychiatric Problems* (Fennell, 1989) and the *Mind over Mood* protocol by Greenberger and Padesky (1995). The adapted protocol is based on groups with 6–10 members who are suffering from depression ranging from subthreshold to moderately severe. Most are referred by their family doctors, and some have attempted a self-help program with telephone coaching but failed to make sufficient improvements. Acceptance into such a group is based on ability to attend regularly, that is, sufficient energy to arrive on time and stay alert during the session and commit to homework between sessions. If there is a history of active or passive suicidal behavior, this needs to be monitored and additional support put in place. For the group to be helpful, all members must have depression as their primary problem. Other problems such as an anxiety disorder can be present so long as the client knows that this issue will not be specifically addressed in the group.

All group members have had a prior intake assessment as well as a pregroup orientation session (Chapter 6 outlines the assessment and orientation process). This orientation focuses on insight into critical thinking patterns and expectations for group participation. Clients are told that the group is primarily educational with the facilitators presenting new information and exercises every week but that ability and willingness to offer and receive feedback from other group members is expected. This creates an opportunity to discuss the level of self-disclosure required for the group, as well as nervousness about interacting with other depressed people.

Psychoeducation

The first two to three sessions are devoted to education about depression and the CBT approach. The initial session includes introductory go-rounds and review of ground rules as outlined in Chapter 1. This is followed by presenting the CBT triangle (see Figure 4.1) and discussing the connection between thoughts, moods, and

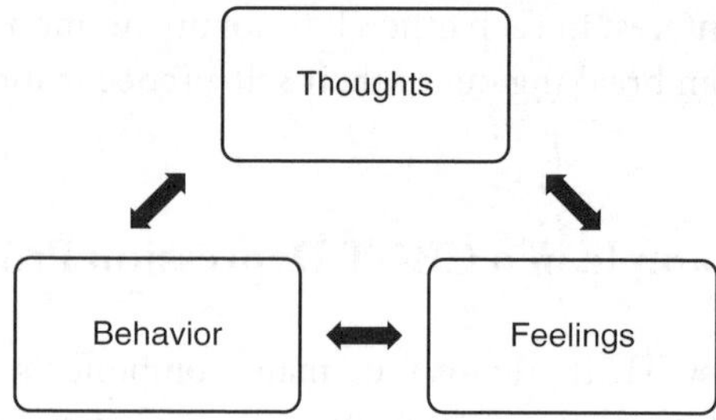

Figure 4.1 CBT triangle.

behaviors. One therapist sketches the triangle on a board or uses other means of visual display. The other therapist explains how the connection is driven by the catalytic impact thoughts have on feelings and behaviors. It is, however, critical to dispel any notion of thoughts causing depression. Thoughts do not cause depression, but are associated with depression.

Not wanting to put anybody on the spot in the first session, the therapists use hypothetical examples of how a certain thought (e.g., Lisa is trying to get out of going for lunch with me) influences how one feels (e.g., sad, upset) and behaves (e.g., goes to bed early instead of out for a walk). A contrasting *healthy thought* response to the same scenario is also derived from prompting the group. The group usually agrees that a person who was not depressed would likely think: "Something is going on for Lisa and she has forgotten our lunch." The group is usually quick to suggest associated feelings of care and concern and a behavior involving making a note to call Lisa tomorrow and carry on with what one had planned to do. The first group session ends with showing a shorter movie based on personal stories of people recovering from depression. The postmovie discussion increases motivation and positive expectations (recommendations for movies are given in Chapter 6).

Depressed clients invariably ask about causes of depression, which is addressed in session 2. While many are convinced they have a biochemical imbalance, most are open to other influences as well. Therapists start this discussion with a statement about all mental health issues being multiply determined and best to avoid oversimplistic beliefs about causality. We talk about genetics, innate temperament, biochemistry, early childhood environment, salient life stressors, and subjective experiences of what is stressful. During this discussion, we refer the group to a handout in their folder (Chapter 1 described the use of folders): *the Cognitive Model of Depression* (Appendix B). One therapist takes the lead in walking the group through the model explaining that CBT therapists tend to understand depression as both a thinking disorder and a mood disorder and that the way we think has profound impact on our feelings and behaviors. The cotherapist may sketch, similar to the first session, the triangle of thoughts–moods–behaviors.

We continue with essentially a mini-lecture on Beck's cognitive model. We use the example in the Cognitive Model of Depression (Appendix B) but encourage clients to insert experiences and examples of dysfunctional thinking from their own life. In fact, we provide them with a "blank" cognitive model for creating their own cognitive model for better understanding their depression (Appendix B). In explaining the cognitive model, we emphasize that early life experiences affect most of us. These may include being unfavorably compared to a sibling, losing contact with a parent due to death or divorce, being bullied, or being unfairly treated by a teacher and of course more extreme experiences of physical or sexual abuse. Because the child's brain is plastic and easily influenced, these critical experiences can lead to personalized beliefs about "not being good enough," "not as smart as others," or "not lovable." We call these beliefs *dysfunctional assumptions* (assumptions can in this model be considered equivalent to *schemas* or *core beliefs*). For many of us, life goes on and we are not that aware of these assumptions. They are in a sense dormant. However, when a critical event happens—and very few people escape those—such as significant conflicts at work, relationship breakups, or serious problems with a child, these assumptions get activated and influence how we cope with the crisis. For example, someone with an assumption of "I'm not good enough" will tend to think that a work or marriage conflict is mostly, or even entirely, their fault. In contrast, people without dysfunctional assumptions or only a modicum thereof (some self-criticalness is healthy, lest we become narcissistic) would understand that all relationships are a two-way street and that one partner taking all the blame may interfere with productive negotiation and compromise. At this point, we see a lot of nodding in the room and often crying.

Therapists new to CBGT for depression frequently ask the primary therapist or their supervisor about how to handle crying in the group. It is a good question and more senior therapists see the discomfort experienced by the junior therapists when one or more members cry in their group. It is best just to let the crying happen without much reaction on the part of the therapists. Other group members tend to beat the therapists to passing on the Kleenex box, or offer their own tissue. Therapists may reflect something like "we appreciate how difficult it can be to reflect back on your life" or "your sadness makes sense; we appreciate you feel comfortable enough here to express it," or "this group can be a helpful place to share some feelings you may not want your close family and friends to be a part of."

We continue by explaining that when these dysfunctional assumptions are not addressed therapeutically, they tend to give rise to an ongoing negative, self-critical commentary: the *negative automatic thoughts* in Beck's language. Clients often talk about this feeling like a tape loop playing in their head or as if some gremlin was sitting on their shoulder commenting critically on every move they make. Some people are able to connect this "voice"[2] of negative automatic thoughts to an actual person of their past, a parent or parental figure, but often there is no specific person. One group therapist coined his own CBT technique of the "eviction notice," which proved quite successful in encouraging group members to "evict" the self-critical voices from their mind. If the negative automatic thoughts are not reigned in, they easily lead to a host of depression symptoms. Each symptom category (motivational, somatic/bodily, cognitive, behavioral, and affective) is reviewed in a group discussion.

The difference between MDD and persistent depressive disorder (dysthymia) is also reviewed at this point. Group members often do not know their diagnosis, but only that they are depressed according to their own understanding, or that of their family doctor. If time permits, group members are invited to reflect on the cognitive model and insert examples from their own life stories. This is voluntary and not assigned as formal homework, but in most groups, clients willingly share their stories and it promotes group cohesion as people listen empathically and relate to each other's stories. We allow this life review and schema insight development to carry over into part of the next session, session 3, but then make it clear that we will be moving from the past to the present. We explain that awareness of the past will continue to inform the rest of the sessions in the group but that we are not going to be reviewing past events in detail. Occasionally, a few people become very interested in their family of origin. This can be a feature of their depression in the form of "searching for a root cause." In that case, it has an unproductive ruminative quality, which usually diminishes as the depression improves. Sometimes, people who recover from their depression continue to be interested in understanding their past better, and it is appropriate to suggest they become connected with a more psychodynamic form of therapy, if available, after the CBT depression group is over.

Behavioral Interventions

Although Beck's cognitive model emphasizes the central role that distorted cognitions play in the development and maintenance of depression, CBGT therapists tend to first target behavioral activation. It is our experience that an increase in energy and the improved self-confidence that comes from accomplishing tasks make it easier to fully engage with the cognitive strategies. Cognitive work involving challenging one's thinking (which will be presented in Chapter 5) can be a strain for a person with compromised resources of the mind (such as difficulty concentrating and/or entertaining multiple perspectives on an issue), so any increase in energy and feelings of self-efficacy helps. Also, the behavioral tasks do not require a deeper examination of one's thinking style and are thus easier to engage with in the beginning of a group when everything and everyone is unfamiliar. The rest of this chapter focuses on behavioral interventions as well the importance of identifying emotions.

Therapists begin the behavioral work in session 3 by explaining that in depression, motivation works backward, that is, the less we do, the more tired and depleted of energy we feel. We deliberately emphasize this as a symptom of depression and encourage people to reflect on why it is incorrect to label themselves "lazy" or "boring." Lack of energy and believing that one cannot do very much without becoming exhausted is probably a hallmark feature of depression. It is crucial to address it in the early part of CBT, including how it can be almost shocking to realize that beliefs about, for example, everyone needing 10 hours of sleep are incorrect. Therapists then stimulate a group discussion of which activities people used to enjoy, have stopped doing, and would like to resume. For group members who are at a loss for which activities give them meaning and joy, therapists can create a handout similar to the one in Appendix C "10 Things I like to Do (Or Used to Like to Do)." Depressed people, by diagnostic definition, do not derive much enjoyment from their days and often feel inadequate as an employee—if working—or as a spouse, parent, or friend. Getting a sense of how group members spend their days is helpful.

Self-monitoring is a classic CBT technique, and the Daily Activity Rating Scale (Fennell, 1989; Greenberger & Padesky, 1995) is a valuable behavioral intervention. We assign it as homework between sessions 3 and 4. This scale asks people to complete a log of what they do hour to hour—using only a few words—in a given day while also rating their feelings of pleasure and mastery on a scale of 0–10. Group therapists can easily make such a log listing each day, broken down into 1-hour segments. We introduce it as an exercise in learning more about oneself. It is in some ways a lot to ask, and it is rare that all group members complete the entire week; however, we keep using it because group members like it and find it helpful. In the group following this homework, the facilitators encourage members to express what they learned about themselves and to offer feedback to each other. For example, one woman was surprised at how good she was at getting her children up and to school (mastery was rated 8/10) but also at how little pleasure this gave her (pleasure rated 4/10). She used this realization to set a goal of getting up 30 minutes earlier and doing a meditation practice for 15 minutes while the house was quiet with everybody else sleeping. Starting the day with some calm moments for herself allowed her to better enjoy the morning routine with her children. Humor usually also gets shared during self-monitoring review. There is almost always one person who will exclaim: "I've mastered the art of sleeping and am very good at lying on the couch—10/10!" We encourage people to be brutally honest about their daily activities including sleeping, watching TV, or doing "nothing." When people feel safe and supported in the group, this kind of honesty is rarely a problem. The results from the self-monitoring become a handy stepping stone for setting more formal goals, often related to increasing pleasurable activities.

Goal setting is pivotal in CBT. This stems from the problem with doing too little when one is depressed. Avoiding pleasurable and other kinds of activities such as necessary ones (e.g., scheduling medical appointments or buying groceries) deprives people with depression of opportunities for positive reinforcement. The avoidance behavior becomes negatively reinforcing. In CBT terms, a behavior is negatively reinforced if it increases because it is followed by the absence of an anticipated aversive event. In depression, the anticipated aversive event could be a fear that one will not be able to complete a task properly, that one will not enjoy starting a new leisure activity, or that other people will be rejecting. Thus, by staying safely at home on the couch, one can be certain none of these feared scenarios will actualize.

Committing to goals for doing more is a critical step in treating depression. Articulating goals and taking steps to accomplish them create momentum in people's lives and offer a way to measure progress. In session 3 or 4, therapists introduce the art and skill of goal setting. One way to do this is by using the concept of specific and achievable SMART goals, based on the acronym SMART (Paterson, Alden, & Koch, 2006):

Specific—I plan to exercise twice a week versus I plan to be more active.
My own—I picked this goal because I want this for me versus I picked this goal because my friend said it would help.
Action oriented—I plan to go to the park for a walk versus I'll go to the park to feel relaxed.
Realistic—I plan to go to the gym once versus I plan to go to the gym every day.
Time defined—I plan to exercise once (it will be on Thursday at 6:00 p.m. at the gym) versus I plan to exercise more.[3]

For more in-depth coverage of goal setting, the excellent CBT-based Changeways program offers many suggestions (Paterson et al., 2006).

In addition to asking each member to set a goal they estimate to have a 95% chance of completion, they indicate a specific time to begin and identify any anticipated obstacles. All of this is written down on a goal sheet handout (Greenberger & Padesky, 1995). Anticipating barriers allows the group to show they are beginning to know each other and stimulates productive interactions. Ensuring that all members have a SMART goal plan for their homework maximizes the chance of the goals being accomplished.

Therapists should make a point of encouraging group members to support one another. The following dialogue involves a missed opportunity for the therapists to work with the process factor of using group members as role models—through *imparting of information*, to use Yalom's language. The therapists are not doing anything particularly wrong and they show empathy for Wendy, but the group is not engaged and Wendy is deprived of learning from others. The example of Wendy is followed by a suggestion for how therapists could include the whole group. First, the missed opportunity.

THERAPIST: Wendy, what goal for the week did you set?

WENDY: I need to get my lazy body off the couch and I'm going to go for a walk every day.

COTHERAPIST: You seem very hard on yourself; remember we just talked about how low energy is a symptom of depression and not a reflection of what you're really like.

THERAPIST: I too am concerned that your goal is a lot to ask of yourself, and maybe a bit unrealistic. I wonder if you could be more specific about the length of your intended walk.

COTHERAPIST: Maybe you could start with three days a week rather than every day. In our experience, that is a big commitment and we want you to succeed and feel good about becoming more active.

WENDY: That makes sense, and I also don't like walking in the rain.

COTHERAPIST: Good to be aware of this barrier—and the forecast is not good, more rain coming.

WENDY: I guess I could buy a new umbrella as I lost my old one.

THERAPIST: That sounds good. All the best, Wendy, and we look forward to hearing how you did.

In the following example, the therapists deflect attention from themselves and intentionally defer to the group to do its process work.

THERAPIST: Wendy, what goal for the week did you set?

WENDY: I need to get my lazy body off the couch and I'm going to go for a walk every day.

COTHERAPIST: Any comments on Wendy's goal of going for a walk every day?

CHARLOTTE: I think it's a great goal and I too need to renew my membership at the gym, but I'm not going to make the same mistake of telling my family I'm going every day.

WENDY: How often are you going to go?

CHARLOTTE: I'm going to start with two days a week. Peter, isn't that also your goal?

PETER: Yes, and two times to the gym will be a challenge for me.

WENDY: OK, I'll start with walking two days a week.

THERAPIST: Any barriers you can anticipate to going for a walk two days a week?

WENDY: I hate walking in the rain.

COTHERAPIST: Me too—how do people cope with that?

LINDA: I find I need to have my rain pants, boots and umbrella all right by the door, otherwise it 's not going to happen. It can be kind of neat to walk in the rain, and I feel good when I come home.

WENDY: OK, I'll get myself a new umbrella and set a goal of walking for 30 minutes two days a week—rain or shine.

RALPH: You've inspired me and I want to change my goal from an inside one of going to the gym to an outside one of walking—even if it rains.

As we see from the aforementioned exchanges, group members often inspire each other, and similar, universal, themes for goal setting in depression groups come up year after year. They usually fall into three categories: (1) routine activities, such as "buy and eat healthier foods"; (2) necessary activities, such as "getting started on my resume"; and (3) pleasurable ones, such as "call up my friend whom I haven't seen in a year" or "sign up for a pottery class." Group therapists educate clients about how people who stay free of depression understand the importance of balancing, and following through with, daily and weekly activities in all three areas. Richards (2010) offers helpful suggestions for how to create graded hierarchies for guiding clients in setting goals in these three areas. It is critical that therapists work with all members in a group in developing their homework goals. To simply give clients a form for "filling in a goal" rarely works in groups for depression or any other CBT group. As

CBT therapists, we actively collaborate with our clients in creating their homework and always inquire about it in the following session. Failure to do so runs the risk of clients becoming unsure of what is expected of them, which can feed into self-defeating thinking and continued avoidance.

Focus on Emotions in Preparation for the Thought Records

In session 4, we turn to a focus on identifying emotional states or feelings. This is introduced as a brief prelude to the Thought Records work, which starts in session 6 (and is the focus of Chapter 5 of this book). The rationale for a discussion of feelings is that the better we are at identifying our feelings, the better we will be at knowing if our feelings are changing as a result of altering our thoughts. Group members are usually intrigued and welcoming of this idea. Therapists can work with the list of feelings outlined in *Mind over Mood* (Greenberger & Padesky, 1995). This list includes 25 different moods. We have found that an expanded list, the Feeling Wheel, with its 78 mood states allows for a richer and more nuanced exercise. The Feeling Wheel is easily downloaded from the Internet (or see Appendix D).[4] The Feeling Wheel works by understanding that the six basic emotions in the center of the pie (mad, sad, glad, scared, joyful, powerful, and peaceful) have several secondary or closely related feelings. It is important to give examples as the therapists explain the Feeling Wheel. For example, a person may feel very angry and be quite in touch with that state of high arousal; however, there may be another feeling driving this anger, a feeling that it is perhaps more difficult to acknowledge or accept. This feeling could be jealousy or insecurity. The group usually does not have problems generating other similar examples of how less socially acceptable feelings may not be recognized, and the idea of broadening one's feeling repertoire is invariably well received. One fair critique of CBT is its tendency to downplay the role of emotions in influencing thoughts and behaviors. Incorporating an emotion-focused therapeutic technique, such as the Feeling Wheel, is one way to overcome this limitation.

The discussion ends with a go-round exercise where each person is instructed to check in with themselves, use the Feeling Wheel as necessary, and identify a dominant feeling as honestly as possible and then say: "Right now, I am feeling ______." Many different feelings are voiced, including attempts to "test" the safety of, and unconditional acceptance by, the group when someone says "I am feeling bored" or "irritated" or "angry." The therapists ensure that all feelings are validated. It is best not to offer comments and simply nod while showing an open, nonjudgmental facial expression—no matter what the person says. Therapists also correct people who express a belief instead of a feeling, a common mistake. For example, a statement like "Right now, I am feeling misunderstood" expresses a belief because it can be challenged and disagreed with. In contrast, genuine feelings cannot be refuted as wrong. Many clients find it interesting to increase their awareness of the difference between thoughts and feelings as this is usually not something to which they had previously paid attention.

This emotion-focused exercise is also based on research showing that many people receiving outpatient treatment have legitimate problems with understanding their feelings, a condition called alexithymia, and that interventions aimed at improving this can enhance other therapy outcomes (Ogrodniczuk, Söchting, Joyce, & Piper, 2012). Moreover, alexithymic people tend to have difficulty connecting with others, often feeling distant. Emotion-focused training, however brief, can thus enhance the cohesion of a group in addition to the individual benefits. Homework involves monitoring five situations where a strong mood was noticed, writing it on the mood-tracking handout from the client folder, listing the associated feelings, and rating their intensity from 0 to 100.

Capitalizing on the Group in CBGT for Depression

CBGT for depression offers endless opportunities for meaningful and productive integration of group process factors. Considering that feelings of hopelessness are common and serious symptoms of depression, the *instillation of hope* is perhaps the most important factor. The therapists offer hope by clearly and transparently educating group members about symptoms of depression, why it is not "their fault," and how this group may offer some help. Therapists, however, must not oversell CBT for depression, as we know remission rates are far from optimal and the risk of relapse is high. Using language such as "this group is one step on your healing journey," "we're going through this together," or "for a number of reasons, it may be difficult for you to follow up with homework between sessions" helps to keep expectations at a realistic level. It is critical to invite group members to share what they find helpful in overcoming problems with motivation and feelings of helplessness. Group therapists explicitly encourage group members to talk among each other, and we take these opportunities during the go-rounds and at any time when it makes sense during the group time. More suggestions for how to deal with realistic expectations for CBGT for depression are offered in Chapter 6.

Opportunities to regain confidence in one's social skills are helpful for people with depression. The group format is uniquely suited for fostering social confidence when group members question their social skills. People with depression get caught in negative self-confirming cycles where, for example, they will berate themselves for cancelling an invitation: "Of course I don't have any friends because I always say no, I screw it up—all the time!" This group member may get feedback from another member: "No, it is not you who screw up, it's your depression getting in the way. You've helped me a lot here in the group, I feel you understand me, and you seem like the kind of person I'd love to be friends with." All group members are challenged to offer feedback and interact with each other. We observe people beginning to reconcile the dissonance between their own harsh and self-critical evaluations and the contrasting positive effect they have on others. A group format offers a number of ways to break out of the self-preoccupation characteristic of depression.

Summary

This chapter shows how the first half of the work in CBGT for depression involves the following components: education and discussion of the connection between thoughts, feelings, and behaviors, Beck's cognitive model of the developmental origins of negative thinking, review of symptoms of depression, self-monitoring of daily activities, introduction to goal setting, and increased awareness of group members' emotions. All this nicely sets the stage for commencing the cognitive restructuring work which follows the behavioral interventions. The next chapter includes several suggestions and clinical illustrations of cognitive restructuring with an emphasis on how to work in a group with Thought Records, which can be a challenging task for group members and therapists alike.

Notes

1. The criteria for a major depressive episode have not changed from the DSM-IV (APA, 2000).
2. The self-critical voice in depression is different in quality from voices people with psychosis may hear. Sometimes in severe depression, however, the depressed person hears voices more consistent with psychosis. This usually requires additional psychiatric management outside of the CBT group and may require the person to leave the group.
3. There are variations on the SMART acronym with M standing for *measurable*, A for *achievable*, and R for *relevant*, that is, my own goal.
4. The Feeling Wheel was developed by Gloria Willcox (1982).

Recommended Readings for Clinicians

Beck, A. T. (1972). *Depression: Causes and treatment*. Philadelphia: University of Pennsylvania Press (Original work published 1967).

Fennell, M. (1989). Depression. In K. Hawton, P. M. Salkovskis, J. Kirk, & D. M. Clark (Eds.), *Cognitive behaviour therapy for psychiatric problem: A practical guide* (pp. 169–235). Oxford, UK: Oxford University Press.

Greenberger, D., & Padesky, C. A. (1995). *Mind over mood: Change how you feel by changing the way you think*. New York: Guilford Press.

Paterson, R. J., Alden, L. E., & Koch, W. J. (2006). *The Changeways clinic core program: Practical strategies for personal change* (3rd ed.). Vancouver, BC: Changeways Clinic. Retrieved from www.changeways.com/ourproducts/store/store.html [accessed on February 21, 2013].

References

American Psychiatric Association (APA). (2000). *Diagnostic and statistical manual of mental disorders, DSM* (4th ed.). Washington, DC: Author.

APA. (2013). *Diagnostic and statistical manual of mental disorders, DSM* (5th ed.). Washington, DC: Author.

Beck, A. T., Rush, A. J., Shaw, B. F., & Emery, G. (1979). *Cognitive therapy of depression.* New York: Guilford Press.

DeRubeis, R. J., Hollon, S. D., Amsterdam, J. D., Shelton, R. C., Young, P. R., Salomon, R. M., et al. (2005). Cognitive therapy vs medications in the treatment of moderate to severe depression. *Archives of General Psychiatry, 62*, 409–416.

Fournier, J. C., DeRubeis, R. J., Hollon, S. D., Shelton, R. C., Amsterdam, J. D., & Gallop, R. (2009). Prediction of response to medication and cognitive therapy in the treatment of moderate to severe depression. *Journal of Consulting and Clinical Psychology, 77(4)*, 775–787.

Hollon, S. D. (2011). Cognitive and behavior therapy in the treatment and prevention of depression. *Depression and Anxiety, 28*, 263–266.

Murray, C. L., & Lopez, A. D. (1996). *The global burden of disease: A comprehensive assessment of mortality and disability from diseases, injuries and risk factors in 1990 and projected to 2020.* Cambridge, MA: Harvard University Press.

National Institute for Health and Clinical Excellence. (2009). *Depression in adults: NICE updated guideline*. London: Author.

Ogrodniczuk, J., Söchting, I., Joyce, A., & Piper, W. (2012). A naturalistic study of alexithymia among psychiatric outpatients treated in an integrated group therapy program. *Psychology and Psychotherapy: Theory, Research and Practice, 85*, 278–291.

Richards, D. A. (2010). Behavioural activation. In J. Bennett-Levy, D. A. Richards, P. Farrand, H. Christensen, K. M. Griffiths, D. J. Kavanagh, et al. (Eds.), *Oxford guide to low intensity CBT interventions* (pp. 141–150). Oxford, UK: Oxford University Press.

Willcox, G. (1982). The Feeling Wheel: A tool for expanding awareness of emotions and increasing spontaneity and intimacy. *Transactional Analysis Journal, 12(4)*, 274–276.

5

CBGT for Depression: Cognitive Interventions and Relapse Prevention

The previous Chapter 4 explained Aaron Beck's model of depression and its use in the psychoeducational and behavioral part of CBGT for depression. This chapter continues Beck's contribution to a better understanding of the role of thinking (cognitions) in depression. The various forms of cognitive interventions all focus on increasing our clients' awareness of the content and quality of their thinking. This chapter will concentrate on how to work with Thought Records in a group but will also review other cognitive strategies. The chapter concludes with a discussion of relapse prevention describing both CBT strategies and the Mindfulness-Based Cognitive Therapy (MBCT) approach. I feel compelled to extend the introduction to this chapter by describing Beck's original contribution to CBT, which has greatly influenced my own commitment to CBT.

Beck had extensive psychodynamic training prior to transforming himself into a cognitive therapist. As a psychodynamic clinician, he understood the importance of paying close attention to all materials produced by a patient, whether emotional or verbal. He became fascinated by what happened *immediately prior* to a patient expressing strong negative emotions and challenged his patients to notice what image or thought, however fleeting, they may have had. Not surprisingly, many patients were unable to name any such cognitive phenomena given that they hover on the border between subconscious and conscious awareness. Since Beck's clinical perceptions, scores of research studies have corroborated the strong influence of preceding thoughts on emotions (see Padesky, 2004, for a detailed review).

Supporting depressed clients in developing cognitive restructuring skills is a key task for CBT therapists. The restructuring of a client's thoughts follows a number of steps. First, therapists support their clients in identifying thoughts or images that are associated with strong negative emotions. This is followed by questioning the

Cognitive Behavioral Group Therapy: Challenges and Opportunities, First Edition. Ingrid Söchting.

thought, a process that encourages the client not to take the thought at face value just because it came from one's mind, but rather to test it in order to determine its accuracy. In the previous Chapter 4, we saw how a strong negative mood can lead to thinking that is not the most accurate reflection of reality. Lastly, the examined thought may lead to the development of an alternative, or more balanced, thought that after some reflection is deemed to be a more realistic appraisal of what "things are really like." This cycle of catch–evaluate–replace characterizes all cognitive work in CBT. Therapists who engage their clients in *cognitive restructuring* use synonymous terms such as *dysfunctional versus functional* or *irrational versus rational* or *realistic versus unrealistic*. It is up to the individual therapist to decide on the vocabulary with which they feel comfortable, and some prefer to minimize jargon when doing therapy. Substitute terms that resonate with clients include *maladaptive versus adaptive* or *unhelpful versus helpful* thinking.

Many CBT therapists object to the use of the term "positive thinking." And clients often say they have heard CBT is about having happy thoughts. Therapists will be guided by their own personal preferences, and depending on what the term happy means to them, they may or may not be comfortable using it in their therapy with depressed people. I usually refute the notion of CBT being a "power-of-positive-thinking therapy" and explain that I prefer to think of it as "reality therapy." Part of engaging clients with CBT is to challenge them to access additional information they are unable to access when they are in the grips of a strong negative mood. Strong moods seem to tighten the cognitive restriction of our thinking, as we saw in the example of Lisa in Chapter 4, who, when upset about the cancelled lunch, locked in to a conviction that her friend secretly did not like her. I might say something like: "Your emotions are real and must be validated by you and others, *but* they are not always the best indicator of what is *really* going on for you and around you. When we are depressed or anxious, our emotional brain tends to override our intellectual one. CBT will help you reconnect with your more rational reasoning abilities. Just because you are feeling depressed or anxious, does not mean you have lost your intelligence or critical reasoning ability." Clients appreciate the idea of using their critical thinking skills, their sound intellect.

Tools called Thought Records are available to help therapists and clients replace unrealistic thinking with more realistic one. Thought Records vary from two to seven columns. The simpler ones—which are often used with children or with adults whose struggles are overwhelming—consist of just two columns contrasting the *unhelpful, untrue thought*, for example, "I can't do anything right", with a *helpful, more true* new thought, for example, "I do many things well and am always interested in learning". The full 7-column Thought Record, developed by Padesky in the 1980s, is frequently used in face-to-face individual and group CBT. It is published in *Mind over Mood*, a self-help manual that teaches all the skills necessary to complete a 7-column Thought Record (Greenberger & Padesky, 1995). This manual is accompanied by a therapist guide, *Clinician's Guide to Mind over Mood* (Padesky & Greenberger, 1995). The 7-column Thought Record is different from other kinds of Thought Records in that it evaluates a *negative automatic thought* or the *hot* thought (e.g., "my friend cancelled lunch because I bore everybody") by examining evidence that may support the hot thought that one is boring (e.g., "It's true that I have stopped going to choir practice and yoga class") and evidence that does not support (e.g., "I know a lot about gardening, especially Japanese designs"). Taking both the pro and the con evidence into account, clients are assisted in developing an alternative and more balanced thought to counter the original hot thought (e.g., "While it is true that I have withdrawn from some things because of my depression, I know I have much to contribute when I hang out with people who share my interests").

The Thought Record in a Group

With the exception of Padesky and Greenberger's section on CBGT in their Clinician Guide (1995) and a CD course on Group Cognitive Therapy: A Balancing Act (Padesky, 2001), it is not easy to find clinical illustrations on how to work with Thought Records in a group. The main difference between using Thought Records in individual and group CBT is that the latter presents an opportunity for the therapists to use other group members to help an individual identify evidence against their hot thought. The individual person's thinking is in a sense pitted against the *reality check* of several real people who offer their questions and perspectives. Also, learning about someone else's hot thoughts, and offering them evidence against it, helps everyone to self-reflect on how easy it is to distort one's own thinking without really being aware of this. Therapists thus tap into this collective pool of collaborative empiricism as group members help one another become curious and more objective as they "check the facts" upon which they base their thinking. The saying about there being strength in numbers rings especially true for this exercise. The following vignette shows how and, I hope, provides therapists with support and inspiration to work with individual Thought Records while engaging the entire group.

THERAPIST: We're now going to work through another Thought Record example. Is there somebody who had a challenging situation last week where they felt a strong mood?

JUANITA: Yes, I did and I'm still upset and scared because it involved my mother and I'm going to see her on the weekend, but have decided I just will not go to this family dinner [starts crying].

COTHERAPIST: It seems very timely, Juanita, and maybe we can review what happened and be able to support you. Can you tell us what the situation was? [Cotherapist goes to the board and sketches the seven columns: 1. Situation, 2. Moods, 3. Automatic Thoughts (images), 4. Evidence That Supports the Hot Thought, 5. Evidence That Does Not Support the Hot Thought, 6. Alternative Balanced Thoughts, 7. Rate Moods Now.]

JUANITA: On Saturday I went shopping with my mom, and she bought a bunch of makeup, and I just bought one small bottle of body lotion. She then called me Saturday evening accusing me of being irresponsible because she knows I have some debt to pay off.

COTHERAPIST: Yes, you've talked about that problem and we can understand how the interaction with your mother was upsetting. Under "Situation," I'll write: at home by myself Saturday night talking to my mother on the telephone. [The therapist reminds the group that it is important that only the bare bone situation is described including who, what, when, and where]. Appendix D shows Juanita's completed Thought Record.

COTHERAPIST: What did you feel? [It makes sense to have the therapist who is starting the Thought Record and standing by the board do much of the questioning for the first three columns].

JUANITA: Upset, angry, scared, threatened, helpless, and depressed.

COTHERAPIST: OK, what would be the most intense feelings and how would you rate their intensity?

JUANITA: Scared, 90%, angry, 70%, and helpless also 90%.

COTHERAPIST: OK, makes sense that these feelings were pretty intense. What was going through your mind when you began to feel questioned by your mother?

JUANITA: That I don't like her, and that she is a selfish person who just happens to have a lot more money than I do. What right does she have to criticize me?

SUSAN: That's like my mother too, I so often feel this disapproval of how I manage my life, and especially my finances, but I don't know how to tell her to back off.

At this juncture, there is potential for the entire exercise to derail and fall apart. This can happen in a number of ways. When people share similar automatic thoughts, the desire to offer mutual support is strong, and the group easily becomes more of a process group. In order to demonstrate the value of working with Thought Records, it is important that at least one individual example gets completed during a group session. The onus is upon the therapists to keep track of time and gently return the attention of the group to the individual example, in this case, Juanita's. However, therapists also take the opportunity to comment on how any individual Thought Record example often has relevance for many people. All group members are encouraged to write down Juanita's example on their own sheets. Another example of derailing is when a therapist accepts a negative automatic thought that is about another person without inquiring further. In Juanita's example, it would be to put the following thought "my mother is selfish" in column 3.

Occasionally, a therapist may mistakenly accept a negative automatic thought about another person and write it down in column 3. This is where cofacilitation is helpful. If one therapist begins to become a bit stuck, the cotherapist can jump in and ensure the Thought Record exercise is brought back on track. This involves a literal return to the drawing board. It is imperative that we do not accept negative automatic thoughts when they are statements about other people. Doing that gets us into trouble as it is impossible to evaluate whether someone else in a client's life is, for instance, "a jerk." They may or may not be. The point is that the negative thought must always be about the person in question. The therapist deals with this by asking what it may mean to the group member to believe that "your brother is a jerk?" The member may say: "That I'm weak and cannot stand up to him." This is an appropriate automatic thought for which evidence for and against can be examined. In the same way, in the case of Juanita, it would not be helpful to engage in a discussion of what her mother is like, but rather to stay with how Juanita's experience of her mother as judgemental and selfish gives rise to a number of self-critical thoughts.

THERAPIST: Juanita and Susan, we understand your frustration and we will have opportunities to work more on your relationship to your mothers, but for this exercise, Juanita, what does it say about you that your mother is being critical of the way you manage your finances?

JUANITA: I worry that my mother is right. I wish I could stand up to her though. I don't trust myself handling money. I'm acting like a child. Maybe I am a selfish person. I'm certainly a financial failure. What if I go broke and become homeless?

RAYMOND: No, Juanita, all that is not true about you. From what I see in our group, you're not selfish.

COTHERAPIST: I appreciate your reaction, Raymond, and if you hang on, we'll soon get to the part of discussing what is or is not true about Juanita. Juanita, of those thoughts and fears you named, which one seems to carry the most energy for you right now? Which one would you like us to work with?

JUANITA: I think the one about being a financial failure—because it comes up a lot for me these days and not just when I'm with my mother.

COTHERAPIST: [Circles the "I'm a financial failure" thought]. Now, I want the group to imagine we are in a sense a judge or a jury in a courtroom and Juanita is on trial for being "a financial failure." How would we arrive at a fair judgment?

BRENDAN: I'm not sure, but I think it would involve looking at the evidence for and against her case.

THERAPIST: Precisely. So based on what we know about Juanita, and what you know about yourself, Juanita, what evidence can we point to in support of this idea of a failure? What questions would we ask to get more information?

BRENDAN: Is it true that you do have debt you want to pay off?

JUANITA: Yes, I have faltered on my debt payment plan for a second time.

COTHERAPIST: OK, that does sound like some hard piece of evidence, so I'll write that down in column 4. Anything else?

JUANITA: I'm also keeping this debt a secret from my husband, and know I'm being dishonest.

THERAPIST: OK, although not disclosing your debt is not necessarily indicative of being a financial failure, we'll write it down as it does provide some evidence for the way you think about yourself. Any other evidence for your being a financial failure?

JUANITA: No, it's mostly about not living within my means and having failed so far to follow the plan for financial recovery as outlined by my bank advisor.

COTHERAPIST: Let's move on to column 5. What is some evidence against Juanita being a financial failure? (Further questions to help with completing column 5 are given in the Mind over Mood protocol (Greenberger & Padesky, 1995)).

DEVIN: Juanita is in therapy and working on her issues. That suggests strength and success to me.

BRENDAN: Yes, and she listens and is open to advice. Remember I suggested she talk to an advisor at her bank as they are free. It sounds like you did that Juanita?

JUANITA: I did—and thanks for that advice, Brendan. My advisor is really helpful and optimistic. I'm certainly far from bankruptcy.

IVANA: Did you say some weeks ago that your work hours have been cut back, Juanita?

JUANITA: Yes, my hours have been scaled back and I've lost about 20% of my income.

IVANA: I think that's important too. I don't know about the rest of you, but I live from paycheck to paycheck and would be in trouble if my income declined.

RICARDO: I'm curious, Juanita, about whether your struggle to stay out of debt has always been a problem or is it more recent?

JUANITA: No I did fine when I was in college and in fact a girlfriend came to me for some advice for saving money [laughs in midst of tears]. It's something that has slowly happened over the past four years. I guess since I began to feel more depressed.

THERAPIST: Excellent questions, Ivana and Ricardo. Juanita, do these examples of evidence against your hot thought fit for you?

JUANITA: It sort of does, but still a bit hard to accept.

COTHERAPIST: OK, I'll write it all down. Juanita, is there anything else you would like to add? [The therapist may comment on how it was easy for Juanita to quickly come up with evidence in column 4 suggesting she is a "financial failure," but much more difficult to offer counterevidence in column 5 without help from the group. This is common and, again, reminds us of how hard people with depression can be on themselves].

JUANITA: Not really, but it's funny how you've all helped me to remember that I wasn't always hopeless at managing my money. I know I can do it; it's just that I've lost what it takes. Although I don't want to blame circumstances, I do see that my lesser income is certainly not making it easier for me either.

COTHERAPIST: Anyone else have a question for Juanita? If not, and in the interest of time, we will now as a group step back and look at the evidence in both columns 4 and 5. [The therapist reads each piece of evidence for and against the possibility that Juanita is a financial failure]. Our next challenge is to come up with a balanced statement about Juanita's money situation, a statement that is fair and takes the evidence both for and against the possibility that she is a "financial failure" into account. How can we put the essence of both columns together into one sentence or statement? [Further questions to help with column 6 are given in the Mind over Mood protocol (Greenberger & Padesky, 1995).]

DEVIN: I'll take a stab at creating the new, balanced thought for Juanita: "Although I, Juanita, do not deny I have a problem with spending more than I and my husband can afford, I'm taking full responsibility and working with a financial advisor and my therapy group on getting back on track."

JUANITA: Thanks, Devin, you captured it. Wow—let me write that down.

COTHERAPIST: How much do you believe your new, balanced thought on a scale from 1 to 100?

JUANITA: I don't know, definitely not a 100%. Maybe 80%.

THERAPIST: That makes sense, and you can pay attention to how this belief may change over the next weeks. Now, let's see how your feelings may have changed. Keeping your new statement about yourself front and center, how intense are the feelings of scared, anger, and helplessness?

JUANITA: They are still there, but I'd say that scared is about 40%, anger 30%, and helplessness only 20%. I feel a lot better and thanks to everyone for your help and support. I also feel I can handle the family dinner and am not going to cancel.

THERAPIST: How might you use this new thought? We would like you to write it down, and even say it to yourself several times a day—it's a bit like learning words in a different language. It will feel awkward at first, but then get easier. Here's a small card, a coping card, [hands Juanita an index-size card] you can write on. That way it's handy for you to take out your card next time the negative thought comes up.

COTHERAPIST: Yes, you're well equipped with your new thought—a kind of shield maybe—and we look forward to hearing how you practice this new thought and how it may help you get through your week and especially the family event.

In another example (which we will not go through in as much detail), a recent immigrant woman cried as she put forth several automatic thoughts related to her 20-year-old son arguing against many of his parents' cultural and religious values. Her thoughts included: "My parenting has been useless; What if he loses his faith? He doesn't see me as a supportive friend." She chose to subject this last thought to "courtroom" scrutiny; and with the help of the group, she arrived at a balanced thought of: "He is growing and finding himself, and despite our differences, we have a close bond." There were several other parents of young adult children in this group, and the example resonated with them as they expressed similar fears of losing connection with a child. We see that the Thought Record is a neutral, universal tool applicable to different cultural and socioeconomic issues. Actively engaging the group, as shown in the aforementioned examples, makes the delivery of a technique feel less didactic and more dynamically interactional.

The group setting provides a unique opportunity for creating a sounding board for reason and fairness—a kind of community reality check. Group members whose Thought Record examples are being demonstrated are often overwhelmed by emotion, which limits their ability to think more flexibly. In contrast, the helping group members are not constrained by their own emotions when the focus is not on them. This emotional distance allows for an effective empathic stance along with other group process factors. The warm and helpful climate in the group room facilitates effective questioning of evidence for and against the negative automatic thoughts. For example, altruism is evident as the group eagerly offers their helpful questions and perspectives on the group member in the "hot seat." CBT therapists agree that group members often ask questions during the thought-challenging process that they themselves had not readily been able to come up with. Not only does this benefit the person whose example is being explored, but because the situations brought up by group members often reflect common themes in depression, many people simultaneously learn new ways to question their own thinking.

Group therapists choosing to work with this 7-column Thought Record must manage session time to ensure each group member gets a turn during the sessions allotted to working with Thought Records. In a given session, which also includes an initial go-round of homework review, there is rarely time for more than two examples. So, depending on the size of the group, it may take several sessions for everyone to complete their example. Thought Records are assigned as homework for everyone, and ideally, each group member will complete three to four in addition to the one they did in the group. Once a member is capable of quickly challenging a particular negative and unrealistic thought, we encourage clients to develop a mental template of the Thought Record by which they can quickly spin a negative thought into a balanced one. Unfortunately, groups are rarely long enough to allow the therapists to witness how members hone their skills, but as will be discussed later, therapists in relapse prevention groups may enjoy the privilege of seeing this consolidation of CBT self-help skills.

Other Cognitive Interventions

After group members have mastered the basic skills of challenging and replacing their unhelpful and unrealistic negative automatic thoughts, there are several additional cognitive interventions aimed at the two other levels of cognition, *core beliefs* and *assumptions* (Figure 5.1).

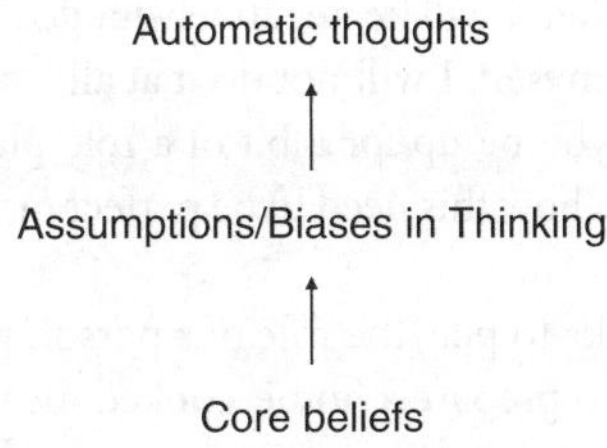

Figure 5.1 Automatic thoughts–assumptions–core beliefs.

Facilitators explain that there are three levels of cognition, with the deepest being the schemas or core beliefs. Schemas and core beliefs are considered equivalent terms in CBT. Core beliefs are characterized by strong, global statements about oneself, for example, "I am incompetent." Core beliefs usually involve one or more of three themes: competency ("I'm not capable"), worth ("I'm inferior to other people"), and lovability ("I'm not lovable"). The midlevel of cognitions is referred to as *assumptions* and characterized by if–then sentences ("If my colleagues found out I'm in group therapy for depression, then they will think less of me"), "shoulds, or other biases in thinking." For example, a person recovering from depression—and still vulnerable—may not be aware that she is thinking and behaving based on an assumption when she says to the group: "If I cannot manage to cook the dinner myself, then I should not bother with inviting people." The third, or most surface level of cognitions, is the ongoing, daily critical commentary, the negative automatic thoughts for which the Thought Record is primarily designed.

Many treatment resources list a number of *Biases in Thinking* or *Faulty Assumptions*, and group therapists can use those to make their own handouts or download them for free (Free, 2007). See Appendix E for a list of *Biases in Thinking*. The most common *Biases in Thinking* are as follows: all-or-nothing thinking, mind reading, disqualifying the positive, magnification and minimization, catastrophizing, the fortune-teller error, and emotional reasoning (e.g., Fennell, 1989; Free, 2007). In addition to group discussions where people are encouraged to say which errors they are especially prone to, group facilitators can also challenge individual group members to increase their awareness of when they may be vulnerable to various biases in thinking. Here is an example of how all-or nothing thinking can be addressed by using the *double-standard* intervention in a *role-play* to help a client work on her all-or nothing thinking.

Testing assumptions

THERAPIST: So, Edith, you have identified your tendency to engage in All-or-Nothing thinking when you told us that you are going to postpone the dinner for some friends; the dinner you in some ways see as a sign of your improving from depression. You are quite aware of having cancelled several socials during your illness.

EDITH: Yes, I see that I fall into the assumption of "if I don't cook the dinner all by myself, then I will be negatively judged by my friends." But if I can't do it all by myself, I will not do it at all.

THERAPIST: Edith, would you be up for a bit of a role-play as a way of getting some feedback on how this need to be perfect may get in the way of your life?

EDITH: Sure.

THERAPIST: Who would like to play the role of a person who is concerned about not being able to prepare a home-cooked meal for her friends?

MAXINE: I'm up for that.

THERAPIST: Great. So, Maxine, please speak to Edith, who is your friend in this role-play.

MAXINE: Edith, I know I had invited you and other friends over for dinner. It has been a long time. I've not been well but am doing better now. But I want to cancel because I'm feeling overwhelmed about what to make. I just don't understand how I used to whip together a meal.

EDITH: [looks at Maxine] Maxine, could you not order something in and we could all chip in?

MAXINE: I don't know. I still really want to be a good host and show my friends that I'm back to my old self.

EDITH: Maxine, I hear you, and I know how hard it is to find the energy to do something that feels like a lot. I just think that your friends really want to be with you and that the food is secondary. Why put so much pressure on yourself when people don't care about the food? I'm not saying that a good home-cooked meal is not great, or that you're not a good cook, it's just about what's more important here.

MAXINE: Yeah, I think I still have this fear of being judged if I'm not the perfect host. I could even ask some friends to bring salad, which could go with the pizzas I'll order.

EDITH: You will be a great role model as many of us could benefit from finding easier ways to get together with our friends over a meal.

THERAPIST: Good work both of you. You see, Edith, how you would not hold a friend to the same high or impossible standard as yourself. The problem of having one standard for ourselves and another for the rest of humanity can be a big challenge, especially as we recover from depression. We call this the *double standard* problem, one standard for us, and another for others.

Testing core beliefs

Core beliefs or schemas are the underlying global statements that infiltrate depressed people's thinking, usually without them knowing, until they enter therapy. Core beliefs have a global and absolute quality, such as "I'm inadequate." Addressing the core beliefs head-on can be productive and satisfying for both client and therapist because of the sense that one is getting at some deeper, core issues. Experienced CBT therapists know that core beliefs in depression tend to cluster around three main types: *I'm unlovable*, *I'm inferior*, or *I'm incompetent*. So therapists usually do not have much difficulty offering them as "interpretations" after having done some Thought Records with a particular group member. Using the Downward Arrow technique is, however, an elegant way to demonstrate how easy it is to go from a relatively surface-level negative automatic thought to a devastating, dark core belief. The Downward Arrow technique is illustrated in both the Fennell chapter (1989) and *Mind over Mood* (Greenberger & Padesky, 1995). Group therapists can create their own handouts with blank spaces for sentences, followed by the line "If that were true, what would it mean to me?"

For example, the group may ask Edith in the aforementioned example: "If it were true that you did not feel like cooking a meal for friends, what would that mean to you?" One imagines the following downward spiral.

ANSWER: "That I was still depressed and not really getting better."
QUESTION: "Suppose that was true, that is, you are not getting better, what would that mean to you?"
ANSWER: "That I'm pretty messed up, with not much hope."
QUESTION: "Suppose it was true that you are pretty messed up and not much hope for getting better, what would that mean?"
ANSWER: "That everyone is right about how incompetent I am when it comes to helping myself, and I don't see any hope."

This is a good place to stop, and the therapist points out how quickly Edith went from an ordinary problem of not feeling like cooking a meal to being "incompetent" and feeling "hopeless." It is easy to see how the Downward Arrow can elicit suicidal ideation (which is the reason why some group CBT therapists do not routinely use it), and it is crucial that the session does not end with a person in the "Downward Arrow Pit." The next step is to generate counters to the core belief and encourage the person to write down on the Core Belief Record all the evidence indicating that this core belief is not 100% true. In the case of Edith, the group will remind her of all that she has accomplished, that she is actively engaged in therapy, that she is competent in knowing her limits, that she has a creative mind, that she problem solves very well, that she is a good role model, and that she gives hope to others, etc. Although core belief work is usually included in CBGT (e.g., Bieling, McCabe, & Antony, 2006), group therapists are aware that increased awareness can lead to strong emotions for some members, especially those who struggle with recovery from depression. Therapists may consider engaging only those members who are clearly improving from their depression in the Downward Arrow exercise.

Behavioral experiments

Behavioral experiments can be used to test all three levels of cognitions (core beliefs, assumptions, and negative automatic thoughts). These experiments offer group members an opportunity to put thoughts and predictions to various real-life tests. Staying with Edith, she could test her assumption of "If I don't make a perfect home-cooked meal, I will be judged." Her experiment would involve homework in the form of inviting her friends for an order-in pizza dinner while asking them to bring a salad. Because the group had already role-played evidence for and against this prediction, there is no need to have another group discussion. In other client examples, such group discussions are fruitful and may seriously question any evidence purported by the person to support the negative prediction. As always, the outcome of any behavioral experiment is reviewed during the homework go-round the following week.

Behavioral experiments are designed using written forms on which clients *state the problem*, their *target cognition* (e.g., "I'll be judged negatively if I don't prepare a home-cooked meal"), their *alternative perspective* ("My friends are more interested in being with me than in what food I cook"), their planned *experiment*, and the *results*. Suggestions for designing behavioral experiments across a wide range of problems are given in the *Oxford Guide to Behavioural Experiments in Cognitive Therapy* (Bennett-Levy et al., 2004).

CBGT Psychodrama

CBGT Psychodrama is a new and optional extension of the more traditional CBT group. Having experienced this intervention firsthand in a training workshop led by Thomas Treadwell, a certified CBT therapist with the Center for Cognitive Therapy at the University of Pennsylvania, I appreciate how the integration of CBT with psychodrama could be a helpful intermediate step toward a real-life behavioral experiment (Treadwell, Kumar, & Wright, 2010). During a psychodrama enactment, the group allows the person to practice testing their new thoughts, as derived from the traditional Thought Record. The CBT psychodrama group attempts to simulate the "real world," including the "real" players in the person's life, as other group members are given instructions on how to act like them. An attractive feature of this intervention is the opportunity for affective expressions in the group—so long as therapists ensure that these are reasonably contained.

Using the aforementioned example of Edith, the CBGT psychodrama may unfold in the following way. Edith, the protagonist who is testing her fear of "I will be judged for being incompetent," would pick members of the group to represent her various friends and give them instructions. For example, one friend may have a habit of dry or sarcastic humor, which Edith easily interprets as critical. Another friend may be very quiet and engage in more nonverbal communication. Other group members are assigned to various *Action Techniques*, including two *Doubles*, the *Contained* and the *Cognitive Double*. The *Contained Double* would be instructed to express negative thoughts and feelings presumed to be felt by Edith but not expressed (e.g., "Edith, careful here, you are feeling very nervous and pretty sure that your friend over here is frowning at the pizza boxes"). The *Cognitive Double* is instructed to express the positive thoughts and feelings that Edith may have but not express (e.g., "You are doing well, Edith, and being genuine when you say it is good to see your friends—without having to prove yourself"). Another person is assigned the *Aside/Automatic Thought*—kind of like the chorus in a Greek drama—who gets to express immediate thoughts and feelings when a change of mood is visible and felt. For example, halfway through the simulated dinner, Edith's mood dips after she picks up the phone. A group member playing her mother called and Edith felt compelled to answer her "mother's" question of what she served for dinner. This led to Edith feeling some shame and anxiety as she realized her real life mother would never have served pizzas for dinner. Edith began to question her own behavior: "I should not have taken this shortcut and they're clearly all just being polite and putting on a good show."

Needless to say, any serious consideration of adding dramatic reenactments to CGBT requires some training and supervision in addition to strong process skills. For a group in which cohesion is strong, experienced group therapists may successfully add this intervention to their CBGT for depression armamentarium and enjoy considerably elevating the energy in the group room.

Relapse Prevention

Preparing for the future is essential given the risk of relapse in depression. Past the halfway mark of a depression group, many members usually express fears about how they will cope after the group ends. Some of these worries can be dealt with by using the same cognitive techniques as for other negative automatic thoughts. The last two sessions in a standard CBGT group are devoted to reviewing strategies for preventing relapse. Appendix G offers a handout for a facilitator-led discussion on what to expect during the recovery phase. This includes preparing clients for *mood traps*. The *dropping-mood trap* prepares group members for inevitable drops in mood and reminds them to not catastrophize by fearing a major setback or the thought that "all is lost." The *rising-mood trap* is also important in that it cautions people to not take on too much too quickly (keep your enthusiasm in check!). Edith did a good thing for herself when she knew her limitation for hosting a dinner party. It is not uncommon for recovered clients to overdo it by planning three course dinners, signing up for full-time university, or refusing a gradual return-to-work plan.

Research findings on relapse rates after individual CBT for depression suggest the risk is not huge, with about an average 30% risk of recurrence. For people who are treated only with medication, their risk of relapse after stopping medication is on average 60% (Gloaguen, Cottraux, Cucherat, & Blackburn, 1998; Warshaw, Dyck, Allsworth, Stout, & Keller, 2001). Research by Robin Jarrett and colleagues suggests that offering continued CBT for clients with residual symptoms of depression after the active CBT treatment is a good investment of resources given the large return in relapse reduction. *Continuation phase cognitive therapy* (C-CT)[1] consists of ten 60–90 minute sessions over 8 months (first four sessions every other week, then the next six sessions monthly). Clients with moderate residual symptoms (e.g., Beck Depression Inventory (BDI) scores from 4 to 9 indicating minimal depression; Beck, Steer, & Brown, 1996) have a 90% better chance of staying free of recurrent depressive episodes compared to about 40% in the noncontinuation treatment groups (Jarrett, Vittengl, & Clark, 2008).

CBGT therapists have new ways of becoming better at identifying those who remain at risk. Jarrett and colleagues are in the process of developing clinical guidelines that will allow therapists to use self-report measures, including the BDI (Beck et al., 1996) and the Hamilton Rating Scale for Depression (HRSD) (Hamilton, 1960) for determining who is at risk for relapse (Jarrett & Thase, 2010). Another option is an ongoing CBT group that could be open, running in a continuous manner. Because all clients in such a continuation group would have had the CBT modules during the active phases, each session would have more of a stand-alone review quality and thus be easier to conduct in an open format. The continuation CBT group is essentially a more intense form of "booster" sessions, which CBGT therapists often already add to their depression groups. Group members are invited to attend a booster group 2, 4, or 6 months after the 12-session CBGT program is completed. Knowing that clients will be reporting back to their group may help them feel motivated to continue to practice on their own. Should there be lapses, this can then be addressed in the booster groups. A continuation CBGT program may consider also welcoming clients from the community who have been managed by their family physician but not had any formal CBT. Research shows that an 8-session relapse prevention CBGT program for clients with four or more previous episodes of depression produced significantly less recurrence compared to clients who did not receive any additional therapy beyond family physician care (Bockting, Spinhoven, Wouters, Koeter, & Schene, 2009). Ideally, depressed people would engage in CBGT after their first episode rather than after four or more, and therapists would have resources to offer continuation therapy for those clients who continue to have residual symptoms after their active CBGT is over.

In the next section, I turn to another form of relapse prevention for depression, MBCT.

Mindfulness-Based Cognitive Therapy (MBCT)

The development of MBCT for depression has offered clinicians an additional approach to relapse prevention (Segal, Williams, & Teasdale, 2002, 2012). I will briefly summarize what mindfulness is, how it works, the importance of facilitator training, and how to use it for relapse prevention in depression, using our group program as an example.

Developers of mindfulness training recognize that although the capacity for mindfulness is inherent in all humans, most of us move through life on "autopilot," performing daily activities based on habitual behavioral patterns while our minds are elsewhere. Mindfulness training can be described as a continual practice of *awakening* to the present-moment experience (Bishop et al., 2004). Whereas traditional cognitive therapy chips away at replacing unhelpful thoughts with helpful ones, mindfulness training is less concerned with the content of the thought (e.g., Juanita's negative automatic thought of "I'm a financial failure") and more with the *acceptance* of the thought and the way the person *relates* to their thought. Mindfulness training helps participants develop a different relationship to their thinking. Similar to CBT, clients learn to not treat thoughts as facts but to instead develop a gentle curiosity about their thoughts, however troubling they may be. Clients are also taught to pay attention to their breath as they engage in slowing down their breathing (*Mindfulness of the Breath*). Various exercises help clients bring a heightened attention to their breath, any body sensations as well as other sensory experiences related to hearing, seeing, feeling, or tasting in the present moment (the *Body Scan* practice, the *Sitting Meditation*). The point is to continually awaken to a full experience of the present moment and redirect one's attention from "mental noise," such as ruminations about past events or worries about future ones. Any difficult sensation, thought, or emotion is accepted rather than resisted or fought (Segal et al., 2012). Ultimately, continued practice supports people in cultivating a stance of radical acceptance of themselves, their thoughts, and the aspects of their lives they are unlikely to be able to change.

Mindfulness teachers help clients understand that even the most distressing thoughts or feelings are transient and will pass—like clouds in the sky, or unexpected visitors to a mind that is experienced only as a guest house, not a permanent residence. To illustrate the helpfulness of accepting and not avoiding difficult thoughts and feelings, I have with selected clients used a poem, The Guest House, in my practice for decades and enjoy seeing it used now also by mindfulness teachers. The Guest House, by the thirteenth-century Persian Sufi poet Jalaluddin Rumi, is a lovely and wise poem (I have a gorgeous handwoven tapestry of the entire poem hanging on my wall) used by therapists (including many, such as myself, who do not consider themselves qualified mindfulness therapists) as a helpful metaphor (Barks & Moyne, 1997). Therapists in MBCT—and other—groups can read this poem while introducing it as an inspiration for becoming more *accepting* of thoughts and moods (Segal et al., 2002).

The Guest House
This being human is a guest house.
Every morning a new arrival.
A joy, a depression, a meanness,
Some momentary awareness comes
As an unexpected visitor.
Welcome and entertain them all!
Even if they're a crowd of sorrows,
Who violently sweep your house
Empty of its furniture,
Still, treat each guest honorably.
He may be clearing you out
For some new delight.
The dark thought, the shame, the malice,
Meet them at the door laughing,
And invite them in.
Be grateful for whoever comes,
Because each has been sent
As a guide from beyond.

From Barks and Moyne (1997).
Reproduced with permission
of Coleman Barks.

The poem can aid clients in bringing an accepting attitude to their internal experience. This may lead to practicing noticing what happens when they stay with this intention of acceptance. A new insight may arrive—"clearing you out for some new delight." Many clients get to this new place by the end of CBGT for depression (and anxiety), but some will benefit from more work, such as mindfulness, on "stepping back" from their thinking and developing new ways of relating to their thoughts.

MBCT for depression relapse is based on the clinical knowledge that although the formerly depressed person resembles a nondepressed person in their mostly reality-based and balanced thinking, depression does leave its mark. Anyone who has been previously depressed is, despite successful recovery, still much more likely to become depressed again compared to someone who has never been depressed. The degree to which negative thinking becomes reactivated plays a key role in predicting relapse. Measuring a formerly depressed person's level of *cognitive reactivity* could thus offer another tool for predicting who is at risk for relapse (Jarrett et al., 2008; Lau, Segal, & Williams, 2004). A difference between the previously and the never depressed person is the tendency of the former to "react to small changes in mood with large changes in negative thinking" (Segal et al., 2002, 2012), that is, the *dropping-mood trap* as previously mentioned.

Studies have replicated initial findings on the effectiveness of an 8-session MBCT group-based intervention on reductions of residual symptoms of depression and up to a 50% reduction in relapse risk (Kingston et al., 2007; Ma & Teasdale, 2004). More recently, Piet and Hougaard (2011) in a review of six randomized controlled group MBCT trials obtained a reduction in relapse of 43% for participants with three or more previous episodes of depression. In the United Kingdom, MBCT is now recommended as an effective intervention for depression relapse prevention by government-approved clinical experts (National Institute for Health and Clinical Excellence, 2009).

In our CBGT for depression program, an MBCT group is recommended for those clients who have residual symptoms of depression. They may have successfully completed the 12-session CBGT program, or they may be directly referred into the MBCT group, which also accepts clients who struggle with anxiety or other issues. Therapists use their clinical judgment, a diagnostic screen, and self-report measures when recommending MBCT for a client who has completed CBGT for depression (or some other form of effective treatment for depression). Our MBCT class follows the approach of Segal and colleagues (2002). It spans eight 2-hour group sessions and includes between eight and 10 members. As with other groups, the cost-effectiveness is inherent, and the class can be expanded to 15 or more members depending on the room size.

Therapists leading MBCT groups must have received formal training as well as demonstrate commitment to a personal mindfulness practice. CBT therapists are increasingly seeking training to lead MBCT groups (e.g., Chartier et al., 2010). Perhaps the most important aspect of doing MBCT in a group is the amount of attention on "the teacher." This is in part due to mindfulness being informed by Eastern spiritual practice, especially Buddhism, with its focus on the personal relationship with a guru and encouraging silence over group "chatting and mingling." In this sense, it is a good fit with the more traditional CBT group and its classroom principles. However, with the focus on the leader, the increased interest in augmenting process factors in more standard CBGT will take on a different form—or not be as applicable—in the MBCT group. The MBCT leader also has the added challenge of embodying the qualities of mindfulness. This is especially relevant during the part of the group when members—after a period of quietly noticing what is going on in their minds and bodies—then give voice to their inner experiences as they noticed them during the sitting meditation. Because of their personal and intimate familiarity with paying attention to body sensations, the MBCT leaders will use that as they relate to the expressions of group members. On the one hand, MBCT follows a protocol and each session includes certain topics, and on the other, it remains open to whatever arises in the moment. Indeed, it is another way of working with integrating structure and process in CBT-based groups.

Summary

This chapter focuses on the standard cognitive therapy interventions for depression and how to implement them in the group setting. The use of the 7-column Thought Record is illustrated with a lengthy group multilog. The chapter also reviews how to adapt interventions focused on assumptions, biases in thinking, and core beliefs to a group setting. Traditional CBGT- and CBGT-based mindfulness approaches to relapse prevention in depression are described. MBCT is gaining in popularity and offers innovative perspectives on working with both structure and process when offered in a group setting.

Although CBT depression groups often work better than clinicians anticipate—and better than the research review in Chapter 3 suggests—there is room for improvement regarding selecting appropriate candidates for the group and ensuring expectations for improvement are realistic. The next chapter turns to these more pragmatic issues of how to present CBGT in general as an attractive treatment option, how to prevent dropouts, and how to evaluate outcome.

Note

1. C-CT is mainly continued cognitive work helping clients to evaluate the validity of negative thinking and generating more realistic alternatives when negative thoughts are not supported.

Recommended Readings for Clinicians

Fennell, M. (1989). Depression. In K. Hawton, P. M. Salkovskis, J. Kirk, & D. M. Clark (Eds.), *Cognitive behaviour therapy for psychiatric problems: A practical guide* (pp. 169–235). Oxford, UK: Oxford University Press.

Free, M. L. (2007). *Cognitive therapy in groups: Guidelines and resources for practice* (2nd ed.). West Sussex, UK: John Wiley & Sons.

Greenberger, D., & Padesky, C. A. (1995). *Mind over mood: Change how you feel by changing the way you think*. New York: Guilford Press.

Padesky, C. A. (2001). *Group cognitive therapy: A balancing act*. Center for Cognitive Therapy. http://store.padesky.com/grp.htm [accessed on February 21, 2014].

Padesky, C. A. (2004). Mind, man, and mentor. In R. L. Leahy Contemporary (Ed.), *Cognitive therapy: Theory, research, and practice* (pp. 3–24). New York: The Guilford Press.

Padesky, C. A., & Greenberger, D. (1995). *Clinician's guide to mind over mood*. New York: Guilford Press.

Segal, Z. V., Williams, J. M. G., & Teasdale, J. D. (2002). *Mindfulness-based cognitive therapy for depression: A new approach to preventing relapse*. New York: Guilford Press.

Segal, Z. V., Williams, J. M. G., & Teasdale, J. D. (2012). *Mindfulness-based cognitive therapy for depression* (2nd ed.). New York: Guilford Press.

Treadwell, T., Kumar, V. K., & Wright, J. H. (2010). Integrating cognitive behavioral with psychodramatic theory and techniques. In S. S. Fehr (Ed.), *In 101 interventions in group therapy* (rev. ed., pp. 395–401). New York: Routledge/Taylor & Francis Group.

References

Barks, C., & Moyne, J. (1997). *The essential Rumi*. San Francisco: Harper.

Beck, A. T., Steer, R. A., & Brown, G. K. (1996). *BDI-II, beck depression inventory: manual* (2nd ed.). Boston: Harcourt Brace.

Bennett-Levy, J., Butler, G., Fennell, M., Hackmann, A., Mueller, M., & Westbrook, D. (2004). *Oxford guide to behavioural experiments in cognitive therapy*. Oxford, UK: Oxford University Press.

Bieling, P. J., McCabe, R. E., & Antony, M. A. (2006). *Cognitive-behavioral therapy in groups*. New York: Guilford.

Bishop, S. R., Lau, M. A., Shapiro, S., Carlson, L., Anderson, N. D., Carmody, J., et al. (2004). Mindfulness: A proposed operational definition. *Clinical Psychology, 1*, 230–241.

Bockting, C. L. H., Spinhoven, P., Wouters, L. F., Koeter, M. W. J., & Schene, A. H. (2009). Long-term effects of preventive cognitive therapy in recurrent depression: A 5.5-year follow-up study. *Journal of Clinical Psychiatry, 80(12)*, 1621–1628.

Chartier, M., Bitner, R., Peng, T., Coffelt, N., McLane, M., & Eisendrath, S. (2010). Adapting ancient wisdom for the treatment of depression: Mindfulness-based cognitive therapy group training, *Group, 34(4)*, 319–327. Special issue: Training in group psychotherapy.

Gloaguen, V., Cottraux, J., Cucherat, M., & Blackburn, I. M. (1998). A meta-analysis of the effects of cognitive therapy in depressed patients. *Journal of Affective Disorders, 49*, 59–72.

Hamilton, M. (1960). A rating scale for depression. *Journal of Neurology, Neurosurgery, and Psychiatry, 23*, 56–62.

Jarrett, R. B., & Thase, M. E. (2010). Comparative efficacy and durability of continuation phase cognitive therapy for preventing recurrent depression: Design of a double-blinded, fluoxetine-and pill-placebo-controlled randomized trial with a 2-year follow-up. *Contemporary Clinical Trials, 31(4)*, 355–377.

Jarrett, R. B., Vittengl, J. R., & Clark, L. A. (2008). How much cognitive therapy, for which patients, will prevent depressive relapse? *Journal of Affective Disorders, 111*, 185–192.

Kingston, T., Dooley, B., Bates, A., Lawlor, E., & Malone, K. (2007). Mindfulness-based cognitive therapy for residual depressive symptoms. *Psychology and Psychotherapy, 80(2),* 193–203.

Lau, M. A., Segal, Z. V., & Williams, M. G. (2004). Teasdale's differential activation hypothesis: Implications for mechanisms of depressive relapse and suicidal behavior. *Behaviour Research and Therapy, 42,* 1001–1017.

Ma, S. H., & Teasdale, J. D. (2004). Mindfulness-based cognitive therapy for depression: Replication and exploration of differential relapse prevention effects. *Journal of Consulting and Clinical Psychology, 72(1),* 31–40.

National Institute for Health and Clinical Excellence. (2009). *Depression in adults: NICE updated guideline*. London: Author.

Piet, J., & Hougaard, E. (2011). The effect of mindfulness-based cognitive therapy for prevention of relapse in recurrent major depressive disorder: A systematic review and meta-analysis. *Clinical Psychological Review, 31(6),* 1032–40.

Warshaw, M. G., Dyck, I., Allsworth, J., Stout, R. L., & Keller, M. B. (2001). Maintaining reliability in a long-term psychiatric study: An ongoing inter-rater reliability monitoring program using the longitudinal interval follow-up evaluation. *Journal of Psychiatric Research, 35,* 297–305.

Part 2

Challenges of Cognitive Behavioral Group Therapy

The next five chapters address some of the challenges that clinicians and program managers who aim to develop strong cognitive behavioral group therapy (CBGT) programs face. We will look at a number of issues, including the technical aspects of CBGT interventions, outcome evaluation approaches, and how to support clinicians in developing sufficient confidence to run CBGT. Chapter 6 outlines an outcome measurement approach to CBGT as well as other topics such as preparing clients for group and preventing dropouts. Chapter 7 deals with the fairly new subject of CBGT transdiagnostic groups. Chapter 8 examines when it makes clinical sense, supported by evidence, to integrate another therapy approach into CBGT. Chapter 9 guides clinicians in a step-by-step fashion on how to develop exposure hierarchies in a group setting, how to improve rates of homework completion, and how to plan for termination of cognitive behavioral therapy groups. Chapter 10 faces the critical issue of developing standards for therapist qualifications. But, first, Chapter 6 begins with perhaps the most important challenge: How to support people with mental health problems in starting CBGT and staying with it.

Cognitive Behavioral Group Therapy: Challenges and Opportunities, First Edition. Ingrid Söchting.

6

How to "Sell" CBGT, Prevent Dropouts, and Evaluate Outcomes

Drawing People into CBGT

When people today hear the words "group therapy," many imagine being trapped in a room with odd and "out-of-control" people, whom even the leaders cannot reign in. This no doubt is influenced by media and movie scenes of group therapy. It is one of the reasons it can be hard to sell any form of group therapy in mental health settings. CBT groups are no exception. Assessment, screening, and pregroup preparation thus play an important role in getting people to engage with CBGT. Ensuring appropriate group member selection reduces dropout rates and enhances attendance, treatment compliance, and outcomes—not only for the individual but the entire group. In addition to having the insight and willingness to assume responsibility for helping oneself, someone entering a CBT group will also need to have some basic level of comfort with and interest in other people. A highly paranoid or angry person is not likely to do well in a CBT group. In general, any presence of strong personality disorder features can impact a person's ability to benefit from CBGT for depression and anxiety. This does not necessarily mean they should be excluded, but the intake assessor needs to make a clinical judgment and also be mindful of how many potentially challenging members there may be in total in the same group. If more than two, it could become problematic.

In Chapter 2, we concentrated on how Yalom and Leszcz's (2005) group process factors mapped onto an obsessive–compulsive disorder (OCD) group. In this section, I will touch on some other group process factors, such as group members' readiness, their motivation, relations to the group therapists, and expectations. These factors all play an important role in group suitability and sustainability. But, first, we need to get people into the group!

Cognitive Behavioral Group Therapy: Challenges and Opportunities, First Edition. Ingrid Söchting.

Dedicated group therapists strongly recommend that mental health programs wanting to offer effective CBT groups not give clients a choice of individual treatment unless there are good reasons for not recommending a group, which of course is sometimes the case. Simply being uncomfortable with or fearful of CBGT is not a clinically sufficient reason for accommodating a client into individual therapy.

Policymakers are aware of the value of promoting group therapy when they point to evidence indicating that, after appropriate pregroup orientation, the outcome from group therapy for the majority of clients is as good as from individual treatment. However, since most people will prefer individual treatment, it is sometimes necessary to put some effort into "selling" group therapy (e.g., B.C.'s Mental Health Reform, 1999). In a recent study on treatment preferences, which included the mental health site where I work, 91% of men and 77% of women expressed a preference for individual therapy versus group (Sierra Hernandez, Oliffe, Joyce, Söchting, & Ogrodniczuk, 2014). Yet, group therapists also know that the vast majority of clients who make it to a group realize their fears were unfounded. They often express relief at having pushed themselves to attend.

To learn more about potential group members' fears, we added a number of questions to a standard CBGT intake assessment. Eighty potential group members were asked, among other things, to indicate their fears (Söchting, Lau, & Ogrodniczuk, 2014). Somewhat surprisingly, when asked directly, most (93%) indicated they were not afraid and "looked forward to group therapy." The fear themes of the more hesitant candidates for CBGT fell into three categories: (1) "I am afraid of being judged and people not liking me," (2) "I'm afraid it will not help me," and (3) "I'm afraid that other people in the group will be too unstable compared to me." These categories likely capture a portion of the same fears expressed by the 38% of OCD patients who refuse CBGT, documented by O'Connor and colleagues (2005) and reviewed in Chapter 3. Not surprisingly, we see similar fears across different group programs.

Preparing Clients for CBGT

All interactions with clients prior to the group are crucial in terms of adequate preparation for CBGT. This first involves an assessment and confirmation of the most likely diagnoses or problems. In programs where CBGT specifically targets specific disorders related to depression, anxiety, obsessive–compulsive, and trauma, it is critical that people end up in the most appropriate group. The assessment is, ideally, done in a face-to-face intake meeting, but other forms of screening such as telephone or online can be reasonable substitutes so long as there is still an added group orientation. This assessment usually takes between an hour and an hour and a half. The time and effort spent up front is worth it, as it is time consuming when people end up in the "wrong" group and need to be redirected. In some outpatient programs, psychiatrists or psychologists initially perform a thorough diagnostic evaluation.

In the absence of a prior psychiatric evaluation, a full structured diagnostic interview following *Diagnostic and Statistical Manual of Mental Disorders* (DSM) criteria is ideal. The Structured Clinical Interview for DSM-IV (SCID; First, Gibbon, Hilsenroth, & Segal, 2004) assists intake clinicians in making sure they do not miss any symptoms, but it can be lengthy to administer and therefore rarely feasible in outpatient community clinics. But developing a template for asking a couple of key screening questions for each disorder is doable and thus ensures that something was not missed. Appendix J offers such a screen, which can be used to guide a face-to-face assessment or support a telephone intake screening assessment. For example, if a client states she has worries about becoming physically ill, it is important to determine if this worry involves obsessions about contamination and excessive washing (OCD) or ongoing worries about health, the uncertainty of life, and difficulty deciding on a course of action (generalized anxiety disorder [GAD]). The intake clinician may also ask the client to complete a self-report measure in order to confirm the primary problem(s). Recommendations for various diagnostic self-report measures are given in *The CORE-R outcome battery* section of this chapter.

The majority of the staff where I work received training in the DSM structured diagnostic interview (SCID). Even though we do not perform full SCIDs, it is helpful to have the diagnostic criteria at our fingertips and understanding key differences between the various anxiety disorders. I thus highly recommend that the staff who do assessments for disorder-specific CBGT receive some basic training in the DSM, now DSM-5 (APA, 2013), even though they do not offer formal diagnoses themselves. Such training can be done in-house by any psychiatrist or psychologist who is required by their professional colleges or boards to be familiar with and use the DSM-5. Ongoing staff education and discussions about the differences and similarities among the various disorders are helpful in order to ensure groups run as effectively as possible and clients get the treatment they need in a timely manner.

In addition to inquiring about present symptoms, the general mental health intake assessment will involve detailed information about the expression of the symptoms or issues over the past to the present, how they interfere with daily functioning, and which coping skills have been tried, including previous mental health contacts. After the intake assessor and the client have established the main problems, the assessment focuses on the client's goals or targets for treatment. The assessor collaborates with the client to ensure the goals are realistic for CBGT and that they include two to three shorter-term goals (during the active treatment phase) and one longer-term goal (where the client would like to be 5 years from now). Any CBT (not just groups) firmly flows from the stated intake goal(s), which must be reasonably specific such as the following: "Learn to control my symptoms better; do more things with friends such as join a book club, and find a physical activity that works for me" (short term) and "when I feel better, I want to review options for a new career" (long term). An ability to state these goals gives an indication of the client's level of motivation, and any ambivalence about treatment can be discussed. So far, this pregroup assessment does not differ from the approach taken in individual CBT, but the last part, which is the *introduction to the group format*, does. This pregroup orientation is critical for maximizing clients' group experience and ensuring they complete their CBT group. The pregroup orientations must include information about the treatment approach, expectations for homework and attendance, and also an opportunity to explore thoughts and feelings about being in a group. As will become apparent in the following text, some clients may have had an introduction to group CBT before their individual assessment if they have participated in a pregroup orientation session delivered in a group setting.

It is also important to discuss group start dates with the client. Often, there is no specific start date. Instead, therapists talk generally about, plans for simply a "fall" or "spring" group, as they need to assemble a sufficiently large group, usually eight members, before beginning. A downside to group therapy is that some members may have to wait for several weeks or even months before their group starts. We find that aiming for two more members than the ideal size is best. One or two people usually drop out just before the group starts, so if eight members is the preferred size, I recommend having 10 people on the list before starting. Clients tend to be accepting as they know wait times for any service in the public system are usually lengthy, up to 10–23 months between referral and start of therapy (Rezin & Garner, 2006). The intake assessors may decide to offer a few telephone check-ins with clients they deem could use support during the wait time. As we see in the following text, a *rapid access* group can also offer support—or actual treatment—while waiting.

Individual pregroup orientation

Pregroup orientation takes various forms: individual orientation, group orientation, and *rapid access* group orientation. The following dialogue illustrates an individual orientation in which a therapist prepares a 25-year-old male for a depression group toward the end of the formal assessment.

THERAPIST: So based on my explanation of what will be covered in this group program, how do you feel about being in a group of about ten people who also struggle with depression, most of them older than you?

TIM: Well, since one of my goals is to become more social, a group would obviously be good for me [laughs]. It's just that I was raised in what you could call a hippie community, and even though it was neat to have many adults looking after us and always doing things in larger groups, I guess, there was also a lot of conflict and people you thought you could trust, but couldn't.

THERAPIST: So from an early age you became familiar with some of the benefits of being part of a close community of people but also some of the possible downsides. How would you handle it, if you began to feel uneasy in the group, perhaps because you felt you could not fully trust the group?

TIM: I know I'm not supposed to leave because that would only hurt myself and I'll stay stuck in my isolation, but it would be hard for me to speak up about that.

THERAPIST: I wonder if there is a way for you to speak about how hard it is for you to trust a group of strangers. What might it sound like [therapist encourages and models a mini role-play in assertive communication using "I" statements].

Group pregroup orientation

In the pregroup orientation, which takes place in a real group format, potential CBGT candidates get all the same information about the content of a particular CBGT program, plus expectations for goal setting and home practice. They also get the *experience* of being in a group. As there is no substitute for actually trying something out, as opposed to only hearing about it or role-playing it, this orientation format is preferred by group therapists—and is the most cost-effective as well. Not only can up to 10 or 15 people get the same information delivered during a 1-hour session by one facilitator (compared to 20 minutes per group member as illustrated in the aforementioned dialogue), it also increases motivation and prevents dropouts. Potential group members have a stronger sense of what they are getting themselves into and what is expected of them. As people leave such a pregroup, we hear comments like "I can't believe how normal everybody else seemed," "The facilitator seemed really nice and knowledgeable," or "I already feel this will give me some skills to help myself." We deliberately do not sign clients up for groups until after this orientation. This lessens the risk of securing a spot in a group to someone who has a high likelihood of dropping out. Thus, in this model, the client referred for group CBT is first invited to a 1-hour pregroup orientation session (offered weekly) and then, if still keen, proceeds to a more formal assessment of suitability for a particular CBT group.

Rapid access group orientation

Rapid access groups expand on the pregroup orientation by inviting potential CBGT clients to enroll in an actual group for two to six sessions. These groups are primarily supportive and offer clients an opportunity to talk about their goals for treatment and get questions about their upcoming groups answered. A rapid access group allows members to become familiar with the basic process in a group and for the therapists to engage in ongoing assessment of suitability. The added benefit is a reduction in wait lists—or the appearance thereof—by getting people into "something" quickly. The downside, however, is that the group rarely offers the more problem-focused CBT that most clients ultimately need. This may lower clients' motivation and their perceptions of treatment credibility. There is evidence that the therapeutic alliance also develops as a *result* of effective CBT (Feeley, DeRubeis, & Gelfand, 1999). That is, as clients improve and attribute their improvement to CBT, they feel better about their therapist. Although the Feeley study involved individual CBT, one would reasonably expect the same to be the case for CBGT. When group members note they are making progress, they feel better about their group and become more motivated and likely to complete treatment with good outcomes. There is a variation of the rapid access group which offers real structured CBT.

A CBT rapid access group has been developed by Hamilton and colleagues (2012). Their *CBT Basics I* is considered a *preindividual therapy* group program primarily designed to reduce wait times for people seeking more intense individual CBT. The program consists of a six-session introduction to the basic concepts and techniques that apply to all depression and anxiety disorders. Although this pregroup was developed for people waiting for individual CBT, it should be just as effective for people waiting for CBGT.

Lastly, the *open intake* CBGT is an option combining *rapid access* with orientation to an actual disorder-specific group. The open intake group maintains the efficiencies of CBGT while offering continued, weekly intake of one or more clients depending on maximum group size. The wait time is typically reduced to only 1 or 2 weeks. This open approach contrasts with more traditional closed group formats in which people begin and end together for a specified number of sessions. The open intake allows flexibility and enables empty places created by premature terminations or *no shows* to be filled more quickly. An additional benefit of open intake groups is that more experienced group members, who have attended a number of sessions, offer support and information about the group to newly entered participants and, hence, serve as peer role models. Anxiety about ending a group (termination) may be mitigated in open groups as clients partake in fellow group members leaving on an ongoing basis. An unavoidable challenge in the open intake group is that psychoeducational material and any treatment rationales will have to be repeated each session for the benefits of newcomers. This format also requires new ways for the therapists to work with the group process factors (clinical observations and research). Chapter 14 discusses an open group for Latino immigrants and Chapter 17 for addiction.

Preventing Dropouts

Once people have committed to a group, the next challenge is to make them stay. Inconsistent attendance or dropping out has been identified as a particularly serious challenge to CBGT. Dropout rates in community outpatient settings tend to be around 20% for depression (Hans & Hiller, 2013a) and about 15% for anxiety (Hans & Hiller, 2013b) but at their extreme can be as high as 30–50% (Erickson, Janeck, & Tallman, 2009; MacNair & Corazzini, 1994). Dropouts are of course not unique to CBGT and also happen in individual CBT—and all forms of individual and group therapy—but are less problematic in individual therapy given the isolated impact.

More than one dropout in a group can disrupt group solidarity and even precipitate a minor cascade of departures. Inconsistent attendance and departing people make remaining group members feel insecure, worried, and angry. As mentioned earlier, it is a good idea to take likely dropouts into account by going above the ideal group size when accepting members. I have experienced one grim scenario in which we started with a depression group of nine and ended with three members and four facilitators! Two psychiatry students participated in addition to the two senior therapists. This was an embarrassingly cost-ineffective group. Fortunately, such experiences are rare.

There is surprisingly little research on why people attend poorly or drop out altogether in CBGT—and other kinds of groups. Some reasons are legitimate and cannot be prevented, such as getting a job that conflicts with the group time, moving, losing childcare coverage, or getting seriously physically ill—or in some cases needing hospitalization for suicide attempts. As for more preventable reasons for dropouts, possible factors have been suggested. They include problems with alcohol (MacNair & Corazzini, 1994), physical health complaints (Bostwick, 1987), difficulty relating in general to others (Miller & Rice, 1993), and low expectations for and fear of group therapy (Yalom & Leszcz, 2005).

In the systematic review of 80 CBGT candidates mentioned earlier, we explored some of these possible reasons for dropping out, but did not find any correlation between health or interpersonal problems and low attendance or dropping out. There was a small correlation between prior alcohol use—but not present—and poor attendance. Overall, 11% of all the clients enrolling in CBGT dropped out. Poor attendance was the case for 7% (less than 50% of total number of sessions), 20% had medium attendance (between 50% and 75% of sessions), and 62% had good attendance (more than 75% of sessions). The dropout rate of 11% from this sample of 80 clients is lower than the rates reported in the literature. Perhaps this reflects clients being well prepared for CBGT, as well as efforts to create a strong group climate allowing for optimal learning of specific CBT interventions. We found a strong correlation between expectations and attendance.

Expectations for CBGT

People waiting for a group were asked, among other things, to rate their expectations on a 1–7-point scale (e.g., "I look forward to beginning group therapy" and "I expect I will stay with the group at least eight weeks"). In other words, looking forward to group therapy and having positive expectations for attendance bode well for completing. Conversely, feeling ambivalent does not. The role of expectations makes intuitive sense and is not a new idea. In his classic text, *Persuasion and Healing*, Frank (1961) argued that mobilization of hope and positive expectations for improvement within the patient seeking help is integral to effective therapy.

There are some studies showing that positive expectation in CBGT for anxiety is related to greater improvements (Dozois & Westra, 2005; Price, Anderson, & Henrich, 2008). In contrast, little is known about the relevance of members' expectations in CBGT for depression. Given that, in our experience, dropouts from depression groups are more common compared to anxiety groups, we took a closer look at expectations in CBGT for depression (Tsai, Söchting, Mirmiran, & Ogrodniczuk, 2014). *The Outcome Expectancy Scale* (OES; Ogrodniczuk & Söchting, 2010) is a three-item self-report questionnaire asking clients to rate their degree of confidence in the helpfulness or expected benefits of therapy on a five-point Likert-type scale ranging from one (not at all) to five (completely). The questions are as follows: (a) How much do you expect to recover from your problems after therapy? (b) How successful do you think the therapy will be in helping you with your problems? and (c) How confident are you that this therapy will help you?

We obtained several results with implications for strengthening CBGT for depression. Overall, expectancy was significantly related to improvement not only in depression but also anxiety, quality of life, and interpersonal problems. Not surprisingly, the more hopeful depressed people benefitted the most and those who felt particularly hopeless and demoralized the least. Another important finding included the relationship between expectancy and feelings about one's connection to the group therapists, *the therapy alliance.*

In our study, the therapy alliance was assessed primarily in regards to how the group members experienced the two group therapists and not the entire group (*the Working Alliance Inventory*; Horvath & Greenberg, 1989). Expectancy immediately prior to starting the group was related to *early-therapy alliance* quality but not *midtherapy alliance.* In other words, people who had positive pregroup expectations that the group would help them experienced a strong working alliance with the therapists in the *initial* phase of the group, but not in the middle phase. We interpret this as perhaps reflecting an attenuation of unrealistically high early expectations. This may simply suggest that group members who are initially quite enthusiastic develop a more realistic perspective about what therapy can and cannot provide. It could also suggest some loss of hope once confronted with the reality that depression is a potentially chronic illness and significant effort is required to keep symptoms at bay. Thus, the third and fourth sessions in CBGT for depression may be an especially critical time for dropping out. Therapists may want to be particularly attentive during these sessions to how individual group members are feeling about their treatment.

Indeed, in our experience, the majority of dropouts happen around the third and fourth sessions. A CBGT outcome study for motor vehicle-related PTSD reported only a few dropouts after session 4 (Taylor et al., 2001). After the introductory sessions, the initial CBGT honeymoon phase has passed and the harder work begins. As mentioned earlier, therapy alliance is a dynamic concept and not just something that is built before the real treatment begins. As people begin to improve, their positive feelings about their therapist(s) increase commensurately. But improvements are most likely to stick if the pace is steady and realistic.

One member in a depression group returned to the second session stating she felt so encouraged after the first session that she had signed up for a yoga class, gone swimming, and resumed contact with a friend. The group therapist shared in her enthusiasm but also paid attention to the pressure she may put on herself to "keep it all up."

What other steps can clinicians take to increase engagement with CBGT and prevent dropouts? We could make more effort in the early group phase to mobilize hope and expectation of improvement, and we must continue to reinforce this in order to support people through the "waning expectations" phase. Realistic expectations are crucial. When group members believe that therapy can bring about desired change, they are more likely to engage in a collaborative working relationship with the group leaders—and the rest of the group. Our efforts could include group discussions and validation of feelings of hopelessness. It could also involve more real-life examples from videos or personal testimonials of recovery from depression through therapy including CBT. For example, the video *Coping with Depression and Manic Depression* by Mary Ellen Copeland (1994) conveys—despite it being two decades old—tremendous credibility and hope (our group clients love it). The newer video *Living Life to the Full* DVD course based on a self-help book, *Overcoming Depression and Low Mood: A Five Areas Approach* (Williams, 2006), also features depressed people speaking about their recovery journey. There are similar videos for most anxiety disorders, and we recommend showing and discussing them during the first three sessions (e.g., Anxiety Disorders Association of Manitoba, 1999; HBO, 1999).

Client Characteristics Impacting CBGT

In addition to more obvious client characteristics such as motivation, readiness to make changes, previous CBT, and severity of symptoms and problems, other client characteristics also play a significant role, in our experience, in some clients receiving limited benefits from CBGT. I will briefly address two of them: chronic pain and gender.

Chronic pain

People with physical complaints in the form of chronic pain (commonly a result of a work-related injury) in addition to depression and anxiety often drop out of CBGT for depression or anxiety. Although group members with chronic pain understand that this will not be the primary focus of the group, they nearly invariably "fall behind" the rest of the group when it comes to actually doing the self-help exercises, whether in the group or at home. Understandably, they explain by saying "when my pain is better, then I will be able to do this." This leaves the therapists and other group members feeling helpless and of course reluctant to gently push as one does not want to exacerbate physical pain. And not keeping up with the rest of the group reinforces negative thinking about hopelessness and exclusion from the group community and the larger society. These clients also miss more sessions due to competing physical health medical appointments or simply being in too much pain to bring themselves to the group. Individual CBT, or group therapy programs with a primary focus on pain, may be a better option than CBGT that targets primarily anxiety and depression (Hofman, Asnaani, Vonk, Sawyer, & Fang, 2012). Clients with chronic pain who also suffer from depression and anxiety voice a strong preference for pain-specific CBGT as opposed to general CBT groups. Specific pain CBGT may not be available in more traditional mental health community settings, but attempts to make this a priority may be worthwhile.

Gender

Another problem in CBGT is the frequent imbalance of gender. Not only are more women than men diagnosed with depression and most forms of anxiety, but women tend to seek therapy more often than men. This results in a typical depression group with seven or eight women and two or three men, or even all-female groups from time to time. A man dropping out is clearly an issue for the one or two remaining men. We have had groups where one man dropping out is followed by the rest of the men. Interestingly, in our CBT group for elderly people, 65 and above, we see a better balance with typically about 40% men. This has a tremendously positive impact on the work of the whole group. Dropout rates among senior men are considerably lower compared to depression groups for men and women ages 19–65. CBGT for anxiety has proven somewhat better, especially for OCD, where we often see a 50–50 gender split or more men than women in about a third of groups (unlike panic disorder, OCD affects men and women equally; in fact, it affects more males in adolescence and early adulthood).

Any gender imbalance has virtually no implication for the *content* part of CBGT but tremendously so for the *process*. Many women in all kinds of CBT groups—and not just posttraumatic ones—have had prior negative experiences with men, which can lead to overgeneralizing beliefs such as "men cannot be trusted." Positive interactions with men in a group help to repair and restore this kind of distorted thinking and build trust, not only in the group but in women's lives outside the group as well. Conversely, men also benefit from the presence of women. A man may fear judgments about not being a good enough husband and father because he is on stress leave from work and therefore a lesser provider (a common presentation). Or a man may say "what's wrong with me as the only man in this group? Am I weak or something?" It is helpful when men hear women express their respect for trying to help themselves through therapy often adding "I wish my husband would be brave like you and go for therapy." This kind of supportive comment is, however, also a reminder to pay attention to our own biases and ensure they do not leak into the group room with the unintended damage of discouraging men even more from attending therapy groups.

Specifically, most group therapists are female and, as professionals, capable of high-level independent functioning. Despite many centuries of lack of equal opportunity for women, we now encounter a reversal in some socioeconomic and cultural groups with women becoming primary wage earners (also, for most degree programs in North American postsecondary institutions—and especially the helping professions—more women than men enroll). Sometimes, men seem to buy into a need to accept being targets for subtle—and not so subtle—ridicule and joking related to "what men are like." We see some of this in our groups, especially the ones for depression.

Male and female group therapists need to pay attention to their own biases and possible "blind spots" and be especially alert to the group not making jokes about, or references to, men that could be misinterpreted as diminishing. Several men have sought the attention of the group leaders after a group saying they felt uncomfortable, and we encourage them to bring their concerns and feelings to the next group. It usually works out. One man in his 60s even wrote a poem and read it to the group. The poem was about his finally daring to stand up and refute characterizations of his gender that he felt were not true. It was well received by all and led to stimulating group discussions over several weeks. Obviously, groups must feel safe for both genders. Both genders understandably need the security of a significant gender subgroup. This point is easily understood when the opposite scenario is sketched of a male gender-dominated group including only one female member, which could be either the leader or a client. Having male cotherapists in depression groups is helpful.

Clinicians' concerns about the difficulties of engaging men in some forms of CBGT have been backed up by research. In a study on short-term supportive group therapy for grief, the men did considerably less well overall than the women. The researchers speculated that if only one or two men are present in a group, they could feel quite isolated and less committed to the group to the point of being treated as fringe members (Ogrodniczuk, Piper, & Joyce, 2004). Although this study was on grief and not on other kinds of emotional distress such as depression, it does raise important questions about whether gender-specific groups, such as a CBT group for depressed men, ought to be offered.

There is a growing recognition that men are increasingly seeking mental health services, but some uncertainty about what kind of support best meet their needs. Many men struggle with asking for advice and often experience this as unmanly and embarrassing. This awareness led therapists from the United Kingdom to develop an exclusive psychoeducational CBT-like group program for young men to address depression, self-esteem, and suicidal thoughts and behaviors. The authors remind us that suicide is four times more common in men than women and the second most common cause of death in young men in Britain after accidents (Pringle & Sayers, 2004). This project was built around football (or soccer) as a metaphor. The project developers were aware of a possible "feminization" in traditional therapy groups, given their emphasis on *talking* over *doing*. These kinds of gender-specific doing groups have not "taken off." There could be a number of reasons for this. But one possibility is that men may be less adverse to traditional talking psychotherapy than popular beliefs may indicate.

Despite the belief that men do not go for psychotherapy as much as women, surprisingly little research has explored this assumption, which is shared by many mental health clinicians. My colleagues and I, somewhat surprisingly, found that among a total of 407 people seeking mental health services, the men were just as interested in psychotherapy (61%) as the women (64%) as opposed to other forms of help, including medication (Sierra Hernandez et al., 2014). I hope these results will stimulate more research that could help therapists make groups more attractive and beneficial for both genders. Questions about the benefits and disadvantages of mixed versus gender-specific groups are largely unanswered at this time.

Evaluating CBGT Outcomes

One of the reasons for the success of CBT and CBGT is the ability of most CBT clinicians to build treatment outcome data into our interventions—and to actually use them (not have them just sit in some box or filing cabinet). At minimum, this consists of using one, but ideally two or three, self-report measures, such as the Beck Depression Inventory (BDI; Beck, Steer, & Brown, 1996), before the first session and after the last session. Not only does this provide another source of valuable feedback to the client in terms of progress, but it also allows the clinician to develop a database of many BDI scores before and after treatment. Simple statistical analyses can then be run to see if clients in a particular program are overall benefitting from the treatment. Positive outcomes can then justifiably be used in proposals for further funding. I mentioned in Chapter 3, and will repeat, that this willingness to let "the numbers" speak, and not just "believe" that one is a competent clinician running effective groups, is a compelling feature of CBT. Group therapists and program administrators will consider various factors when choosing their final battery. These factors include cost, ease of scoring, interpretation, meaningful feedback to the client, time to complete, and whether clinicians wish to also use their outcomes for larger networks, by contributing to the scientist–practitioner literature.

In the following section, I discuss the benefits of integrating clinical outcome measures in CBGT and share some outcome measurement recommendations from the *Science to Service Task Force of the American Group Psychotherapy Association (AGPA)*. (Burlingame et al., 2006), which are highly relevant for CBGT clinicians.

The benefits of outcome measures

Clinicians with an interest in self-assessment and self-reflection easily list reasons for integrating outcome evaluation into regular clinical practice (Asay, Lambert, Gregerson, & Goates, 2002). Outcome measures offer another source (in addition to the clinician's opinion) of information on a client's progress. Clients may communicate information on a questionnaire that they would otherwise not state verbally. We get a fair share of direct, constructive suggestions for improvement in our *client satisfaction surveys* at the end of all CBT groups. If more than five people over a reasonable period of time express a similar sentiment, we take steps to tweak our group intervention if at all possible. Midterm evaluations are also helpful, especially if they reveal a lack of progress. This can lead to increased collaboration and revision of initial goals, or to troubleshooting other reasons for why the CBGT is not helping. In this way, clients become not just passive recipients of treatment but active collaborators.

It is good practice to share all results from outcome measures with clients. This can be done either on a one-to-one basis outside of the group or integrated into a group session. The latter is preferred and can be done by giving each group member a summary of their scores (nobody knows each other's scores) and inviting them to share any reactions to their scores.[1] For example, one person in a group did not understand why her self-reported depression score on the BDI came out in the *severe* range. She received feedback that she might be puzzled because she tries hard to cope in front of others by "putting on a good face" and that she maybe needs to be more accepting of being quite ill. Another person with obvious and severe OCD scored in the nonclinical range on a self-report measure of OCD symptoms. He showed some insight and was able to articulate a fear of having to actually confront his obsessions. He also acknowledged he had been ambivalent about starting therapy and had thought about dropping out. He received feedback from the group about perhaps being in some denial about his illness. Group therapists enjoy listening to insightful feedback and attempt to let the group members offer this first before doing it themselves.

In addition to improving individual outcomes, measures can also be used to review overall outcomes for a particular CBGT treatment service. This can provide a more meaningful perspective for expectations of improvements compared to relying solely on benchmarks from the literature. Clinicians working in community settings may feel demoralized if their outcomes do not match those reported in the literature, and it is easy to forget that high-level outcome research often involves carefully selected clients. Community clinicians cannot "cherry-pick" clients and thus need to include people who may be less motivated or who have a number of other issues in addition to the one for which they seek CBGT help. The majority of community clinicians are nevertheless keen to be informed by the literature on effective interventions and outcomes. In a national Canadian survey, there was considerable interest in bridging the *practitioner–scientist gap*. Clinicians expressed a desire to partake in larger practice research networks where they could feel supported in their daily clinical decision making, especially with regard to how to measure outcomes (Lau, Ogrodniczuk, Joyce, & Söchting, 2010; Ogrodniczuk, Piper, Joyce, Lau, & Söchting, 2010). Clinicians in the United States have similarly shown an interest in practice research networks (Borkovec, Echemendia, Ragusea, & Ruiz, 2001).

The CORE-R outcome battery

The AGPA task force recognized that any outcome battery must be brief, comprehensive, easy to administer, free from theoretical bias, sensitive to change, have established reliability and validity, and be widely used. Their recommended battery, the CORE-R, takes about 30–45 minutes for the client to complete. The CORE-R includes the following: (a) a symptom-focused outcome measure, the *Outcome Questionnaire-45* (OQ-45; Lambert et al., 1996), (b) *Inventory of Interpersonal Problems-32* (IIP-32; Horowitz, Alden, Wiggins, & Pincus, 2000), (c) *Target Complaint Scale* (Battle et al., 1966), (d) *Group Evaluation Scale* (Hess, 1996), (e) *Rosenberg Self-Esteem Scale* (Rosenberg, 1965), (f) *Quality of Life Enjoyment and Satisfaction Questionnaire* (Endicott, Nee, Harrison, & Blumenthal, 1993), and (g) *Personal Health Questionnaire-9* (PHQ-9; Kroenke, Spitzer, & Williams, 2001). There are several helpful discussions covering how clinicians can incorporate this battery, or a portion of it, in their group practice (e.g., Strauss, Burlingame, & Borman, 2008). Most measures in this battery are available at no cost. The OQ-45 requires the purchase of one license (about US$ 100), which allows unlimited individual test usages. All the aforementioned measures are translated into at least one other language, with the OQ-45 in 12 languages including Dutch, Spanish, and Arabic and the IIP-32 in German, Swedish, Norwegian, and Danish. The Rosenberg Self-Esteem Scale includes Polish and Mandarin.

While the CORE-R is appropriate for older clients and adolescents, it is not for younger children. An alternative battery for children has been recommended (Friedberg, 2007). This includes the BDI, but it is also worth considering the *Children's Depression Inventory* (CDI), the *Multidimensional Anxiety Scale for Children* (MASC), the *Screen for Child Anxiety Related Emotional Disorders* (SCARED), and the *Conners Parent Rating Scales* (CPRS).

Effective CBGT programs tend to be informed by the aforementioned CORE-R battery recommendation and include (a) measures of symptoms (e.g., BDI, Beck Anxiety Inventory (BAI), PHQ-9, OQ-45, or other symptom measures relevant to the specific group), (b) measures of interpersonal functioning (the IIP-32 does not seem to have any competing measures), and (c) measures of life quality. Most programs also ask for three target complaints at the initial assessment. It is rare that CBGT programs include measures of self-esteem and group cohesion. I hope this will change given CBGT therapists' observations that the effectiveness of CBGT often goes beyond symptom relief. The *Group Evaluation Scale* mentioned earlier is one such group cohesion measure. Another group cohesion self-report measure is the *Group Climate Questionnaire—Short Form* (MacKenzie, 1983, 1990). The scale assesses the perceived interpersonal climate using three scales that address the extent to which group members work constructively together (Engaged Scale), the degree of their perceived tension and conflict (Conflict Scale), and degree to which group members avoid working on their problems (Avoidance Scale). *The Therapeutic Factors Inventory—Short Form* (Joyce, MacNair-Semands, Tasca, & Ogrodniczuk, 2011) reviewed in Chapter 2, is yet another adequate substitute or addition to either the *Group Evaluation Scale* or the *Group Climate Questionnaire.*

There are various symptom measures for specific diagnoses that can easily be included in the outcome battery for CBGT. Any research on the assessment of various disorders will offer suggestions for both clinician-administered and self-report measures. In CBGT, we are primarily interested in self-report symptom measures that do not take longer than 5–10 minutes to complete. My suggestions below are thus not comprehensive, but simply examples of frequently used symptom outcome measures (Table 6.1).

Table 6.1 Recommended symptom measures for evaluating CBGT outcomes

Depression	*Beck Depression Inventory* (BDI; Beck et al., 1996)
	Personal Health Questionnaire (PHQ; Kroenke et al., 2001)
	Hamilton Rating Scale for Depression (HRSD; Hamilton, 1960)
OCD	*Yale–Brown Obsessive Compulsive Scale* (Y-BOCS; Goodman et al., 1989) is the gold-standard self-report outcome measure
SAD	The *Social Phobia Scale* (SPS; Mattick & Clarke, 1998) assesses fears of being observed and evaluated
	The *Social Interaction Anxiety Scale* (SIAS; Mattick & Clarke, 1998) assesses anxiety when engaging in social interactions with different kinds of people
GAD	*Why Worry Scale II* (Freeston, Rheaume, Letarte, Dugas, & Ladouceur, 1994)
	Intolerance of Uncertainty Scale (IUS; Buhr & Dugas, 2002; Freeston et al., 1994)
	Penn State Worry Questionnaire (PSWQ; Meyer, Miller, Metzger, & Borkoved, 1990)
Panic disorder	*The Panic Attack Questionnaire* (Cox, Norton, & Swinson, 1992). Assesses frequency and distress of panic attacks
	Mobility Inventory (Chambless, 1985) assesses the extent of agoraphobic avoidance
	Beck Anxiety Inventory (BAI; Beck & Steer, 1990)
PTSD	*The Impact of Event Scale* (Weiss & Marmar, 1997)
	Posttraumatic Diagnostic Scale (PDS; Foa, Cashman, Jaycox, & Perry, 1997). This is mapped to the DSM-IV diagnostic criteria and may need revision for DSM-5
Compulsive hoarding	*Saving Inventory—Revised* (SI-R; Frost, Steketee, & Grisham, 2004)
	Clutter Image Rating (CIR; Frost, Steketee, Tolin, & Renaud, 2008) addresses the extent to which living space is cluttered
Substance abuse	*Drinking Expectancy Questionnaire* (DEQ; Young & Oei, 1990)
	Drinking Refusal Self-Efficacy Questionnaire (DRE-SEQ; Young, Oei, & Crook, 1991)
Psychosis	*Positive and Negative Syndrome Scale* (PANSS) is widely used in clinical settings (Kay, Fiszbein, & Opler, 1987). This is not a self-report but a clinician-administered measure

Outcome measures are primarily used to measure individual clients' progress. Secondarily, several individual outcome measures can be reviewed together and thus evaluate a specific CBGT program. Outcome measures can also be valuable at a third level, namely, that of larger national or international practice networks. I alluded to research showing that the majority of clinicians are eager to join with their research colleagues and bridge the scientist–practitioner gap. Using the same CBGT outcome battery allows programs or clinics to pool data, which in turn can lead to analyses and comparisons across sites and countries. Such multisite, multicountry outcome data collections will support the evaluation of CBGT effectiveness across programs. They also permit comparisons with results from more rigorous, controlled outcome studies. In this way, networks comprised of both practitioners and researchers work together to improve the effectiveness of CBGT in clinical settings. These partnerships encourage research into clinically relevant frontline questions such as the following: Do people with social anxiety benefit more from homogeneous versus heterogeneous (transdiagnostic) groups? Or what is the correlation between group process factors and symptom improvement across different CBGT programs? Are different factors more relevant for certain problems? The ultimate goal would be to create a network in which CBGT clinicians would be directly involved in the design and implementation of research, with researchers ensuring adherence to the protocol, managing the database, and taking the lead on statistical analyses.

Summary

This chapter reviews a number of issues pertaining to drawing people into CBT groups and minimizing dropouts. In addition to careful screening and CBGT preparation, addressing group members' fears and expectations, especially during the first four sessions, is critical. Client characteristics including chronic pain and gender are used as examples of additional factors that impact successful group participation and completion.

The chapter addresses how to measure outcomes in CBGT. At a minimum, outcomes should include one relevant symptom measure and a quality of life measure. Specific symptom outcome measures exist for each disorder covered in this book. Group therapists may wish to include additional outcome measures of interpersonal functioning and clients' perceptions of the group climate.

The next chapter turns to the challenge of having people with different diagnoses in the same group. It explores the literature and examples from community clinics.

Note

1. In transdiagnostic groups (reviewed in Chapter 7), group members get somewhat different outcome measures, which does not matter given the individual focus on sharing results within the group.

Recommended Reading and Viewing for Clinicians

Anxiety Disorders Association of Manitoba. (1999). *Panic disorder: Frightening, disabling, treatable*. Manitoba, Canada: Lank Beach Productions.

Copeland, M. E. (1994). *Coping with depression*. Oakland, CA: New Harbinger Publications.

HBO Home Video (1999). *Panic: A film about coping*. New York: America Undercover.

Williams, C. J. (2006). *Overcoming depression and low mood: A five areas approach* (2nd ed.). London: Hodder Arnold.

References

APA. (2013). *Diagnostic and statistical manual of mental disorders, DSM* (5th ed.). Washington, DC: Author.

Asay, T. P., Lambert, M. J., Gregerson, A. T., & Goates, M. K. (2002). Using patient-focused research in evaluating treatment outcome in private practice. *Journal of Clinical Psychology, 58*, 1213–1225.

Battle, C. C., Imber, S. D., Hoehn-Saric, R., Stone, A. R., Nash, E. R., & Frank, J. D. (1966). Target complaints as criteria of improvement. *American Journal of Psychotherapy, 20*, 184–192.

Beck, A. T., & Steer, R. A. (1990). *Manual for the Beck anxiety inventory*. San Antonia, TX: Psychological Corporation.

Beck, A. T., Steer, R. A., & Brown, G. K. (1996). *BDI-II, Beck depression inventory: manual* (2nd ed.). Boston: Harcourt Brace.

Borkovec, T. D., Echemendia, R. J., Ragusea, S. A., & Ruiz, M. (2001). The Pennsylvania practice research network and future possibilities for clinically meaningful and scientifically rigorous psychotherapy effectiveness research. *Clinical Psychology: Science and Practice, 8*, 155–167.

Bostwick, G. (1987). "Where's Mary?": A review of the group treatment dropout literature. *Social Work with Groups, 10(3)*, 117–131.

British Columbia Ministry of Health and Ministry Responsible for Seniors. (1999). *BC's mental health reform: Best practices*. Retrieved from http://www.health.gov.bc.ca/mhd/best.html [accessed on February 21, 2014].

Buhr, K., & Dugas, M. J. (2002). The intolerance of uncertainty scale: Psychometric properties of the English version. *Behavior Research and Therapy, 40*, 931–945.

Burlingame, G. M., Strauss, B., Joyce, A., MacNair-Semands, R., MacKenzie, K., Ogrodniczuk, J. S., et al. (2006). *Core battery-revised: An assessment took kit for promoting optimal group selection, process and outcome*. New York: American Group Psychotherapy Association.

Chambless, D. L. (1985). The relationship of severity of agoraphobia to associated psychopathology. *Behaviour Research and Therapy, 23*, 305–367.

Cox, B. J., Norton, G. R., & Swinson, R. P. (1992). *The panic attack questionnaire: revised*. Toronto, Canada: Clark Institute of Psychiatry.

Dozois, D. J. A., & Westra, H. A. (2005). Development of the Anxiety Change Expectancy Scale (ACES) and validation in college, community, and clinical samples. *Behaviour Research and Therapy, 43*, 1655–1672.

Endicott, J., Nee, J., Harrison, W., & Blumenthal, R. (1993). Quality of life enjoyment and satisfaction questionnaire: A new measure. *Psychopharmacology Bulletin, 29(2)*, 321–326.

Erickson, D. H., Janeck, A., & Tallman, K. (2009). Transdiagnostic group CBT for anxiety: Clinical experience and practical advice. *Journal of Cognitive Psychotherapy: An International Quarterly, 23(1)*, 34–43.

Feeley, M., DeRubeis, R. J., & Gelfand, L. A. (1999). The temporal relations of adherence and alliance to symptom change in cognitive therapy for depression. *Journal of Consulting and Clinical Psychology, 67*, 578–582.

First, M. B., Gibbon, M., Hilsenroth, M. J., & Segal, D. L. (2004). The structured clinical interview for DSM-IV axis I disorders (SCID-I) and the structured clinical interview for DSM-IV axis II disorders (SCID-II). In M. J. Hilsenroth & D. L. Segal (Eds.), *Comprehensive handbook of psychological assessment: Vol. 2. Personality assessment* (pp. 134–143). Hoboken, NJ: John Wiley & Sons, Inc.

Foa, E., Cashman, L., Jaycox, L., & Perry, K. (1997). The validation of a self-report measure of PTSD: The Posttraumatic Diagnostic Scale (PDS). *Psychological Assessment, 9*, 445–451.

Frank, J. D. (1961). *Persuasion and healing: A comparative study of psychotherapy*. Baltimore, MD: The John Hopkins Press.

Freeston, M. H., Rheaume, J., Letarte, H., Dugas, M. J., & Ladouceur, R. (1994). Why do people worry? *Personality and Individual Differences, 17*, 791–802.

Friedberg, R. D. (2007). Group cognitive-behavior therapy in outpatient settings. In R. W. Christner & J. L. Stewart (Eds.), *Handbook of cognitive-behavior group therapy with children and adolescents: Specific settings and presenting problems* (pp. 129–143). New York: Routledge/Taylor & Francis Group.

Frost, R. O., Steketee, G., & Grisham, J. (2004). Measurement of compulsive hoarding: Saving Inventory–Revised. *Behaviour Research and Therapy, 42*, 1163–1182.

Frost, R. O., Steketee, G., Tolin, D., & Renaud, S. (2008). Development of an observational measure of hoarding: The clutter Image Rating. *Journal of Psychopathology and Behavioral Assessment, 30*, 193–203.

Goodman, W. K., Price, L. H., Rasmussen, S. A., Mazure, C., Fleischmann, R. L., Hill, C. L., et al. (1989). The Yale-Brown Obsessive-Compulsive Scale: Development, use, and reliability. *Archives of General Psychiatry, 46*, 1006–1011.

Hamilton, K., Wershler, J., Macrodimitris, S. F., Bakcs-Dermott, B. J., Ching, L. E., & Mothersill, K. J. (2012). Exploring the effectiveness of a mixed-diagnosis group cognitive behavioral therapy intervention across diverse populations. *Cognitive and Behavioral Practice, 19(3)*, 472–482.

Hamilton, M. (1960). A rating scale for depression. *Journal of Neurology, Neurosurgery, and Psychiatry, 23*, 56–62.

Hans, E., & Hiller, W. (2013a). Effectiveness of and dropout from outpatient cognitive behavioral therapy for adult unipolar depression: A meta-analysis of nonrandomized effectiveness studies. *Journal of Consulting and Clinical Psychology, 81(1)*, 75–88.

Hans, E., & Hiller, W. (2013b). A meta-analysis of nonrandomized effectiveness studies on outpatient cognitive behavioral therapy for adult anxiety disorders. *Clinical Psychology Review, 33(8)*, 954–964.

Hess, H. (1996). Zwei Verfahren zur Einschatzung der Wirksamkeit von Gruppenpsychotherapie [Two methods to assess the effectiveness of group psychotherapy]. In B. Strauss, J. Eckert, & V. Tschuschke (Eds.), *Methoden der empirischen Gruppentherapieforschung – Ein Handbuch [Methods of empirical group psychotherapy research–A user guide.]* (pp. 142–158). Leverkusen, Germany: Westdeutscher Verlag.

Hofmann, S. G., Asnaani, A.,Vonk, I. J. J., Sawyer, A. T., & Fang, A. (2012). The efficacy of cognitive behavioral therapy: A review of meta-analyses. *Cognitive Therapy and Research, 36*, 427–440.

Horowitz, L. M., Alden, L. E., Wiggins, J. S., & Pincus, A. (2000). *The inventory of interpersonal problems-32 (IIP-32)*. Menlo Park, CA: Mind Gardens.

Horvath, A. O., & Greenberg, L. S. (1989). Development and validation of the Working Alliance Inventory. *Journal of Counseling Psychology, 36(2)*, 223–233.

Joyce, A. S., MacNair-Semands, R. R., Tasca, G. A., & Ogrodniczuk, J. S. (2011). Factor structure and validity of the Therapeutic Factors Inventory-Short Form. *Group Dynamics: Theory, Research and Practice, 15(3)*, 201–219.

Kay, S. R., Fiszbein, A., & Opler, l. A. (1987). The Positive and Negative Syndrome Scale (PANSS) for schizophrenia. *Schizophrenia Bulletin, 13*, 261–276.

Kroenke, K., Spitzer, R. L., & Williams, J. B. (2001). The PHQ-9: Validity of a brief depression measure. *Journal of General Internal Medicine, 16(9)*, 606–613.

Lambert, M. J., Hansen, N. B., Umphress, V., Lunnen, K., Okiishi, J., Burlingame, G.M., et al. (1996). *Administration and scoring manual for the Outcome Questionnaire (OQ-45)*. Wilmington, DL: American Professional Credentialing Services.

Lau, M. A., Ogrodniczuk, J., Joyce, A., & Söchting, I. (2010). Bridging the practitioner-scientist gap in group psychotherapy research. *International Journal of Group Psychotherapy, 60(2)*, 177–196.

MacKenzie, K. R. (1983). The clinical application of a group climate measure. In R. R. Dies & K. R. MacKenzie (Eds.), *Advances in group psychotherapy: Integrating research and practice* (pp. 159–170). New York: International Universities Press.

MacKenzie, K. R. (1990). *Group climate questionnaire*. Unpublished scale, Department of Psychiatry, University of British Columbia, Vancouver, Canada.

MacNair, R. R., & Corazzini, J. G. (1994). Client factors influencing group therapy dropout. *Psychotherapy, 31(2)*, 352–362.

Mattick, R. P., & Clarke, J. C. (1998). The development and validation of measures of social phobia scrutiny fear and social interaction anxiety. *Behaviour Research and Therapy, 36*, 455–470.

Meyer, T. J., Miller, M. L., Metzger, R. L., & Borkoved, T. D. (1990). Development and validation of the Penn State Worry Questionnaire. *Behavior Research and Therapy, 28*, 487–495.

Miller, G., & Rice, K. (1993). A factor analysis of a university counseling centre problem checklist. *Journal of College Student Development, 34*, 98–102.

O'Connor, K., Freeston, M. H., Gareau, D., Careau, Y., Dufour, M. J., Aardema, F., et al. (2005). Group versus individual treatment in obsessions without compulsions. *Clinical Psychology and Psychotherapy, 12*, 87–96.

Ogrodniczuk, J. S., Piper, W. E., & Joyce, A. S. (2004). Differences in men's and women's responses to short-term group psychotherapy. *Psychotherapy Research, 14(2)*, 231–243.

Ogrodniczuk, J. S., Piper, W. E., Joyce, A. S., Lau, M. A., & Söchting, I. (2010). A Survey of Canadian Group Psychotherapy Association members' perceptions of psychotherapy research. *International Journal of Group Psychotherapy, 60(2)*, 177–196.

Ogrodniczuk, J. S., & Söchting, I. (2010). *Outcome expectancy scale*. Unpublished scale. University of British Columbia, Vancouver, Canada.

Price, M., Anderson, P., & Henrich, C. C. (2008). Greater expectations: Using hierarchical linear modeling to examine expectancy for treatment outcome as a predictor of treatment response. *Behavior Therapy, 39*, 398–405.

Pringle, A., & Sayers, P. (2004). It's a Goal!: Basing a community psychiatric nursing service in a local football stadium. *The Journal of the Royal Society for the Promotion of Health, 124(5)*, 234–238.

Rezin, V., & Garner, C. (2006). A survey of psychological therapy waiting lists in secondary adult mental health services throughout UK NHS Trusts. *Clinical Psychology Forum, 163*, 30–33.

Rosenberg, M. (1965). *Society and the adolescent self-image.* Princeton, NJ: Princeton University Press.

Sierra Hernandez, C. A., Oliffe, J. L., Joyce, A. S., Söchting, I., & Ogrodniczuk, J. S. (2014) Treatment preferences among men attending outpatient psychiatric services. *Journal of Mental Health, 23(1)*, 83–87.

Söchting, I., Lau, M. A., & Ogrodniczuk, J. (2014). Use of the Group Therapy Questionnaire to predict treatment compliance. Manuscript in preparation.

Strauss, B., Burlingame, G. M., & Borman, B. (2008). Using the CORE-R battery in group psychotherapy. *Journal of Clinical Psychology: In Session, 64(11)*, 1225–1237.

Taylor, S., Fedoroff, I., Koch, W., Thordarson, D., Fectau, G., & Nicki, R. (2001). Posttraumatic stress disorder arising after road traffic collisions: Patterns of responses to cognitive-behavior therapy. *Journal of Consulting and Clinical Psychology, 69(3)*, 541–551.

Tsai, M., Söchting, I., Mirmiran, J., & Ogrodniczuk, J. (2014). Forecasting success: Patients' expectations for improvement and their relations to baseline, process, and outcome variables in group CBT for depression. *Clinical Psychology and Psychotherapy, 21*, 97–107.

Yalom, I. D., & Leszcz, M. (2005). *The theory and practice of group psychotherapy* (5th ed.). New York: Basic Books.

Young, R. M., & Oei, T. P. S. (1990). *Drinking expectancy profile: A manual.* Brisbane, Australia: University of Queensland.

Young, R. M., Oei, T. P. S., & Crook, G. M. (1991). Development of a drinking self-efficacy questionnaire. *Journal of Psychopathology and Behavioral Assessment, 13*, 1–15.

Weiss, D. M., & Marmar, C. R. (1997). The impact of event scale-revised. In J. P. Wilson & T. M. Keane (Eds.), *Assessing psychological trauma and PTSD* (pp. 339–411). New York: Guilford Press.

7

Transdiagnostic and Other Heterogeneous Groups

CBGT started out with highly homogeneous groups and those are still considered the easiest to run. However, research shows that groups including people with different diagnoses (transdiagnostic) can yield acceptable outcomes too—along with other practical benefits and efficiencies. Transdiagnostic group interventions are welcomed by many CBGT therapists and are gaining ground in community mental health settings, probably faster than the research literature can keep up.

Clinicians' main hesitancy toward transdiagnostic approaches may have more to do with this intervention not being part of the training of most senior CBT clinicians. As a result, when senior clinicians today talk about CBT groups, we are still usually talking about specific groups for specific disorders, such as depression, obsessive–compulsive (OCD), social anxiety (SAD), generalized anxiety (GAD), and panic disorder. The few existing guides on general group CBT (e.g., Bieling, McCabe, & Antony, 2006; Scott, 2011) reflect this categorical approach. A transdiagnostic option thus requires some effort to change one's habitual approach to designing and running a CBT group.

This chapter will first review the existing transdiagnostic approaches. It will take a transdiagnostic tour, beginning with the initial rationale for transdiagnostic groups, a content discussion, and finally a look at evidence of their efficacy. This research review will be followed by two clinical examples from the community program where I work. The first example is a group that combines social anxiety and panic disorder. The second brings together different types of posttraumatic stress disorder (PTSD), such as motor vehicle accident and sexual assault. The latter is an example of the challenge of combining different types of trauma—despite the same shared diagnosis of PTSD.[1] I refer to this kind of mixed group as a *heterogeneous* group. The many terms for transdiagnostic can be confusing. Transdiagnostic is the

Cognitive Behavioral Group Therapy: Challenges and Opportunities, First Edition. Ingrid Söchting.

most commonly used term, but others, such as *unified*, *mixed*, *heterogeneous*, and *blended*, are equivalent terms. A transdiagnostic group can include people with different diagnoses (e.g., some have panic disorder and some have GAD) and people who have more than one diagnosis (e.g., a group member may have both social anxiety and depression).

Subsequent chapters will continue the transdiagnostic theme. Chapter 11 describes how older adults with depression and/or anxiety can be successfully treated in the same CBT group. Chapter 12 shows how children with different anxiety disorders can be accommodated in the same group. Chapter 13 describes how impulse control or OCD-related disorders, such as trichotillomania (hair pulling) and body dysmorphic disorder, can be mixed into an otherwise pure OCD group.

Clinicians are aware that commonalities across emotional disorders often seem to outweigh the differences. They also know that similar CBT components are applied to different mental health issues. Putting people with different problems in the same CBT group—such as GAD and depression or social anxiety and panic disorder—thus seems like an attractive option for several reasons. Clinicians are, however, also concerned about how to practically implement such blended groups and how much mixing and matching is allowed. This concern stems from the strong CBT tradition of diagnostic-specific interventions. CBT clinicians take some pride in having developed different interventions for each and every diagnosable disorder, or defined problem.

But the need for a transdiagnostic approach has been apparent to many clinicians for some time. One of the first published guides for transdiagnostic groups (without calling it transdiagnostic) was the *Group Cognitive Therapy Program* (Free, 2007), a 24-session generic group therapy manual emphasizing cognitive techniques. This program is suitable for people with depression, anxiety, and anger. Since Free's group program, additional CBGT guides for transdiagnostic problems have been published and will be introduced in this chapter.

Why Consider Transdiagnostic Groups?

Transdiagnostic treatment outcomes have until recently come from two main types of mixed groups: anxiety disorders with mood disorders (depression) and different anxiety disorders within the same group. Research has repeatedly demonstrated that anxiety and depression often go "hand in hand." Early research showed that 50–80% of individuals report simultaneous symptoms of anxiety and depression (Kendall & Watson, 1989), and ongoing research continues to find high overlap—including in elderly people (Blazer, 2002; Hinrichsen & Emery, 2005). This has led to the development of CBGT interventions targeting both depression and anxiety. Thus, this kind of transdiagnostic group would include people who struggle with depression or anxiety or with both depression and anxiety.

A second body of research that supports the move toward transdiagnostic groups focuses on conceptualizations of a *core pathology* primarily for anxiety disorders but also relevant for depression. Core pathology researchers posit that our diagnostic classification system, based on the DSM-IV (American Psychiatric Association [APA], 2000) with its 12 distinct anxiety disorders, all share the same vulnerability, namely, "a perceived inability to predict, control, or obtain desired results" (Barlow, 1988). Perceptions of uncontrollability and unpredictability are also a common underlying factor in depression and may indeed explain the high rates of comorbidity and similarity between mood and anxiety disorders (Clark, Steer, & Beck, 1994). The term *negative affectivity* is sometimes used to describe the common personality characteristics of people prone to anxiety and depression. It is defined as "a stable, heritable trait tendency to experience a broad range of negative feelings such as worry, anxiety, self-criticisms, and a negative self-view" (Keogh & Reidy, 2000). Our increased understanding of what is commonly shared by all types of anxiety disorders—while not losing sight of their unique distinguishing aspects—has led to successful implementation of transdiagnostic CBGT for anxiety. However, as we shall see, not all types mix equally well.

A further argument supporting transdiagnostic treatment involves the concept of treatment generalizability. Experienced clinicians are familiar with how CBT can bring about improvements even in problems not specifically targeted. For example, clients in panic disorder groups are often surprised—but encouraged—to note that their depression also improved, even though it was not specifically addressed.

In addition to the theoretically driven research, many pragmatic reasons compel clinicians to consider moving from homogeneous to transdiagnostic CBGT in community mental health settings. There are benefits to both clinicians and clients. For the clinicians, consolidating multiple diagnosis-specific protocols into fewer protocols simplifies efforts to teach and implement treatments. A transdiagnostic approach is more easily mastered by a *generalist clinician* who may not have received specialized, supervised CBT training during their education. This is usually the case for the majority of frontline mental health group therapists. They may have had supervised CBT training on individual cases, but rarely for CBT groups. Continuing education for staff in a transdiagnostic approach is thus more practical—and cheaper—than education in 12 diagnosis-specific treatments (Erickson, Janeck, & Tallman, 2009). However, juggling several different types of anxiety in the same group can be an enormous challenge for generalist clinicians, especially if they have not had much specific CBT experience. I say this to validate clinicians who often find that running transdiagnostic groups is not as easy as it may sound from some of the existing manuals.

Clients benefit from the efficiency of only one course of therapy, which targets both their primary and secondary concerns (e.g., agoraphobia and GAD or panic disorder and depression), rather than undertaking sequential treatment for each disorder. Clients also get improved access to services when clinics do not have to wait to get enough people with SAD, as an example, to fill a group. A more transdiagnostic group approach can allow quicker access and reduce waitlist time. In many less populated areas, it is simply not feasible to run pure groups for sexual assault survivors since—fortunately—there are not enough demands for such a therapy service. Even though we still need more conclusive evidence from direct comparisons of transdiagnostic versus diagnosis-specific CBGT, the aforementioned practical advantages encourage clinicians to experiment with developing their own transdiagnostic groups informed by the available outcome research.

What Do Transdiagnostic CBGT Protocols Include?

Transdiagnostic CBGT includes basic CBT components, which at minimum include (a) psychoeducation, (b) self-monitoring, (c) awareness and replacement of dysfunctional thinking, and (d) graded exposure to internal or external triggers. These components run across all CBT for various problems but tend to take different forms depending on the disorder. Thus, the common components differ in *content* but not *function*, and their treatment rationale remains the same. For example, with GAD, exposures may include imaginary future and worst-case scenarios, such as worrying about one's child not marrying within the same ethnic group. For panic disorder, the exposure is to concrete places such as buses, commuter trains, movie theaters, or concert halls.

The rationale for both kinds of exposure is the same. It involves increased tolerance (desensitization) to repeatedly putting oneself in the feared situation (whether real or imagined) *and* realizing that one is not harmed or that the feared scenario is not as "horrible or devastating" as previously thought. A man with panic disorder realizes that feeling trapped in the middle of a row in a concert hall may be uncomfortable but not life-threatening and certainly not a sufficient cause for concern to forgo a favorite Beethoven symphony. A woman with GAD realizes that she can "survive" the possibility of her child marrying outside the family's ethnic group. With successful exposure treatment, both clients will experience a decrease in symptoms. The man with panic disorder notices that his heart rate does not accelerate as quickly, his throat is less dry, and his legs are less wobbly. The woman with GAD notices that she is not consumed with "what if" worries about future scenarios she is unlikely to control and that her sleep is better and jaw and shoulders are less tense. In the following text, we will look at protocols for mixing anxiety disorders with depression and then different anxiety disorders in the same CBGT program.

Mixing anxiety with depression in the same group

Some of the first attempts to mix people with anxiety and depression were done by Kush and Fleming (2000). They evaluated a 12-session CBGT program designed to conjointly treat individuals with comorbid depression and anxiety. Their program was primarily targeting cognitions, with less emphasis on behavioral interventions such as the exposures mentioned earlier. Their program followed a *content specificity* approach. This approach recognizes that people with depression or anxiety have different *cognitive profiles*. Anxious people tend to hold beliefs about excessive vulnerability and elevated perceptions of threat, especially future ones. Depressed people hold beliefs about inadequacy and personal failure, especially ruminations about past events.

When dysfunctional thinking was addressed in the groups, members received different handouts and instruction for addressing their thinking depending on their primary diagnosis. For example, anxious group members were helped to identify and challenge beliefs about danger related to present or upcoming life events (e.g., "I'll be so anxious that I cannot swallow my food during the business lunch meeting"), events nonanxious people would consider ordinary. Depressed group members were helped to identify and replace self-critical thinking (e.g., "Forgetting to bring my daughter to her friend's birthday party shows what an incompetent parent I am"), events nondepressed people would consider ordinary. Results from a total of four groups showed significant improvement on measures of depression and anxiety and thus point to the clinical and practical utility for a combined CBGT approach.

Similar to Kush and Fleming (2000), McEvoy and Nathan (2007) also reported good results from their 10-week 2-hour session CBGT for anxiety and depression. A total of 143 clients referred to a community mental health clinic received the same CBGT protocol, which was an integration of two individual CBT manuals: Beck's *Depression* manual (1967/1972) and Barlow and Craske's (1994) *Mastery of Your Anxiety and Panic* manual. Treatment components included psychoeducation about anxiety and depression, calming techniques, behavioral activation, exposures, and cognitive restructuring. Unlike in the Kush and Fleming groups, there were no diagnosis-specific, or content-specific, interventions. The achieved outcomes were compared to those from diagnosis-specific treatments reported in the literature and were found to be similar. As a result, the clinician researchers concluded that this transdiagnostic CBGT evaluation benchmarked the effectiveness of mixed depression and anxiety CBGT.

Based on these and similar successful outcomes in combining depressed and anxious clients in the same group, we now have full transdiagnostic protocols (which include workbooks for clients and guides for therapists; Barlow et al., 2011). The Barlow transdiagnostic protocol, which Barlow and colleagues refer to as a *unified approach*, instructs clinicians on how to increase their clients' awareness of their emotions and emotion-driven behaviors. Concepts from mindfulness training (reviewed in Chapter 5), such as nonjudgmental and present-focused emotion awareness, run throughout this therapist guide. There is less emphasis on exposures to different situations and triggers and on how to develop exposure hierarchies. Informed by the work of Barlow and colleagues, a number of innovative transdiagnostic CBGT programs have enjoyed successful dissemination and evaluation. One such example includes an inspiring version of the rapid access group discussed in Chapter 6.

Hamilton and colleagues (2012) developed a two-part CBGT program for people with anxiety and depression, the CBT Basics I and CBT Basics II. As described in

Chapter 6, CBT Basics I is considered a *preindividual therapy* group program primarily designed to reduce wait times for people on lists for more intense individual CBT. The additional program, CBT Basics II, was developed by the same group of clinicians and is a stand-alone CBT group adding an additional four weekly 2-hour sessions to the six sessions comprising CBT Basics I. In addition to the standard behavioral and cognitive interventions, a mindfulness component is included based on accepted knowledge of mindfulness practice reducing risk of relapse in individuals recovered from depression. Since its inception in 2005, over 160 clients have completed these programs in six different clinics located in a Canadian province. Several clients were severely depressed or anxious and also struggled with chronic medical illnesses such as diabetes. Fifty-eight mental health practitioners have been trained including psychiatrists, psychologists, nurses, and social workers. The reductions in symptoms of depression and anxiety suggest that such transdiagnostic groups may be an effective intervention in general mental health programs.

Mixing different anxiety disorders in the same group

Erickson et al. (2009) created a mixed anxiety group in a community outpatient service in a large metropolitan area. Their initial protocol involved transdiagnostic techniques such as psychoeducation about anxiety and general principles of graded exposure. Diagnosis-specific techniques were administered to the various subgroups within the larger group. These included (a) interoceptive exposure for panic disorder with or without agoraphobia, (b) assertiveness skills for SAD, and (c) worry-time and thought-stopping for GAD. Worry-time involves taking control of one's worries by setting aside a certain block of uninterrupted time, for example, 30 minutes a day, to immerse oneself in worry. It tends to have the somewhat paradoxical effect of experiencing less worry outside of this dedicated worry-time. Thought-stopping involves the person imagining yelling "STOP–STOP!" the moment the worry-thought enters their mind; they may also snap an elastic band on their wrist upon noticing the arrival of a worry-thought.[2]

All group members engaged with all the treatment components, that is, they all did worry-time and role-plays regardless of diagnosis. A later protocol by the same clinician researchers reflected advances in the CBT anxiety disorders field and included more cognitive techniques, which were not developed at the time of the first protocol. The newer cognitive techniques replaced the older interventions of assertiveness and role-playing. These cognitive interventions—now standard in almost any anxiety protocol—include *probability overestimation* ("What are the odds of my dying next time I have a panic attack?") and challenging *catastrophic* automatic thoughts ("What if people notice I'm anxious? That would be terrible"). Worry-time and imaginary exposure for GAD were still used as an example of a diagnosis-specific techniques.

This revised protocol was applied to 152 clients in a total of 12 groups (social anxiety, GAD, OCD, and PTSD). Overall results revealed significant changes on outcome measures between the wait-listed group members and those who completed group treatment. These treatment benefits were maintained at 6 months follow-up. Conclusions from this evaluation state that transdiagnostic CBT groups could be effective, but that this particular protocol was not ready for dissemination.

In particular, Erickson and colleagues caution that people with OCD and PTSD require a more intense and specific treatment focus compared to other anxiety presentations. For example, PTSD group members were more labile in their anxiety. Their reexperiencing of traumatic memories often occurred in the group sessions, distracting other clients from their exercises. The OCD clients struggled with motivation and were not as willing to let go of their compulsive behaviors as would be needed in order to engage in effective exposures. It is indeed our experience that clients with OCD need constant attention and encouragement to stay "on task" for their exposures. It is therefore not surprising to hear of their tendency to "hide" behind participation in apparent anxiety-reducing tasks such as relaxation training, when this has only minimal, if any, therapeutic value in reducing obsessions and compulsions.

Similar to Erickson et al. (2009), Norton (2008) also obtained good results from 52 clients across the anxiety disorders. The strongest response to treatment was with the social anxiety and panic disorder clients, and the poorest was with GAD, OCD, and specific phobias (e.g., a fear of heights, dogs, or spiders). There were no PTSD clients in this trial. The 12-week 2-hour group session protocol emphasized three core ingredients of CBT: (1) psychoeducation and self-monitoring, (2) cognitive restructuring, and (3) exposure to feared stimuli. Similar to the Erikson study, Norton did not have sufficient OCD participants to conduct a specific treatment response analysis for this subgroup. Norton (2009) concludes that the initial developers of the transdiagnostic approach are hesitant to include clients with OCD and PTSD. Norton has since 2009 conducted a randomized controlled study on transdiagnostic versus diagnosis-specific CBGT and concluded that mixed groups of social anxiety, generalized anxiety, and panic disorder meet the same gold standard outcome as diagnosis-specific CBGT (Norton & Barrera, 2012). In his *Group Cognitive-Behavioral Therapy of Anxiety: A Transdiagnostic Treatment Manual*, Norton (2012) offers a 12-session transdiagnostic CBGT manual suitable for all anxiety disorders including OCD. There is an emphasis on exposure and many helpful examples of how to conduct those in the groups.

The transdiagnostic literature on anxiety disorders encourages CBGT clinicians to consider combining the different disorders into the same group. However, despite some research supporting including OCD into a transdiagnostic group, the experience of many clinicians, including myself, is that OCD and PTSD do not mix well with other disorders and are best treated separately. The DSM-5 reinforces this with both of these disorders having their own category separate from the anxiety disorders category. I am familiar with successful transdiagnostic community programs offering groups with different combinations of anxiety disorders, usually panic disorder, separation anxiety, GAD, and social anxiety. But I have yet to hear positive outcomes from mixing PTSD and OCD with the rest of the anxiety disorders. These two disorders express themselves in highly varied ways even within their own diagnosis. Combining, for example, different traumas such as motor vehicle accident and assault in the same group often feels and looks like a transdiagnostic group. The same is true for an OCD group where someone will have obsessions involving molesting young boys and another group member will repeatedly check to ensure a hair straightener is turned off.

We will return to the option of a heterogeneous trauma group at the end of this chapter. This discussion will be included because clinicians often wonder about combining different traumas, given that it can be hard to fill groups with the same trauma in a timely manner. First, though, I review a typical transdiagnostic approach involving combining people with social anxiety and panic disorder. Both types of mixed groups can make valuable additions to community CBGT settings.

CBGT for Social Anxiety and Panic Disorder

The diagnosis of social anxiety disorder

Community programs offering CBT for anxiety find that they can fill groups faster, and thus reduce wait lists, if they combine socially anxious and panic disorder clients into the same group. Other than quicker access to treatment, this combination works because those two disorders share many features. Further to practical benefits, however, clinical experience suggests that group members with social anxiety may derive improved treatment gains compared to a pure social anxiety group. A panic disorder and social anxiety CBGT program is admittedly a minor version of the transdiagnostic approach given that only two disorders are combined.

SAD involves a persistent fear of one or more social and performance situations in which the person is exposed to unfamiliar people or possible scrutiny by others. Individuals fear they will act in a way (or show anxiety symptoms) that will be humiliating or embarrassing. Social anxiety can be specified as "performance only."[3] The "performance only" specification recognizes that people whose social fears are limited to performing in front of an audience seem to represent a distinct subset of SAD. Perhaps more than other anxiety disorders, people with social anxiety are at higher risk for substance abuse, an understandable coping mechanism or safety strategy. Chapter 17 presents a CBGT protocol for comorbid social anxiety and substance use.

Despite high prevalence compared to other anxiety disorders, 3–13% (APA, 2000) of people with social anxiety rarely seek treatment, and when they do, they often do not engage well. From Chapter 3, we learned that the research generally supports a group format for SAD so long as the protocol offers both exposure and restructuring of socially anxious thinking. We also learned that these groups are likely most effective if exposure is especially emphasized, and practiced, in and between sessions. Many clinicians, however, remain skeptical about group CBT for social anxiety, and dropout rates can be high, up to 35% (Blanco, Heimberg, Schneier, & Fresco, 2010). Clinicians who have experience with both pure and mixed social anxiety groups find that the group climate in the pure groups can be heavy and unpleasantly intense. Socially anxious people, despite their gentle and shy presentation, often harbor anger and can come across as intimidating, suspicious, and critical.

Why groups can be challenging for people with social anxiety

Considering that many people with social anxiety have strong memories of social situations associated with extreme distress, their guardedness in groups makes sense. These social moments are etched into the socially anxious person's psyche and can have a near-trauma quality. In addition to ridicule or emotional abuse from parents, it can also be an unexpected embarrassing moment, such as forgetting to zip one's fly before giving a class presentation and one's 15-year-old buddies "killing themselves laughing." People with preexisting sensitive temperaments understandably recover more slowly than those blessed with robust dispositions. For the vast majority, the problem starts before age 20, which also suggests that for many the development of their social anxiety was layered on top of the already unpleasant experiences of awkwardness and insecurity in adolescence. Although their anger may be a legitimate response to being, in a sense, robbed of a more carefree youth, it can interfere with benefiting from group treatment.

Erwin, Heimberg, Schneier, and Liebowitz (2003) found that socially anxious people, who in addition to their social anxiety admitted to frequent feelings and expressions of anger, were less likely to do well in a 12-session CBGT program. Those who attempted to suppress their anger also did not benefit as much. Alden, Taylor, Laposo, and Mellings (2006) shed further light on some of the reasons for their anger and poorer treatment response. They were interested in the alliance between the socially anxious group members and the therapists and found that self-reported childhood parental abuse (e.g., frequent criticism, put-downs, or corporal punishment) was associated with a more negative patient–therapist relationship and poorer treatment outcome.

Why a transdiagnostic group is attractive for people with social anxiety

This defensive anger, with its message of "don't get too close to me" or "don't put demands on me," is understandable but is rarely the main focus of a CBGT group for social anxiety. This is likely one of the problems in CBGT for social anxiety. Part of the solution can indeed involve a transdiagnostic approach.

We notice a palpable difference when our groups have a mix of people with panic disorder and SAD, ideally half-and-half. Panic disorder clients tend to be—or have been—high-functioning, socially skilled, positive people who strongly desire to enjoy their lives more by overcoming fears of fainting, dying, etc. Despite their significant fears, they contribute to a lighter atmosphere in the group and serve as positive social interaction role models. One might suspect that the socially anxious people would get more upset by this appearance of an easier life and ability to connect socially. If that were so, the group process would clearly be impacted. Interestingly, we find this not to be the case. Instead, we find that the socially anxious group members fairly quickly become comfortable with those who have panic disorder.

The group members with social anxiety are often mildly shocked at how frequent and debilitating are the attacks for the panic disorder group members. Typically, people with panic disorder report—at least in the first half of the group—4–15 or more attacks a week as recorded on their *Panic Attack Records* (a simple self-monitoring sheet where the person records the number and intensity of panic attacks in a given week). People with social anxiety rarely experience more than one or two panic attacks a week but usually intense sensations or fears of *coming close*. This eye opening allows the socially anxious people to realize they are far from alone in their suffering, and their expressions of empathy are well received. When group members with social anxiety realize that others respond positively to them and seem to like them, these "real-life" events in the group provide evidence countering their beliefs that "others think I'm goofy or disgusting" or "others will not be interested in me if I try to connect." We commonly see improvements in interpersonal comfort and self-esteem for the socially anxious people when they complete this kind of transdiagnostic group. The group format provides opportunities for positive interpersonal interactions for all the members, but may be especially therapeutic for those with social anxiety. These observations are supported by interpersonal social psychology research on the dynamic interaction between self-evaluation and other's judgments of likability (Srivastava & Beer, 2005).

Key features of a mixed social anxiety and panic group

The recommended protocol for this kind of 12-week 2-hour session group follows an integration the approach of Barlow and Craske's (2007) *Mastery of Your Anxiety and Panic* with components from *The Shyness and Social Anxiety Workbook: Proven Techniques for Overcoming Your Fears* (Antony & Swinson, 2000). Both protocols were developed for individual CBT. In this group, not everybody gets the same unified approach (unless of course they are comorbid with panic disorder and social anxiety), but rather, some *content specificity* is included. Everybody gets psychoeducation about the physiology of panic attacks, breathing and relaxation, exposure to feared body sensations (interoceptive exposure), cognitive restructuring focusing on *overestimation of probability* (e.g., "I'm 95% sure I will die of a heart attack next time I panic") and *decatastrophizing* (e.g., "It would be completely unacceptable if I lost my train of thought in front of others"), and graded exposure following a hierarchy of rank-ordered fears from 0 to 100 on a subjectively rated anxiety scale. The panic disorder group members will create hierarchies, including a number of situations they avoid such as going to shopping malls, movie theaters, public transit, and long-distance travel. The socially anxious members will have different items on their hierarchy, including asking someone for direction, saying hello to the cafe barista, giving a toast, speaking up in a staff meeting at work, and attending a party with unfamiliar people.

Content specificity is reflected in the way exposures and behavioral experiments are carried out. Two standout features of the exposure to anxiety-provoking situations component of this mixed group are as follows: (a) the socially anxious people do most of the in-session exposure, whereas the panic people simply plan their exposures to be done outside of the session, and (b) there is lots of group feedback on the socially anxious people's catastrophic cognitions and their accompanying *safety behaviors*. Safety behaviors are any acts that help the socially anxious person cope with an uncomfortable situation. They take many forms, such as looking busy with one's phone so as to avoid small talk in the beginning of the group, hiding half of one's face in a turtleneck sweater, or coming late when the group is safely and "formally" in process (another way to avoid small talk). People with panic disorder have their own safety behaviors, which are also discussed during the psychoeducation part and throughout the group. A typical panic disorder safety behavior is to bring water bottles into the group room. This helps relieve sensations of a dry mouth, choking, and lightheadedness. The two components of exposure and thought challenging are combined during the in-session exposures. For group members with panic disorder, this especially involves exposure to bodily sensations such as hyperventilation while testing beliefs about not being able to cope. For group members with social anxiety, a number of real-life exposures can be executed during the group time.

Successful in-session exposures for group members with panic attacks and social anxiety lead to continued practice between group sessions. Group therapists ensure that homework exposure is carefully planned and is a meaningful extension of what was practiced in the previous session. As mentioned earlier, people with panic disorder do fewer in-session real-life exposures other than the ones to internal body sensations. Instead, they make plans for daily exposure goals based on their hierarchies, and they set up behavioral experiments to test their predictions. For example, a group member may predict that she will be so anxious at an upcoming staff lunch meeting that she will be unable to eat. Or another person planning to go with a friend to a movie theater may predict that his anxiety in the form of accelerated heart rate and choking sensations will cause him to be completely unable to focus on the show. The results of these behavioral experiments and predictions are then shared with the group in the following session.

In-session social anxiety exposures

The in-session exposures are both interoceptive and "real life." In Chapter 1, we reviewed how a group for panic disorder together practices interoceptive exposure such as restricted breathing and hyperventilation. We do the same in a mixed group. For panic disorder clients, most of the triggers for their feared body sensations are outside of the group room (e.g., riding on a bus, going to the grocery store), while for the socially anxious, the triggers are right there in the room. A wide range of exposures are thus available for creative therapists, motivated clients, and a healthy group climate. Therapists capitalize on as many process factors as possible, which also usually include panic clients being more than willing to serve as a "mock audience."

For example, typical graded social exposures in nearly all groups involve giving a 2-minute presentation on *the best vacation I have had* or *my favorite movie*. Moving up the fear hierarchy to increased challenges, a socially anxious person may agree to exposures such as *express my opinion about a social or political issue I care about* or to role-playing a disagreement with someone, asking for a favor, or even to role-play part of a job interview. Group therapists can also create exposures involving eating, drinking, or writing in front of others. Therapists prepare the exposures ahead of time, including arranging for necessary items or props and what instructions are to be given to the rest of the group. For example, the group may be told to have neutral expressions during the presentation and only offer feedback after. The panic disorder clients readily get these instructions and enjoy participating in role-plays. These social exposures address a number of issues simultaneously.

In-session social anxiety exposures offer the opportunity for desensitization. At the same time, they also implicitly challenge unhelpful beliefs and safety behaviors based on the exposed group member receiving direct feedback from the group. Typically, the member doing the exposure fears not only critical and judgmental reactions from others but also body sensations such as dry throat, shaky voice, and trembling hands. A member doing a little speech may have beliefs about others being unable to hear what he says due to a shaky voice or a fear of looking nervous if hands are trembling. The actual feedback from the group can lead to a more adaptive thought, such as "I was anxious, but still able to give my speech, and they said I did not look as anxious as I felt." The group may also encourage the person to give their presentation while dropping the safety behavior of, for example, putting hands in pockets or covering part of face with a baseball cap. The decatastrophizing, rational response is an important part of cognitive restructuring. Members are encouraged to write down both the fearful thought and the adaptive, rational coping response. Another example could be "I will look anxious, my hands will tremble, and I'll go blank," which is countered with "So what if I look anxious. It shows that I care and am not full of myself. If I go blank, I can take a pause, which shows I'm thoughtful, or even say I'll come back to that point later."

In addition to furthering desensitization and countering unhelpful beliefs, these kinds of social exposures can also support members in practicing self-disclosures and letting others get to know them. Invariably, the group will engage with the presented topics. After the mini-presentation, a discussion ensues and group members share their thoughts about a movie or vacation destinations. A transdiagnostic group of panic disorder and social anxiety has the potential for offering opportunities for simultaneously targeting several aspects of SAD.

CBGT for Different Types of Trauma

The diagnosis of posttraumatic stress disorder (PTSD)

In this section, I show how different kinds of trauma can be successfully treated in the same group—as long as all group members have some basic understanding of the impact of trauma on the body and mind as well as some skills for calming themselves and staying grounded when triggered. CBGT has been established as an effective intervention for people who meet full or partial criteria for PTSD (see, for example, a recent meta-analytic study by Barrera, Mott, Hofstein, and Teng, 2013). Clinicians agree that people who have some, but not all, of the required diagnostic criteria for PTSD can be included in a trauma group. The diagnosis of PTSD in the DSM-5 includes a helpful expansion from the DSM-IV and is therefore reviewed in some detail in the following.

The diagnosis of PTSD in the DSM-5 (APA, 2013) differs somewhat from the one in DSM-IV (APA, 2000) but does not question the continued use of CBT interventions based on DSM-IV criteria. In fact, the changes to DSM-5 only strengthen the CBT treatment rationale. In DSM-5, the traumatic event is more clearly defined compared to DSM-IV. The traumatic event must involve exposure to actual or threatened death, serious injury, or sexual violence either by directly experiencing it oneself, or witnessing in person the event as it occurred to other(s), or learning that the traumatic event occurred to a close family member or close friend, or experiencing repeated or extreme exposure of aversive details of the traumatic event (e.g., first responders collecting human remains, police officers repeatedly exposed to details of child abuse).

DSM-5 has four symptom clusters (whereas DSM-IV had three). The *reexperiencing* cluster includes intrusive memories, nightmares, a sense of reliving the trauma (flashbacks), and psychological distress in response to reminders of the event (a reminder trigger could be seeing the same kind of car in which one was sexually assaulted). The *avoidance* cluster includes attempts to avoid feelings or thoughts related to the trauma as well as numbing, in the sense of feeling detached from one's own feelings and from other people. The *persistent negative alterations in cognitions and mood* cluster is new in *DSM-5*. It includes symptoms such as exaggerated negative beliefs or expectations about oneself, others, or the world (e.g., "I am disgusting," "No one can be trusted," or "The world is completely dangerous"). Lastly, the fourth cluster, *hyperarousal*, includes symptoms of being on edge, hypervigilant, easily startled, irritable, and angry, as well as aggressive or self-destructive behavior. There are options for specifying if the PTSD is accompanied by dissociative symptoms, depersonalization, or derealization. PTSD may also be diagnosed with *delayed expression*, if the full diagnostic criteria are not met until at least 6 months after the event. The new cluster of persistent negative alterations in cognitions and mood is welcomed by clinicians who practice *Cognitive Processing Therapy* (CPT). As I explain shortly, the CPT approach directly addresses the devastating beliefs about oneself that can result from trauma. In the United States, the lifetime risk for PTSD is 8.7% (APA, 2013).

Like most groups, groups for trauma work best when the group setting feels predictable, contained, and safe. In trauma groups, the group serves the additional purpose of a symbolic community witness to each victim's story. A successful group experience can thus provide a tremendous healing opportunity as people feel believed and stop blaming and silencing themselves as they work through their trauma and its impact (Johnson & Lubin, 2000). To achieve this level of safety, the majority of clinicians have until recently thought it best to make CBT trauma groups as homogeneous as possible, that is, one group for those with motor vehicle accidents and one for those with sexual assaults. In Chapter 3, we saw that the outcome literature on effective CBGT for trauma is based on homogeneous groups.

From homogeneous to heterogeneous trauma groups

Some of the first CBT groups my colleagues and I developed were highly homogeneous: sexually assaulted females only. Consistent with the literature (e.g., Chard, Resick, & Wertz, 1999), they were reasonably successful. Similar to other programs, we experienced community and organizational pressure to extend this trauma group to other kinds of trauma, especially motor vehicle accidents. This, in a sense, forced experimentation with a heterogeneous trauma group for different traumas for both men and women. It was a valuable experience in staying open to innovation in one's group practice.

However, extremely careful assessment and pregroup preparation are needed as one puts together a heterogeneous trauma group. It is not recommended to offer this heterogeneous group in the absence of an in-depth, in-person clinician-driven assessment and pregroup orientation. Two main components have shaped our heterogeneous trauma groups: (1) a prerequisite group focused on self-care skills and (2) the inclusion of in-session exposures.

Self-care skills as a prerequisite

Despite pressure in community mental health programs to accept clients with multiple and complicated needs—including a history of suicidal or self-harm behaviors-clients should not be accepted into CBGT involving exposure unless they have sufficient ability to stay reality focused (using grounding and other self-care skills) and regulate their emotions. Offering such a skill-based group as a prerequisite is one way to increase the probability of a successful heterogeneous trauma group but would also help clients going into a homogeneous trauma group.

The field of trauma research and treatment is increasingly recognizing the impact on both body and mind for the traumatized individual. The concept of the "body remembering or storing" the trauma is widely accepted, including its implications for treatment (van der Kolk, 1994). The focus is on the limbic brain system and especially the role of the amygdala, the brains' fire alarm, and the hippocampus, the brain's long-term memory storage. Thus, when someone who has been traumatized is faced with a trigger reminding them of the original trauma (e.g., hearing a siren), the amygdala overreacts—like a fire alarm set to detect the tiniest bit of smoke from the kitchen in absence of a real fire—while the hippocampus tries to reign in the amygdala, reminding the person that the original trauma was a while ago and the present siren is this time not paired with any danger to the person. There is research showing that severe and ongoing trauma in childhood may lead to long-term damage to the brain's ability to regulate the stress hormone, cortisol, creating a situation where the autonomic nervous system becomes overreactive (e.g., Gillespie & Nemeroff, 2007). This may, in part, explain the challenge traumatized people face with putting their trauma into a temporal context and not going into alarm mode every time they encounter a reminder. "Trauma destroys time," as Stolorow reminds his patients (Stolorow, 2007).

Effective trauma treatment often involves both a talking (verbal processing) part and a body-focused (calming) part. The latter can be hands-on treatment offered by a yoga teacher with additional trauma training, or it can be exercises in body awareness based on instructions from the therapist without any touching of the client. Based on the work of Ogden, Minton, and Pain (2006) and Haskell (2003), we offer such a pre-CBGT group called *Self-Care Skills After Trauma*. The eight group modules include education about reactions to trauma, such as the role of the limbic system in the "fight, flight, or freeze" responses, staying present in the "here and now" as opposed to becoming detached (minimizing the trauma, sleeping too much, numbing with drugs or alcohol, and various forms of dissociating), or becoming overwhelmed (emotional flooding, hyperalertness, panic attacks, and reliving the trauma in flashbacks). Clients are taught a range of self-calming skills, such as the *Five to One*, which asks them to become grounded by identifying and saying to themselves at any chosen moment, "Five things I see, Five things I hear, and Five things I feel," and continuing down with *Four Things* to *One Thing*. A person in a group may say: "I see the red frame of the drawing board, the clock above the door, the church steeple through the window, the crack on the wall, and the face of Chelsea." Talking about one's actual trauma during this skills group is discouraged, but all disclosures are validated. The facilitators may say: "We understand how painful it was for you and appreciate your being willing to trust the group as a safe place to work through it, but remember that there will more opportunities to do so some weeks from now. Are you OK with primarily working on how to calm yourself when you get that intense feeling of being flooded with memories and anxiety?"

Cognitive processing therapy (CPT) in heterogeneous CBGT for trauma

After the self-care skills group, clients deemed ready for actually confronting and processing their traumas are invited to join the *processing trauma group* based on a *CPT* approach (Resick & Schnicke, 1993), which was developed for individual trauma treatment. Some clients repeat the self-care skills group in order to be ready for CPT. In a CPT group, we typically have four to six members. Two-thirds tend to be female. The most common traumas are motor vehicle accidents, injuries at work, witnessing or experiencing physical or sexual assault from strangers, family members, or intimate partners. We are hesitant to invite people with childhood sexual abuse into this group and suggest other treatment resources if possible. The CPT approach is most effective for recent traumas but not inappropriate for childhood trauma.

Following the Resick and Schnicke CPT protocol (1993) for trauma, everyone gets the same intervention components but with different content. To allow for more exposure than this original protocol was designed for, we alter the session schedule by continuing the *remembering the trauma* component through sessions 4–8. We also combine the discussion of safety and trust, instead of devoting a separate session to each topic. In contrast to the Resick and Schnicke manual, we encourage actual in-session exposure. Some CBT group therapists are concerned about allowing such group exposures. They instead prefer to have individual group members write about their trauma and share only with the facilitators. These alterations are noted in italics in the Session Themes outline for CPT. They show a flexible use of this protocol adapted to a group setting.

Session Themes for CPT (Resick & Schnicke, 1993)
Session 1: Introduction and Education Phase
Session 2: The Meaning of the Event
Session 3: Identification of Thoughts and Feelings
Session 4: Remembering the *Trauma*
Session 5: Identification of Stuck Points plus *Remembering Your Trauma*
Session 6: Challenging Questions plus *In-Session Trauma Exposure*
Session 7: Faulty Thinking Patterns plus *In-Session Trauma Exposure*
Session 8: Faulty Thinking Patterns plus *In-Session Trauma Exposure*
Session 9: Safety and Trust Issues plus *In-Session Trauma Exposure*
Session 10: Power and Control Issues plus *In-Session Trauma Exposure* if Needed
Session 11: Esteem and Intimacy Issues
Session 12: Review, Relapse Prevention, and the Road Ahead

The first phase is the education phase about posttraumatic stress symptoms. We review the diagnostic symptoms of posttraumatic stress disorder inviting examples from the group members in the discussion. We especially focus on how unwanted reexperiencing of the trauma in the form of intrusions or nightmares (or "daymares," as one client referred to the feeling of reliving the trauma) can be seen as the mind *nudging* the person to do the healing work, to process unfinished business, so to speak. This is a powerful treatment rationale for exposure therapy, which forms a major component of our CBGT for trauma. This is followed by a basic introduction to the connection between thoughts, feelings, and behaviors.

Group members complete work sheets called "A–B–C sheets" based on recent events that do not have to be trauma related but often are. "A" stands for activating event, "something happens"; "B" for belief, "I tell myself something"; and "C" for consequence, "I feel and do something." For example, a person who had emigrated from a country undergoing war indicated that his activating event was "Taking my kids trick-or-treating on Halloween night and becoming startled by a loud fire cracker." In column "B" for beliefs, he wrote "Something dangerous is happening." In column "C" for consequence, he noted that "I feel scared and unsafe and tell the children we must return home right away." These introductory A–B–C exercises help to increase group members' awareness of the powerful influence of beliefs on subsequent feelings and behaviors. Following this part of the protocol, the deeper cognitive work begins.

This part involves increased understanding of what the traumatic event *meant* to each person and what their *stuck points* may be. For example, a recent 45-year-old immigrant from China was stuck in his beliefs that "I am a safe and totally defensive driver and can prevent all accidents" and thus struggled with overcoming a non-life-threatening accident, for which he was found primarily responsible. His complete avoidance of driving interfered greatly with his family life, given that he was the only driver in the family. Next to him was a 19-year-old woman whose *stuck point* was "You cannot get sexually assaulted by someone you are dating." She held a belief about being "stupid" for agreeing to go home to his apartment on a second date. The development of negative, trauma-related beliefs is well documented (Clark & Beck, 2010) and imperative to address in any trauma treatment. The aforementioned woman's schema of believing you cannot get assaulted by someone you choose to go out with was seriously challenged when she became assaulted. To make sense of what happened, to reconcile this cognitive dissonance, she would have to either (a) alter the event and minimize or deny she was assaulted or (b) begin the slow process of integrating the new information (the fact that she was assaulted by her date), which was not congruent with her schema of a more just-world belief. This work of reprogramming beliefs based on conflicting information is the crux of CPT. We find that the CPT approach is especially well suited for the cognitive restructuring part of CBGT for trauma. The Resick and Schnicke manual includes excellent handouts for challenging stuck points and faulty thinking.

The middle sessions are devoted to *remembering your trauma*, which is classic exposure therapy. They involve go-rounds of group members listening to each other's narratives, which involve a beginning, middle, and an end part to the trauma they have chosen to work on. More and more sensory details are added during the 6 weeks of exposure, and eventually, the stories are told in the present tense (e.g., "I see bright light coming right at me, I hear myself scream as I slam the breaks, my hands slide on the wheel in cold sweat"). The compassionate witnessing of a whole group is powerfully healing. After the exposure sessions, *CPT* returns to a focus on *faulty thinking patterns* (e.g., overestimation of danger on the roads or the degree to which men in general can be trusted). The final sessions are devoted to group discussions on issues relevant to all traumas, such as *safety*, *trust*, *control*, *self-esteem*, and *intimacy*. The *CPT* approach includes all of the recommended treatment components in CBT for motor vehicle accidents (education, challenging faulty beliefs, imaginal and in vivo exposures) except for applied relaxation (Taylor et al., 2001). However, this component, along with many other calming skills, is offered in the prerequisite group.

The role of exposure in CBGT for trauma

There is some debate about whether to encourage trauma exposures during the group, as opposed to having group members simply write about their trauma without sharing them with the rest of the group. We find that not sharing the exposure potentially deprives the group of its full working and social support power. Social support is a critical factor in recovery from PTSD, and group exposures allow members to overcome individual shame as they feel heard and validated by a small community of people, not just by one or two therapists. Therapists are understandably worried that allowing for in-session exposure can become too intense, with group members becoming vicariously traumatized and dropping out. With adequate group preparation, and ensuring the group follows a highly structured, time-managed, and formalized approach (e.g., first the bare-bones, or lay-of-the-land story, then gradually adding more sensory detail) worries about vicarious traumatization rarely become a reality. Not everyone necessarily gets to share during any one group session, but facilitators ensure that time is fairly allocated so that everyone gets to repeat their story at least three times. Occasionally, a group member chooses to not share verbally but prefers written iterations of their trauma. Therapists continuously watch for signs of any vicarious retraumatization, that is, someone developing signs of trauma from listening to the stories of others. Therapists encourage group members to monitor their emotional reactions, and they use clinical judgment regarding arranging for additional individual treatment. So far, we have not had any instances of retraumatization necessitating a person to leave the group. Our dropouts rarely happen after exposure begins, but tend to be after the first one or two sessions.

We believe in the benefits of sharing trauma scripts with the whole group as opposed to individual group members sharing only with the facilitators. Not sharing with the whole group runs the risk, however inadvertently, of supporting beliefs about it being "best to keep traumas secret." At worst, this may prevent a person from reporting a physical or sexual assault. Commonly, group members will have been told by family members to not tell anybody about their trauma as a way of preventing shame befalling the family. Shame also stems from other kinds of trauma, including motor vehicle accidents or believing one did not do enough and was merely a "passive bystander" when witnessing an assault or accident. A large part of trauma work in CBGT is to promote an atmosphere where members can overcome faulty beliefs about their trauma and associated feelings of shame.

Therapists in CBGT for trauma take an active and directive approach. This ensures that the group stays grounded and the group container tight and safe. Homework is assigned and often involves real-life exposures. For the motor vehicle people, these can include returning to the intersection where the accident happened and gradually resuming driving. For women who have been sexually assaulted, it can similarly include a return to the place where the assault took place and gradually returning to socializing—especially with men. It is rare to have men with sexual assaults in these groups, but when it happens, they do as well as the other group members.

This mixed trauma group probably poses the greatest challenge when it comes to running a "tight yet process-based CBGT ship." Needless to say, it requires two experienced therapists, with a possible third in a trainee role. Results from a large meta-analytic review of the role of exposure in CBGT for trauma support clinicians' experiences with the benefits of including exposure. The conclusions from this study stated that concerns about the potentially negative impact of group exposure may be unwarranted and that exposure-based CBGT is a promising treatment option for PTSD (Barrera et al., 2013). Some clinicians may be hesitant to engage in group exposures because they do not feel adequately trained in offering exposure therapy, even though they understand it theoretically and support its use. A new kind of anxiety disorder, *exposaphobia*, has humorously been suggested (Schare & Wyatt, 2013). Exposaphobia refers to the extreme fear (and associated avoidance) among many trained mental health professionals toward using exposure therapy procedures. More seriously, Share and Wyatt urgently call for better training and dissemination of exposure-based CBT protocols.

Capitalizing on the group in heterogeneous CBGT for trauma

Heterogeneous trauma groups include strong elements of process factors, such as instillation of hope, interpersonal learning, and universality, to name just a few. The heterogeneous component seems to be more effective in supporting victims, or survivors, to move beyond clinging to a *shared victim identity* (Johnson & Lubin, 2000), whether this relates to a fear of men, institutions, roads, robberies, or natural disasters. In an all-female group for sexual assault, for example, the bonding is naturally strong, and the fear of reentering society often equally, if not, stronger. When female group members who have been harmed by men connect with the male members, and begin to challenge strong beliefs about not trusting men, this helps them move closer to their ultimate goal of feeling more safely connected to the world outside of the group. The challenging of beliefs, which usually includes inflated estimates of the dangerousness of any particular man, or gross generalization of what "men are like" plays a key role in this mixed-gender cognitive processing trauma group. The success of this mixed-gender trauma group depends to a large extent on careful screening, assessment, group readiness, and ongoing monitoring. Group therapist Susan Gantt (2013) offers a similar, and moving, perspective in reflecting back on her mixed-gender trauma groups: "To see the look on some of these women's faces while these men worked so hard to move past their abuse, especially because it had sometimes led them to be abusive, was quite reparative. We were all touched by how men in general could be held by women or women in general held by men."

Although it is our clinical experience that an adapted *CPT* is effective for a mixed trauma group including both men and women, the ultimate test is empirical. Beyond gender, a systematic evaluation of a wide variety of mixed trauma groups against both a wait-list control group and established benchmarks for homogeneous trauma groups seems overdue.

Summary

This chapter reviews the development of transdiagnostic approaches to CBGT and how traditional CBT principles can be creatively and effectively applied to a range of heterogeneous groups both across and within diagnostic categories. The strongest support for transdiagnostic groups includes combinations of panic disorder, SAD, and GAD. OCD and PTSD seem best treated with a homogeneous group approach, although different types of trauma can, provided careful preparation and prior skills training, be included in the same CBT group for trauma. The chapter offers clinical illustrations of a transdiagnostic group mixing panic disorder and SAD and a heterogeneous group mixing different kinds of trauma. The next chapter stays with the theme of mixing. But this time the focus is on blending treatments. Chapter 8 explores how some CBT groups benefit from augmentation with other approaches, such as mindfulness and interpersonal therapy (IPT).

Notes

1. Technically, this is not a true transdiagnostic group given that all group members share the diagnosis of PTSD, but they have different types of trauma.
2. Thought-stopping is no longer considered an evidence-based approach to GAD.
3. This specifier was not available in the DSM-IV (APA, 2000).

Recommended Readings for Clinicians

Antony, M., & Swinson, R. P. (2000). *The shyness & social anxiety workbook: Proven techniques for overcoming your fears.* Oakland, CA: New Harbinger Press.

Barlow, D. H., & Craske, M. C. (2007). *Mastery of your anxiety and panic* (4th ed.). New York: Oxford University Press.

Barlow, D. H., Farchione, T. J., Fairholme, C. P., Ellard, K. K., Boisseau, C. L., Allen, L. B., et al. (2011). *Unified protocol for transdiagnostic treatment of emotional disorders: Therapist guide*. Oxford, UK: Oxford University Press.

Bieling, P. J., McCabe, R. E., & Antony M. A. (2006). *Cognitive-behavioral therapy in groups*. New York: Guilford Press.

Free, M. L. (2007). *Cognitive therapy in groups: Guidelines and resources for practice* (2nd ed.). West Sussex, UK: John Wiley & Sons.

Norton, P. J. (2012). *Cognitive-behavioral therapy for anxiety: A transdiagnostic treatment manual*. New York: Guilford Press.

Resick, P., & Schnicke, M. (1993). *Cognitive processing therapy for rape victims*. Newbury Park, CA: Sage.

Scott, M. J. (2011). *Simply effective group cognitive behaviour therapy: A practitioner's guide*. London: Routledge.

References

Alden, L. A., Taylor, C. T., Laposo, J. M., & Mellings, T. M. B. (2006). Impact of social developmental experiences on cognitive-behavioral therapy for generalized social phobia. *Journal of Cognitive Psychotherapy: An international Quarterly, 20(1)*, 7–16.

American Psychiatric Association (APA). (2000). *Diagnostic and statistical manual of mental disorders, DSM* (4th ed.). Washington, DC: Author.

APA. (2013). *Diagnostic and statistical manual of mental disorders, DSM* (5th ed.). Washington, DC: Author.

Barlow, D. H. (1988). *Anxiety and its disorders: The nature and treatment of anxiety and panic*. New York: Guilford Press.

Barlow, D. H., & Craske, M. C. (1994). *Mastery of your anxiety and panic* (2nd ed.). New York: Oxford University Press.

Barrera, T. I., Mott, J. M., Hofstein, R. F., & Teng, E. J. (2013). A meta-analytic review of exposure in group cognitive behavioral therapy for posttraumatic stress disorder. *Clinical Psychology Review, 33(1)*, 24–32.

Beck, A. T. (1972). *Depression: Causes and treatment*. Philadelphia: University of Pennsylvania Press (Original work published 1967).

Blanco, C., Heimberg, R. G., Schneier, F. R., & Fresco, D. M. (2010). A placebo-controlled trial of phenelzine, cognitive-behavioral group therapy and their combination for social anxiety disorder. *Archives of General Psychiatry, 67*, 286–205.

Blazer, D. G. (2002). *Depression in late life* (3rd ed.). New York: Springer.

Chard, K., Resick, M., & Wertz, J. J (1999). Group treatment of sexual assault survivors. In B. H. Young & D. D. Blake (Eds.), *Group treatments for post-traumatic stress disorder* (pp. 35–50). Philadelphia: Brunner/Mazel.

Clark, D. A., Steer, R. A., & Beck, A. T. (1994). Common and specific dimensions of self-reported anxiety and depression: Implications for the cognitive and tripartite models. *Journal of Abnormal Psychology, 103*, 645–654.

Clark, D. M., & Beck, A. T. (2010). *Cognitive therapy of anxiety disorders*. New York: Guilford Press.

Erickson, D., Janeck, A., & Tallman, K. (2009). Clinical experience and practical advice. *Journal of Cognitive Psychotherapy, 23(1)*, 34–43.

Erwin, B. A., Heimberg, R. G., Schneier, F. R., & Liebowitz, M. R. (2003). Anger experience and expression social anxiety disorder: Pretreatment profile and predictors of attrition and response to cognitive-behavioral treatment. *Behavior Therapy, 34*, 331–350.

Gantt, S. (2013). *Relational neuroscience and the power of the group: An interview with Bonnie Badenoch, PhD, LMFT*. The Group Circle, Winter Issue. New York: American Group Psychotherapy Association.

Gillespie, C. F., & Nemeroff, C. B. (2007). Corticotropin-releasing factor and the psychobiology of early-life stress. *Current Directions in Psychological Science, 16(2)*, 85–89.

Hamilton, K., Wershler, J., Macrodimitris, S. F., Bakcs-Dermott, B. J., Ching, L. E., & Mothersill, K. J. (2012). Exploring the effectiveness of a mixed-diagnostic group cognitive behavioural therapy intervention across diverse populations. *Cognitive and Behavioral Practice, 19(3)*, 472–482.

Haskell, L. (2003). *First stage trauma treatment: A guide for mental health professionals working with women*. Toronto, Canada: Centre for Addiction and Mental Health (CAMH).

Hinrichsen, G. A., & Emery, E. E. (2005). Interpersonal factors in late-life depression. *Clinical Psychology: Science and Practice, 12(3)*, 264–274).

Johnson, D. R., & Lubin, H. (2000). Group psychotherapy for the symptoms of posttraumatic stress disorder. In R. H. Klein & V. L. Schermer (Eds.), *Group psychotherapy for psychological trauma* (pp. 141–169). New York: Guilford Press.

Kendall, P. C., & Watson, D. (1989). *Anxiety and depression: Distinctive and overlapping features*. San Diego, CA: Academic Press.

Keogh, E., & Reidy, J. (2000). Exploring the factor structure of the Mood and Anxiety Symptom Questionnaire (MASQ). *Journal of Personality Assessment, 74*, 106–125.

van der Kolk, B. (1994). The body keeps the score: Memory and the evolving psychobiology of posttraumatic stress. *Harvard Review of Psychiatry, 1*, 253–265.

Kush, F. R., & Fleming, L. M. (2000). An innovative approach to short-term group cognitive therapy in the combined treatment of anxiety and depression. *Group Dynamics: Theory, Research, and Practice, 4(20)*, 176–183.

McEvoy, P. M., & Nathan, P. (2007). Effectiveness of cognitive behavior therapy for diagnostically heterogeneous groups: A benchmarking study. *Journal of Consulting and Clinical Psychology, 75(2)*, 344–350.

Norton, P. (2008). An open trial of a transdiagnostic cognitive-behavioral group therapy for anxiety disorder. *Behavior Therapy, 39(3)*, 242–250.

Norton, P. (2009). Integrated psychological treatment of multiple anxiety disorders. In M. Antony & M. Stein (Eds.), *Oxford handbook of anxiety and related disorders* (pp. 441–450). New York: Oxford University Press.

Norton, P., & Barrera, T. L. (2012). Transdiagnostic versus diagnosis-specific CBT for anxiety disorders: A preliminary randomized controlled noninferiority trial. *Depression and Anxiety, 29(1)*, 874–882.

Ogden, P., Minton, K., & Pain, C. (2006). *Trauma and the body: A sensorimotor approach to psychotherapy*. New York: W.W. Norton & Company.

Schare, M. L., & Wyatt, K. P. (2013). On the evolving nature of exposure therapy. *Behavior Modification, 37(2)*, 243–256.

Srivastava, S., & Beer, J. S. (2005). How self-evaluations relate to being liked by others: Integrating sociometer and attachment perspectives. *Journal of Personality and Social Psychology, 89*, 966–977.

Stolorow, R. D. (2007). *Trauma and human existence: Autobiographical, psychoanalytic, and philosophical reflections.* New York: Taylor & Francis Group.

Taylor, S., Federoff, I., Koch, W., Thordarson, D., Fectau, G., & Nicki, R. (2001). Posttraumatic stress disorder arising after road traffic collisions: patterns of responses to cognitive-behavior therapy. *Journal of Consulting and Clinical Psychology, 69*, 541–551.

8

Augmenting CBGT with Other Therapy Approaches

Just as it is becoming common to blend components within CBT to target multiple disorders—the transdiagnostic approach—there is increasing experimentation with blending CBT with another treatment tradition. This chapter introduces the idea of integrated treatment.

Good reasons for integrated CBT approaches have increased over the past decade. Integrated CBT has proved helpful for "hard-to-treat" disorders where too many clients receiving only CBT do not reach desired levels of improvement within a reasonable time period. An integrated approach to CBT is also useful for client populations where symptom expressions clearly covary with interpersonal factors above and beyond what is the case for most mental health issues. In addition, integrated CBT is helpful for client populations where improvement in functioning is just as high a priority as better symptom control and where it is reasonable to expect that symptoms decrease as functioning improves (Chapter 16 on psychosis offers examples of a paramount focus on improving functioning).

Many therapists already recognize that "pure" CBT can be tricky to deliver, especially in group settings, where supportive and interpersonal therapy approaches inevitably sneak in, even when not encouraged. It would, however, not be helpful, or appropriate, to add other forms of therapy to a CBGT protocol simply because we think "more is better" for our clients. When clinicians consider more integrated approaches, they must be mindful of the pragmatic, research-informed reasons for doing so.

In this chapter, I will review how CBGT for generalized anxiety disorder (GAD) can benefit from formally integrating a mindfulness component. First, however, I describe a pure CBGT approach to GAD. This is followed by a discussion of how to integrate components of mindfulness training. The latter part of the chapter

Cognitive Behavioral Group Therapy: Challenges and Opportunities, First Edition. Ingrid Söchting.

explores how CBGT for perinatal depression becomes enriched by including elements from interpersonal therapy (IPT).

Integrating CBGT and Mindfulness: Generalized Anxiety Disorder (GAD)

The diagnosis of generalized anxiety disorder

GAD involves excessive anxiety and worry for more days than not for a period of at least 6 months about a number of present or future events or activities. In order to be diagnosed, according to the DSM-5,[1] people must find it hard to control their worry and experience at least three additional symptoms, such as (a) restlessness or feeling on edge, (b) being easily fatigued, (c) difficulty concentrating or mind going blank, (d) irritability, (e) muscle tension, or (f) sleep disturbance (difficulty falling or staying asleep or restless unsatisfying sleep). About 5% of people will be affected by GAD (lifetime prevalence rate). Similar to most anxiety disorders, the majority of people suffering from GAD say it started in childhood or adolescence. In the absence of treatment, GAD tends to be chronic with worsening during times of feeling stressed.

A core feature of GAD is the person's belief in their inability to control their worries, which then often get compounded by worrying about worrying. For example, a father in a job dependent on global financial markets may worry about losing his job (the *content* of his worry) and becoming unable to support his two daughters in university. He may then begin to worry about the impact his restless sleep and lack of concentration has on his physical health (the *meaning* or *interpretation* of his worry). This example is consistent with the *metacognitive model of GAD* developed by Wells (1997). Interestingly, and further to the metacognitive model, beliefs in the benefits about worrying can be a predisposing factor to GAD.

Positive beliefs about worry can include seeing it as an attractive personality trait. For example, the above father may have assumptions along the lines of "Worrying about my children all the time shows how much I love them." Positive beliefs can also take the form of protection from negative emotions: "If I worry a lot now, then it will not be so shocking when I do lose my job." The latter is an example of how people hold beliefs about investing in a sort of "worry bank" hoping they will save themselves some grief when their fears become true. Another rationalization for worry has to do with fear of losing motivation and ability to function: "If I didn't worry every day about the next task or deadline, I might become complacent and unproductive."

CBGT for GAD

There are separate but related CBT interventions for treating GAD: the traditional, the metacognitive, and a new approach focused on tolerating uncertainty. The traditional CBT approach is outlined in *Mastery of Your Anxiety and Worry* therapist guide

(Zinbarg, Craske, & Barlow, 2006) and client workbook (Craske & Barlow, 2006). Techniques include monitoring specific worries, relaxation training, challenging overestimation of the probability of a worry coming true, and exposure to worst-case scenario worries. Elements of this approach were used in the transdiagnostic CBT protocol used by Erickson, Janeck, and Tallman (2009) reviewed in Chapter 7.

The metacognitive approach keeps a primary focus on negative—and positive—beliefs about worries and offers techniques for supporting clients in challenging those beliefs. The father who worried about being unable to support his daughters in university would learn to identify his different kinds of worries (positive, negative, and metacognitive) and how to rein them in to a more manageable level.

A more novel CBT approach, *targeting intolerance of uncertainty* (CBT-IU), includes elements of the more traditional CBT and the metacognitive approach as well as new ones (Dugas & Robichaud, 2006; Dugas et al., 2003). This approach explicitly emphasizes that *intolerance of uncertainty* (IU) is the general vulnerability that drives different kinds of worries. This approach has also been specifically tested in a group format (Dugas et al., 2003) and works well in community CBGT programs.

Key treatment components in group CBT-IU include (a) psychoeducation about GAD and worry (including metacognitive worries); (b) IU and behavioral exposure; (c) problem-solving training; (d) cognitive, or imaginal, exposure; and (e) relapse prevention. I will limit the discussion of these treatment components to uncertainty recognition, problem-solving training, and imaginal exposure, and illustrate how these various techniques work in a group setting. Further discussion of these three, plus the other treatment components, can be found in the helpful GAD manual by Dugas and Robichaud (2006), *Cognitive-Behavioural Treatment for Generalized Anxiety Disorder: From Science to Practice.*

Intolerance of uncertainty

Few people are entirely comfortable with the idea that, no matter how much we try to plan, we cannot create certainty in our lives. It is hard to accept that we cannot be certain that our otherwise carefully thought-through decisions will have the desired consequences. People with GAD are especially intolerant of uncertainty, even compared to the other anxiety disorders. IU is the *fuel* that keeps the worry engine going. Thus, once individuals become more tolerant of uncertainty, they worry less in general. Targeting the *underlying* problem of uncertainty intolerance seems more productive than focusing on trying to control specific worries, which more traditional CBT for GAD does. CBT therapists working with GAD clients recognize that the content of a person's worries changes constantly (yesterday, it was about my 12-year-old not wanting to play football; today, it is about my VISA card bill; and tomorrow, it will be about when I should retire). Instead, therapeutic gain is increased when the focus is directly on the underlying problem that is causing intolerance of uncertainty. Clients who manifest IU are constantly developing strategies for approaching worries and for avoiding worries.

Their approach strategies include excessive information gathering, looking for reassurance, questioning a decision one has already made, and double-checking.

Paradoxically, seemingly impulsive behavior often follows a long period of indecisiveness. For example, a woman new to the city in which her GAD group took place spent months researching a suitable restaurant for lunch with an old friend who was coming through town. She looked up restaurants in the local food magazines, searched the web, talked to people (including group members), and even visited a few places to look at their menu. She surprised the group when she announced having gone to the restaurant "just across the street" from the building where her group took place, a decent but not particularly special place. For a fuller discussion of the construct of IU, see Carleton, Sharpe, and Asmundson (2007).

In addition to approach strategies, the worry-prone individual also uses avoidance as a way of coping. Avoidance can be cognitive or emotional. In cognitive avoidance, people may try to avoid watching the news, or reading newspapers, or active financial planning with an advisor. Interestingly, parents who worry a great deal tend not to engage their children; they just avoid connecting with them on certain topics. Children whose parents have GAD say they would never bring up certain issues with them, because they fear the parents could not control their worries. Sadly, the parents thus deprive themselves of becoming more effectively engaged with their children's struggles, which only encourages the growth of their worried imaginations. In emotional avoidance, the worry may serve the function of actually distracting people from their feelings and detaching them from noticing sensations in their bodies. In this sense, worrying becomes a defense against getting more in touch with one's emotional and inner life. GAD people are sometimes referred to as "emotion phobics." In the shorter term, their avoidance strategies may offer some relief for distress, but they tend to maintain the worry in the longer term because a fuller emotional processing of their fears does not take place.

Typical avoidance strategies in GAD include evading fully committing to certain tasks or people, finding "imaginary" reasons for not doing things, procrastinating, and asking others to make one's decisions. When IU is targeted in treatment, it may involve asking clients to do some homework, such as not checking emails in their "sent" box, buying an item without researching it, and not calling a child's or spouse's cell phone multiple times in a day. People high on IU overestimate threat and underestimate their ability to cope. IU is also addressed in all other GAD treatment components, such as problem-solving training and using exposure to reverse cognitive and emotional avoidance and more recently also through mindfulness training.

Problem solving

Protocols emphasizing problem solving lend themselves to a group because of the rich opportunities for group members to brainstorm and offer mutual support as members confront their worst fears. Problem-solving training involves five steps: (1) problem definition, (2) goal formulation, (3) generation of alternative solutions, (4) decision making, and (5) solution implementation. The book called *Problem Solving Therapy: A Social Competence Approach to Clinical Interventions* (D'Zurilla & Nezu, 1999) is an excellent resource for clinicians wishing to offer their clients better problem-solving tools, something that is not unique to GAD. Here is an illustration of what problem solving in a CBT group for GAD can look like.

THERAPIST: Barry, you've asked the group for some help with your mother.

BARRY: Yes, I just can't stand visiting her anymore because she keeps buying stuff from all the flea markets she goes to, and it's getting close to impossible to even make a dinner in her cluttered kitchen not to mention clearing some space for plates on the dining table. She just laughs, and does not think she has any problems. She says she likes her stuff and that I'm an uptight neat-freak.

THERAPIST: Sounds like you and your mother have a difference of opinion here.

COTHERAPIST: Using our five-step problem solving framework, how would you define your present problem with your mother?

BARRY: My present problem is that I don't feel like visiting my mother, and the truth is that I have actually avoided her for four months now. I worry a lot about her, and I don't know what to do. My goal would be to visit her once a week.

THERAPIST: We can see how this sure adds to your worries, and why you would prefer to stay away from your mother and her apartment. Do you have some ideas for solutions that would help you meet your goal of getting back to a regular connection schedule?

BARRY: No. I'm kind of stuck, other than just trying to force myself to go as I obviously feel terrible about myself for neglecting her. I lose so much sleep over this and have had to get a mouth guard because I grind my teeth at night.

COTHERAPIST: [goes to board and writes *brainstorming*] OK group, let's do some brainstorming! When we brainstorm we try not to think about how good or practical an idea is. That comes later.

LESLIE: How about having a frank conversation with your mother explaining why you are not coming as much.

NATE: A friend of mine has joined a support group for family members of hoarders. You may get a lot out of attending as you're not alone with this problem.

BARRY: I had no idea we had such support groups. Do you have a name or number I could call?

JEANNIE: How about offering to pay to have a helper come in? There are services for helping people de-clutter their space.

BARRY: Maybe I could get my children involved, as my daughter did say she would like to help grandma. My daughter is very organized and tidy.

THOMAS: How about just accepting your mom, if she really does not think she has a problem. Maybe this is more your problem than hers.

MOHAMMED: Yes, you could sort of make it a bit of a fun adventure. You could even bring a picnic basket and just spread out a cloth somewhere—and sort of camp out and bring the dirty dishes home with you.

COTHERAPIST: All good suggestions, and we now have about five alternative solutions. Let's talk about the pros and cons of each, keeping in mind questions like: How effectively will it solve the problem of "Barry wants to overcome his avoidance of his mother?" What is the time and effort involved for Barry? What might be some emotional consequences, or relationship consequences?

The group engages with Barry, who feels encouraged to implement a solution, knowing that it is not perfect but a pretty good one to at least try. Invariably, the person in question thanks the group for offering ideas they could not have come up with themselves.

Imaginary exposure

Exposing someone with GAD to their *core fear* follows the same rules as other CBT exposures. It involves gradually working up to the worst fear, writing it out as a coherent narrative or script with beginning, middle, and end, using information about all senses as much as possible, and reading the script out loud in the group in the present tense. This worry script looks a lot like the trauma exposure discussed in Chapter 7. With daily home practice of about 45 minutes, it generally takes about 2 weeks for habituation to occur. Most worries about hypothetical situations involve the same underlying fears. Imaginal exposures thus tend to be needed for only one or two scenarios. Clients in CBGT for GAD are asked to write several drafts of their chosen scenario while increasingly adding details about their sensory and body sensations. For example, a husband worrying about his wife dying in a car crash may in his first draft write: "I pick up the phone and it's a call from the police. They tell me to sit down and I do." In the final draft, he may write: "I pick up the phone and when I hear it's the police, I shake all over and can barely hang onto the phone; my legs are so wobbly I cannot stand up; I am unable to speak because my throat is so dry and tight. I whisper, 'Is she alive?'"

In the GAD group, members take turns reading their drafts and offering comments and suggestions to each other, especially on the earlier versions of their scenarios. Peer support and modeling become crucial during these difficult exposure tasks. The group facilitators ensure that clients record and track their level of anxiety using the standard 0–100 scale—as they read their scenarios. They can also record their exposure scenarios on tapes and listen to them repeatedly. Similar to other exposures, the peak level of anxiety during a reading of a worry script is the most indicative of progress. Over time, group members will see that their peak anxiety is steadily decreasing as they confront and become more tolerant of their worst fears. Helpful downloadable forms for clinicians on "How to write a worry script" and "How to tolerate uncertainty" are available for free from www.anxietybc.com.

Group facilitators of GAD often remark at how the group turns into a gathering of mutually supportive mini Buddhas! Transformative statements abound: "Life is too short to waste energy on things that are clearly beyond my control." "I am so much more productive now that I try to enjoy each day and not always think about tomorrow." "When I am calm and centered, I can actually really help others." Or "I am more accepting of developments in my life." Although GAD group members can get to this calmer place by relying on CBT techniques with support from the group, there are good reasons to explicitly include elements of Eastern philosophy-informed practices, such as mindfulness, to make CBGT for GAD even more effective.

GAD and mindfulness

Another novel approach to GAD is mindfulness training. In what follows, I sketch what it looks like to integrate aforementioned Dugas and Robichaud CBGT approach with mindfulness.

Despite the effectiveness of CBT and CBGT for GAD, some research clinicians convincingly argue that GAD remains the least successfully treated of all the anxiety disorders. On average, only slightly more than half of the GAD clients who have received CBT score in the "nonworried and anxious" range on GAD outcome measures after having completed treatment (Borkovec & Castello, 1993; Ladouceur et al., 2000). A theoretical rationale for including mindfulness approaches into CBT for GAD has been articulated by Orsillo, Roemer, and Barlow (2003). These clinician researchers agree with other GAD CBT researchers and clinicians on what characterizes people with GAD.

First, people with GAD spend a great deal of effort avoiding distressing thoughts and feelings. Secondly, they use worry as a strategy to prepare for, or avoid, the occurrence of low-probability future negative events. Orsillo and colleagues remind us that mindfulness—and other similar new therapy approaches such as acceptance and commitment therapy (ACT) (Hayes et al., 1999)—helps people become fully observant and tolerant of external and internal sensations in the present moment (Segal, Williams, & Teasdale, 2013).[2] The ability to notice an upsetting feeling, and just let it be without straining to figure out what it may mean and what one could do, is precisely what is extremely difficult for people with GAD. They find it difficult to just *notice* feelings, body tensions, and concerns without *distracting* themselves by staying busy with worries and action. For example, a parent with GAD may feel intense anxiety about a teenage child being 15 minutes past her curfew and have a strong urge to do something—such as call either her cell phone or the local hospital to check for new admissions. Not surprisingly, many people with GAD are high-functioning, highly productive people at work and at home—always busy with something *important*—but at the expense of being able to slow down into some leisure activity that may not be seen as productive by them.

In their individual CBT treatment of four individuals with GAD, Orsillo and colleagues (2003) included progressive muscle relaxation (PMR), self-monitoring of worries, awareness of the present moment through the mindfulness exercise of physical sensation awareness (body scan), and increasing awareness of avoidant behavior. Therapists help clients overcome their avoidant behaviors by encourage them to commit to what is important in their life and to set goals to be accomplished in the service of a particular valued life direction (*finding your values*). For example, one client was chronically worried about his relationship with his partner but also pushed away thoughts of his relationship unhappiness. Through exploration of values, he became aware of yearning for a more intimate relationship than his partner was willing to provide. He then translated this into action by formulating a plan for achieving his goal of increased intimacy. Although the four cases in the Orsillo study all made improvements, the authors point out that more research is clearly needed in order to determine just how beneficial these new elements are to traditional CBT. Lastly, they point to group as a viable mode of treatment delivery, if at all feasible.

Integrating mindfulness into CBGT

Clinicians who have created their own integrated CBGT-mindfulness protocols for GAD report good results and a dropout rate of about 20%. More systematic outcome evaluations are needed in order to determine the added benefits of mindfulness. Here is an example of what a session agenda in the middle of a 12-week 2-hour CBT group protocol may look like based on integrating mindfulness (Marchand, 2012; Roemer & Orsillo, 2002) and CBT for GAD (Dugas & Robichaud, 2006):

1. Go-round on homework review
2. Mindfulness practice in session, such as a body scan or 5–15 minutes of meditation followed by discussion of noticing and tolerating physical sensations
3. New CBT-mindfulness skills introduced, for example, *thoughts are not facts* or *finding your values*
4. CBT practice in-session, such as *problem-solving* exercise for each group member in turn OR *exposure working with worry scripts*
5. Assigning homework

Although this integration is both attractive and doable, there are nevertheless challenges when designing and implementing such a group protocol. An integrated CBT-mindfulness protocol for groups would be strengthened by ensuring that any mindfulness skills be introduced early to allow for sufficient practice time and skills consolidation. CBT-mindfulness focus is inevitably on the individual—as each person quietly enters into their own mind and has potential for undermining the cultivation of a strong group climate. Facilitators can try to overcome that by encouraging postexercise discussions, where members can review what was helpful or challenging. This gives group members opportunities to support and learn from each other.

Staying with silence can be almost impossible for some people with GAD, and they may experience distress in the form of *relaxation-induced anxiety*. Some clients with GAD reject any groups involving a requirement to meditate for at least 15 minutes. However, seeing that one is not alone is an advantage that individual CBT for GAD does not offer. Group members often talk about leaning on the group and feeling held and supported by it—even when there is no talking—as they work on becoming more comfortable with silence and stillness. It is easy to relate. (I for one cannot seem to develop a yoga practice at home, but am utterly dependent on my class to get me going.)

As with any integrated protocol, there is a risk of offering a half-and-half approach, a watered-down version depriving clients of a fair dosage of a full treatment. When time is limited, as it is in CBGT, and especially in public settings, it is important that clients receive a whole course of a treatment with demonstrated efficacy. Thus, based on research to date, this protocol is best built *around* the basic CBT for GAD treatment protocol, which means that enough time will have to be devoted to practicing in-session CBT interventions including exposures. Full integration of exposure can indeed be a challenge. It can feel disruptive to the gentle, quiet flow of mindfulness practices. Mindfulness-trained clinicians often express some hesitation to engage in the more aggressive, full-on, worst-case scenario exposures right after a more contemplative exercise. Pairing facilitators—with one being primarily mindfulness trained and the other CBT—helps.

It will be interesting to follow outcome evaluations on mindfulness-enhanced CBGT for GAD. One also anticipates other forms of silence-and-stillness interventions as a way of augmenting the CBT protocol. *Compassion-focused therapy* (CFT) is another candidate for an integrated approach, which is reviewed in Chapter 16. Mindfulness was the first spiritually informed practice to make its way into secular psychological treatment protocols, but many other wisdom or faith traditions—and secular, common sense approaches to slowing down and being more present with one task at a time—have similar potential. The positive psychology movement, with its emphasis on what makes individuals *flourish* as they try to overcome their worries (and other problems with anxiety), encourages clinicians to support their clients in engaging with absorbing and personally meaningful activities in a free-flowing, unrestrained, and nonjudgmental manner. These could be anything from meditative walking, listening to music, dancing, or quietly working with one's hands, as with painting, knitting, woodwork, pottery, or cooking.

CBGT and Interpersonal Therapy: Perinatal Depression

About 10–15% of women experience a clinically significant major depressive episode in the perinatal period, the time from pregnancy to the first months after the child is born. Given that many pregnant women are reluctant to take medication, a psychological intervention is an attractive alternative. The symptoms are the same as in MDD or persistent depressive disorder (as listed in Chapter 4). Individual CBT has shown good results for depressed mothers. Given that social support is frequently cited as a risk factor for perinatal depression (Nielsen, Videbech, Hedegaard, Dalby, & Secher, 2000; O'Hara & Swain, 1996), it is no surprise that CBGT has emerged as helpful (Goodman & Santangelo, 2011). The group format not only breaks social isolation. It also offers opportunities to have feelings and worries normalized, as well as to receive tips and helpful advice from other mothers. New mothers who are not depressed also benefit from joining regular support group meetings.

The *Perinatal Depression Cognitive Behavioral Therapy Treatment Group Model* (Fraser Health, 2009, September) is an example of a standard CBGT protocol for perinatal depression. This protocol is based on integrating material from a number of CBT depression protocol resources, including *Mind over Mood* (Greenberger & Padesky, 1995), *Antidepressant Skills Workbook* (Bilsker & Paterson, 2005), and *Coping with Depression in Pregnancy and the Postpartum: A CBT-Based Self-Management Guide for Women* (Haring, Smith, Bodnar, & Ryan, 2011). It can be downloaded from the web at www.fraserhealth.ca. The group session themes are as follows.

Perinatal Depression Cognitive Behavioral Therapy Treatment Group Model (Fraser Health, 2009, September)

Session 1: Introduction to the CBT Group Model and Learning about Perinatal Depression
Session 2: Risk Factors and Making the Connections
Session 3: Introducing CBT and Goal Setting: NEST-S (**N**utrition, **E**xercise, **S**leep and Rest, **T**ime for Yourself, and **S**upport)
Session 4: The Five Aspects of Our Life Experiences and Goal Setting beyond NEST-S
Session 5: Identifying Our Moods, Situations, and Hot Thoughts
Session 6: Defining and Understanding Our Automatic and Hot Thoughts
Session 7: Gathering the Evidence
Session 8: The Balancing Act
Session 9: Solving Problems Effectively
Session 10: Relapse Prevention

The *Perinatal Depression Cognitive Behavioral Therapy Treatment Group Model* follows the general CBGT protocol for depression outlined in Chapters 4 and 5, including each session being 2 hours long and group size being ideally eight members. The goal-setting part is expanded to first focus on self-care skills such as nutrition and rest, which is then followed by goals that increase a sense of pleasure, mastery, and social connection. The cognitive restructuring work is also similar, with its focus on identifying negative automatic thoughts and replacing them with more adaptive and realistic thinking. It does not use the 7-column Thought Records reviewed in Chapter 5 but a shorter version of only three or a maximum of five columns. Therapists running these groups find that expectant and new mothers find shorter Thought Records more manageable. The manual does not provide any specific suggestions for how to work with the group climate. It does encourage the mothers to arrive 30 minutes in advance, to allow for socializing as well as to prepare the babies for childcare, which is provided by community volunteers. The screening and outcome measure is the *Edinburgh Postnatal Depression Scale* (EPDS; Cox, Holden, & Sagovsky, 1987).

Some clinicians offering the *Perinatal Depression Cognitive Behavioral Therapy Treatment Group* have found it useful to augment the protocol by inviting partners and other loves ones to attend an education and information session. The group members do not attend this session for confidentiality reasons. The session is led by the two cotherapists and takes place around sessions 4–6. The format for this evening session is roughly the following:

7:00–7:45 p.m. Provide education regarding signs, symptoms, and risk factors for perinatal depression
7:45–8:15 p.m. Partners and loved ones speak about their own experiences of supporting their partners struggling with depression.
8:15–8:45 p.m. Worksheets on "needs and requests" completed by the group members are shared with respective partners. A sheet may involve a woman asking for attention ("Ask me how my day was"), love ("Hug me, but please do not assume this will lead to anything"), or support ("Let's check in once a week to talk about the week to make sure we give each other time alone and together").
8:45–9:00 p.m. Closure—what will I walk away with tonight?

Integrating interpersonal therapy (IPT) into CBGT

Clinicians implementing this partner-augmented CBGT protocol for perinatal depression find that the interpersonal component of inviting the partners to a separate session is well received, often so well that the women who are in the group ask for additional strategies for how to connect and communicate with their partners. *IPT* offers many strategies for improving connection and communication. IPT is a shorter-term form of therapy that directly addresses the nature and quality of people's relationships. It is a rare couple that does not struggle to at least some degree with staying close and mutually supportive during the perinatal period. New mothers tend to feel they don't get the *kind* of support they especially need, and new fathers tend to feel emotionally neglected, excluded from the intensely intimate mother–child connection. Fathers are often left trying to figure out how they can offer the *right* kind of help (e.g., one father was very pleased with himself for surprising his wife on a Friday evening—one month after the birth of their child—with having booked a table at an expensive restaurant, only to be taken aback by her bursting into tears because of "not having anything to wear").

It is not difficult to empathize with each partner in this couple nor to understand their communication challenges in recovering from this episode, keeping in mind that the woman is suffering from depression. It is common sense that an explicit interpersonal component becomes part of the CBGT protocol. Recent systematic reviews also encourage clinicians to experiment with IPT and CBT integration. A few words about IPT before we look at these reviews.

What exactly is IPT?

IPT is derived from attachment theory (Ainsworth, 1969; Bowlby, 1977). IPT is based on the premise, which in some ways is obvious yet not always fully appreciated by lay persons and professionals alike, that interpersonal function is a critical component to psychological adjustment and well-being (Klerman, Weissman, Rounseville, & Chevron, 1984; Stuart & Robertson, 2003). Early attachment issues (secure vs. insecure) with caregivers are not directly addressed in IPT, but a sense of the client's attachment style is helpful in understanding their relationships and communication problems. In attachment research, 65% of children are referred to as secure and the remainder 35% as insecure. Insecure attachments broadly take the form of having either an anxious/ambivalent or an anxious/avoidant attachment to the main caregiver (Ainsworth & Wittig, 1969). According to the attachment theory, children gradually construct increasingly complex internal models of themselves and others. Bowlby refers to this process as the construction of *internal working models*, a process essentially involving confidence or lack of confidence in the caregiver's accessibility and responsiveness to the needs of the child, as well as the child experiencing itself as worthy or not worthy to be attended to. Once an attachment style is consolidated, these internal models provide the individual with certain cognitive patterns, or biases of information processing, about interpersonal cues. An assumption of attachment theory is that early attachment relationships continue to be important throughout life. People who were insecure as children tend to struggle more in their adult relationships (Bartholomew, 1993). Bowlby's *internal working model* concept influenced Beck's understanding of *schemas* as described in Chapter 5 where we reviewed how Beck came to understand a person's *schema* about, for example, not being "lovable," as influenced by childhood factors including the quality of the relationship to parents or other caregivers.

IPT was originally developed in the 1970s for depression. It is most often used for this disorder, but attempts to apply it to eating and anxiety disorders are promising. Similar to CBT, IPT is a shorter-term (typically 16 sessions), evidence-based, therapist-directed, and manual-driven therapy. Although developed for individual therapy, it can also be offered in group format (Stuart & Robertson, 2003, 2012). Much like CBT, IPT does not claim to bring about fundamental changes in personality or attachment style. However, in contrast to CBT, the main focus is not on the depressed person's thinking style or their daily activities, but on the relationships in their lives. The assumption is that the quality of our relationships is directly connected to changes in our moods and that otherwise insightful and mature people—when depressed—fail to recognize this connection. For example, when IPT therapists establish a time-and-interpersonal-event chronological line with their client, clients often express not having realized certain connections. They might say: "Now I see that the ongoing friction and lack of communication with my coworker led to my feeling more depressed" or "I realize that I started to become depressed when I retired even though I had looked forward to it." IPT seeks to help clients improve their interpersonal relationships or change their expectations of them, as well as improve social support networks.

IPT focuses on four main interpersonal areas, and suitable clients must acknowledge that at least one of those areas is troublesome for them. They are *interpersonal disputes* (conflict between the client and another person stemming from either poor communication or unrealistic expectations), *role transition* (change in social role and support during life-phase transitions such as leaving home, becoming a parent, or retiring), *interpersonal sensitivity* (difficulty forming satisfying relationships and feeling socially isolated), and *grief* (the death of a loved one, where grief has developed into complicated bereavement). Each area includes the opportunity for therapists to introduce various IPT techniques such as role-playing, problem solving, and communication analysis (Stuart & Robertson, 2003). In a second edition of the Stuart and Robertson IPT guide, the area of interpersonal sensitivity has been eliminated and incorporated into the remainder three areas (Stuart & Robertson, 2012). This makes sense to several IPT therapists, who find that the area of *interpersonal sensitivity* often gets the least attention in therapy because the other areas tend to cover it.

Administration of IPT requires foundational skills in psychopathology and psychotherapy as well as at least 40 hours of didactic IPT training and ongoing supervision for a minimum of two cases. The training required to become a competent IPT group therapist follows a similar approach to that described for CBT in Chapter 10. The Interpersonal Psychotherapy Institute offers information about training and certification (www.iptinstitute.com). Adding one or two partner nights to the aforementioned CBGT protocol does not require full IPT training, but CBGT therapists interested in a fuller integration of CBT and IPT for their perinatal groups may consider becoming IPT trained.

Research support for IPT and CBT in treating perinatal depression

Recent systematic reviews have further consolidated the use of both IPT and CBT in treating perinatal depression. The evidence for a group format, however, is mixed but generally positive.

Based on 27 studies of individual and group therapy, Sockol, Epperson, and Barber (2011) concluded that IPT and CBT in individual format—but not group—were equally helpful and superior to other forms of therapy, including group. The authors speculate on why the group format for IPT or CBT did not do as well. They noted that women were hesitant about the idea of groups. They worried about lack of confidentiality, not getting enough individual attention, and being uncomfortable at the thought of sharing with strangers. These pregroup fears are common but were perhaps not assuaged during the actual group experience.

In contrast, Goodman and Santangelo (2011) found that many forms of group therapy were all effective for postpartum depression. They reviewed 11 studies (some but not all were randomized control studies). The group interventions included CBT, IPT, and psychodynamic. All but one study (a group described as unstructured social support) showed statistically significant improvement in depression scores immediately after the group ended and also at 6 months follow-up. No modality emerged as superior to others. The authors advise, however, against making generalized interpretations of their findings, given the considerable heterogeneity of the studies and the varying degrees of methodological quality. The researchers noted that for some groups the full benefit did not emerge until about 6 months after the end of the group.

Goldvarg and Kissen (2011) have responded to this research suggesting that both CBT and IPT are effective for postpartum depression. They wonder if combining CBT and IPT may make a group format more attractive. Their group case study seems to be the first published evidence of an integrated IPT and CBT postpartum group.

Example of combined IPT and CBGT for perinatal depression

Goldvarg and Kissen (2011) report good outcomes in a case study involving a group of six mothers with postpartum depression. The group was offered in a community outpatient program serving primarily people of lower socioeconomic status. The IPT focused on each woman's relationship with her baby, with her partner, and the transition back to work if relevant. The CBT part focused on education about the link between mood, thoughts, and behaviors, relaxation techniques, challenging negative beliefs, and identification and ranking of anxiety-provoking situations. There were no dropouts. Unfortunately, their case study does not include illustrations of the various CBT or IPT techniques, nor any outcome measures other than qualitative statement, such as "I never thought I would speak to my mother again. Being here helped me understand the importance of being a mother; it's a special bond. It helped me reconnect with Mom" (Goldvarg & Kissen, 2011).

In the following text, I describe an example of how a CBGT group for postpartum depression can be expanded to include an IPT component. This community outpatient program is similar to the one described by Goldvarg and Kissen. It follows the *Perinatal Depression Cognitive Behavioral Therapy Treatment Group Model* (Fraser Health, 2009) described earlier in this chapter. The CBT group was augmented by a specific integration of IPT communication analysis. This technique helps clients identify their communication patterns, recognize their contribution to communication problems, and motivate them to communicate more effectively. The technique is described in the widely used IPT manual by Stuart and Robertson (2003, 2012) and can easily be adapted to a group setting. Group therapists rely on several sources to get a sense of the group members' style of communication: the client's description of their communication, the quality of the client's narrative to the therapists and the group, the client's in-group communication, and reports from significant others such as partners who attend the partner evening. Here is an example of how the IPT communication analysis technique can be included in perinatal CBGT.

THERAPIST: Let's review how helpful the partner evening last week was.

JASMEET: My husband said it was the first time he felt understood as trying to be supportive, but not getting it right. He really appreciated learning more about depression too, and how I am often "not myself [indicates quotation marks with hands]." He feels he has lost me and it scares him.

COTHERAPIST: Anything in particular you think he learned about depression, and your depression in particular?

JASMEET: He found the information helpful about how depression can make someone always think and assume something negative; I guess he felt better about it not being all his fault when I got upset and cried instead of being happy that he wanted to invite me—and baby Preet—out for dinner. I know he is right when he says that I need to relax and not worry about everything being perfect, and who cares if I'm still wearing my maternity clothes to a restaurant. He knows my family, and where this obsession with looking proper is coming from.

COTHERAPIST: So, he was able to identify some of your negative automatic thinking. Did you tell him about the Thought Record we did in group where you countered the belief that "I cannot be the kind of mother my family deserves?"

JASMEET: No, because every time we start to talk, I begin to cry and I don't know how to tell him that I really love and appreciate what he is doing, and the insight he has about me and my family. I just feel like such a burden to him.

LAURA: I totally relate, and I feel like this burden to my mother, who comes every day for three hours. She is so helpful, and shops and cooks, but I also feel she is quietly critical of me. Yesterday I blew up at her, and she called me ungrateful. I know I'm not good at showing my appreciation, but I just feel so bad about myself.

THERAPIST: People in this group have noted that it often is hard for both of you, Laura and Jasmeet, to express yourselves, and you even got some feedback about some people not being sure if you enjoyed their company here in the group. I wonder if you would be up for role-playing some communication with the people who try to help you, but seem confused about what you want?

JASMEET: Sure, I'm up for that. What do I do?

COTHERAPIST: Let's start with my being Jasmeet's husband, and you, Jasmeet, will first be yourself and simply respond the way you usually do. We will then do a second role-play, where you try to express your feelings as directly and honestly as you can. You will use "I" statements such as "I have trouble" or "I really appreciate, but…"

Role-playing this kind of communication with a loved one is a powerful group intervention, and clients often return to the group saying that by rehearsing the lines, it "came out" more naturally at home. Role-playing invariably elevates the energy in the group and supports members in expressing themselves strongly and genuinely ("it feels so real" is often said). When members experience the group as a secure place for emotional expressions, role-playing strengthens cohesion and allows members to model new ways of communicating. Therapists in this kind of augmented CBGT group will often suggest that the group members take the initiative to organize more regular talk times with their partners even if they are just asking about each other's day and how they are doing. Group therapists can offer further instructions about the importance of each partner, in turn, simply listening to the other and validating what the partner said by repeating it. For example, a husband may demonstrate this kind of reflective listening by saying: "I hear that your day was tough because our baby cried a lot." Both the men and the women in the group report that such communication feels validating and that it often leads to an increase in talking and connecting as a couple.

Summary

This chapter shows how basic CBGT can be enriched by integrating other therapy approaches that are likely to make the group format more attractive and engaging and thus improve individual group members' outcomes. The chapter includes examples of augmenting CBGT for GAD with mindfulness and CBGT for postpartum depression with IPT. For GAD, therapists find that their clients are increasingly familiar with mindfulness and curious to try such an integrated CBT group. Considering how difficult it can be for people with GAD to "be still," the opportunity to practice mindfulness exercises in a supportive and safe group is helpful. For postpartum depression, an interpersonal focus on partners—and other loved ones—in the new mother's life may help them in overcoming hesitation about group therapy. In such an integrated group, the women feel an increased sense of universality when they realize they are not alone in their struggles with their partners and other family members.

Lastly, no psychotherapy approach benefits from becoming static and insular. Psychotherapy theory and practice are similar to other scholarly disciplines, where the "survivor" therapies maintain their staying power through the slow and organic process of revising their approaches based on new research findings and clinicians' collective experiences. The added opportunity for thoughtful, evidence-and-practice informed integration of different treatment modalities into CBGT not only helps group members but also therapists as they commit to ongoing professional growth.

The next two chapters return to a specific focus on CBT, with an emphasis on how to hone critical CBGT skills, and how to develop and maintain and develop competence as a CBGT therapist.

Notes

1. The essential feature and diagnostic criteria of GAD remain unchanged from DSM-IV (2000) to DSM-5 (2013).
2. Chapter 5 offered a detailed explanation of the use of mindfulness in preventing relapse from depression. The practice is the same, but in GAD, mindfulness is used to augment CBT and offered simultaneously, whereas for depression, mindfulness follows the active CBT treatment.

Recommended Readings for Clinicians

Dugas, M., & Robichaud, M. (2006). *Cognitive-behavioral treatment for generalized anxiety disorder: From science to practice*. New York: Routledge.

D'Zurilla, T. J., & Nezu, A. M. (1999). *Problem solving therapy: A social competence approach to clinical intervention*. New York: Springer Publications.

Fraser Health (2009, September). *Perinatal depression cognitive behavioral therapy treatment group model*. Fraser Health, BC: Author. Retrieved March 10, 2013, from www.fraserhealth.ca [accessed on February 22, 2014].

Greenberger, D., & Padesky, C. A. (1995). *Mind over mood: Change how you feel by changing the way you think*. New York: Guilford Press.

Haring, M., Smith, J. E., Bodnar, D., & Ryan, D. (2011). *Coping with depression in pregnancy and the postpartum: A CBT-based self-management guide for women*. Vancouver, Canada: Mental Health & Addictions Services (Reproductive Mental Health). www.carmha.ca [accessed on February 22, 2014].

Stuart, S., & Robertson, M. (2003). *Interpersonal psychotherapy: A clinician's guide*. London: Hodder Arnold.

Stuart, S., & Robertson, M. (2012). *Interpersonal psychotherapy: A clinician's guide* (2nd ed.). London: Hodder Arnold.

References

American Psychiatric Association (APA). (2000). *Diagnostic and statistical manual of mental disorders, DSM* (4th ed.). Washington, DC: Author.

APA. (2013). *Diagnostic and statistical manual of mental disorders, DSM* (5th ed.). Washington, DC: Author.

Ainsworth, M. D. (1969). Object relations, dependency, and attachment: A theoretical view of the infant-mother relationship. *Child Development, 40*, 969–1027.

Ainsworth, M. D., & Wittig, B. A. (1969). Attachment and exploratory behavior of one-year-olds in a strange situation. In B. M. Foss (Ed.), *Determinants of infant behavior* (Vol. 9, pp. 111–136). London: Methuene.

Bartholomew, K. (1993). From childhood to adult relationships: Attachment theory and research. In S. Duck (Ed.), *Understanding relationship processes*, Vol. 2. *Learning about relationships* (pp. 30–62). Newbury Park, CA: Sage Publications.

Bilsker, D., & Paterson, R. (2005). *Anti depressant skills workbook*. Vancouver, Canada: Centre for Applied Research in Mental Health & Addictions. Retrieved from www.carmha.ca [accessed on February 22, 2014].

Borkovec, T. D., & Castello, E. (1993). Efficacy of applied relaxation and cognitive-behavioral therapy in the treatment of generalized anxiety disorder. *Journal of Clinical and Consulting Psychology, 61*, 611–619.

Bowlby, J. (1977). The making and breaking of affectional bonds: Etiology and psychopathology in the light of attachment theory. *British Journal of Psychiatry, 130*, 201–210.

Carleton, R. N., Sharpe, D., & Asmundson, G. J. G. (2007). Anxiety sensitivity and intolerance of uncertainty: Requisites of the fundamental fears? *Behaviour Research and Therapy, 45*, 2307–2316.

Craske, M. G., & Barlow, D. H. (2006). *Mastery of your anxiety and worry: Client workbook* (2nd ed.). New York: Oxford University Press.

Cox, J. L., Holden, J. J., & Sagovsky, R. (1987). Detection of postnatal depression: Development of the 10-item Edinburgh Postnatal Depression Scale. *British Journal of Psychiatry, 150*, 782–786.

Dugas, M. J., Ladouceur, R., Leger, E., Freeston, M. H., Langlois, F., Provencher, M. D., et al. (2003). Group cognitive-behavioral therapy for generalized anxiety disorder: Treatment outcome and long-term follow-up. *Journal of Consulting and Clinical Psychology, 71*, 821–825.

Erickson, D., Janeck, A., & Tallman, K. (2009). Clinical experience and practical advice. *Journal of Cognitive Psychotherapy, 23(1)*, 34–43.

Goldvarg, E., & Kissen, M. (2011). Group psychotherapy for women suffering from postpartum depression. *Group, 35*, 235–246.

Goodman, J. H., & Santangelo, G. (2011). Group treatment for postpartum depression: A systematic review. *Archives of Women's Mental Health, 12*, 277–293.

Hayes, S. C., Bissett, R., Korn, Z., Zettle, R. D., Rosenfarb, I., Cooper, I., et al. (1999). The impact of acceptance versus control rationale on pain tolerance. *The Psychological Record, 49(1)*, 33–47.

Klerman, G., Weissman, M., Rounseville, B., & Chevron, E. (1984). *Interpersonal psychotherapy of depression*. New York: Basic Books.

Ladouceur, R., Dugas, M. J., Freeston, M. H., Leger, E., Gagnon, F., & Thibodeau, N. (2000). Efficacy of a new cognitive-behavioral treatment for generalized anxiety disorder: Evaluation in a controlled clinical trial. *Journal of Consulting and Clinical Psychology, 68*, 957–964.

Marchand, W. R. (2012). Mindfulness-based stress reduction, mindfulness-based cognitive therapy, and Zen meditation for depression, anxiety, pain, and psychological distress. *Journal of Psychiatric Practice, 18(4)*, 233–252.

Nielsen, F. D., Videbech, P., Hedegaard, M., Dalby, S. J., & Secher, N. J. (2000). Postpartum depression: Identification of women at risk. *British Journal of Obstetrics and Gynaecology, 107*, 1210–1217.

O'Hara, M. W., & Swain, A. M. (1996). Rates and risk of postpartum depression—A meta-analysis. *International Review of Psychiatry, 8*, 37–54.

Orsillo, S. M., Roemer, L., & Barlow, D. H. (2003). Integrating acceptance and mindfulness into existing cognitive-behavioral treatment for GAD: A case study. *Cognitive and Behavioral Practice, 10*, 222–230.

Roemer, L., & Orsillo, S. M. (2002). Expanding our conceptualization of and treatment for generalized anxiety disorder: Integrating mindfulness/acceptance based approaches with existing cognitive behavioral models. *Clinical Psychology: Science and Practice, 9*, 54–68.

Segal, Z. V., Williams, J. M. G., & Teasdale, J. D. (2013). *Mindfulness-based cognitive therapy for depression: A new approach to preventing relapse* (2nd ed.). New York: The Guilford Press.

Sockol, L. E., Epperson, C. N., & Barber, J. P. (2011). A meta-analysis of treatments for perinatal depression. *Clinical Psychology Review, 31*, 839–849.

Wells, A. (1997). *Cognitive therapy of anxiety disorders: A practice manual and conceptual guide*. West Sussex, UK: Wiley & Sons.

Zinbarg, R. W., Craske, M. G., & Barlow, D. H. (2006). *Mastery of your anxiety and worry: Therapist guide* (2nd ed.). New York: Oxford University Press.

9

How to Fine-Tune CBGT Interventions

The previous chapters looked at a number of challenges in developing strong CBGT programs—such as how to prepare people for group treatment, ensure their expectations are positive and realistic, combine different mental health problems in the same group, and augment CBT by integrating it with elements of another therapy approach. This chapter offers suggestions for how to fine-tune common CBGT interventions. CBT therapists, especially if they were primarily trained to do individual therapy, can feel a bit thrown off their otherwise confident CBT stance when having to transfer their skills from individual to group settings. The following topics reflect some of the more technical struggles. I have often been asked about by therapists who lead CBT groups. We will review how to develop exposure hierarchies, support homework completion, and prepare clients for becoming their own therapists after the group is over.

Why Exposure Hierarchies are Important

Supporting clients in systematically facing their fears is one of the fundamental principles of CBT. It is the feature that most distinguishes CBT from other forms of psychotherapy. CBGT therapists can introduce the concept by describing how exposure therapy is based on the principle of extinguishing fears by preventing an escape from experiencing them. When human beings engage fully with unpleasant emotions and associated uncomfortable body sensations, these will, over time, diminish. This process is referred to as habituation or desensitization, but really means to become used to a feeling, to become bored with it! The therapist can go on to explain that, when humans are too quick to avoid unpleasant feelings, we deprive ourselves of the opportunity to

Cognitive Behavioral Group Therapy: Challenges and Opportunities, First Edition. Ingrid Söchting.

learn that those feelings and body sensations are time limited and not harmful. New parents, for example, often remark how unpleasant and even disgusting it at first is to change a baby's diaper. But because escape is not an option, it surprisingly quickly becomes routine and boring. However, as grandparents will say, after several years of having "escaped" changing diapers, it may take a little while to get used to it again.

Despite research consistently confirming the robustness of this evidence-based therapeutic procedure, many CBT and other clinicians seem to struggle with the implementation of exposure and are at times hesitant to engage in its practice (Schare & Wyatt, 2013). And exposure interventions for different kinds of disorders can without doubt be challenging to implement in a group setting. Hence, the majority of CBGT therapists will need to spend some time preparing their clients—and themselves—for the exposure part of group treatment.

In the first couple of CBGT sessions, where group therapists cover education about a particular illness and its treatment approach, they repeatedly tell group members their exposure will be gradual and systematic and that they will always be in charge. Therapists may add: "You will not be doing anything you do not agree to. Our job as therapists is to work with you to find the place where you push just a bit beyond your comfort zone. We will never push you to do anything that is not safe."

There are some exposure approaches that rely on *flooding* instead of *graded* exposure. As the word implies, in flooding the client is basically thrown into their worst fears right away. An example could be going to a dog obedience training class if one has a fear of dogs or being forced to use a public bathroom 24 hours a day every day for a 2-week summer camp. With sufficient time in flooding, anxiety will gradually come down. It can be a faster way to get to the ultimate goal of tolerating what one is avoiding, but since it can require hours of exposure in a given day, it is often not practical to implement in community settings. Flooding is usually limited to more intense treatment programs, where people stay all day or overnight.

Graded exposure is by far the most common approach in CBGT. The key technique involves building an exposure hierarchy that lists a range of situations the client fears or may be entirely avoiding. Each situation is given a subjective anxiety rating from a range of 0 to 100, where 100 is the most intense anxiety one can imagine and 0 is completely relaxed. Clients can also rate the intensity of their avoidance, where 100 would be complete avoidance, 50 would be avoiding half the time, and 25 about a quarter of the time. These anxiety ratings are called SUDS, an acronym for Subjective Units of Distress Scale. Since this term sounds technical, some therapists prefer to avoid it and instead just talk about degrees of anxiety or fear. Other therapists and clients have fun with the acronym and turn it into a verb: "I was *sudsing* at 60 during the public toilet exposure."

The exposure hierarchy becomes the master plan from which individual exposure exercises are derived. Not everything on the hierarchy is necessarily turned into an exposure challenge, and it is important to remind clients of that. Some clients will be reluctant to put their worst fears down on paper, assuming the therapists are going "to make me do it." Therapists can assuage group members' anxiety by again reminding them that they are in control and may not get to their top items during their group treatment, but that it is helpful to get a sense of the full range. Hierarchies are most commonly used in groups for panic disorder, social anxiety disorder (SAD), obsessive–compulsive disorder (OCD), and compulsive hoarding and of course any groups for specific phobias such as fear of heights, dogs, or injections. It is important to dedicate at least one group session in the early part of treatment, usually session 3 or 4, to developing exposure hierarchies.

Groups for posttraumatic stress disorder (PTSD) may or may not include hierarchies. If several clients have strong avoidance of specific situations, for example, driving a car or visiting the place where the accident took place, a hierarchy may be helpful. But because many people in a PTSD group do not avoid any places, other than the memory places in their mind, this kind of group usually does not include the development of hierarchies. Groups for GAD tend to also not use hierarchies but rather focus on one or two worst-case scenarios as explained in Chapter 7.

Although there is often overlap, each group member has unique fears and no two hierarchies will be identical. The greatest overlap in fear themes are in panic disorder and social anxiety disorder. Typical entries on the panic disorder client's hierarchy are as follows:

	SUDS (fear)	*(Avoidance)*
Spending 20 minutes by myself in the shopping mall	60	75
Contacting a travel agent about an airplane trip	90	100

Typical entries on the socially anxious client's hierarchy are as follows:

	SUDS (fear)	*(Avoidance)*
Initiating small talk with a person in coffee shop lineup	35	35
Hanging out with my boyfriend's friends	50	20

Working on hierarchies in an OCD group can be trickier because there are many different subtypes of fears in a typical OCD group. The following two example entries are from two different clients' hierarchies. As the reader will see, there is no thematic overlap between their fears.

	SUDS (fear)	*(Avoidance)*
One group member: Doing some research in local library on pedophiles	85	100
Another group member: Shake hands with all my group buddies	30	55

CBGT therapists wanting to develop groups for OCD often find it difficult to prepare for having to implement a wide range of exposures. It would be easier if the entire group had, for example, contamination obsessions. However, if therapists keep in mind that the *function* of the symptoms is more important than the *content*, as we learned in Chapter 7, then it is easier to cope with hierarchies that look vastly different.

In that sense, therapists should maintain a transdiagnostic group atmosphere, as Norton (2012) reminds, and encourage group members to look for the commonalities in what drives their fears as opposed to individual differences in expression. With this reminder, therapists will become more relaxed (and notice their own SUDS dropping). However, there is another factor that complicates hierarchy building even more: many OCD group members have more than one type of OCD. A person may primarily seek treatment for their checking behaviors and concerns with safety at home but may also engage in an inordinate amount of rearranging and ordering of items in their home and avoid going to church because of fears of saying something inappropriate. Each distinct subtype will need its own, separate hierarchy. In the following text we focus on building hierarchies in an OCD group followed by a panic disorder group. The principles are the same across different disorders.

How to develop exposure hierarchies in the group

The hierarchy-building session is often the most challenging session in an OCD group and definitely not the session where your cotherapist can be on vacation or sick! In OCD groups, unlike other anxiety groups, the therapists take some time during the session before the hierarchy development session to review each client's OCD subtypes or themes based on information from the intake assessment. This is further discussed with each client during the group. An OCD group member may list a first theme as a concern with ordering and rearranging, a second as fear of contamination, and a third as concerns about harming others. Sometimes, group members prefer to first work on a less distressing OCD theme, although therapists may encourage starting with the most distressing. They remind clients of the likely generalizing effects, where secondary obsessions—not directly addressed in treatment—end up improving as a result of successful treatment of other obsessions and compulsions.

In a hierarchy development session, we start like this after the go-round:

THERAPIST: As you note on your group schedule, today we are going to help you develop a sort of master treatment plan. We call it a hierarchy. It will help you get a sense of the range of your fears, and it will help us plan individual exposure and response prevention exercises as we move forward.

COTHERAPIST: Your hierarchy is not cast in stone, and you will have plenty of time to revise it. Also, we know you cannot put everything down as we've limited the sheet to 12 entries. That's OK. We just need to get a sense of the types of fears you have, and we can then derive other related fears from the ones you put down.

THERAPIST: First, let's just get comfortable with the SUDS scale we just introduced. It's all about your own inner anxiety thermometer and not about comparing to others. How about going around the room and have each of you say where your SUDS are at right now, sitting here, about to fill in your hierarchy form. Jonah, are you OK with starting us off?

JONAH: Uuhh, that's hard to say as I've never asked myself this question before. How anxious do I feel now on a scale from 0–100? Well, I feel pretty good here in the group, but also not quite sure what it is you want me to do. I'm going to say I'm at 35.

THERAPIST: Thanks Jonah. Louise, how about you?

After this go-round, the cotherapist proceeds:

COTHERAPIST: "Please write your first name on top of the form [for OCD, we also ask for clients to write down the name of their theme, e.g., contamination, checking, or aggression]. Let's establish some anchor points on your hierarchy. What would be something in the middle, in the 50 SUDS range—a situation you have trouble with and are probably not facing, but the thought of facing it is not completely overwhelming?" [Group members are writing down their 50 SUDS item and the other therapist circulates the room and offers individual help as needed.]

COTHERAPIST: OK, let's move to what would be a 100. That is the kind of situation or place you have a lot of trouble imagining that you can manage. But you also know your life would be a lot more enjoyable and anxiety-free if you could tolerate it. Lastly, let's get the lowest items, something in the 5–10 SUDS range.

THERAPIST: From walking around, I can tell you're all on a pretty good track in terms of writing down situations related to your theme. Does anybody want to share his or her first three items?

After having established these three low, middle and top items, clients are instructed to fill out the rest of their hierarchy on their own. At this point, the two therapists circulate the room. They may also be receiving help from a third trainee therapist. As needed, the therapists sit down with individual clients who may seem a bit stuck. Some clients get stuck when they are unable to identify the specific fear trigger, as in the case of Adam who has OCD.

TRAINEE THERAPIST: I note, Adam, that you have two similar entries: "Coming home from work" is 80 and "Greeting my wife and kids" is 90. I'm curious what it is about those situations that make you anxious?

ADAM: Well, I don't want to bring contamination into our home, and have asked my wife to set out some clean clothes so that I can change in the garage.

TRAINEE THERAPIST: I see, and I get how stressful it must be for you to come home if you worry about contaminating your family. What about changing this item to something like: "Keeping all my clothes on, except for my shoes, as I enter my home?" What SUDS rating would you give that one item?

ADAM: That would be up there, I'm going to say 95.

Another common problem is clients having items bunched either at the top or the bottom of their hierarchy. The therapist may inquire about a range of variables that could modulate anxiety, as in this example of a person with both panic disorder and agoraphobia.

THERAPIST: You have a lot of situations above 70. You have been driving outside of your neighborhood, walking more than four blocks away from your home, and going to the mall. What are some things you struggle with that are less anxiety provoking?

GILLIAN: I can't think of anything. It all seems to be about getting myself to those places I listed.

THERAPIST: What about going with someone? Would that make some of this easier?

GILLIAN: Not sure if I have somebody. But it would be easier for me to drive if I was not alone in my car as I'm afraid of fainting. If I was with someone it would be about 40 SUDS.

THERAPIST: OK, let's add that as an item.

Therapists can also inquire about the time of day. Many people who worry about panic attacks, not surprisingly, find it easier to go to shopping malls and supermarkets when they are less crowded, such as Tuesday mornings as opposed to Saturday afternoons.

After offering about 30 minutes of help with group members' hierarchies, the therapists explain that they will photocopy each hierarchy, but people are free to add items or make changes at home. The therapists further elaborate that they will use the hierarchies to plan in-session exposure exercises. Therapists also keep copies of the hierarchies in order to use them as an additional outcome measure. In one of the last sessions, it is a good idea to distribute everyone's original hierarchy and ask clients to rerate their SUDS for every item. The following is an example of an excerpt from an OCD hierarchy with rerated items. Joshua has OCD with pedophilic sexual obsessions. Similar to other people with these kinds of obsessions, Joshua had no history or signs whatsoever of any *pedophilic disorder*. But his OCD made him terrified of the possibility of becoming a pedophile. He therefore did everything he could to avoid contact with children and material related to pedophilia. This avoidance decreased chances of becoming triggered with obsessions such as "Does finding that girl cute mean I'm a pedophile?"

Joshua's harm hierarchy	*SUDS (fear)*	*SUDS (fear)*
	Beginning of group	*End of group*
Going to a playground	15	0
Sit next to a child on a bench	20	5
Say something nice to a child	25	5
Reading about pedophiles in newspaper	70	15
Researching pedophile profiles in a library	80	15
Bumping into a child	25	10
Put a child on my lap	100	25

Joshua was pleased to see that he had overcome many of his fears about whether he secretly was a pedophile. Through a series of increasingly challenging exposures, Joshua's distress decreased as he realized he did not "turn into a pedophile" but was able to genuinely enjoy having more contact with children and trusting himself. He found the exposures helpful, many of which involved hanging out in places with children around, including family members he had previously avoided because of his obsessions. But he was also aware of not feeling as much in control of his OCD as he had hoped. He realized he needed to continue to engage in exposure tasks as much as possible in order to keep the feeling of being just an ordinary person (and not a pedophile) foremost on his mind. He developed a new hierarchy with any trigger situation that still had a rating of 5 or above and planned to use this for his self-directed exposure practice after the group was over.

How to Support Homework Completion

CBT undeniably involves homework, the *sine qua non* in CBT. CBT would not be CBT without it and it is the reason why some people—including therapists—love it or hate it. But homework, or the idea of practicing something between therapy sessions, is not unique to CBT. In psychodynamic therapy, for example, a client may be encouraged to practice specific ways of being less accommodating to a perceived authority figure in their life. But whereas other therapies, including IPT, keep between-session work as only an option, it is mandatory in CBT and must be consistently implemented every week. Therapists present the rationale for homework as involving the idea of becoming one's own therapist and therefore better able to maintain treatment gains and prevent relapse. Therapists need to emphasize that CBT is a shorter-term treatment aimed at self-help. Because time is limited and dependency on the therapist(s) is discouraged, daily self-initiated practice is essential.

The assignment of homework in CBT can be misunderstood by CBT therapists themselves. It is important to never just ask a client to, for example, "read some chapters in this book." It is worse to give them a handout and tell them to "try and do a Thought Record," without first having gone through an example in a session. Instead, we constantly collaborate with our clients, and any homework follows naturally and logically from what they worked on in our session with them. Clients need to be crystal clear about their homework, or it will certainly not get done. Discussing what homework means to the client earlier in treatment can be helpful in anticipating avoidance or barriers.

Persuading clients to comply with CBT homework can be challenging in individual treatment, but perhaps even more challenging in a group setting. This is an issue, considering that good outcomes from CBGT are predicated upon clients engaging in at least an hour of daily homework between sessions. There is quite a body of literature highlighting how clients' *willingness* to do their homework is a strong predictor of good outcome (e.g., Neimeyer, Kazantzis, Kassler, Baker, & Fletcher, 2008).

Experience has led us to wonder if a main reason for lack of homework compliance in CBGT may originate with varying degrees of psychological trauma related to memories of primary-school classrooms.

Unlike individual CBT, CBGT undeniably resembles a classroom, and for many clients, it may be their first return to such a setting since graduating from high school or leaving without graduating. Painful memories of struggling academically, or downright bullying by teachers or peers, may surface in the group setting. Where I work, some group members over age 65 have shared that they associate classroom settings with punitive authority, including corporal punishment. A few have dropped out of a CBT group stating they could not tolerate being treated "like children." Not surprisingly, we see the highest comfort and compliance with homework in younger people. A classroom setting is familiar to them, and homework seems to still be just part of life. Since homework is critical in CBT, what can CBGT therapists do to make it more positive?

One partial solution is to refer to homework as *home practice* and have a group discussion about what it means to have a home practice of anything. Facilitators may continue to use the term homework because it is so engrained in the CBT vocabulary, but they can at least engage in a discussion about people's thoughts and feelings related to practicing, ideally every day. Supporting clients in increasing their willingness to do homework is critical. Clients fairly easily talk about practicing a range of activities they want to get better at. This could be learning a new language, broadening one's cooking, playing golf or tennis, or having a meditation practice. There is something about the concept of "practice" that suggests more volition, willingness, internal desire, and drive compared to "homework," which is easily associated with an external imposition by an authority figure. Truly, how many CBT therapists would enjoy being assigned homework in mid and later life?

There are several less traumatic reasons for lack of homework compliance. Often, even when people feel good about doing their homework, unexpected barriers interfere. There simply is not enough time in the group to review every possible obstacle to a homework assignment. Again, this can be specifically addressed in the group as was shown in Chapter 4, where goal setting in CBGT for depression was described. In that example, the group member, Wendy, was able to anticipate that poor weather could be a barrier to her goal of walking. With help from the group, she created a plan allowing her to still pursue her goal despite rain. Furthermore, the therapists may introduce the 95% rule. This rule challenges clients to ask themselves if they are fairly sure there is at least a 95% probability their chosen homework is doable.

When homework is incomplete or not done at all, it is important to set clients free from any *all-or-nothing* burden of homework expectation. Group therapists do this by discussing that people often learn valuable lessons about homework that did not get done. This can lead to clients becoming aware of, for example, any tendency to prioritize the needs of others over their own. Some clients find it hard to dedicate themselves to working on something that is important to them—for a full 12 or more weeks. As therapists, we learn a great deal about our clients when we sensitively inquire "What got in the way?" as opposed to potentially shutting down our clients by saying "Why did you not do your homework?" The following example illustrates how valuable information can be gained from incomplete homework.

THERAPIST: Paula, how did your practice of progressive muscle relaxation for 20 minutes twice a day go?

PAULA: Not good. I couldn't do it, and almost didn't come to group today because I knew you were going to ask about it.

THERAPIST: I recall that you were quite eager to try this form of relaxation after we did it as a group in our last session. We're curious about what got in the way of you doing it at home.

PAULA: Well, I'm not really sure. I tried one day in our bedroom before dinner, but then my husband yelled, asking how long before we were going to eat. I felt selfish for just disappearing, and I kind of forgot about it after that.

THERAPIST: So, it sounds like you struggled with some feelings of guilt for taking time to do something that is mostly important to you and not benefiting the whole family?

PAULA: Yeah. Who wants to be selfish?

COTHERAPIST: Any suggestions from the group on how Paula could make her relaxation training work better for her?

LEONARD: Well, I can relate because my wife has also wondered about what it is I am doing in this panic disorder group. So, I sat her down and told her all about it, including that I really want to dedicate one hour a day to practicing skills, and that I need her support. I was surprised at how little she knew about my anxiety—because I'm quite good at protecting her from it.

PAULA: I'm pretty sure my husband is supportive, and he certainly is happy to look after our 4-year-old daughter every Monday evening when I go to group.

LEONARD: Maybe your husband doesn't fully get that you need his support above and beyond the 2-hour a week group time.

THERAPIST: Paula, do you think you could sit down with your husband and explain what this group program involves and what you need from him in terms of support?

PAULA: I know it is hard for me to take time to do something that is just for me, so I would like to get better at this and not feel guilty.

COTHERAPIST: Sounds like you're not the only person who struggles with that, and it is something that comes up in other groups too. So, maybe we could spend some time talking about how being concerned with neglecting our families may get in the way of doing homework.

This discussion is a common one in CBGT and invariably leads to group members getting better at predicting and troubleshooting any obstacles to their homework. Allowing time and patience to ask clients about what interfered—as opposed to offering them quick solutions, which can be a tendency for CBT therapists—yields valuable information about the clients' patterns of thinking and behaving, patterns that are likely to persist if not addressed. Young, Grant, and DeRubeis (2003) similarly argue that any slowing down of treatment by allowing clients to solve their own problems ultimately saves time. In CBGT, therapists create opportunities as much as possible for group members to problem solve with the group. This time and effort is well spent and reduces the chance of the whole group having to return at a later time to explore barriers to completing homework. Group members also show relief when they realize that nobody is judging them for "just coming up with excuses." The discussion helps everyone take seriously how difficult it can be to add home practice to other demands and responsibilities.

The problem of too much praise can also interfere with how clients feel about the group and can lead to incomplete homework. Overenthusiastic therapists who are quick to say "fantastic!" or "good for you!" can be experienced as off-putting and disingenuous and at worst patronizing and infantilizing. Adults with mental health issues are painfully aware of having fallen below their own expectations—and certainly those of society's. Thus, praise is best offered when it is specific, directly tied to the person's stated goals, and respectful of the adult as an otherwise intelligent and mature person. For example, a therapist may say: "We know how important it is to you to be able to go to the grocery store without having to wait for your wife to come home and accompany you. Last week you went twice on your own for the first time in years. You exceeded your homework goal. We hope you give yourself lots of credit for your hard work in the group paying off." A refreshing discussion of the issue of therapist enthusiasm is offered by Young and colleagues (Young et al., 2003). Therapists can of course not control the rest of the group, and spontaneous applause often breaks out as group members report on their homework successes. This is usually very well received by the member being celebrated.

How to Plan for Termination

The encouragement of homework practice is closely tied to the inevitable ending—or termination—of any form of therapy. But termination is especially relevant in CBGT. In individual CBT, there is some flexibility for the therapist and client to negotiate the date of the last session depending on how therapy proceeds. However, in CBGT, this date has been firmly determined by the therapist(s) long before the first group session even took place. The nature of CBGT is such that groups need to start and end at certain times. It gives people on wait lists a specific start time, often weeks or even months in advance, which many appreciate as it makes the wait more tolerable. There are rare exceptions in which group facilitators will extend a group from 12 to 14 sessions provided that everyone in the group is in agreement and able to attend. Although the fixed end date is undeniably rigid, and can create discomfort for clients and therapists alike, it does have benefits.

One advantage of the preset termination date is that issues of termination simply do not become a dominant issue in the therapy with all that this can entail.

In open-ended treatments, clients may wonder just how unwell the therapist thinks they are. They may start to worry their therapists do not care much for them and secretly want to get rid of them. In longer-term therapies, these issues of course provide grist for the dynamic mill. Proponents of shorter-term therapies such as CBT and interpersonal therapy (IPT) agree that setting a termination date in advance can facilitate the therapeutic work. In CBGT, members have a printed schedule indicating the precise dates of all sessions, including the last one. CBT therapists reason that when a certain task or opportunity comes with a deadline, most humans will notice acceleration in their motivation to get as much from it as they can. For the majority of clients, the time-fixed nature of CBGT provides the spark to pour their hearts and minds more fully into it.

CBGT therapists work with termination from the beginning of any group, but in a matter-of-fact way. First, it becomes part of the rationale for homework, with emphasis on how people are not likely to benefit much if they only dedicate themselves to the 2 hours of weekly group time. Second, taking responsibility for making personal changes as opposed to relying on an external agent such as a therapist—or medication, for people who want to come off that—becomes a real and consistent part of CBGT. This encouragement of individual responsibility looks different depending on the type of CBGT a person is in.

Becoming one's own therapist

In CBGT, just past the midway mark, therapists introduce the concept of becoming your own therapist. Clients are expected to come up with their own ideas for home practice and sometimes for in-session practice as well. In an OCD or social anxiety group, where in-session exposures figure prominently, this can at first be challenging. But group members are by then quite aware of what increases their anxiety and creates opportunities for developing better tolerance. They will sometimes come up with incredibly effective and clever exposure ideas for self-directed homework.

For example, an OCD sufferer who feared that he would hurt someone's feelings and therefore spent a lot of time and energy repeatedly asking people for reassurance suggested that he make a comment that could be perceived as slightly critical for each and every person in the room, including the facilitators. He wrote all the comments down on individual pieces of paper. A box with the comments was then passed around and each group member in turn read it out aloud. Nobody knew to whom a specific comment was directed at, but they all knew that they had been expressed by Robert. There were comments like "Occasionally you interrupt others," "You sometimes seem to ignore me during our breaks," and "The color black especially suits you." Robert found it harder than anticipated (SUDS were around 75 during the in-session exposure), but the hardest thing for him was to refrain from calling the facilitators before the next group to inquire—seek reassurance—if anyone had been hurt or offended. The entire group cooperated as they completely understood Robert's obsessions and compulsions. They handled his questions to them by saying the following: "You handled that exposure really well" or "It was fun to participate in your exposure."

Similarly, clients are encouraged to come up with homework practice on their own and mostly use the facilitators and other group members for a brief check on whether their chosen task seems realistic or whether there are any obstacles to completing it.

Formal and informal booster sessions

After CBT treatment has formally ended, booster sessions are common. The promise of booster sessions offers an incentive for clients to independently practice their acquired skills, ensuring they are becoming increasingly consolidated. Thus, meeting with the therapist 3, 6, or more weeks after termination allows the therapist to determine if this has taken place. It also increases motivation when clients know they will be reporting back. This can, for sure, prolong the dependency, but it is reasonable to allow for this weaning off the therapeutic relationship. Booster sessions are considered a basic part of CBT. Group therapists can also preplan or, more spontaneously, respond to a request for such group boosters. Some CBGT programs build in booster sessions for all graduates of any CBGT program four times a year, for example. In Chapter 5, we reviewed how *continuation* CBT, a formal booster program, can greatly decrease rates of relapse for people with depression. Booster sessions provide an opportunity for people to set themselves goals to report back on, and get feedback on, something they have become unsure of. Sometimes booster sessions are not as well attended as clinicians would like, especially for those clients who have recovered from anxiety. We would hope the poor attendance means that most graduates of CBGT programs are doing well on their own and do not need the boosters.

A group will sometimes agree to form their own peer follow-up group. Group members are often not sure if this is allowed. But it is indeed permitted. Facilitators may even encourage a piece of paper be passed around so that those who are interested can write their name and phone number. It obviously requires that one member is willing to be the coordinator. Therapists make it clear that they will not provide anybody's name and phone number after the group. It has happened that a group member coordinator of on ongoing peer support group calls the program secretary or a therapist for this information, but legal acts pertaining to privacy and confidentiality usually prevent such sharing of client information.

Group therapists may also be invited to join a peer follow-up support group. Most will likely not be able to due to time constraints and already having enough groups to run. If they do join a peer follow-up support group, it does create issues pertaining to ethical responsibility for the clients. The therapist should set clear boundaries and limitations to any follow-up contact and how this will or will not be documented. In my workplace, therapists have declined requests to attend follow-up groups as facilitators, but we have been able to work with administration to make a group room available for ongoing peer-support groups. Such initiatives can include secretarial support in the form of sending letters to all past members of certain groups informing them of any peer follow-up group meetings.

How to Handle the Last CBGT Session

Although the date of the last session is no surprise, it often does seem to arrive sooner than the group and the facilitators are ready for. When a group is going well, 12 sessions, or 4 months, progress quickly. Group facilitators understandably may feel some sadness, wishing this group would continue instead of having to, again, start all over. In the spirit of CBT therapist transparency, warmth, and directness, it makes sense that the group facilitators thank the group for the privilege of their having been part of it and being able to support everyone on their journey to better health. I and my cotherapists add group-specific comments if this at all feels genuine, as it most often does. We usually give a standard line such as "As you know we work with many groups, and it is part of our jobs, however, as you can probably easily imagine, each group is quite different even though we cover the same basic material." In this group, we have been especially impressed with…" It seems important to not single out any members, but rather say things like "We were impressed with how quickly the group warmed up to each other. We noted that there was a lot of talking during the tea break starting in the first session; sometimes this takes several weeks." Or "We found this group to be very creative in the way you offered input on each other's exposures." Group members also express what the group has meant to them. This group validation is well received. Group members tend to hang on every word spoken—one can hear a pin drop. It is the final emphasis on the process of the group with the hope that the acknowledgment will create a lasting positive memory for each member, a memory that can be accessed and offer support to people for years as they move on into their ongoing self-help practice.

The last session does not have a homework assignment per se, but rather this go-round involves the question: what are your plans for keeping up the good work? Clients are encouraged to write down specific steps they intend to take. This can be as follows: (a) make sure I keep my group folder where I can see it and review it, (b) ask my wife if she is willing to be a support person for my home practice, and (c) join a local support group for mood disorders. For some clients, more formal group or individual treatment is needed. This is also openly discussed in the group, with a reminder that one of the therapists will be in touch by telephone to review further.

Summary

This chapter deals with how to implement a number of traditional CBT interventions in the group setting. Group therapists can understandably find certain CBGT tasks daunting: developing eight different exposure hierarchies, working within the constraint of an imposed deadline, and understanding individual group members' barriers to homework—to name just a few challenges related to adapting CBT techniques to a group setting. Most of these group adaptations are reasonably straightforward, but it helps to anticipate potential challenges in order for therapists to not lose self-confidence. Unfortunately, there is not much written about these more technical aspects of CBGT implementation, but consulting and talking with other CBGT therapists is helpful. A web-based forum for questions, answers, and mutual support for CBGT therapists would also be valuable.

References

Neimeyer, R. A., Kazantzis, N., Kassler, D. M., Baker, K. D., & Fletcher, R. (2008). Group cognitive behavioural therapy for depression outcomes predicted by willingness to engage in homework, compliance with homework, and cognitive restructuring skill acquisition. *Cognitive Behaviour Therapy, 37*, 199–215.

Norton, P. J. (2012). *Cognitive-behavioral therapy for anxiety: A transdiagnostic treatment manual.* New York: Guilford Press.

Schare, M. L., & Wyatt, K. P. (2013). On the evolving nature of exposure therapy. *Behavior Modification, 37(2)*, 243–256.

Young, P. R., Grant, P., & DeRubeis, R. J. (2003). Some lessons from group supervision of cognitive therapy for depression. *Cognitive and Behavioral Practice, 10*, 30–40.

10

Who Is Qualified to Offer CBGT?

There is no easy answer to this question. Becoming a CBGT therapist requires a combination of two different skill sets: ability to implement CBT interventions for a range of disorders and ability to facilitate groups. Thorough knowledge of individual CBT is a logical and necessary prerequisite for being a lead therapist in CBGT, but the added complexity of the group format demands additional skills not necessarily offered in CBT training centers. While there are organizations offering certification, separately, in CBT and group therapy, the ones listed in this chapter do not offer formal certification in both, with a title of *Certified CBGT Therapist*.

Standards for Training and Qualifications

Ideal CBGT therapists are those who have had extensive, supervised CBT as part of their mental health education. Usually, this involves a minimum of at least 1 year, full-time supervised CBT training in the form of an internship in a formally approved hospital-based program or community mental health center. The majority of CBT internship programs in North America meet standards for approval by the American Psychological Association (APA) or the Canadian Psychological Association (CPA). Equivalent training is, however, also widely available to practicing and regulated health-care professionals who want to extend their scope of practice. They can seek this training through private training centers, such as the *Beck Institute for Cognitive Behavioral Therapy and Research* in Philadelphia, United States, or the *Oxford Cognitive Therapy Centre*, Oxford, United Kingdom. Clinicians are encouraged to check with their local CBT associations (some are listed at the end of this chapter)

Cognitive Behavioral Group Therapy: Challenges and Opportunities, First Edition. Ingrid Söchting.

for training opportunities in their area. Admission to this type of training is usually restricted to mental health practitioners who already demonstrate strong foundational skills in the assessment and treatment of mental health problems. After completing formal internships or equivalent supervised training, CBT therapists can seek additional certification as a CBT therapist. In the United States, the *Academy of Cognitive Therapy* offers such certification, which is available to individuals who have demonstrated an advanced level of expertise in cognitive therapy. The academy's certified membership includes social workers, psychiatrists, psychiatric nurses, psychologists, counselors, and other mental health professionals from around the world. This certification recognizes expert levels of, and leadership in, the field of cognitive therapy. Great Britain, Canada, and Australia also offer certification in CBT. Other countries in northern Europe—and China—are likely to follow suit as CBT is making significant inroads in those countries and is often even more accessible to the public compared to North America.

Ideally, the expert CBT therapist would also have received certification in group therapy by a recognized training institute. The *American Group Psychotherapy Association* (AGPA), for example, offers the title of *Certified Group Psychotherapist*, which allows one to be recognized as a specialist in group psychotherapy as well as affirm commitment to a certain standard of practice for group psychotherapy. Group psychotherapy associations offer certifications for a wide range of therapy approaches, problems, and disorders. Thus, it is impossible—without inquiring—to know what *kind* of therapy a *Certified Group Psychotherapist* offers for what kind of client. However, clients can be confident that certified group therapists have a solid understanding of what makes therapy groups safe and helpful. Organizations such as the *Canadian Group Psychotherapy Association* (CGPA) and the AGPA offer training courses on the basics of group therapy covering issues such as developmental stages in a group's life, group dynamics, processes, client selection and preparation, etc. CBGT therapists often find these courses helpful and inspiring. They offer CBGT therapists a broader appreciation for the potential healing capacity of the group process and how to best deliver the content of a CBT protocol in a group setting.

CBGT would be a scarce resource if mental health centers required the top level of training sketched in the beginning of this chapter. At the same time, it is best to avoid the opposite extreme in which health professionals whose formal training did not include CBT, or any form of supervised psychotherapy, are asked to develop and run CBT groups. It does happen that such professionals are offered one or two CBT workshops in order to take on leadership of a CBT group. Although many professionals are fully capable of reading, understanding, and presenting any CBT manual, overreliance on any manual or guide, without prior supervised experience with a range of clients, can quickly undermine therapist confidence and be potentially harmful to group members. The unexpected always happens, and when therapists become unsure and anxious, group members immediately sense this and their anxiety about the group increases.

A significant portion of CBT and CBGT involves presenting often complicated interventions, such as graded exposures. Even when these interventions progress well for most or all group members, deviations from any group manual are usually necessary. Group therapists are constantly faced with the challenge of accommodating individual group members' symptom expressions and needs within the group context. The consequences of insufficient CBGT training can tarnish CBGT with a negative reputation. This is unfortunate when the problem is not CBGT per se. As with any craft or service, whether cabinet making, midwifery, or heart surgery, it is optimal to provide initial classroom teachings of basic knowledge followed by graduated, supervised training.

Somewhere in the middle of these two training poles are rich opportunities for mental health practitioners from varied backgrounds to become responsible and competent CBGT therapists. In thriving, dedicated mental health CBGT programs across many countries, there is typically a CBT champion with significant CBT and group therapy training providing formal or informal leadership. One or two such leaders can, if given the necessary resources, train other mental health practitioners to become qualified and confident CBGT therapists. In what follows, I propose how CBGT can be incorporated into staff training. I then review issues pertaining to student training in CBGT and how to implement ongoing staff supervision, consultation, and professional development.

How to Become a CBGT Therapist

Qualifications of the competent CBGT therapist

A competent CBGT therapist will have had a combination of didactic learning and direct supervision. This combination can also be referred to as blending foundational or *declarative knowledge*, the kind gained through courses, workshops, and reading, with *procedural knowledge*, the kind obtained from ongoing and direct supervision (Newman, 2013). I elaborate on these two approaches in the following text. In any CBT group, it is critical that at least one of two group facilitators have had extensive CBT training for the particular type of group they are running.

Since mental illness is a serious matter, similar to a physical illness such as heart disease, clients with mental health issues need effective treatment delivered by qualified practitioners. It is not professionally rewarding to be in charge of eight depressed group members if neither leader has had prior supervised experience with depression, including in a group setting. Compared to individual therapy, much more is at stake when an entire group breaks down, as it is not easy to transfer a whole group to another therapist. Individual clients are easier to transfer when therapists feel out of their depth or for other reasons do not believe they are the most qualified to offer treatment.

In settings where one therapist has had formal training in mental health; at least 1 year of supervised CBT training, including CBGT; and an additional 2–3 years of ongoing CBT practice, this therapist can begin to train cofacilitators. A cofacilitator is often a mental health therapist who has a solid grasp of psychopathology, assessment, and mental health issues based on a formal education in psychiatric nursing, social work, counseling, psychology, or psychiatry. This clinician is familiar with diagnostic criteria for the various mental health disorders and all the personal and environmental variables influencing the functioning of people with mental illness. Such a cofacilitator knows how to engage in a client-centered manner, how to support the client in setting goals, and how to work collaboratively with the client in working toward improved well-being and symptom management. Many cofacilitators have had various group therapy experiences. These experiences may be supportive groups, psychoeducational groups, or interpersonal process groups.

A cofacilitator who is being trained by the primary CBGT therapist will learn to add specific CBT skills to their already broad base of general knowledge about mental health. A cofacilitator will develop CBT skills—or declarative CBT knowledge—by taking courses and workshops and engaging in assigned readings and discussions. Mental health practitioners who already have a professional degree, including foundational skills in psychotherapy and are working independently within their scope of practice as they become cofacilitators, are obviously limited in how much additional declarative CBT knowledge they can add to their already busy workload, but if their goal is to become primary therapists in CBT groups, this didactic CBT training must be a priority. If they are comfortable with being cotherapists in a secondary role, they may not need the same amount of additional training outside of their work setting. The primary therapist will be able to offer recommendations for where gaps in knowledge need to be filled.

Declarative knowledge about core CBT competencies

Didactic training aimed at increasing declarative knowledge usually takes the form of a series of workshops on core CBT skills. For example, an introduction to CBT can, minimally, exist of five full-day (or 40 hours) workshops focusing on (a) *introduction to CBT*, (b) *behavioral techniques*, and (c) *cognitive techniques*. The introduction to CBT will cover its historical development, theoretical learning principles, the range of disorders and problems for which there is evidence to support CBT, appropriate client populations, characteristics of the therapist, and how to communicate the CBT model and treatment rationales. The coverage of behavioral techniques will include monitoring of symptoms, ongoing improvement, outcomes, hierarchy development in exposure therapy, and goal setting. The review of cognitive techniques will touch on dysfunctional assumptions and thinking (e.g., black-and-white thinking) and the use of Thought Records to challenge unhelpful thinking. In this kind of introductory course, some interventions are demonstrated by the workshop instructors, who also use the participants for role-play. Mental health professionals new to CBT who enroll in such a course enjoy having a better sense of the foundational CBT principles. Although the course is primarily a theoretical overview, it nevertheless offers a solid framework, which can be hard to get on one's own.

There may be initial education and training costs for programs that hire staff without prior CBT experience. However, this investment quickly pays off. When staff feel supported and confident in their CBT skills, they are more likely to enjoy a higher level of job satisfaction. The didactic part of CBT training is ideally done before entering into any CBT group as a trainee, but, if this is not possible, a concurrent approach is also workable. Following courses on CBT core skills, staff may seek more specialized knowledge on specific disorders depending on what groups they are involved in. For example, a program specializing in obsessive–compulsive disorder (OCD) would want their group facilitators to get as much specific knowledge about this disorder, especially given that CBT is the gold-standard intervention for OCD. And a program wishing to prioritize mixed diagnostic groups may want to send their staff to workshops on the new transdiagnostic protocols reviewed in Chapter 7. With some basic declarative knowledge of core CBT skills, the staff trainee will be able to add procedural knowledge, which is the process by which one implements acquired CBT skills to an actual group.

Implementing declarative knowledge into real groups

This implementation follows a graded approach. A first helpful step would be to "silently" observe a CBT group. This could be done from behind a one-way mirror, which is ideal, but not always available in community centers (one-way mirrors are more common in academic psychotherapy training clinics). The group is told that there are trainees watching behind the mirror and that they participate in the post-group therapist debriefing discussion. Group members may not easily be in a position to refuse this, if the program presents itself as also being a teaching site. It is, fortunately, a rare member who objects to having trainees involved. Groups are most often quite agreeable after having had an opportunity to discuss their concerns. In public settings, where clients appreciate getting high-quality therapy services for free, they are usually more than willing to offer "payment" in the form of going along with having trainees or students present.

If a mirror is not connected to the group therapy room, the trainees can silently sit away from the group table so that it is clear they do not play an active role. It is important that the role of the trainees is explained during the first CBGT session. Therapists may tell clients to not worry about establishing eye contact or turning to the trainees when they talk. They can just ignore them. Such instructions are helpful. It is also best if the trainees do not mingle too much with clients during the break so as to minimize confusion about who is in or who is "out of" the group. It is a bit awkward and counter to the group spirit. It is one of the reasons why many supervisors prefer that trainees observe behind mirrors.

Watching videotapes of groups in action is also helpful. But it is a less dynamic experience, since all group sessions have usually taken place by the time the video is presented to trainees. Trainees often have excellent questions, which the group facilitators take into account and may incorporate in their subsequent CBGT sessions.

This kind of interaction is complicated to do if videos are used, but not impossible. With the appropriate equipment, each CBGT session could be reviewed by many trainees on a screen immediately after it took place, or simultaneously. This would allow the group facilitators to more actively work with issues that come up in the postgroup session debriefing and transfer it into the next group session. One could also imagine broadcasting videotapes of CBGT sessions with a wide trainee audience that teleconnects or Skypes from various sites and engages in a large debriefing discussion. With advances in technology, it is easier for therapists in more remote areas to access training and supervision.

Before graduating to a real group, there is the possibility of conducting a mock group. This training approach has been described by Clarke (2010). Mock groups typically consist of several trainees preparing to lead independent groups taking turns being the leader with the remainder trainees role-playing clients in a particular group. In the Clarke example, the trainees role-played depressed adolescents.

The trainee takes on a more active facilitation role after observing one or two groups—and perhaps running a mock group—and reading the CBT manual and any other relevant material assigned by the primary therapist. The trainee often does so as a third therapist in addition to two main cotherapists. The trainee therapist sits around the table and is expected to actively participate but not at the same level as the cotherapists. In the first CBGT session, the therapists carefully explain to the group who the main therapists are and who the trainees are. This frankness is critical so as to avoid any discomfort related to why one therapist barely speaks and seems nervous when they do. When introducing themselves, the trainee therapist will often say something like:

> I have just graduated as a social worker and am new to this program. I'm very excited about the opportunity for group therapy and although I did do one group during my training, it is my first time in a CBT depression group. Although I am mostly learning, I will from time to time take the lead on introducing new material. I may be a bit nervous, but hope you'll forgive me.

CBGT group members tend to react positively to this, and there may be some therapeutic value in how trainees model dealing with their own anxiety.

Ongoing observational learning and supervision

The formal inclusion of the trainee provides ample opportunity for direct supervision and observational learning from more experienced therapists. Unlike individual therapy, where the trainee mostly hears about how well (!) their supervisor would have handled a certain challenge, in group therapy, the trainee gets to directly observe, something that can make even the most seasoned group therapist slightly nervous too. Sometimes, the senior therapist may not be "in the mood" for having a whole group plus one or two trainees hang at their every move and word. Senior group therapists—somewhat jokingly—occasionally express a longing for the private, individual therapy room. And even that can be intense. According to psychiatrist and Freud biographer, Anthony Storr (1989), Freud chose to sit behind his patients, who were on the couch, to facilitate free associations but also because he could not tolerate the self-consciousness he felt from having his patients stare at him hour after hour.

Adequate time needs to be allocated to support the learning needs of the trainee. This usually involves having both a pregroup meeting and a postgroup debriefing. In the pregroup meeting, the two main therapists review the agenda with the trainee, the specific material to be covered, and any expectations and responsibilities from the trainee for a given session. For example, in a depression group, the trainee may be asked to introduce the SMART goal component of the group (reviewed in Chapter 4) and rehearse this with the facilitators before the group starts. The trainee may also be asked to take the lead on the homework go-round and review ways to prevent derailing in a time-consuming way by group members who have trouble limiting their turn to just their homework. The trainee will be reassured the main therapists will jump in whenever needed. It is also helpful to assuage trainees' anxiety about saying the *right* thing when they have their moment in the group. Helpful words to that effect may be something like:

> You need to remind yourself of your basic good skills and clinical instincts; we are confident that nothing you say will be harmful, so just go for it. Even experienced therapists can often think of slightly better ways they could have explained something or offered feedback. That's the good stuff we talk about in our postgroup debriefing.

In the debriefing, the therapists along with the trainee review how the session went. This provides the opportunity to get comfortable with feedback. Feedback is essential for developing skills, and it is naturally also a salient aspect of any group therapy. Group therapists who are uncomfortable with receiving and offering their own feedback will likely have a tough time cofacilitating groups. The senior therapist emphasizes both corrective and confirming feedback and models his or her own ability to reflect on what they thought they handled well and not so well in the session. Scott's *General Group Therapeutic Skills Rating Scale* (Scott, 2011) introduced in Chapter 2 is a helpful tool for this feedback process.

The first item on Scott's rating scale, for example, involves reviewing homework and setting the agenda. The lowest score of 0 would be given if the following description was true: *Therapist did not set an agenda/did not review homework.* The senior therapist may ask the trainee how he or she felt about their presentation of the agenda and their homework go-round management. The trainee may say that he felt he worked well with everyone's homework and especially was able to support two members in solving problems related to their homework. The therapists and the trainee may also agree that they ensured all group members had roughly equivalent airtime. Thus, the therapists and the trainee may give themselves the highest score of 6 in the area referred to as *Review of Homework/Agenda* on

Scott's rating scale. The wording for a score of 6 is as follows: *therapists set an agenda that was suitable for the available time. Established priorities and tracked the agenda. Difficulties with previous session's homework were effectively problem solved.* One therapist may praise his fellow therapist—or trainee—for effectively handling a particular problem in the homework review:

> I liked how you gently redirected Ben and brought him back to the topic.
>
> Or:
>
> I appreciated how you commented on Lara's dosing off, as I had not really noticed, and it gave Lara an opportunity to give Brenda permission to poke her. I don't think she felt scolded by you, and I liked how you just reflected on it being hard for her to stay alert.

Learning from what did not go so well is perhaps the most productive part of the debriefing. This requires a sufficiently healthy cofacilitator dynamic in order to ensure that feedback is not perceived as criticism but rather as an opportunity for mutual learning. If it does not feel safe to offer feedback to one's cotherapists, any steps to remedy this would be beneficial and in the best interests of the group members. It can be difficult to share a concern about one's group therapist colleague. A concern could be about a didactic or process intervention. The following is an example of two group facilitators reviewing a missed opportunity for both of them. Using Scott's rating scale, they realized they could have done better in *Utilising Group Members as Role Models*. In the postgroup discussion after a social anxiety group, one therapist shared this observation about how a particular situation could have been better handled.

THERAPIST, ROSA, SPEAKING TO HER COTHERAPIST: Henry, I liked how you referred to Kim when Hanna spoke about becoming more and more focused on what the woman she was talking to was thinking of her. Hanna said she became convinced that this woman found her "uninformed" and "silly." Just before that Kim had also talked about self-preoccupation in terms of how he thinks others evaluate him. Kim mentioned that he had good success with trying some externalizing behaviors. Remember, Kim said he focused on the slight accent the person had, and the pattern of her shirt. Now, you only spoke about Kim having done well in his social interaction, but you did not point out that it was his externalizing behaviors that helped him. I just wonder if that may not have been important for Hanna to be reminded of. Kim was doing some good role modeling there.

HENRY: I was trying to use Kim as a helpful example of how to deal with social anxiety, but I just sort of blanked a bit and couldn't quite remember exactly what it was Kim did that was so helpful. It's a bit intense trying to not miss anything in this group. I totally see it now. You're right, it was a great example of engaging in some external focus as a way of distracting from one's self-critical thinking.

ROSA: Well, I regret that I didn't jump in, and help you out. That was my blanking, and I apologize. Let's all be reminded to look for opportunities for helpful role modeling whenever we can. This group is doing well in terms of supporting each other. I guess we can only give ourselves a 2 on this item in Scott's rating scale for today's session. Does that make sense to you? Let's pay more attention and do better next week!

On Scott's rating scale, a score of 2 on the *Utilising Group Members as Role Models* is given when *therapist made fleeting reference to the positive behavior of a group member but without making it explicit to what other member that behavior might be particularly relevant*. In the exchange between Rosa and Henry, it makes sense that they agreed to give themselves a lower score in that they failed to fully create the opportunity for Hanna to learn from Kim's use of coping skills when feeling socially anxious. The example also shows how both therapists share in the responsibility of this missed opportunity. When we feel something is not going quite as well as it could, the onus is upon all of the group therapists to attempt to remedy.

Equal Cofacilitation

Although it is hard to put an exact number on how many training groups should be required in order for a therapist to be capable of independent and equal cofacilitation, three to four groups of the same kind are usually necessary. It depends on the nature of the group and the comfort level of the trainee. Once the trainee develops sufficient expertise to be a primary therapist, supervision may occur through observation of video recordings of sessions or, more traditionally, weekly meetings. Once supervision is over, equal cofacilitation is a reality, and what remains is ongoing peer support and consultation.

Equal cofacilitation can be a pleasure. A strong and special relationship usually develops and can be completely independent of what else those two cotherapists may, or may not, share when they are not doing groups together. Doing the same groups with the same cotherapist year after year has many benefits and a few downsides. The benefits involve a high level of comfort with one another and excellent communication. You begin to know what kind of questions are best handled by which one of you, a slight nod passes the ball of communication to your partner, and you gently tease each other while also pointing out which one of you has special knowledge and expertise. Thus, the dynamic between the cotherapists becomes a model for interpersonal comfort, respect, direct communication, support, and humor. At times, it is necessary to respectfully disagree with your cotherapist, which is fine, and clients usually do not have problems with different perspectives on an issue.

An example of a slight difference of opinion could be one cotherapist saying that a diet without meat is healthier for the body and helps to regulate the sleep–wake cycle, which is a common problem in depression. The cotherapist may say that she admires people who can give up steaks and that most people probably could benefit from less meat; however, there is to the best of our knowledge no research support explaining the role of meat in depression.

It goes without saying that you never put down or even make a subtle dig at your cotherapist. You may not think anyone notices, but people do, and those struggling with mental health issues may be especially perceptive and attuned to the nuances of tensions in relationships. If you realize you may have felt some irritation toward your cotherapist, this must be immediately addressed in the postgroup debriefing.

The downsides of cofacilitation with the same person year in and year out are of course mostly about becoming too predictable to one another and possibly a bit stuck in a certain approach and manner. This may be sufficient reason for programs to agree to some form of rotation if feasible. A new person—even with the same level of CBT skills—will invariably bring a different approach and energy to the group. Similar to other roles, such as a university lecturer who has taught the same course in the same way for years, some professional renewal in the form of challenging oneself with the unfamiliar is important in CBGT.

Questions occasionally come up about how much equality is necessary between cotherapists. Specifically, it is not always clear how therapists prefer to be addressed by the group members. Do they want to be called by their first name or their last? Or if they have MD or PhD qualifications, do they want to be addressed as Dr. So-and-so? This latter may be more of an issue when one therapist is a "Dr." and the other not. How may it possibly impact the group climate if one therapist is "Dr. Castle-Smith" and the other is "Bob?" It is hard to know, and I am not aware of any study addressing this issue in the group therapy literature. So, in the absence of guidelines, facilitators are free to do what they prefer, and hopefully be in agreement. The only reason the issue of titles is a potential problem in group therapy is that many clients become more deferential toward "the doctor," which can undermine the strength of cofacilitation and thus the entire group climate.

My personal view is that a large part of what makes groups successful is the inherent assumption of equality, competence, and respect. I thus prefer that group leaders present themselves by profession and suggest they strongly align with their profession. In interdisciplinary teams, which is increasingly the norm, this also helps avoid perceptions that everyone is doing the same thing and are the same kind of therapist. For example, in a depression group with a psychiatrist or a psychiatry trainee, a clinical counselor may say that he is pleased to lead this group with someone who has knowledge about medication. In an OCD group, an occupational therapist may say she is especially skilled in developing creative exposures.

Students in CBGT Training

Students in many ways follow the same training approach as that of a staff member outlined earlier. However, the training needs to be tailored to the length of stay of the student in any CBGT program. If the placement is only 3 months, there may only be an opportunity to observe a group. Also, we decline requests by students who want to "just spend four weeks to get an idea of CBGT." If a student cannot stay for an entire group, we will not offer them the privilege of a training spot. If the student has not already taken courses in the principles of CBT, the onus is on the senior supervisor to offer this didactic knowledge base separate from the group experience. Supervisors will typically follow a review of core CBT competencies similar to the workshop schedule outlined earlier. It is helpful to ask students to do their own CBT homework. That is, ask the student to monitor their own moods and thoughts and do Thought Records and exposures depending on what group they are involved with. Not only does this bring home how helpful self-directed CBT can be for all us, but it also increases empathy for the client position. It does seem odd to be enthusiastic about asking group members to engage with certain tasks if we ourselves have no real feel for the exercise. Similarly, in psychodynamic training, it is common to encourage students to seek their own therapy if for no other good reason than that they develop empathy for what it is like to sit in "the other chair."

Similar to the training of staff clinicians, students should engage in role-play with senior therapists and other forms of rehearsing their delivery of a particular CBGT intervention. Students require evaluations, and many are building their psychotherapy portfolio as part of their training. Evaluation of students in CBGT involves both their grasp of specific CBT skills and ability to implement in a group. It is important to indicate limits of competency by clearly stating on any evaluation what specific disorder(s) the student had supervised exposure to and what they still need supervision with. Or in cases where a student is not seeking to become a CBGT specialist, the supervisor discusses with the student which areas of CBGT they have reasonable competence in and the limits of their competence. Evaluation forms are cosigned by the student and the supervisor so that the record indicates limits to competence. For example, a student may be aware that they can work as an equal cofacilitator with panic disorder clients but would need supervision if they were to be a cotherapist in CBGT for trauma.

How to Stay Competent as a CBGT Therapist

In addition to training, group debriefings, and peer supervision, tremendous opportunities exist for ongoing professional and personal development. Group therapists support each other and aim to improve both the content and process aspects of their groups. A content improvement may involve adding a new intervention that seems to have sufficient support in the literature. One therapist may have taken a workshop on the topic and like to modify the CBGT protocol. For example, a therapist may have completed mindfulness training and want to revise a CBGT protocol for generalized anxiety disorder (GAD) by including this component. Process improvements involve ongoing discussions of questions such as "how do we manage clients who are 'too silent,' or 'too talkative,' who do not complete homework, who may be critical of other members, or who are not likely to benefit from the group?" Process issues also involve ongoing attention to the relationship dynamic between the cotherapists.

CBGT therapists also benefit from connecting with colleagues outside of their local area. Conferences and workshops are excellent ways to stay abreast and fresh in the field of CBGT. But they can be costly. A less expensive option is to form local group therapy practice networks. A national group therapy organization may have local chapters, which can create opportunities to discuss CBGT specifically. It can be helpful for therapists to share CBGT protocols and discuss common issues that come up in CBGT. It is also professionally rewarding to take turns offering more formal presentations on specific groups or issues pertaining to CBGT.

Summary

This chapter grapples with the question of who is qualified to lead CBT groups. Competence in either individual CBT or general group psychotherapy does not imply competence in CBGT. I sketch a commonsense and ethically responsible approach to defining a competent CBGT therapist. Completing a degree and obtaining a certain level of training is one major achievement, but staying engaged with and interested in new CBGT applications and developments is equally important. Initial training—even at the highest level—is no guarantee that a clinician remains a strong and evolving CBGT therapist.

I hope the last part of this book, Part 3, will inspire competent CBGT therapists to appreciate the many opportunities for creative, effective, and socially conscious applications of CBGT.

The following is a list of some of the major organizations in various countries offering information about and training in CBT and group therapy.

Recommended Resources for Clinicians

www.agpa.org	The American Group Psychotherapy Association
www.cgpa.org	The Canadian Group Psychotherapy Association
www.cabct.ca	The Canadian Association of Cognitive and Behavioural Therapies
www.academyofct.org	The Academy of Cognitive Therapy
www.babcp.com	The British Association of Behavioural and Cognitive Therapies
www.abct.org	The American Association for Behavioral and Cognitive Therapies
www.eabct.org	European Association for Behavioural and Cognitive Therapies
www.aacbt.org	The Australian Association for Cognitive Behaviour Therapy
www.cacbt.org	The Chinese Association of Cognitive Behaviour Therapy
www.beckinstitute.org	Beck Institute for Cognitive Behavioral Therapy and Research, Philadelphia, PA
www.octc.co.uk	Oxford Cognitive Therapy Centre, Oxford, UK

References

Clarke, G. (2010). Low intensity targeted group prevention of depression in adolescents and children. In J. Bennett-Levy, D. A. Richards, P. Farrand, H.Christensen, K. M. Griffiths, D. J. Kavanagh, B. Klein, M. A. Lau, J. Proudfoot, L. Ritterband, J. White, & C. Williams (Eds.), *Oxford guide to low intensity CBT interventions*. Oxford, UK: Oxford University Press.

Newman, F. C. (2013). *Core competencies in cognitive-behavioral therapy: Becoming a highly effective and competent cognitive behavioral therapist*. London: Routledge.

Scott, M. J. (2011). *Simply effective group cognitive behaviour therapy: A practitioner's guide*. London: Routledge.

Storr, A. (1989). *Freud: A very short introduction*. Oxford, UK: Oxford University Press.

Part 3

Cognitive Behavioral Group Therapy Across Ages and Populations

When cognitive behavioral therapy (CBT) and cognitive behavioral group therapy (CBGT) were first developed, their target populations were similar to those for other forms of psychotherapy: adults who spoke English within a Western cultural tradition with its emphasis on the individual's well-being, separate from their family, interpersonal, and socioeconomic context. The research participants informing CBT treatment protocols tended to be White, middle-class adults, as well as undergraduate students. However, CBT, and especially CBGT, continue to evolve. Encouraging attempts are well underway to consider the larger contexts of clients receiving CBT or CBGT such as family, stage-of-life, culture, and socioeconomic status. Part 3 will focus on how CBGT lends itself to emerging mental health care priorities beyond its initial scope.

First, Chapters 11–13 will show how CBGT can be expanded from the traditional age range of 19–65 to successfully include older adults, children, and adolescents. Chapter 14 starts a discussion of how to offer CBGT for cultural and language minorities. With increased immigration into English-speaking countries, any adaptation of CBGT to meet the language and cultural needs of newcomers will reduce the mental health burden for individuals and societies. This is also the case for immigrants to countries where CBT protocols have already been translated, such as the Netherlands, but where cultural adaptations may still be needed. Lastly, Chapters 15–17 review how CBGT has been further diversified to also benefit society's most vulnerable and marginal members, who face significant challenges in daily functioning. This section will cover the struggles of people with compulsive hoarding in accessing and benefiting from CBGT, and of people with addictions and psychosis. Specific CBGT interventions will be presented, along with the latest evidence informing these topics.

Cognitive Behavioral Group Therapy: Challenges and Opportunities, First Edition. Ingrid Söchting.

11

Later Life Depression and Anxiety

This chapter resumes the discussion in Chapter 7 on the viability of transdiagnostic groups. It does so by outlining how depression and anxiety often coexist in elderly people. It will become apparent why it makes sense to offer a CBGT approach for both of these mental health problems and why, for elderly people, a group format is preferable to individual CBT.

Depression and Anxiety in the Elderly

Depression and anxiety are common mental health problems among older adults—with prevalence from 6–9% for severe depression and 17–37% for milder (Seritan, McCloud, & Hinton, 2009) and 10–15% for anxiety disorders (Hendriks, Oude Voshaar, Keijsers, Hoogduin, & van Balkom, 2008). For all age groups, depression and anxiety often coexist, but this is especially the case among the elderly (Ames & Allen, 1991; Blazer 1997, 2002; Hinrichsen & Emery, 2005). Not only are rates of comorbidity higher than previously thought, but rates of suicide from untreated depression are also surprisingly high and increase steadily with age for both men and women. Critical risk factors for suicide include, among others, being male, elderly, and socially isolated (Seritan et al., 2009).

Symptoms of depression[1] (e.g., disturbance in sleep patterns, poor appetite, poor concentration, feelings of guilt, ruminating about the past, and lack of joy) and anxiety (e.g., increased heart rate, chest tightness, racing thoughts, excessive worry about ordinary things or matters beyond one's control) are similar across the age

Cognitive Behavioral Group Therapy: Challenges and Opportunities, First Edition. Ingrid Söchting.

spectrum. However, they are often overlooked or misdiagnosed in older adults. This may have to do with older adults being less likely to show emotional symptoms and more likely to present with bodily symptoms (Fiske, Wetherell, & Gatz, 2009; Seritan et al., 2009). The DSM-5 option of diagnosing major depressive disorder (MDD) with a specifier of *with anxious distress* (American Psychiatric Association, 2013) seems fitting for many people in the CBGT program described in the following text.

There are understandable reasons why older people may be reluctant to admit to depression and a need for help. Some have survived substantial economic hardship, wars, and immigration and view mental health issues as signs of moral or personal weakness or even character flaws. Others have simply not developed an attunement to their emotional lives, growing up in times and places where communication about such matters was not encouraged. Also, many older people themselves succumb to ageism and beliefs such as "depression is an expected part of growing older" (Laidlaw, 2010).

Clinicians working with older adults suggest that attending to certain issues specific to depression and anxiety in later life may be more useful for detecting psychological distress than simply reviewing symptoms (Laidlaw, 2010; Munk, 2010). Such issues include conflicts with adult children; a number of losses including of physical abilities, productivity, status, spouse, and close friends; substance or prescription drug misuse; meaning-of-life crises (including questioning whether one's life was worthwhile); and, ultimately, unresolved fear of death. Typical CBT protocols for depression and anxiety must be adapted to address these unique stage-of-life issues.

Psychotherapy for the Elderly

Until recently, psychotherapy for the elderly has not been easy to access. This is the case despite elderly people perceiving psychotherapy as an attractive treatment—without the side effects that medication often produces (Hanson & Scogin, 2008; Kuruvilla, Fenwick, Haque, & Vassilas, 2006). Elderly people's responses to antidepressant medication may further be impaired by comorbid anxiety, thus pointing to the need for alternatives to pharmacotherapy (Greenlee et al., 2010). Although the problem in accessing appropriate treatment, in part, has to do with issues such as difficulty detecting psychological distress, the tradition of psychotherapy itself may until recently not have placed much value on "talking therapy" for older people. For instance, Freud was pessimistic about the prospects of elderly patients benefiting from therapy, saying, "Near or above the age of 50 the elasticity of mental processes, on which the treatment depends is as a rule lacking—old people are no longer educable" (Freud, 1905/1957). Such an attitude likely influenced generations of psychiatrists and psychotherapists. Yet, while few clinicians today are likely to agree with Freud's opinion, professionals and laypersons alike—including elderly people themselves—do unfortunately buy into ageist myths, such as "older adults are not capable of learning new information due to limited brain plasticity."

In contrast to these beliefs, there is growing evidence that psychotherapy can greatly benefit elderly people struggling with depression and anxiety. Most of the research has focused on single-disorder therapy with an individual format. Within this context, two major psychotherapy approaches, CBT and interpersonal therapy (IPT), have been evaluated for individual treatment for either depression or anxiety (IPT, Carreira et al., 2008; Hinrichsen, 2008; Hinrichsen & Emery, 2005; CBT, Laidlaw, Thompson, Dick-Siskin, & Gallagher-Thompson, 2003; Laidlaw et al. 2008). CBT has received most research attention, with evidence suggesting it is a promising approach with elderly patients suffering from depression (Mackin & Arean, 2005; Morris & Morris, 1991) or anxiety, especially generalized anxiety disorder (GAD) (Ayers, Sorrell, Thorp, & Wetherell, 2007; Hendriks et al., 2008; Laidlaw et al., 2003; Wetherell et al., 2009).

Group therapy

Group therapy for older adults has been available for a few decades in a variety of forms, including activity focused, reminiscence and life review, and cognitive behavioral. As studies on group therapy for older adults continue to grow, we may well see stronger support for groups in treating elderly people with depression and anxiety (Kennedy & Tanenbaum, 2000; Mohlman, 2004).

Considering that social isolation is a significant risk factor for onset and maintenance of depression in elderly people compared to other age groups, a group format has for decades been suggested as inherently more therapeutic (Sherbourne, Hays, & Wells, 1985). According to Leszcz (1997), it is not just the provision of social support provided by the group that is beneficial but also the opportunities to acquire and develop interpersonal skills. These skills can then be used to generate and sustain more successful social integration as a buffer against depression relapse.

For elderly people with mild depression, a CBGT program consisting of eight weekly 2-hour sessions yielded promising results. Compared to a control group, the CBT group (10 clients) showed a significantly greater reduction of depressive symptoms and greater improvement of functional impairment (Hsu et al., 2010). A recent meta-analysis of CBGT for depression in the elderly based on six qualifying trials found an overall significant effect although this effect was "at best modest," suggesting that there is room for improvement in order to make CBGT for the elderly even more effective (Krishna et al., 2010).

With regard to treating anxiety among older adults, Radley and colleagues studied an 8-week CBGT program that was offered to six elderly females in the form of psychoeducation and self-help skills training. Follow-up booster sessions were held at 4 and 12 weeks. Results showed a significant drop in anxiety symptoms, with the greatest change for cognitive symptoms, for example, the interpretation of body sensations as less dangerous (Radley, Redston, Bates, Pontefract, & Lindesay, 1997). There does not seem to be any meta-analysis on group therapy for anxiety in the elderly.

CBGT for the elderly

Although sparse, the literature encouragingly suggests that CBGT can successfully be offered to people over age 65 and with no upper limit. Any community outpatient program should thus be able to adapt a traditional CBT protocol to an elderly population. The following criteria are typically used for evaluating whether a person aged 65 and above (our oldest member was 91) may be appropriate for CBGT. It is preferable that clients meet criteria for either a depression or anxiety disorder, or both, as determined by the intake assessment and that they have only mild cognitive impairment, if any, and no substance abuse that will interfere with group attendance and homework. Further criteria for admission include an ability to set goals for treatment and an ability to commit to regular and timely attendance. During the intake assessment, it is also important to distinguish normal grief from depression. Clients are often referred for treatment after the loss of a spouse. The distinction between normal grief and depression helps clinicians to avoid pathologizing grief. Grief can be explained to the client as involving a broken heart but an intact mind, including an absence of the kind of self-denigrating thinking usually seen in depression and anxiety. In the groups I am involved with, we do not exclude people with grief only, especially not if clinical judgment indicates that the person may be at risk for their grief morphing into clinical depression. This could be the case if the bereaved has poor social support, difficulty engaging with enjoyable activities, a tendency to feel helpless and hopeless, or a proclivity to ruminate about the deceased in an angry or self-blaming way.

The demographics from our CBGT for the elderly over the past several years show that 65% are women and the average age is 70 (Söchting, O'Neal, Third, Rogers, & Ogrodniczuk, 2013). The higher number of men in these groups, 35%, is encouraging and in contrast to our CBGT for depression in younger adults, where the men comprise at best only 20% of any group. In the elderly groups, the level of education tends to be high, with over 88% having completed high school. About 40% are married, 22% divorced, and 30% a widow or widower. Most are Caucasians (85%) but other ethnic groups include Asian, East Indian, people from the Middle East, African, and Hispanic. About 60% of people who successfully complete this CBGT program have had previous psychiatric treatment, 20% have experienced psychiatric hospitalization, and 9% present with passive suicidal thoughts. These elderly people who successfully complete CBGT thus have fairly significant mental health issues. Considering that many continue to have decades ahead of them, any investment in skills for managing their anxiety, depression, health issues, and social isolation is highly worthwhile.

CBGT Protocol for the Elderly

The *Changeways Geriatric Participant Manual* is an example of a CBT protocol for both depression and anxiety that has been adapted by several community programs for CBGT in the elderly (Geriatric Psychiatry Outreach Team, 2004; Paterson, McLean, Alden, & Koch, 1996). The *Changeways Geriatric Participant Manual* is especially well suited for people who are primarily depressed and whose secondary symptoms are along the lines of generalized and social anxiety. If an elderly person has a primary panic disorder with frequent, uncontrollable panic attacks and no significant symptoms of depression, a pure panic disorder protocol would be the responsible treatment and not the protocol described in the following text. The geriatric CBGT protocol is highly structured and covers specific session-by-session material. They include goal setting, understanding the nature of stress, the role of one's social life, introduction to assertiveness, worry control, and identifying and overcoming distorted thinking and faulty assumptions, such as "I'm worthwhile only so long as I'm doing something for someone else" or "I can change people." Final sessions include education about planning for the future and how to deal with minor (and major) setbacks in symptom recurrence. Our CBGT program further adapted the Changeways protocol by inviting professional guest speakers on topics relevant to older adults, such as nutrition (dietician), medication (pharmacist), and spiritual/religious (hospital chaplain). Other topics such as falls prevention, exercise and leisure, and chronic disease management are addressed by offering clients information about community resources. Goal setting and homework are assigned in each session. All sessions begin with a go-round, where group members take turns reporting on how their week was and how they did with their homework. CBGT for the elderly typically involves 12–14 weekly group sessions each lasting 2 hours. The following outline shows common session themes for CBGT for the elderly in a 13-session group.

Session Themes in Later Life CBGT (Adapted from Paterson et al., 1996)
Session 1: Introduction to Cognitive Behavioral Therapy and the Relationship between Thought, Feelings, Behaviors, *and Health*
Session 2: Transforming Problems into Goals
Session 3: Setting Attainable Goals
Session 4: The Role of Leisure
Session 5: Thinking about Thinking: Part 1—Catch It!
Session 6: Thinking about Thinking: Part 2—Check It! This module also includes information on Managing Worries.
Session 7: Thinking about Thinking: Part 3—Change It! Managing Worries
Session 8: The Role of Your Social Life
Session 9: Introduction to Assertiveness
Session 10: The Sustaining Lifestyle
Session 11: Guest Speaker
Session 12: Guest Speaker
Session 13: Review, Relapse Prevention, and the Road Ahead

The major treatment components in this geriatric protocol are reviewed in the following text.

Psychoeducation in CBGT for the elderly

As highlighted in italics above, CBGT for the elderly has the option of expanding the three-part model of CBT to include physical health. Facilitators may introduce this expanded CBT model by saying (Figure 11.1):

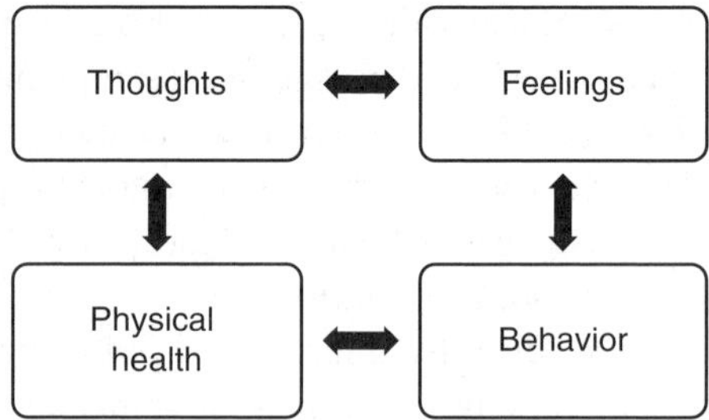

Figure 11.1 Interconnection between thoughts, feelings, behavior, and physical health.

> Thoughts, emotions, physical health and behavior are powerfully connected to one another. In fact, we can picture our personal lives as a square. The four sides of the square represent four aspects of our lives. The sides of the square are connected. These connections are critical factors in personal change.

This square is illustrated with the following example from the *Changeways Geriatric Participant Manual* (Geriatric Psychiatry Outreach Team, 2004):

> Doris is a 66-year-old, retired woman who has weekend plans to go shopping with a friend. Unfortunately, she wakes up feeling ill on Saturday morning (*physical health*) and isn't able to go shopping (*behaviour*). She thinks: "My friend will think that I really don't want to go shopping. She'll never invite me to go shopping again (*thought*). This belief raises her anxiety (*emotion*) as well as her frustration about not feeling up to par. This makes it even harder for Doris to figure out how to face the day, and consequently, she stays in bed (*behaviour*), which in turn only serves to raise her anxiety *(emotions)* and strengthens her negative thoughts about her friend's reaction (pp. 12–21).

Goal setting in CBGT for the elderly

The two goal-setting modules start with group members first writing a problem list, from which they then pick just one problem at a time for turning into a goal. For example, 81-year-old Heather's problem list was the following:

Family: Every day I feel sad and miss my husband who died last year
Friends: I say no to friends who invite me out because I don't feel I have the energy
Health: I have just been diagnosed with Parkinson's Disease
Lifestyle: I often don't leave my home for 3 days; I have stopped playing bridge at the seniors' center, and I skip meals because I don't feel hungry
Finances: I have not seen my financial planner since my husband died. I am afraid my daughter will find out that I give my son money for his rent every month

Within the framework of picking one problem at a time and breaking it down to manageable chunks, Heather decided to start her goals with calling a friend from whom for months she had refused phone calls. Other later goals included *having a conversation with my son about money* and *contact the local Parkinson's Disease Support Group.*

The module on the *Role of Leisure* expands on goal setting by first offering education on the importance of making time for enjoyable and fun activities. The facilitators explain that when we have mood problems, our energy reserves are low. Removing things we normally enjoy can feel like a way of conserving energy for more important tasks, but giving up enjoyable activities actually reduces energy in the long run. What would happen if we asked someone who is not depressed to do as little as many depressed individuals do—to have few social contacts, to get out rarely, and to give up many pleasant activities. This person would likely begin to show signs of depression! Michael, age 75, found this resonated with him:

> I used to think that if I was struggling, straining and sweating I must be doing the right thing, and that anything easy, fun, or just leisure was 'shallow' and not worthwhile. When I look back on it I think this idea was guaranteed to make my life miserable. Now I make sure I include fun as part of my life. (Geriatric Psychiatry Outreach Team, 2004, p. 47)

Challenging unhelpful thinking in CBGT for the elderly

The *Thinking about Thinking* modules follow a modified Thought Record. The 7-column Thought Record was illustrated in Chapter 5. The modified approach involves a 4-column Thought Record, which if often preferred by clinicians dealing with older people. Although older people can manage working with seven columns, this comprehensive approach does require sustained focus and attention for quite some time. Sustaining concentration can be a challenge in this group in which fatigue due to medication and physical health complications is more present compared to groups of younger adults. Another reason for choosing a shorter record has to do with its better applicability to both depressive and anxious thoughts. The usefulness of a 4-column Thought Record for groups where problems with depression and anxiety are combined is illustrated in two examples.

Alice, a primarily depressed 78-year-old woman, wrote this answer in column 1 to the question *Where and When Were You?* "I was waiting in a restaurant for Shirley and she did not show." In column 2, she answered "sad and rejected" to the question *What Was I Feeling?* In response to the third column, which asks the question, *What Was I thinking*? Alice wrote, "Shirley didn't want to spend time with me. She doesn't like me. No one likes me. I'll always be alone." Lastly, the fourth column challenges clients to determine if their thinking may contain *Thinking Errors*, such as *jumping to conclusions, personalization*, or *catastrophizing* (Appendix F offers a handout of common Biases in Thinking for depression and anxiety). With support from the group, Alice came to see that she was indeed jumping to the conclusion that Shirley did not like her, without putting any effort into "checking the facts." It turned out that the facts offered a whole other interpretation. Shirley had waited for Alice in a different restaurant, where she and Alice usually meet, and had completely forgotten that Alice suggested they try to mix up their routine by trying a new place. The group chuckled at how we can learn from younger people in terms of getting comfortable with cell phones.

Bruce, an 81-year-old divorced man with GAD and occasional panic attacks, worked on an episode in which, after 2 weeks of intense worrying, he had cancelled an invitation to his daughter's choir performance. In column 1, he wrote: "I was at home calling my ex-wife saying I was not well enough to attend, and that she should not come and pick me up." As to the question *What was I Feeling?* Bruce wrote "anxious and pathetic." In terms of what he was thinking, he wrote: "What if I feel some shortness of breath, become dizzy? What if I start to panic? It will be too embarrassing to get up from my seat with everyone noticing that I'm leaving." With help from the group, Bruce realized he was doing a lot of *catastrophizing* with all the "what ifs." He became able to decatastrophize and began to prepare himself for not cancelling when the next opportunity to attend a social function with his daughter came up. He became able to counter his anxious anticipation with adaptive statements like "So what if I get anxious? It's no big deal to get up and step outside for a few minutes to do some deep breathing. So what if people notice I look anxious? The main thing is that I'm there for my daughter and not what other people may think."

The *Role of Your Social Life* module helps clients make an inventory of close friends, intimates, other friends, acquaintances, and familiar faces. Group members may discover that they have no close friends with whom they feel they can share their vulnerability but have many acquaintances; or they may realize that their main social support revolves around only one person. Suggestions for ways to broaden or deepening friendships are presented and discussed.

The *Sustaining Lifestyle* module helps clients evaluate how they spend their time and energy and take care of their bodies and minds. A number of topics are included ranging from diet, sleep, alcohol, prescription medication, sexuality, and spirituality. Guest speakers such as a pastoral counselor, dietician, or pharmacist can offer helpful presentations that stimulate group discussions.

Capitalizing on the Group for the Elderly

The following case shows a common client presentation in CBGT for the elderly and how the group format offers unique opportunities for therapeutic gains.

John is an 80-year-old retired business man whose spouse of 52 years passed away 1 year earlier. His diagnoses include MDD and GAD. A World War II veteran, he spent his adult life as a sales executive with several large corporations before retiring at age 70. John is becoming increasingly socially withdrawn to the point of avoiding family functions. His somatic complaints are accumulating and now include weight loss and difficulty sleeping. Despite his adult children's encouragement, he refuses to accept help with meals and other daily activities. He is preoccupied with the loss of his wife and has abandoned his former social and leisure activities, including reading, watching the History Channel, and walking. John admits to an increase in worries about smaller issues, for example, paying bills on time, as well as larger issues related to his difficulty with daily functioning and increased loneliness.

In the group, members encouraged John to set goals related to meeting people who shared his interests. He did begin to meet regularly over coffee with a man from his neighborhood after they had attended the same European history lecture at the local library. From the *Role of Your Social Life* module, John realized he no longer had friends he considered close. Initially, in the group, he was reluctant to speak to "strangers" and held some beliefs about how talking about it would only make his pain worse. Over the first 5 weeks of the program, a shift began and he came to see that sharing personal information about his wife actually made him feel closer to others in the group and better about himself and his ability to cope. The following dialogue illustrates how John began to realize that, despite missing the company of his wife, he needed and wanted to work on getting closer with others.

THERAPIST: Let's complete the work on your Thought Record, John. It's an interesting example because it's actually about our here and now group. So far you have noted that your situation was [therapist writes on the board]: "I was in my therapy group and there was pressure on me to talk." What were your feelings?

JOHN: Irritated and angry—especially with you therapists!

THERAPIST: OK, got that. What was going through your mind as you are sitting in this group feeling pressure to talk and becoming angrier?

JOHN: I was thinking that it does not help to talk about my loneliness, it only makes it worse. If I start talking about it, I will become unable to cope with this group and also feel worse when I'm home by myself.

COTHERAPIST: That's a powerful belief, and we understand your reluctance to tell us more about your wife and what you miss about her. Now, based on the Thinking Errors we talked about—and they are listed in your handout—is there a possibility that you may be giving into one of those errors?

JOHN: Not sure.

COTHERAPIST: Would you be OK with the group offering some help? You know how it can sometimes be easier for others than ourselves to identify these errors.

JOHN: Sure.

AUGUST: John, it seems to me that you anticipate that things will turn out badly if you talk about your wife, and you're pretty sure your prediction is accurate. I used to also think that talking about my own pain from losing my daughter to cancer would make it worse, and make me seem weak to others.

SHELLEY: I too for the longest time was sure that talking about my problems with my son would not make a difference; in fact I was quite convinced talking about him would make it worse.

JOHN: Well you two seem to understand where I'm coming from. I'm been thinking about other things people in here have said. It sort of makes sense. I'm willing to tell you all more about my wife. Would it be OK if I brought some photos of our last trip together?

DAVID: It seems to me that the *Fortune-Teller Error* sort of applies to many of us.

JOHN: Is that listed on one of the handouts we have? I'll go home and study it!

THERAPIST: Yes, John, you may find it helpful to review the sheet in your folder on Biases in Thinking. We look forward to hearing more about your wife during the first go-round in our next group.

The *Fortune-Teller* Error can also be referred to as the *Unjustified Negative Prediction* Error (Free, 2007). John was able to see that he had been mistaken about his beliefs related to how much to share. He became increasingly comfortable and connected to the other group members, and in the last group he offered the following thanks:

> Just coming here and meeting all you folks has made such a difference. I've learned a lot about the importance of not falling into self-pity, and instead staying active and reaching out to people. When my GP first mentioned this program, I wondered if he had lost his mind: me in group therapy sitting around in a circle talking about my feelings! He worked on me for eight months before I agreed to the referral. This group has really been helpful [wipes eyes with a Kleenex].

Common Challenges in Later Life CBGT

Although later life CBGT follows the same basic format as that for other kinds of CBGT in terms of assessment, pregroup orientation, outcome measures, and ground rules, there are issues unique to the later life group which therapists need to take into account.

Decline in all senses is an expected part of aging and needs to be highlighted. Handouts should have larger fonts, and everyone in the group should be reminded to talk louder than they usually do as there is invariably at least one group member who has trouble hearing. Therapists may need to encourage people to say "louder please" or make a motion with their hands. It is not uncommon for a group member to say toward the end of a group session that they did not follow, or get much of, what took place. This is a problem and needs to be prevented as much as possible. The group room also needs to be accessible to walkers or wheelchairs.

Contrary to what some clinicians new to CBGT for the elderly tend to think, homework and the more didactic focus of CBGT for the elderly tend to be well received. Many older people grew up at a time, and in environments, where emotional expressions were discouraged. They find that the CBGT approach feels a bit safer as they realize the focus is on didactic instructions and less on emotional expressions. CBGT offers an implied respect for previous coping mechanisms that could be considered more "strong-mind focused," as opposed to "whining and complaining." Elderly people, who have coped with significant challenges during their lives, are often fearful of being seen as "complainers." Over time, they begin to see that emotional expressions do not equate with weaker character. Many also value the satisfaction of a sense of returning to school as they realize they are able to understand the presented material, successfully complete homework, and achieve their goals. Occasionally, elderly people have strong negative reactions to CBGT, finding it demeaning to be treated like a child and fearing they will be scolded for not doing their homework. This is especially the case if they were part of a generation that endured corporal punishment. The therapists encourage group members to voice their resistance to homework and discuss an alternate way to think about it (Chapter 9 addresses this not uncommon issue in more detail).

As was apparent in the clinical examples, grief, social isolation, and conflict with adult children are recurring themes among the elderly. We saw that in the case of Heather, who felt guilty about giving one child more money than the other and afraid of addressing this with her children. Similarly, another man was supported by the group to challenge his beliefs about "helping" his drug addicted son by continuing to pay off the son's debts.

As group leaders working with seniors, we have encountered many variations on these themes, including guilt related to decades-old marital affairs or to having initiated a divorce. Regret also arises over not having divorced, or to not having accepted a career opportunity. As for the theme of grief, every group has included at least two members with recent loss of spouse. Sometimes, people lose a spouse during the group, or a group member dies.

Role transitions invariably figure prominently in our groups. Retirement often seems to be followed by becoming a full-time caregiver for a spouse. Men especially seem to find it challenging to spend most of their time attending to domestic chores. These same men are also reluctant to ask for outside help in form of government-supported respite, but they often respond well to gentle pressure from the group to get such help. Role transitions involve a sense of loss, including of former professional or socioeconomic status. In addition, we increasingly see group members who have lost significant amounts of retirement savings and worry about their financial security. Other losses include physical health and subsequent implications for gross or minor motor skills or vision and hearing (e.g., doing less cycling, struggling with reading, playing piano, or knitting). Fears about dying are also addressed. Several group members have thanked the group for helping them to set goals to get their personal affairs and wills organized.

CBGT offers many opportunities for supporting older adults in challenging their thinking and behavior about these issues, while also working actively with the group in terms of support, role modeling, and universality, to name just a few. However, just as CBGT for perinatal depression, which was discussed in Chapter 8, can benefit from a formal inclusion of an IPT approach, so can CBGT for later life depression and anxiety be enhanced by an explicit interpersonal focus. One such augmentation involves adding a parallel IPT group in addition to the CBGT one. With this augmentation, older adults get a total of 3 hours of group therapy—half CBT and half IPT—over a 16-week period (Söchting et al., 2013).

Summary

This chapter reviews a CBGT protocol, that can be considered transdiagnostic in that it targets symptoms of depression and anxiety in the elderly. The chapter offers examples of how group therapists present psychoeducation, goal setting, and cognitive restructuring for this population. It also shows how to actively work with the group process. As the percentage of people over age 65 continues to increase in many populations, so will the demand for treatment for depression and anxiety in otherwise physically well older adults. In Canada, this percentage was 14.5% in 2011 but it is projected to be 18.5% in 2021 and 24% in 2041 (Statistics Canada, 2011). The demand for psychotherapy targeting both symptoms and stage-of-life issues, coupled with the increased risk of social isolation after retirement, makes CBGT an attractive option for seniors. Any community mental health program ought to consider including CBGT for the elderly.

The next two chapters turn to the other end of the age spectrum to review developments in CBGT for children and adolescents.

Note

1. Symptoms of the major mood and anxiety disorders were described in previous chapters.

Recommended Readings for Clinicians

Geriatric Psychiatry Outreach Team. (2004). *The Changeways participant manual*. Vancouver, Canada: Vancouver Coastal Health.

Laidlaw, K. (2010) Are attitudes to ageing and wisdom enhancement legitimate targets for CBT for late life depression and anxiety? *Nordic Psychology, 62*, 27–42.

Laidlaw, K., Davidson, K., Toner, H., Jackson, G., Clark, S., Law, J., et al. (2008). A randomized controlled trial of cognitive behaviour therapy vs treatment as usual in the treatment of mild to moderate late life depression. *International Journal of Geriatric Psychiatry, 23(8)*, 843–850.

Laidlaw, K., & McAlpine, S. (2008). Cognitive behaviour therapy: How is it different with older people? *Journal of Rational-Emotive & Cognitive Behavior Therapy, 26(4)*, 250–262.

Laidlaw, K., Thompson, L. W., Dick-Siskin, L., & Gallagher-Thompson, D. (2003). *Cognitive behaviour therapy with older people*. New York: John Wiley & Sons.

Leszcz, M. (1997). Integrated group psychotherapy for the treatment of depression in the elderly. *Group, 21(2)*, 89–113.

Paterson, R. J., McLean, P. D., Alden, L. E., & Koch, W. J. (1996). *The changeways programme*. Vancouver, Canada: Vancouver Hospital and Health Sciences Centre -UBC Pavilions. Retrieved from www.changeways.com [accessed on February 25, 2014].

References

American Psychiatric Association. (2013). *Diagnostic and statistical manual of mental disorders, DSM* (5th ed.). Washington, DC: Author.

Ames, D., & Allen, N. (1991). The prognosis of depression in old age: Good, bad or indifferent? *International Journal of Geriatric Psychiatry, 6(7)*, 477–481.

Ayers, C. R., Sorrell, J. T., Thorp, S. R., & Wetherell, J. L. (2007). Evidence-based psychological treatments for late-life anxiety, *Psychology and Aging, 22(1)*, 8–17.

Blazer, D. G. (1997). Generalized anxiety disorder and panic disorder in the elderly: A review. *Harvard Review of Psychiatry, 5(1)*, 18–27.

Blazer, D. G. (2002). *Depression in late life* (3rd ed.). New York: Springer.

Carreira, K., Miller, M. D., Frank, E., Houck, P. R., Morse, J. Q., Dew, M. A., et al. (2008). A controlled evaluation of monthly maintenance interpersonal psychotherapy in late-life depression with varying levels of cognitive function. *International Journal of Geriatric Psychiatry, 23(11)*, 1110–1113.

Fiske, A., Wetherell, J. L., & Gatz, M. (2009). Depression in older adults. *Annual Review of Clinical Psychology, 5*, 363–389.

Free, M. L. (2007). *Cognitive therapy in groups: Guidelines and resources for practice* (2nd ed.). West Sussex, UK: John Wiley & Sons.

Freud, S. (1957). *On psychotherapy*. In J. Strachey (Ed. & Trans.), *The standard edition of the complete psychological works of Sigmund Freud* (Vol. 7, pp. 257–68). London: Hogarth Press (Original work published 1905).

Greenlee, A., Karp, J. F., Dew, M. A., Houck, P., Andreescu, C., & Reynolds, C. F., III (2010). Anxiety impairs depression remission in partial responders during extended treatment in late-life, *Depression and Anxiety, 27*, 451–456.

Hanson, A. E., & Scogin, F. (2008). Older adults' acceptance of psychological, pharmacological, and combination treatments for geriatric depression. *Journal of Gerontology Series B: Psychological Sciences and Social Sciences, 63(4)*, 245–248.

Hendriks, G. J., Oude Voshaar, R. C., Keijsers, G. P. J., Hoogduin, C. A. L., & van Balkom, A. J. L. M. (2008). Cognitive-behavioural therapy for later-life anxiety disorders: A systematic review and meta-analyses, *Acta Psychiatrica Scandinavia, 117*, 403–411.

Hinrichsen, G. A. (2008). Interpersonal psychotherapy as a treatment for depression in later life. *Professional Psychology: Research and Practice, 39(3)*, 306–312.

Hinrichsen, G. A., & Emery, E. E. (2005). Interpersonal factors in late-life depression. *Clinical Psychology: Science and Practice, 12(3)*, 264–274.

Hsu, C. T., Weng, C. Y., Kuo, C. S., Lin, C. L., Jong, M. C., Kuo, S. Y., et al. (2010). Effects of a cognitive-behavioral group program for community-dwelling elderly with minor depression. *International Journal of Geriatric Psychiatry, 25(6)*, 654–655.

Kennedy, G. J., & Tanenbaum, S. (2000). Psychotherapy with older adults. *American Journal of Psychotherapy, 54(3)*, 386–407.

Krishna, M., Jauhari, A., Lepping, P., Turner, J., Crossley, D., & Krishnamoorthy, A. (2010). Is group psychotherapy effective in older adults with depression? A systematic review. *International Journal of Geriatric Psychiatry, 26*, 331–340.

Kuruvilla, T., Fenwick, C. D., Haque, M. S., & Vassilas, C. A. (2006). Elderly depressed patients: What are their views on treatment options? *Aging and Mental Health, 10(2)*, 204–206.

Mackin, R. S., & Arean, P. A. (2005). Evidence-based psychotherapeutic interventions for geriatric depression. *Psychiatric Clinics of North America, 28*, 805–820.

Mohlman, J. (2004). Psychosocial treatment of late-life Generalized Anxiety Disorder: Current status and future directions. *Clinical Psychology Review, 24(2)*, 149–169.

Morris, R. G., & Morris, L. W. (1991). Cognitive and behavioural approaches with the depressed elderly. *International Journal of Geriatric Psychiatry, 6(6)*, 407–413.

Munk, K. P. (2010). New aspects of late life depression. *Nordic Psychology, 62(2)*, 1–6.

Radley, M., Redston, C., Bates, F., Pontefract, M., & Lindesay, J. (1997). Effectiveness of group anxiety management with elderly clients of a community Psychogeriatric team. *International Journal of Geriatric Psychiatry, 12(1)*, 79–84.

Seritan, A. L., McCloud, M. K., & Hinton, L. (2009). Geriatric depression: Review for primary care. *Current Psychiatry Reviews, 5*, 37–142.

Sherbourne, C. D., Hays, R. D., & Wells, K. B. (1985). Personal and psychosocial risk factors for physical and mental health outcomes on course of depression among depressed patients. *Journal of Consulting and Clinical Psychology, 63(3)*, 345–355.

Söchting, I., O'Neal, E., Third, B., Rogers, J., & Ogrodniczuk, J. S. (2013). An integrative group therapy model for depression and anxiety in later life. *International Journal of Group Psychotherapy, 63(4)*, 503–523.

Statistics Canada. (2011). *Human Resources and Skills Development Canada (HRSDC) calculations.* Ottawa, Canada: Employment and Social Development Canada. Retrieved March 5, 2012, from www.statcan.gc.ca/cansim [accessed on February 25, 2014].

Wetherell, J. L., Ayers, C. R., Sorrell, J. T., Thorp, S. R., Nuevo, R., Belding, W., et al. (2009). Modular psychotherapy for anxiety in older primary care patients, *American Journal of Geriatric Psychiatry, 17(6)*, 483–492.

12

Youth with Anxiety and Depression

CBT is the treatment of choice for a range of disorders and problems in childhood. The focus on self-rewards (positive reinforcement), goal setting, behavioral modification, and skills training makes CBT a natural intervention for children. Although most parents turn into amateur CBT therapists as we try to encourage and shape positive behaviors in our children and extinguish negative ones (classic behavioral therapy terms), professional help is often still needed. Age seven is generally considered an appropriate age for starting CBT, but some children less than seven can benefit from some aspects of CBT.

This chapter and the following, Chapter 13, present examples of several successful CBGT approaches to treating and supporting anxious and depressed children and adolescents. Challenges in successful implementation of CBGT include the role of parents and the degree to which different disorders and different ages can be mixed into the same group. For younger children, it seems obvious that the parents become a key part of treating children given children's dependency on their parents and home environment. However, for older children, the role of peers may be more important than that of parents. A group format may therefore be especially helpful for children ages 12 and above.

Anxiety and Depression in Children and Adolescents

Childhood anxiety disorders are common, with estimates that about 10% of school-age children suffer from one or more (Reynolds, Wilson, Austin, & Hooper, 2012). The most frequent types of anxiety in children include social

Cognitive Behavioral Group Therapy: Challenges and Opportunities, First Edition. Ingrid Söchting.

anxiety, generalized anxiety disorder (GAD), panic disorders, obsessive–compulsive disorder (OCD), and separation anxiety. All of these disorders are described elsewhere in this book (Chapters 1, 7, 8, and 13), except for separation anxiety.

Separation Anxiety Disorder is now listed under *Anxiety Disorders* in the DSM-5 (APA, 2013).[1] According to the DSM-5, separation anxiety disorder involves at least three of the following eight symptoms: recurrent excessive distress when anticipating or experiencing separation from home or major attachment figures, worry about losing attachment figures or about possible harm to them, worry about experiencing an untoward event (e.g., getting lost, being kidnapped, having an accident), reluctance or refusal to be away from home and go to school or work because of fear of separation, fear of being home alone without attachment figures, reluctance or refusal to sleep away from home, nightmares involving the theme of separation, and complaints of physical symptoms (e.g., headaches, stomachaches, nausea) when separation from attachment figures occurs or is anticipated. In order to be diagnosed, the problems must last at least 4 weeks in children and at least 6 months in adults and must cause clinically significant distress or impairment in social, academic, occupational, or other important areas of functioning.

Untreated anxiety of any kind in children can interfere significantly with academic and vocational achievements, as well as with achieving satisfying peer and family relations. Social isolation is one of many devastating consequences of untreated anxiety. Although the focus has primarily been on developing effective treatment for childhood anxiety, depression also often develops as a result of or secondary to the anxiety. Protocols targeting depression will, therefore, also be reviewed in this chapter. Although these protocols recognize the overlap between anxiety and depression, they can also be used for children who seem to only struggle with depression.

Child-Focused CBT

For children, CBT has for decades been recognized as a preferred treatment option to medication. Because the long-term effects of antidepressant and antianxiety medications for children are yet unknown, most parents are reluctant to agree to pharmacotherapy for young children. Although other forms of psychotherapy, such as psychodynamic (Target & Fonagy, 1994), are also effective, they usually take longer to achieve desired outcomes. 12–16 sessions of CBT is often sufficient for children to make impressive changes—provided they spend time practicing what they learn in sessions. CBT thus has a cost-effective advantage, which is important when the goal is to offer help to as many children and families as possible.

A number of trials—including some randomized controlled ones—comparing individual and group CBT to other forms of treatment or placebo treatments have consistently yielded strong support for both individual and group CBT in children (e.g., Manassis et al., 2002; Mendlowitz et al., 1999; Reynolds et al., 2013; Silverman et al., 1999). These studies all contribute to the growing popularity for CBT as an effective treatment, especially of CBGT for older children. Indeed, there is some evidence that CBGT may lead to better maintenance of treatment gains 1 year after treatment compared to individual CBT (Flannery-Schroeder, Choudhury, & Kendall, 2005). On the other hand, there are also some child anxiety disorders that may not respond as well to a group format.

The child-focused CBT manuals for anxiety disorders include, to name the most widely used, the American *Coping Cat* program (Kendall, 1990), the Australian *Coping Koala* program (Barrett, 1995), the Canadian *Taming Worry Dragons* program (Garland & Clark, 2009), the Australian *Freedom from Obsessions and Compulsions Using Special tools* (FOCUS) program (Barret, Healey-Farrell, & March, 2004), and the Australian FRIENDS program (Barrett, Shortt, Fox, & Wescombe, 2001). These protocols all offer a number of similar CBT strategies and techniques about *what to do* when adapting CBT to younger people, but less about *how to* do it. Clinicians are often left struggling with figuring out the best process for delivering CBT to younger persons. Simply taking an adult CBT protocol and trying to extend it downward to children does not work well. Not only do children become bored, but this also fails to acknowledge important developmental issues that need to be taken into account in child-focused CBT. In his excellent clinician guide, Paul Stallard (2005) addresses a number of process issues regarding CBT for children, such as when and how to include parents, how to present adult-based techniques in a simpler and more fun way, and when to emphasize behavioral interventions over cognitive ones. Although Stallard primarily deals with individual CBT, many of his suggestions can be woven into the group format, as this chapter will show.

The role of parents

As for the role of parents, the child-focused CBT approaches we will be discussing do this in different ways. Raising children is at best humbling. The saying "I was a great parent until I had kids" resonates with many. Thus, parents readily admit to feeling helpless, and it is not difficult to get at least one parent interested in learning more about their child's CBT and how to best offer support. Clinicians seem to differ in their opinions about the helpfulness of involving parents. The older literature is more critical of the involvement of parents (King et al., 1998; Toren et al., 2000), whereas newer studies are supportive. However, a meta-analysis of 55 studies of high-quality randomized controlled trials of psychological therapies for anxiety disorders in children and youth[2] concluded that parental involvement in the child's therapy was not associated with differential effectiveness (Reynolds et al., 2012). Despite this meta-analytic study conclusion, several clinical research trials on treating anxious children show that the involvement of parents makes a positive difference.

Barrett, Dadds, and Rapee (1996) treated 79 children with anxiety individually using a variation of the Coping Koala CBT protocol. They found that parental involvement in children's anxiety treatment resulted in 95.6% of children being declared diagnosis-free after treatment, compared to 70.3% for children whose parents were not involved. The involvement of parents in this study consisted of their being enrolled in separate, parallel parent sessions where they were taught how to reward their children when they engage in courageous behaviors, how to not encourage excessive anxiety, how to deal with their own emotional upsets, how to gain awareness of their own anxiety in stressful situations, and how to model problem solving. After each separate child CBT and parent anxiety management session, they would come together as a family with a therapist (*family anxiety management*) and review what they had each learned and discuss new skills and how they would resolve hypothetical ambiguous situation (e.g., "On the way to school, you (your child) feel(s) funny in the tummy. What do you think is happening? What would you (your child) do?"). The positive effect of parents' involvement was stronger for the younger children and for girls.

In another study on parental involvement in individual CBT for children ages 12–17 with OCD, the parents attended every session along with their children, that is, the parents were coclinicians. Although both groups, children alone and children with family, achieved significant reductions in symptoms of OCD, the parent-involved group did better (Reynolds et al., 2013). The way in which clinical trials include parents obviously differs, which may have contributed to the lack of a significant finding in the Reynolds meta-analysis (Reynolds et al., 2012).

Parents can be involved in various ways. They can be (a) facilitators, (b) coclinicians, or (c) clients in their own right (Stallard, 2005). The parental facilitator role is the least involved and usually consists of offering the parents a few sessions separate from and in parallel with those of their children. The focus is on educating the parents about the CBT model and the specific skills the children are learning. When parents are coclinicians, they attend a number of sessions in the same group as their children, and they play an active role in encouraging and monitoring homework between sessions. Parents can also be clients themselves, as we saw earlier in the Barrett study, and attend sessions without their children. In those sessions, parents are taught skills to help them better manage their children's behaviors, problem solve, and negotiate with their children. These sessions also deal with parental thinking styles and help correct any unhelpful beliefs regarding attribution (e.g., "My child not wanting to go to school has absolutely nothing to do with me or us as parents") or about the origins of the problem ("She is refusing school to get back at me"). The focus in these sessions inevitably becomes the parents' own anxiety and how this may impact their response to and management of their child's anxiety. This will be further addressed in the discussion on a specific CBGT protocol for anxiety.

Before delving into the various CBGT manuals, a note on the limitation of CBT for childhood problems seems fitting. CBT is not a panacea for all childhood disorders. Child-focused CBT is especially suitable for the childhood *internalizing* disorders such as depression, GAD, social anxiety, separation anxiety, and school refusal. In regard to *externalizing* disorders, such as attention deficit hyperactivity disorder (ADHD), aggression, and anger, the evidence for child-focused CBT is less strong.

However, CBT may be part of a comprehensive treatment approach toward externalizing problems. Such approaches usually involve a parent education component.

Using CBT, parents learn how to set limits on their children's behaviors, how to show consistency, and how to reward adaptive and positive behaviors. CBT is also insufficient when there are larger family system issues at play. For example, the child's behavior may become the focus that unites and diverts the parents' attention away from their own relationship conflicts. A not uncommon example is of a 12-year-old child who is scared of sleeping alone in his own bed and insists on being in the parental bed. He may have overheard the parents arguing many a time in their bed and thus attempt to be a peacekeeper. This of course prevents the parents from addressing their own intimacy issues as they focus on their "anxious" child. Or a child's "distorted" thinking about being overly criticized, rejected, or not supported and loved may prove to be a reality. In such cases involving other struggling family members, there is a risk of the therapist colluding with an unwell family and mistakenly pathologizing the child (Stallard, 2005).

CBGT for children and adolescents with anxiety

It has been encouraging to follow the developments in CBGT for children. For younger people, belonging to a group of peers where one feels accepted contributes greatly to healthy psychological development. However, the actual group climate likely matters in different ways for different ages. For younger children, support and praise from parents and group therapists may be more important than for older children. For children ages 12 and above, although parental and therapist support and praise are necessary, this is rarely sufficient. Peers matter, and the group format with all its opportunities for bringing out that sense of connection and togetherness allows CBT to become even more popular at a time when childhood mental health problems are on the rise. Groups for children tend to be transdiagnostic and include various anxiety disorders in the same group. Similar to adults, however, OCD does not mix so well with other anxiety disorders and is best treated in a separate group. Chapter 13 outlines a CBGT approach for youth with OCD.

Barrett (1998) developed the first study on the efficacy of CBGT for children ages 7–14 with anxiety disorders, including separation anxiety, generalized anxiety, and social anxiety. The children were randomly assigned to three groups: CBGT alone, CBGT plus family management, and a wait list. The number of children who no longer met diagnostic criteria for an anxiety disorder after treatment was significantly higher for those in the treatment groups—with 85% no long symptomatic in the CBGT group and 65% in the CBGT plus family management. For those on the wait list, only 25% improved. These clinical outcome studies led to the creation of the program called FRIENDS, a family- and peer-based CBGT program for anxious children. The program consists of 10 weekly sessions and two booster sessions at 1 and 3 months following completion of the group treatment. Although initially designed for school-age children in Australia, the FRIENDS program is now widely used in the United States, Canada, and—with translation—various European countries, including Holland, Germany, Belgium, and Portugal (Shortt, Barrett, & Fox, 2001).

The name FRIENDS is an acronym for the strategies taught: F, feeling worried; R, relax and feel good; I, inner thoughts; E, explore plans; N, nice work so reward yourself; D, don't forget to practice; and S, stay calm, you know how to cope now. The FRIENDS program encourages children to (a) think of their body as their friend because it tells them when they are feeling worried or nervous by giving them clues; (b) be their own friend and reward themselves when they try hard; (c) make friends, so that they can build their social support networks; and finally (d) talk to their friends when they find themselves worrying about difficult situations (Shortt et al., 2001).

Similar to other anxiety programs for children, such as *Coping Cat* and *Taming Worry Dragons*, FRIENDS is based on core CBT interventions, such as exposure, relaxation, cognitive strategies, and contingency management (self-rewards). In addition, the FRIENDS program has some unique features. The program recognizes that cognitive abilities vary in younger children compared to older children, and it therefore comes in two forms: FRIENDS for children (ages 6–11) and FRIENDS for adolescents (ages 12–16). The FRIENDS program explicitly incorporates a family skills component, which includes helping parents cope with their own anxiety, communication and problem-solving skills, as well as how to offer positive reinforcement to their children. Strategies for how families can build supportive social networks are emphasized. Parents and children are encouraged to practice the skills learned in FRIENDS as a family on a daily basis.

The developers of the FRIENDS program reasonably assumed that cognitive strategies would be most attractive and effective for adolescents, whereas behavioral and self-reward strategies would be more effective for younger children. However, the clinician expectations were not fully born out (Barrett et al., 2001). Parents of younger children rated identifying inner thoughts (cognitive strategy) as more useful for their child than did parents of adolescents. The younger children and the adolescents themselves did not differ significantly in their ratings. But the younger children found the behavioral techniques with self-reward to be the most useful. Contrary to expectations, the adolescents also rated the behavioral technique of developing a graduated exposure hierarchy to be more useful than the cognitive techniques. This finding of behavioral preferences is consistent with our experience in youth OCD groups, which I discuss in Chapter 13.

Similar to other CBGT programs for children, the developers of FRIENDS encourage clinicians to emphasize a number of group process factors. These take the form of group exposure through discussion, role-playing common threatening experiences, and group conversations about successes and difficulties. I have already stated in previous chapters that a CBGT format lends itself especially well to the more behavioral and *doing* parts of CBT. With this in mind, it may be less surprising that the behavioral exercises resonated with the FRIENDS adolescents and allowed them to form lasting positive memories, which likely influenced their later evaluation of their group experience.

Most anxiety disorders are welcome in the FRIENDS and other child CBT programs. However, the evaluations have primarily been done on children in transdiagnostic groups with separation anxiety, social anxiety, and generalized anxiety. Similar to transdiagnostic CBGT in adults, it appears that childhood OCD and posttraumatic stress disorder (PTSD) are best treated in homogeneous groups. In a study on transdiagnostic anxiety disorders (but not including PTSD) in youth (Lumpkin, Silverman, Weems, Markham, & Kurtines, 2002), the only child who did not improve was the one with OCD. But as the clinician researchers noted, at least this child did not have a deleterious effect on the treatment efficaciousness for the other children. As recognized by Barrett and colleagues (2004), children with OCD require additional attention with a specific focus on their obsessions and compulsions. Childhood PTSD is also best treated separately in its own group (Jones & Stewart, 2007). Similar to the situations for adults, OCD and PTSD require a qualitatively different approach to developing effective exposures. Interestingly, in the Reynolds meta-analysis (Reynolds et al., 2012), the seven studies for PTSD which did not include CBT yielded a nonsignificant effect size and thus suggest that any PTSD therapy for children ought to involve CBT.

Although research shows that social anxiety in children can be successfully treated in a group, some clinicians question the efficacy of mixing children with social anxiety into heterogeneous child anxiety CBGT. Manassis and colleagues (2002) found that children with social anxiety responded least favorably to a CBT group format. They speculate that the reassurance and social approval provided by a single concerned adult—the individual CBT therapist—may have enhanced treatment gains for children with social anxiety, whereas the group may have been somewhat overwhelming for them, at least initially.

Therapists who are eager to offer CBGT for social anxiety for children and adolescents may consider a homogeneous group. It is possible that for children, a pure social anxiety group is more helpful. Some clinicians who have successfully treated adolescents with social anxiety in CBGT have found that it is easier to address the situation-specific anxiety if the content of the group is solely on social anxiety (Albano, Marten, Holt, Heimberg, & Barlow, 1995). Whether CBGT for pure social anxiety is as successful for younger children as it is for adolescents remains to be determined.

CBGT for children and adolescents with depression

Evidence suggests that childhood depression can often be a consequence of high levels of anxiety (Cole, Peeke, Martin, Truglio, & Seroczynski, 1998). This high level of secondary depression, or comorbidity, is taken into account by clinicians who have developed treatment manuals for childhood depression (e.g., Lewinsohn, Clarke, Hops, & Andrews, 1990). Those manuals tend to overlap with the more specific anxiety manuals such as *Coping Koala* and *Taming Worry Dragons* in that they include stress management and cognitive restructuring. Children who receive treatment for anxiety may experience a concomitant improvement in their depression (Manassis et al., 2002; Muris, Meesters, & van Melick, 2002), but comorbid depression has also been linked to poor treatment outcome for anxious children (Last, Hansen, & Franco, 1997).

Indeed, comorbidity is the rule in childhood and adolescent depression. Anywhere from 40% to 90% of adolescents with a diagnosable depression also have another psychiatric disorder, including anxiety or substance abuse. Thus, a commonly used protocol for depression in adolescence takes a broad approach. The *Adolescent Coping with Depression* (CWD-A) course (Clarke, Hops, & Lewinsohn, 1990) provides training in a number of skills, including social skills, relaxation training, cognitive restructuring, and problem solving. This protocol runs over 16 2-hour group sessions for 8 weeks. Recognizing the high overlap of depression and anxiety, other approaches to depression in adolescence are similarly broader than the typical CBGT approach for adults in depression as described in Chapters 4 and 5. For example, relaxation training and problem solving are not typically part of an adult CBT group for depression. But problem-solving tools are helpful for a vulnerable adolescent. The basics of problem solving are illustrated in a workbook for depressed adolescents, *Dealing with Depression: Antidepressant Skills for Teens* (Bilsker, Gilbert, Worling, & Garland, 2005).

Using *Dealing with Depression: Antidepressant Skills for Teens*, the adolescent works with a sheet labeled *Problem Solving*. First, the problem must be stated, for example, "My teacher is always targeting me; I think it's unfair." Next, the person thinks about people who are supportive and writes this down: "My parents, the school counselor, my good friend in that class." This is followed by reflecting on *What I Want to Happen*. The person may write: "I just want to be treated the same as everyone else in the class." After some brainstorming, the last part of the sheet asks about three things the adolescent could do. The youth may come up with the following ideas: (a) I could give a sarcastic answer next time my teacher picks on me, (b) I could just stay quiet in class and hope she forgets about me, or (c) I could talk to the counselor about the situation. In a group setting, the facilitators will engage the entire group as everyone helps with brainstorming ideas and weighing the advantages and disadvantages of possible solutions. A fuller discussion of how to do problem solving for GAD in a CBT group was provided in Chapter 8.

How effective are booster sessions or parental involvement in CBGT for depressed adolescents? The answers are not clear. Clarke, Rhode, Lewinsohn, Hops, and Seeley (1999) found a couple of booster sessions did not prevent future recurrence of depression at any better rate than for those adolescents who did not receive booster sessions. The clinician researchers discuss how these results are somewhat counterintuitive, given clinical beliefs about the benefits of booster sessions in all kinds of CBT. They acknowledge that booster sessions are helpful for those who have not fully benefited from treatment, but in this case, they are more like a treatment continuation, as described in Chapter 5 for adult depression, as opposed to "prophylactic."

As for the role of parents, Rhode, Clarke, Lewinsohn, Seeley, and Kaufman (2001) did not find that including parents improved outcomes for the depressed adolescents whether they were comorbid or not. These clinician researchers obtained similar results in an earlier validation of their CBGT protocol for depressed adolescents (Clarke et al., 1999). Clinicians treating adolescents tend to agree that a majority voice a preference for not having their parents present in their sessions, but they do not mind separate education sessions for their parents.

CBGT Protocol for Anxious Children

A standard CBT protocol for childhood anxiety will include the following elements: psychoeducation, emotional identification, relaxation training, identifying anxiety-increasing cognitions and replacing them with anxiety-reducing cognitions, positive praise and reinforcement, development of a fear hierarchy, and systematic desensitization via exposure (Stallard, 2005). The CBGT protocol presented here for children with various anxiety disorders includes all of these components.

The *Taming Worry Dragons* manual (Garland & Clark, 2009) was developed to help children, parents, therapists, and other coaches. The manual includes nine chapters describing the different kinds of dragons (e.g., the Shy Dragon, the Habit Dragon, and the Phobia Dragon) along with basic and advanced tools for *taming* the dragons (e.g., trapping the worry dragon by creating a "worry box," learning to relax and breathe deeply by "blowing bubbles," changing what the worry dragons say by countering negative self-talk with positive self-talk). A typical group involves 10 weekly sessions with 6–8 children ages 8–10. There is a version for older children, *Worry Taming for Teens* (Garland & Clark, 2002), which is nearly identical to the younger child version but with language and examples adapted to older children. After education about anxiety, each group session teaches one or two new skills. Final sessions include education about planning for the future and how to deal with minor (and major) setbacks in symptom recurrence. The protocol was further adapted by including more emphasis on the *facing the worry dragons* skill by developing fear ladders and implementing real life (in vivo) exposures.

In the younger child program, parents are involved as coclinicians and attend three sessions along with their children: one in the beginning, the middle, and toward the end. Parents are also offered their own separate, parallel group, which runs alongside the group for their children (making parents clients in their own right). In such parallel groups, parents meet with therapists who are not the facilitators of the group, but who are knowledgeable about CBT for children and adults. These separate groups provide parents with an opportunity to address their own worries and anxieties. They also offer parents suggestions on how to encourage their children and deal with common problems, such as regular bedtime. Parents in these groups enjoy hearing from others parents, which makes them feel less alone in their own struggles.

The outline of a typical CBGT protocol for a mixed anxiety group for children is presented in the following text, along with elaboration on how therapists can modify the psychoeducation sessions and teach coping skills to a level where children can best understand their anxiety. The majority of CBGT protocols for children are developed for transdiagnostic groups with a mix of social anxiety, generalized anxiety, separation anxiety, and specific phobias. The downside of this more general approach is that the introduction of a wide range of skills may preclude a more intense focus on more primary concerns. For example, the *Taming Worry Dragons* approach may be a helpful primer for an intensely socially anxious child. This child may subsequently need a single topic social anxiety group to complete a full course of treatment. The Reynolds meta-analysis (Reynolds et al., 2012) did find that homogeneous anxiety groups led to greater treatment effects compared to the trans-diagnostic groups, even though both types are considered effective overall.

Session Themes in the Worry Dragons CBGT (Adapted from Garland & Clark, 2009)

Session 1: Psychoeducation: The Nature of the Beast and How You Get Worry Dragons

Session 2: Psychoeducation: A Tour of the Zoo: Generalized Worries, Phobia Dragons, Panic Attacks, the Shy Dragon, and the Habit Dragon

Session 3: Basic Tools for Dragon Trapping: Scheduling and Overcoming Procrastination

Session 4: Basic Tools for Dragon Trapping: Mental Imagery: Worry Boxes, Off Switches, and Relaxation

Session 5: Advanced Tools: Knowing When the Dragons Come Around, Checking It Out: Are You a Perfectionist?

Session 6: Advanced Tools: Facing the Dragons: Mental Rehearsal and Fear Ladders

Session 7: Advanced Tools: Working with Fear Ladders to Face the Dragons

Session 8: Extra Tools: Exercise, Laughter and Self-Rewards

Session 9: The Quest: Taking Back Your Life

Session 10: The Care and Feeding of Pet Dragons

Psychoeducation

Similar to psychoeducation in CBGT for adults, the facilitators draw the triangle showing the connection between thoughts, feelings, and behaviors. There is an emphasis on what worrying does to your body and mind, with the idea of helping children become better able to notice initial signs of anxiety. The metaphor of the alarm system that becomes overactive is introduced: "It's like those car alarms which go off at the slightest breeze." Facilitators explain to the children and the parents that while it is good to be able to detect real danger, having an overactive alarm system in our body that goes off when there is no real danger turns us into masterful worriers. To further increase children's awareness of body sensation signaling "danger," they are asked to draw a body and indicate which parts get impacted. Some children draw butterflies in the stomach, and others create figures with large, shaky hands.

To show how worry dragons originate, the group therapists educate the parents and children about how *dragons are born in the minds of very creative and talented worriers and that they trick us by scaring us into thinking they are real.* Therapists may say that dragons feed on worries and misinformation. They may also say to some parents: "It sounds like the worry dragon is roaming freely in your home, bullying everybody." Parents are educated about how two forms of behaviors especially feed worry dragons: avoidance and excessive reassurance seeking.

Parents may realize they support avoidance by too quickly allowing the child to miss school or withdraw from a new leisure activity. Another parent may for the first time understand how subtle reassurance can be when they say to their child who is expressing worry about going to a first tennis lesson: "Don't worry about starting your new tennis class; it really should all be just fine—I know you'll do so well and that it will be lots of fun!" It is a fine line between helpful encouragement and unhelpful offers of reassurance. Repeated reassurances do feed and maintain the worries by validating—or even dignifying—them as special and deserving of attention.

Parents also learn to respect children's developmental level and realize that emotions often lag behind intellectual maturation. Children may, as a result, develop reality-based fears but lack the ability to calm themselves emotionally and put their fears into a perspective. For example, the most appropriate response to a 5-year-old constantly worrying about her mother dying may be to simply say that mom is healthy and is not going to die. For a 13-year-old worrying about a parent dying of cancer, the parents may opt for introducing the concept of probabilities. Therapists offer CBT teaching about probabilities and emphasize how we humans often give disproportionate worry time to something with an extremely low probability. To make this more visual, child therapist can use the *popcorn technique* informally developed by a colleague and myself. This technique includes first figuring out what the real probability for a feared outcome is. Many children with anxiety are preoccupied with death and especially of a parent dying. An example may be a child fearing their mother will die of cancer. If we take breast cancer as an example, a report from the National Institute of Health (1997) indicates that a 40-year-old woman has a 2% chance of being diagnosed with invasive breast cancer within the next decade of her life. The probability of dying from breast cancer during this time span is much lower, 0.3% or 3/1,000. To illustrate this small probability, the therapist can pop 1,000 popcorn and paint 3 of them blue or, more simply, pop 333 and paint 1 blue. This helps children to see that their big fear is based on a small likelihood—just one tiny blue popcorn—among 333 white ones.

Basic and advanced tools for combating anxiety

I will review two important tools from the *Taming Worry Dragons* protocol, the basic tool of *sticking with schedules* and the advanced one of *facing the dragons.*

Child therapists emphasize the importance of structure and weekly schedules. Doing constructive, positive activities such as playing indoor and outdoor games with parents, sibling, and friends leaves less time for the dragons to take over. Active routines *oil the calm engine.* Therapists teach children and their parents that humans do best when we are calm. For example, a parent may get anxious about a 13-year-old child having a spelling test in school. In an attempt to manage their own worries, the parent may allow the child to stay up until midnight and practice for the test and insist on waking the child up early. Referring to the importance of a calm engine, the therapist will encourage the parent to set a time limit of 7:00 p.m. for studying, followed by sticking to the usual bedtime, and then one review only in the morning. In general, bedtime and other routines are emphasized throughout the program for anxious kids. Routines help children relax. Lack of routines and regular rhythms for sleeping and eating tend to feed worry dragons because it makes us less rested. Battling dragons require a well-nourished and well-rested warrior! Parents in the beginning of the program often do not see a connection between emotional dysregulation and lower ability to stand up to the dragons. They quickly get it and begin to benefit from more regular routines themselves.

Facing the dragons takes the form of a behavioral experiment, or putting the dragon's roar to a real test. Standing up to the dragon, talking back to it, help children over time to learn that their fears do not come true. A 10-year-old girl with social anxiety, Monica, may let her Shy Dragon bully her into believing that she will be laughed at if she asks a girl, Mia, who she would like to be friends with, to play at recess. In the group, the facilitators may draw the dragon on the board with a talk bubble saying, "Mia will laugh at you if you say anything to her—you better believe me!" With Monica's agreement, she could role-play her behavioral experiment in the group with another group member playing Mia. The therapists will do their best to determine how likely it is that the feared outcome will come true. If any significant likelihood, they can encourage role-plays of various scenarios such as Mia saying she had plans to play with someone else today. This can lead to more behavioral exposures and the importance of sometimes having to "throw out our fishing line" several times before we get a catch. This is a helpful reminder to many socially anxious children and adolescents who are sensitive to perceived social rejection and easily recoil after only one unsuccessful attempt.

In developing fear ladders, which are the child equivalent of exposure hierarchies, parents are trained to catch overt and subtle reinforcement of avoidance. A blatant example of supporting avoidance is the mother who says to her 12-year-old daughter who refuses to go to school because her stomach hurts: "Well—if you're not going to school you'll have to come to the mall with me." A less obvious example of supporting avoidance is the concerned and caring parent who keeps saying, "Do you think trying school today will work for you, sweetie?" A more helpful approach may be "I'm impressed with how you practiced *blowing bubbles* [a deep breathing exercise] last evening and look forward to hearing how that may help you today in school when you may get that funny feeling in your tummy." In this approach, the parent reminds the child of using a coping skill. The parent helps the child be realistic about expecting discomfort as opposed to hoping all will be fine, and the parent expresses confidence in the child.

Self-rewards

The basic CBT principle of rewarding good behavior works well for all child-focused CBT. However, therapists have much to say—including to parents—about how to implement a reward system. It is important to keep the rewards small and delivered after each step toward an overall goal. For example, a child may accumulate 10 points each time he wins a battle with the Phobia Dragon. The ultimate goal worth 100 points is to be able to sleep away from home, that is, a sleepover at a friend's place, which will be rewarded with a video game. Like all parts of CBT for children, the rewards ought to be fun. These rewards offer external incentives, but child CBT therapists find that children become internally motivated or self-motivated surprisingly quickly.

Capitalizing on the Group for Youth with Anxiety and Depression

Similar to groups for adults, children benefit from seeing other children facing the same challenges. Many group process factors operate and support the work of the CBGT clinicians. Opportunities to watch peers engage in positive modeling of coping skills may be especially reinforcing (Albano et al., 1995). For younger children, CBGT therapists frequently note that having fun and laughing together is the group process magnet that keeps them coming back. Anxious children are serious children, and their bodies and minds benefit tremendously from laughing and having fun with other children. Considering how hard it is to laugh and "become less serious" in one's own company—or that of anxious family members—whether one is a child or adult, the group format for anxious children is uniquely therapeutic. The group processes of universality and belonging run strongly through these child CBT groups. In groups for young children, there is usually at least one "crier" and one who cannot initially tolerate separation from their parent. Even these kids begin to relax, smile, and laugh more as the group develops—provided the therapists make it fun using all the props needed, such as puppets, storytelling, crayons, paper, games, etc.

Adult CBT therapists admire how their child CBT colleagues keep the energy levels in their groups elevated. It is no small task to constantly be looking for creative and imaginative ways to keep the interest of the children and inspire them to take risks to overcome their fears and to be doing so while keeping all the parents calm and engaged.

Common Challenges in CBGT for Children and Adolescents

As discussed, a couple of major challenges facing child-focused CBGT therapists are how to include parents and how to adapt adult CBT protocols to the developmental level of children.

Parental involvement may be especially helpful for younger children. When parents become directly involved and receive exactly the same information as the children, treatment outcomes are much better as demonstrated, among others, by Mendlowitz and colleagues (1999). However, if the parents are quite anxious themselves, the benefits of participating in their child's treatment diminish. Parental psychopathology in the form of depression and anxiety is often the greatest barrier preventing positive change in the child (Stallard, 2005).

Anxious parents tend to be overprotective. Overprotection deprives the child of developing adequate coping skills at age-appropriate levels for navigating a world full of complicated events and people. Whether more parents are becoming anxious and overprotective is a good question to be determined. The trend toward abandoning recess in many American states and keeping children safely indoors focused on structured activities—often in front of computers—instead of rough-and-tumble play is not helpful. It may serve to further feed worry dragons. Child clinicians wonder if they are beginning to see some of the consequences of this. Scenarios are common in which parents text their 10-year-old three times as he walks to the corner store, or forbid their 11-year-old to walk to school with a friend and no adult, or warn their youngsters of not talking to anybody on the bus. Child clinicians find themselves increasingly arranging for parents to be referred for their own CBT in addition to participating in their child's.

Recent work by child and family CBT clinician researcher Anne Marie Albano and colleagues offers promising innovative ways to support anxious parents. In the **C**oaching, **A**pproach behavior, and **L**eading by **M**odeling (CALM) program (Comer et al., 2012), parents are offered *live* coaching to help reshape their interactions with their children. A therapist sits behind a one-way mirror offering immediate feedback to the parent, who has a bug-in-the-ear receiver while being present with their child in the same room. The therapist behind the mirror offers suggestions, which the parent then tries out. This allows parents to continually adjust their reactions and communication until it becomes more habitual. For example, the parent may be coached to support bravery and improve the child's confidence by saying, "I know it's hard, but you can do it." Using the CALM approach, about 80% of children achieve improvements and no longer meet criteria for an anxiety disorder (Comer et al., 2012). One wonders about extending this approach to children in a group. Several parents could be receiving support from individual coaches as they interact with their children in the group.

The CBT child literature for both therapists and parents is increasingly emphasizing the family context in which the anxious child lives. Parents are often eager to learn more, and clinicians can recommend books such as *You and Your Anxious Child* (Albano & Pepper, 2013) and *Treating Childhood and Adolescent Anxiety: A Guide for Caregivers* (Lebowitz & Omer, 2013). This latter is primarily for therapists but parents can also benefit as they learn about CBT interventions for children.

The question of whether child-focused CBT clinicians need to include as many cognitive techniques as the equivalent adult CBT protocol includes is important. Generally, child clinicians agree that cognitive change occurs indirectly through behavioral techniques, such as exposures, and that any explicit cognitive focus without exposure is less effective (Kendall et al., 1997). But that does not preclude the importance of identifying budding formations of faulty appraisals, core beliefs, and negative automatic thoughts. How to do that most effectively in young children is one of many clinical challenges. Some clinicians and researchers argue that explicit targeting of cognitions may not be as useful in young children because they lack the cognitive maturation for adequate engagement (e.g., Barrett et al., 2001), whereas others find that children's cognitive development is sufficiently flexible to engage with cognitive approaches so long as those are appropriately adapted to a child level (Quakley, Reynolds, & Coker, 2004). There does not seem to be an unequivocal answer to this question of how to balance cognitive versus behavioral interventions for children and youths.

Summary

This chapter reviews a number of CBGT programs for children with various forms of anxiety and depression. The most common type of group is for mixed anxiety, including generalized anxiety, separation anxiety, and social anxiety. Most protocols have a transdiagnostic quality. The chapter discusses the Taming Worry Dragons program. It also introduces protocols for depressed youth. Although a group format may be especially helpful for older children for whom peers matter a great deal, younger children also benefit from some of the aspects unique to the group setting. The role of parents has yielded inconsistent results. When clinicians include parents directly in the same group as their children, the outcomes are better—especially for younger children. New experiments with live coaching for parents also seem to make a substantial positive difference in the child's anxiety. Considering that "an ounce of prevention is worth a pound of cure," any effort to increase access to child-focused CBGT will improve the well-being of individuals, families, and societies. It will also reduce the costs associated with untreated anxiety and depression in adults.

Chapter 13 on youth OCD continues several of the themes from this chapter.

Note

1. Separation anxiety was listed under *Other Disorders of Infancy, Childhood, and Adolescence* in the DSM-IV (APA, 2000), but this section has been entirely eliminated in the DSM-5 (APA, 2013).

Recommended Readings for Clinicians

Albano, A. M., & Pepper, L. (2013). *You and your anxious child.* New York: Avery/Penguin Group.

Barrett, P. M. (1995). *Group coping koala workbook.* Unpublished manuscript, Griffith University of Brisbane, Queensland.

Bilsker, D., Gilbert, M., Worling, D., & Garland, E. J. (2005). *Dealing with depression: Antidepressant skills for teens.* Vancouver, BC: Ministry of Children and Family Development. Retrieved from http://www.mcf.gov.be.ca/mental_helath/current_initiatives.htm [accessed on February 25, 2014].

Clark, S. L. (2008). *Tools for taming and trapping worry dragons* (2nd ed.). Vancouver, BC: BC' Children's Hospital. Retrieved from http://bookstore.cw.bc.ca [accessed on February 25, 2014].

Garland, E. J., & Clark, S. L. (2002). *Worry taming for teens.* Vancouver, BC: BC Children's Hospital.

Garland, E. J., & Clark, S. L. (2009). *Taming worry dragons: A manual for children, parents, and other coaches* (4th ed.). Vancouver, BC: BC Children's Hospital. Retrieved from http://bookstore.cw.bc.ca [accessed on February 25, 2014].

Kendall, P. C. (1990). *The coping cat workbook.* Ardmore, PA: Workbook Publishing.

Lebowitz, E., & Omer, H. (2013). *Treating childhood and adolescent anxiety: A guide for caregivers.* Hoboken, NJ: John Wiley & Sons.

Stallard, P. (2005). *A clinician's guide to think good—Feel good: Using CBT with children and young people.* West Sussex, UK: John Wiley & Sons.

References

Albano, A. M., Marten, P. A., Holt, C. S., Heimberg, R. G., & Barlow, D. H. (1995). Cognitive-behavioral group treatment for social phobia in adolescents: A preliminary study. *Journal of Nervous and Mental Disease, 183*, 649–656.

American Psychiatric Association (APA). (2000). *Diagnostic and statistical manual of mental disorders, DSM* (4th ed.). Washington, DC: Author.

APA. (2013). *Diagnostic and statistical manual of mental disorders, DSM* (5th ed.). Washington, DC: Author.

Barrett, P. M. (1998). Evaluation of cognitive behavioral group treatments for childhood anxiety disorders. *Journal of Clinical Child Psychology, 27(4)*, 459–468.

Barrett, P. M., Dadds, M. R., & Rapee, R. (1996). Family treatment of childhood anxiety: A controlled trial. *Journal of Consulting and Clinical Psychology, 64*, 333–342.

Barrett, P. M., Healy-Farrell, L., & March, J. S. (2004). Cognitive behavioral treatment of childhood obsessive compulsive disorder: A controlled trial. *Journal of the American Academy of Child and Adolescent Psychiatry, 43*, 46–62.

Barrett, P. M., Shortt, A. L., Fox, T. L., & Wescombe, K. (2001). Examining the social validity of the FRIENDS treatment program for anxious children. *Behaviour Change, 18(2)*, 63–77.

Clarke, G. N., Hops, H., & Lewinsohn, P. M. (1990). *Adolescent coping with depression course.* Eugene, OR: Castalia Press.

Clarke, G. N., Rhode, P., Lewinsohn, P., Hops, H., & Seeley, J. R. (1999). Cognitive-behavioral treatment of adolescent depression: Efficacy of acute group treatment and booster sessions. *Journal of the American Academy of Child and Adolescent Psychiatry, 38(3)*, 272–279.

Cole, D. A., Peeke, L. G., Martin, J. M., Truglio, R., & Seroczynski, A. D. (1998). A longitudinal study of the relation between depression and anxiety in children. *Journal of Consulting and Clinical Psychology, 66*, 451–460.

Comer, J. C., Puliafico, A. C., Aschenbrand, S. G., McKnight, K., Robin, J. A., Goldfine, M., et al. (2012). A pilot feasibility evaluation of the CALM Program for anxiety disorders in early childhood. *Journal of Anxiety Disorders, 26*, 40–49.

Flannery-Schroeder, E., Choudhury, M. S., & Kendall, P. C. (2005). Group and individual cognitive-behavioral treatments for youth with anxiety disorders: 1-year follow-up. *Cognitive Therapy and Research, 29(2)*, 253–259.

Jones, A., & Stewart, J. L. (2007). Group cognitive-behavior therapy to address post-traumatic stress disorder in children and adolescents. In R. W. Christner, J. L. Stewart, & A. Freeman (Eds.), *Handbook of cognitive-behavior group therapy with children and adolescents: Specific settings and presenting problems* (pp. 223–249). New York: Routledge/Taylor & Francis Group.

Kendall, P. C., Flannery-Schroeder, E., Panichelli-Mindel, S. M., Southam-Gerow, M., Henin, A., & Warman, M. (1997). Therapy for youths with anxiety disorders: A second randomized clinical trial. *Journal of Consulting and Clinical Psychology, 65(3)*, 366–380.

King, N. J., Tonge, B. J., Heyne, D., ritchard, M., Rollings, S., Young, D., et al. (1998). Cognitive-behavioural treatment of school-refusing children: A controlled evaluation. *Journal of the American Academy of Child and Adolescent Psychiatry, 37*, 4, 395–403.

Last, C. G., Hansen, C., & Franco, N. (1997). Anxious children in adulthood: A prospective study of adjustment. *Journal of the American Academy of Child and Adolescent Psychiatry, 36*, 645–652.

Lewinsohn, P. M., Clarke, G. N., Hops, J., & Andrews, J. (1990). Cognitive behavioral treatment for depressed adolescents. *Behavior Therapy, 21*, 385–401.

Lumpkin, P. W., Silverman, W. K., Weems, C. F., Markham, M. R., & Kurtines, W. M. (2002). Treating a heterogeneous set of anxiety disorders in youths with group cognitive behavioral therapy: A partially nonconcurrent multiple-baseline evaluation. *Behavior Therapy, 33*, 163–177.

Manassis, K., Mendlowitz, S. L., Scapillato, D., Avery, D., Fiksenbaum, L., Freire, M., et al. (2002). Group and individual cognitive-behavioral therapy for childhood anxiety disorders: A randomized trial. *Journal of the American Academy of Child and Adolescent Psychiatry, 41(12)*, 1423–1430.

Mendlowitz, S. L., Manassis, K., Bradly, S., Scapillato, D., Miezitis, S., & Shaw, B. (1999). Cognitive behavioral group treatments in childhood anxiety disorders: The role of parental involvement. *Journal of the American Academy of Child and Adolescent Psychiatry, 38*, 1223–1229.

Muris, P., Meesters, C., & van Melick, M. (2002). Treatment of childhood anxiety disorders: A preliminary comparison between cognitive-behavioral group therapy and a psychological placebo intervention. *Journal of Behavior Therapy and Experimental Psychiatry, 33*, 143–158.

National Institute of Health. (1997). Breast cancer screening for women ages 40-49. *NIH Consensus Statement, 15(1)*, 1–35.

Quakley, S., Reynolds, S., & Coker, S. (2004). Visual cues and age improve children's abilities to discriminate between thoughts, feelings and behaviours. *Behaviour Research and Therapy, 42*, 343–356.

Reynolds, S. A., Bowers, G., Norton, E., Clark, S., Smith, H., Langdon, P. E., et al. (2013). Randomized controlled trial of parent-enhanced CBT compared with individual CBT for obsessive-compulsive disorder in young people. *Journal of Consulting and Clinical Psychology, 81*, 1021–1026.

Reynolds, S. A., Wilson, C., Austin, J., & Hooper, L. (2012). Effects of psychotherapy for anxiety in children and adolescents: A meta-analytic review. *Clinical Psychology Review, 32*, 251–261.

Rhode, P., Clarke, G. N., Lewinsohn, P. M., Seeley, J. R., & Kaufman, N. K. (2001). Impact of comorbidity on a cognitive-behavioral group treatment for adolescent depression. *Journal of the American Academy of Child and Adolescent Psychiatry, 40(7)*, 795–802.

Shortt, A. L., Barrett, P. M., & Fox, T. L. (2001). Evaluating the FRIENDS Program: A cognitive-behavioral group treatment for anxious children and their parents. *Journal of Clinical Child Psychology, 30(4)*, 525–535.

Silverman, W. K., Kurtines, W. M., Ginsburg, G. S., Weems, C. G., Lumpkin, P. W., & Carmichael, D. H. (1999). Treating anxiety disorders in children with group cognitive behavioral therapy: A randomized clinical trial. *Journal of Consulting and Clinical Psychology, 67*, 995–1003.

Target, M., & Fonagy, P. (1994). Efficacy of psychoanalysis for children with emotional disorders. *Journal of the American Academy of Child and Adolescent Psychiatry, 33*, 361–371.

Toren, P., Wolmer, L., Rosental, B., Eldar, S., Koren, S., Lask, M., et al. (2000). Case series: Brief parent-child group therapy for childhood anxiety disorders using a manual based cognitive-behavioural technique. *Journal of the American Academy of Child and Adolescent Psychiatry, 39(10)*, 1309–1312.

13

Youth Obsessive–Compulsive Disorder (OCD)

In Chapter 12, we learned that CBGT for children with anxiety and depression is an effective form of treatment. This chapter, with its focus on youth obsessive–compulsive disorder (OCD), also emphasizes the benefits to adolescents, families, and society of "catching" early tendencies to develop a serious mental health problem. It can be near heartbreaking to listen to adults successfully treated with CBT for OCD wishing this had been available to them sooner, thus mitigating many painful years of suffering.

OCD is a disorder which, similar to other mental health problems, often shows manifestations in childhood above and beyond normal OCD-look-alike behaviors. For example, it is normal for kids to have a high need for certain bedtime rituals being performed in exactly the same way and order every night. First, daddy reads the same story two times, then mommy chases away the monsters under the bed, and then daddy kisses good night tree times and mommy four times. It is also normal for children to engage in mildly superstitious obsessive thinking, such as "If I see three patterns of 3 s before entering my classroom, I will do well on my test." For those kids who do not spontaneously outgrow these kinds of normal obsessions and compulsions around age 10 and become stuck at what could be termed a prerational stage of cognitive development, a lifelong battle with fears and senseless rituals can start (Söchting & March, 2002).

In this chapter, I show how CBGT for OCD in youth is becoming a highly effective intervention for a potentially devastating and not well-understood disorder. I summarize relevant research and present a specific CBGT protocol. I am including this chapter because OCD is more serious and disabling than any other anxiety disorders (Kessler, Chiu, Demler, & Walters, 2005). It is as prevalent as schizophrenia (DSM-5,

Cognitive Behavioral Group Therapy: Challenges and Opportunities, First Edition. Ingrid Söchting.

APA, 2013), yet far fewer treatment resources and public education are available. At most about 25% of youth with OCD receive mental health treatment (Whitaker et al., 1990). When young adults receive effective CBT, they are able to manage their OCD symptoms and prevent the illness from becoming more severe. Although this chapter focuses on CBGT for youth, many adults would benefit from the same treatment approach—with only slight modifications.

OCD used to be considered an anxiety disorder, but with the advent of DSM-5 (APA, 2013), it has now become distinct from the anxiety disorders and has its own category: *Obsessive–Compulsive and Related Disorders*. The related disorders include several body-focused problems such as hair-pulling, skin-picking, nail-biting, and body dysmorphic disorder. OCD and related disorders share features such as the experience of an overwhelming urge to engage in certain behaviors, whether excessive hand washing, picking at one's skin, or constant checking for facial asymmetries in mirrors. The section on treatment later in this chapter shows how people with body dysmorphic and hair-pulling behaviors can be included in the same group as those with OCD. OCD clinicians and researchers are pleased to see OCD getting a distinct diagnostic category. We view it as progress toward a better understanding of, and treatment for, people with OCD and related disorders.

OCD in Children and Adolescents

OCD in children and adolescents looks remarkably similar to the disorder in adults. It follows the same diagnostic criteria with the exception of the requirement of insight. Preadolescent children are not expected to recognize that their obsessions and compulsions are unreasonable and due to a psychiatric disorder, but in mid-adolescence, a growing awareness begins. Many treatment manuals for OCD across the age span are based on the older versions of the DSM, but according to both the DSM-IV (APA, 2000) and DSM-5 (APA, 2013), OCD consists of recurrent and persistent thoughts, urges, or images that are experienced as intrusive and unwanted and that in most individuals cause marked anxiety or distress. Compulsions are defined as repetitive behaviors (e.g., hand washing, ordering, checking) or mental acts (e.g., praying, counting, repeating words silently) that the individual feels driven to perform in response to an obsession or according to rules that must be applied rigidly. The obsessions and compulsions are time consuming and take up more than 1 hour per day or cause clinically significant distress or impairment in social, occupational, or other important functioning. DSM-5 allows clinicians to specify whether the person with OCD has *good*, *fair*, *poor*, or *absent insight*. Absent insight may be coupled with *delusional beliefs*. The broader range of insight specification in DSM-5 is especially helpful for those OCD sufferers with absent or delusional insight. This improves the chance they can be diagnosed correctly with the kind of OCD involving *absent insight/delusional beliefs*, as opposed to being diagnosed with a psychotic disorder. For example, a youth may be convinced that the water in his local community is undrinkable and "contaminated." He will avoid any drinking of tap water at all costs and engage in elaborate compulsive behaviors to ensure no tap water gets into his food or mouth, ear, and nose when bathing. This person resembles, but is different from, someone with psychosis who believes city engineers are plotting to poison her with contaminated water.

OCD affects about 2% of children and adolescents and interferes with school performance and relationships with friends and family (Valleni-Basile et al., 1994). This means that 1 in 50 children in any elementary or high school would meet criteria for OCD and experience significant distress as a result. Boys are more likely to have onset of OCD before they reach puberty, in contrast to girls who tend to develop the disorder during their adolescent and young adult years (Swedo, Rapoport, Leonard, Lenane, & Cheslow, 1989). Similar to adults, the course of OCD in children is usually gradual and influenced by the child's more general abilities to cope with stress. In the absence of treatment, spontaneous recovery is rare, and a diagnosis of OCD in childhood tends to continue into adulthood and is associated with a higher probability of developing other anxiety, mood, or personality disorders (Thomsen & Mikkelsen, 1993).

CBT for Youth OCD

Given the similarity of expression of OCD in children and adults, recommended treatment protocols are nearly identical for both age groups whether pharmacological or behavioral or a combination. The CBGT protocol outlined in this chapter can thus also be used, with some modification, for adult CBGT for OCD. Several clinical trials have shown that pharmacological treatment is as effective for children with OCD as it is for adults but that symptoms usually recur after discontinuation of medication treatment (March et al., 1998). As we saw in Chapter 3, there is strong empirical support for the efficacy of CBT and CBGT for adults with OCD. The evidence for individual (Reynolds et al., 2013) and group CBT for children and adolescents is also strong and growing (to be reviewed in the following text) as more rigorous studies are carried out.

Behavioral interventions

The CBT treatment principle of *exposure and response prevention* (ERP) has proven just as effective for younger people with OCD as for adults. ERP involves facing the feared or avoided stimulus (exposure) and refraining from performing the compulsive activity (response prevention). For example, a child sitting in a classroom will begin to doubt whether she locked her locker properly (obsession) and will feel a strong need to leave the room and check that she did (compulsion). She may repeat this OCD cycle several times, leaving the classroom up to five times, which renders her unable to focus on what is being taught. When this child engages in ERP, she will learn **not** to take her obsession at face value, trust herself more, and develop skills helping her refrain from giving into her compulsive need to get up and go check her locker. She will remain in the classroom and become better able to focus. Over time, with repeated exposures, she learns to tolerate anxiety and realize that her worst fear (e.g., someone will break into my locker because I forgot to lock it) is extremely unlikely to come true. In addition to the ERP intervention described earlier, cognitive interventions are also used in CBT for childhood OCD.

Cognitive interventions

Cognitive interventions for OCD are designed to target a number of beliefs people hold about the *appraisal* or meaning of their obsessions. Three broad beliefs have been identified: (1) inflated sense of responsibility, (2) importance of thoughts, and (3) control of thoughts (Obsessive-Compulsive Cognitions Working Group, 1997, 2001). The beliefs interact with the obsessions. That is, when cognitive intrusions (thoughts, images, or impulses) occur, they are likely to be misinterpreted as signaling that this particular thought is very important, that the person is responsible for the thought or its outcome, and that he or she should control the thought. For example, a common child obsession involves uncontrollable images of parents being in a deadly car accident. The child interprets the mere presence of this thought or image to mean that the likelihood of the feared scenario is extremely high. Hence, the child needs to *undo* the image with various rituals, such as having to count to five or replacing the gruesome image with a happy one of playing monopoly safely at home with the parents.

The girl mentioned earlier felt responsible for her locker and wanted to prevent at all costs a break-in. This sense of inflated responsibility is common in children and youth with OCD. They feel personally responsible for a number of things that could go wrong in their lives, far more than what even quite conscientious youngsters feel. There are cognitive techniques designed to discuss the realistic amount of responsibility that can reasonably be attributed to one person. One technique aimed at an inflated sense of responsibility is the *pie technique*.

In the *pie technique*, the therapist works with the client (or the group) and lists all factors potentially and realistically contributing to the feared consequence. For example, a 13-year-old girl may fear that her puppy will get a fatal infection from contaminated food and that the death of the puppy will be her fault and responsibility. The girl may check twice an hour for signs that her puppy is getting ill, which include insisting on getting up during the night. She may refuse to go to school or may text her father at home several times a day to get reassurance that her puppy is fine. This girl has what is considered an *inflated sense of responsibility*, which is common in OCD. Perhaps a previous pet died, or her parents had told her they did not think she was old enough to take care of a puppy. A number of factors can contribute to inflated responsibility, or there may not be any easily identifiable predisposing reasons. In regard to the obsession about the puppy eating contaminated food, the therapist works with the child to identify other factors that reasonably could contribute to a scenario of the puppy becoming ill from eating contaminated food. The therapist writes them all down: the producer of the pet food, the packaging, the transport of the food, the shopkeeper who sold the food, and the fridge it was stored in. After a circle is drawn on the board, the 13-year-old fills in pieces of the pie that differ in size relative to the importance of each contributing factor. All factors should be pieces of the pie with the girl's own contribution drawn last. At the end of the exercise, there is often little of the circle left for the person's personal responsibility or control over the event. This girl may realize that her role in whether the puppy lives or dies because of what it eats may be only 5% in contrast to the previous belief of 90%.

Although the *pie* and various other cognitive techniques can be valuable in any CBT and CBGT for OCD (Salkovskis, 1996; Söchting, Whittal, & McLean, 1997; Wilhelm & Steketee, 2006), research clinicians for childhood OCD agree that the behavioral component in CBT, the ERP, seems to be the key driving force for successfully treating younger people (Barrett, Healey-Farrell, & March, 2004; March, Mulle, & Herbel, 1994). But clinicians acknowledge that faulty beliefs often change indirectly and spontaneously as children have success with their exposures. So, although clinicians may not spend as much time on specific, explicit cognitive interventions for youth as they do with adults, they pay attention and inquire about the kinds of meaning and beliefs the youngsters with OCD hold.

CBGT for youth OCD

A CBGT format has consistently shown great promise from the first uncontrolled, naturalistic evaluations (Chowdhury, Caulfield, & Heyman, 2003; Fisher, Himle, & Hanna, 1998; Thienemann, Martin, Cregger, Thompson, & Dyer-Friedman, 2001) to more rigorous comparisons with individual CBT (Barrett, Farrel, Pina, Peris, & Piacentini, 2008; Barrett et al., 2004) followed by randomized controlled trials (Asbahr et al., 2005; O'Leary, Barrett, & Fjermestad, 2009). The O'Leary study (O'Leary et al., 2009), comparing CBGT to individual CBT, involved 38 participants aged 13–24, who were followed up to 7 years after they completed their CBT for OCD. For those treated with CBGT, 95% no longer met criteria for OCD versus 79% in the individual CBT group. It is rare to get such impressive and long-term follow-up in any CBT treatment outcome study. Clinician researchers evaluating CBGT for OCD in children and adolescents agree that a group format is highly effective and preferable. Given the developmental stage of adolescents, peers are an enormously important source of feedback and support. A group approach thus provides a context conducive to sharing experiences with peers. For these reasons, it has become hard for me to imagine offering CBT to adolescents in anything but a group format.

CBGT Protocol for Youth OCD

Similar to CBGT for other disorders, CBGT therapists interested in running groups for youth with OCD must take an established individual protocol and adapt it to a group setting. In what follows, I show an example of such a protocol based on three existing CBT manuals for OCD. The rationale for this particular adolescent OCD manual was based on a couple of key considerations informed by both the literature and prior experience with individual CBT for children, as well as with CBGT for adults with OCD.

For this adolescent CBGT manual, we first decided to make it primarily a behavioral protocol with emphasis on ERP. An earlier adult OCD CBGT study in which I served as one of the group therapists compared a pure cognitive CBGT condition to a pure ERP CBGT condition (McLean et al., 2001). Results from this study suggested that those treated with ERP improved more on the Yale–Brown Obsessive–Compulsive Scale (Y-BOCS; Goodman et al., 1989) with an average Y-BOCS score of 15.9 after treatment compared to an average score of 18.43 for the cognitive treatment condition.[1] Although the difference is not huge, the research clinicians running the ERP groups found that the atmosphere was more alive and engaged and that the opportunities for interactions and support among group members were richer compared to the cognitive groups. Although we did not measure the impact of the group climate itself on symptom improvement, our clinical hunch was that the therapists and group members alike found the ERP more interactive—and even fun on occasion. This seemed important when designing a group for youngsters where any overly dry and clinical atmosphere could be a deterrent for full and willing participation. This hunch has been backed up by research showing that—contrary to expectations—adolescents treated for anxiety disorders (not OCD) found the behavioral interventions, such as graded exposure, more useful than the cognitive ones (Barrett, Shortt, Fox, & Wescombe, 2001).

Second, we had to figure out how to make ERP more attractive for young people so that they did not drop out of the group. Although our comparative adult study showed ERP CBT to be slightly superior to cognitive CBT, ERP seems to result in more dropouts. The overall dropout rate in our adult CBGT for OCD study was 13%, which is not too bad, but in the ERP condition, it was 19% (McLean et al., 2001). Having close to 20% of people drop out of treatment begins to become a concern. CBT therapists agree that a significant number of people with OCD are not helped by exposure therapy. There is a need for improving our interventions and making them more tolerable for our clients.

We decided to develop a protocol based on classic CBT ERP therapy adapted for younger people, but with an important twist that would make it easier for the adolescent to tolerate difficult exposures. It is tough to tell a 14-year-old to "just stand there" after he has touched walls in a public washroom and his anxiety is at a 95% level. So we borrowed an idea from the work of University of California, Los Angeles, neuropsychiatrist Jeffrey Schwartz. In his popularized book *Brain Lock*, Schwartz permits clients who have exposed themselves to take part in a new activity, something that feels engaging and positive. When we do not specifically allow this *refocusing*, we find that adolescents with OCD will invariably try to distract themselves anyway by chatting, joking, attempting to leave the room, etc. However, the *refocusing* option must not actually *distract* clients from their exposure—as that could interfere with the process of desensitization. Instead, it becomes a means to facilitate enduring the full exposure, to stay emotionally engaged with it, and not to give in to compulsive behaviors. The therapeutic window is the place where clients are able to push and challenge themselves but not become so overwhelmed that they begin to disengage, numb out, flee treatment or give the impression of working hard when they are in fact engaging in task-avoidant behaviors. In a group, therapists must pay attention to the members who may initially seem helpful to others and eager to be a peer model *but* who are in fact avoiding their own work. Exactly how the refocusing option works in ERP will be illustrated in the section *Exposure, response prevention, and refocusing.*

Thus, the final CBGT adolescent protocol became an integration of (a) an OCD protocol for individual CBT in children (March & Mulle, 1998), (b) the psycho-biobehavioral approach for adults popularized in *Brain Lock* (Schwartz, 1996; Schwartz, Martin, & Baxter, 1992), and (c) traditional exposure therapy designed for adults (Foa & Franklin, 2001; Foa & Wilson, 2001). A more formal test of this integrated adolescent protocol was done in a pilot study consisting of a group of seven adolescents, some of whom were comorbid with ADHD, body dysmorphic disorder, Tourette's disorder, or depression (Söchting & Third, 2011). The CBGT protocol consists of two main components, psychoeducation and ERP. The group, consisting of between five and eight members, meets for 12 2-hour weekly sessions. The optimal age range for group membership is 14–18, but younger people can be included so long as they understand the treatment rationale for ERP and are able to attend sessions and engage in homework. It is, by the way, a good idea to offer this group during the summer months when children are out of school. Dropout rates are low and some groups have none, suggesting this group treatment is acceptable and tolerable to youth. In the following text, I discuss each of the two key components in the protocol—psychoeducation and ERP.

Psychoeducation in CBGT for adolescent OCD

The facilitators begin by engaging the group in a discussion of what defines an obsession and a compulsion and how the two phenomena are connected. A model is sketched on the board starting with a trigger, which is followed by an obsession, which is followed by a range of distressing emotions which in turn leads to a compulsion as a way of neutralizing the distressing emotions (Figure 13.1).

For example, one adolescent's trigger was attending a religious service with his parents. His obsessions took the form of a repeated and relentless mental image popping into his mind of "God as a jester." Based on his appraisal of this image as meaning he was a "blasphemous person who secretly had no respect for God"

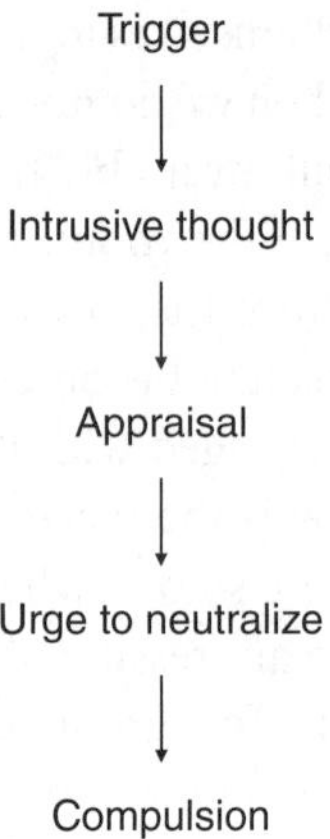

Figure 13.1 Cognitive behavioral model of OCD.

(an example of attaching overimportance to thoughts), he was overwhelmed with guilt and anxiety, which diminished as he engaged in quiet compulsive praying, over and over again. (Incidentally, part of his exposure involved drawing exactly what this jester image looked like, which was at first terrifying for him but later became easier as he came to see the image was "just an obsession" and had nothing to do with his and his family's actual understanding of what God is about.) Looking at the model on the board, we ask the group where they think treatment ought to intervene in order to interrupt the vicious OCD cycle, with its short-term relief but long-term worsening of OCD. Invariably, some suggest intervening at the level of obsessions.

This creates an opportunity for the facilitators to provide education about how common obsessions are. For example, most people will admit to once in a while having a weird thought about how easy it would be to, for example, pull the bow of a performing violinist, or wonder if it was okay to sit down on the toilet seat in a pretty messy public washroom, or even the fleeting thought of how easy it would be to suffocate a screaming baby. The difference between people who do not have OCD and those who do is that the former just smile at their "silly" thoughts, trusting themselves to not act them out. In contrast, people with OCD believe that *just* because the thought came to them means it must be super important, probably true—and worse—that they may act it out. The youngsters also engage in animated discussions of how the illness of OCD is incredibly sneaky and cruel, trying to get them where it hurts the most. The young fellow with God jester obsessions came to see that it was precisely because his religious practice was important and sacred that OCD would zoom in on that instead of something he cared less about.

Youngsters with OCD (and also adults with OCD) are often surprised to hear that there is no recorded incident in history of a person with bona fide OCD causing harm to anybody. Indeed, OCD sufferers are among the gentlest, most conscientious, and careful people—which is one of the reasons therapists enjoy working with them. Charles Darwin likely had OCD, but was nevertheless able to keep it at bay and remain productive in his field. He did, however, struggle. Anecdotes suggest he would wake up in the middle of the night—upset—because he had not written back to somebody in a timely manner or that he had perhaps allowed himself to be misunderstood by not fully explaining an argument or an idea. In other words, Darwin's conscientiousness hovered just on the border of a more debilitating OCD.

After a rich discussion, the group usually agrees that if the OCD cycle is to be broken, treatment will have to be placed *after* the obsessions but *before* the compulsions. The facilitators proceed to explain that the treatment principle of ERP is exactly that, namely, to welcome the obsession but to take the power away from it by **not** neutralizing it with compulsive behaviors. The facilitators further elaborate that over time, group members will begin to see that nothing terrible happens if they just stay with their fear, carry on with more important tasks, and realize it is just an obsession and has nothing to do with the truth about themselves (they are not potentially dangerous people) or how things really are (fatal diseases cannot be contracted from ordinary use of public washrooms).

To further help young people diminish the power of obsessions, March and Mulle (1998) introduced the idea of cultivating *mindful detachment* and of externalizing the OCD. Schwartz also encourages externalizing techniques with his *relabeling* practice. Relabeling—or mindful detachment—teaches clients that their obsessions are not ordinary thoughts but rather the symptoms of OCD and, therefore, they must be *relabeled* and referred to as what they are, namely, obsessions. Clients are encouraged to distance themselves from these obsessions and view them as bizarre "messages" that "do not belong to me" and could be experienced as "passing clouds in the sky." To enhance this idea, and inspired by the March and Mulle protocol, we instruct our clients to make graphic representations of what their OCD looks or feels like and to discuss this with the group (Chapter 2 included an example of such a representation).

Exposure, response prevention, and refocusing

After about three sessions of psychoeducation, the latter nine are devoted to ERP. The first step involves building a master treatment plan in the form of an *exposure hierarchy* to guide a systematic approach to the ERP exercises to be practiced both in the group sessions and between them. In Chapter 9, I reviewed how to build an exposure hierarchy, and it is the same process for younger people. Based on the completed hierarchies, the group facilitators meet before the group session and plan individual, paired, or trio exposures for all group members. This enhances treatment compliance due to the support, humor, and sense of shared experience. To further improve treatment compliance, the facilitators strive to develop *creative exposures*.

As a psychologist with an admitted tendency to be more comfortable with sitting in my chair, hands in lap, I have greatly benefited from cofacilitating CBGT for OCD with an occupational therapist. Occupational therapists get up from their chairs, move around, and magically create all sorts of wonderful and highly therapeutic props for OCD exposures, such as look-like-blood pieces of gauze, flowers that need to be potted in "dirty" soil, and clay for sculpting a particular sexual or aggressive obsession, to name just a few.

Some examples of effective exposures in our groups have included a 14-year-old girl with contamination fears who collected various junk and garbage items from the street before using art supplies to create her *contamination collage*. A veritable piece of modern art! A 13-year-old girl with obsessions about getting cancer contacted the local cancer agency to inquire about volunteering there. She also drew a story board depicting herself receiving treatment for cancer in a hospital. A 15-year-old boy with obsessions about everything being "just so" and neatly ordered was eventually able to tolerate group members writing personal and encouraging messages on his group folder. He had been especially distressed by spelling mistakes and messy erasing.

A 17-year-old young man who obsessed that he was gay directed a skit with various roles assigned to all the group members, where he played the role of a gay man attempting to pick up another. During the debriefing, he expressed relief from having acted out his worst fears, which then lessened their grip on him. For any youngster who obsesses about being lesbian, gay, bisexual, or transgender (LGBT), it is obviously important to have at least one thorough assessment (a second opinion is helpful too) to ensure that the obsessions are indeed consistent with OCD and not related to the emergence of an LGBT identity, which must not be pathologized.

The refocusing option in ERP allows people to do something engaging and wholesome for at least 15 minutes after their exposure. Instead of performing compulsions, group members refocus on an alternative behavior, a behavior that is constructive and enjoyable, such as walking, exercise, crafts, or listening to music. Alternatively, they can refocus by trying to continue the activity that their compulsive urge had interrupted. This is especially relevant for doing ERP at home outside of the group sessions. Reviewing one's success with battling OCD in the form of repeating positive self-talk is another highly portable refocusing option. Optimal activities require concentration and the involvement of other people and are thus incompatible with the compulsive behavior. After 15 minutes, group members notice that the urge to perform the compulsion has diminished. The aim of refocusing on an alternative behavior is to facilitate response prevention, not to interfere with the process of desensitization. This approach has also been successfully used in a wait-list-control telephone-administered CBT for OCD (Taylor et al., 2003). Here are two examples of refocusing activities following an exposure.

A 15-year-old has repacked several garbage bags as part of his exposure and is struggling with a strong need to go and wash his hands. He eases this urge by engaging in a card game with two other group members. There is usually lots of laughter during such a game and the added therapeutic benefit of a kind of "double exposure" as the "contaminated" cards are passed around. After 15 minutes, his anxiety has decreased from an initial rating of 95/100 to 50/100, and he feels more confident he can manage the rest of the group and return home without washing his hands. A 17-year-old girl who has written a poem on the board with several deliberate mistakes for "the world to see" (her OCD included perfectionism) may attempt to cope with her urge to go and correct the mistakes by making some candles (the occupational therapists need to have all supplies available prior to the group starting). As she returns and sees the board, her anxiety increases, but it does not seem as important as she simultaneously admires the candles she made and receives compliments about them.

The facilitators strive to work with group members' particular interests as this increases compliance and motivation. The *Leisure Skills Inventory*, an occupational therapy tool, is a helpful aid in planning exposures with refocusing. Clients can fill it in at the same time they complete other pregroup measures. It asks people about a wide range of leisure activities, from golfing, dancing, and knitting to political involvement (see Appendix H).

New research on brain plasticity may offer further support for the benefit of pairing an adverse experience (the exposure) with a pleasant one (the refocusing). Similar to scores of other neuroscientists interested in brain plasticity, Rick Hanson (2009) describes how mental activity can change neural structure. Hanson argues that because of the brain's well-known negativity bias—like Velcro for the bad but Teflon for the good—this cultivation needs to be skillful and sustained. Otherwise, positive experiences wash through the brain like water through a sieve, while negative ones are caught every time. People can learn to turn positive mental states into positive neural traits by (a) having a good experience in the first place, (b) helping it last 10 or more seconds while feeling it in your body, and (c) sensing that it's sinking into you. It is not about denying or being unaware of what is unpleasant and anxiety provoking but about also—simultaneously—accessing what feels good and pleasant. By taking in the good, you can weave some of these gems into the fabric of your brain and your life. As you build up inner strength and fulfillment through this gradual cultivation, there is less need for the ancient survival reaction of fear and anxiety.

The refocusing option has the added benefits of supporting adolescent clients in increasing their self-esteem as they begin to engage with new interests or leisure activities—making less space, in a sense, for their OCD. Any clinician who has worked with OCD clients knows how their lives are usually impoverished. It is difficult for many to answer the question: what will you do when OCD takes up less time in your life? In fact, my experience with OCD has included many examples of adolescents (and adults) who are reluctant and feel ambivalent about what getting better will entail, perhaps fearing they will become just *ordinary* people. A more comprehensive treatment approach, which supports the client in developing new interests and talents, is therefore highly therapeutic. It has been invigorating for my practice to follow the research in brain plasticity, which was not available when I was a student. More research directly comparing the refocusing option to traditional ERP, ideally in a randomized controlled design, would be helpful.

Capitalizing on the Group for Youth OCD

CBGT for youth OCD can enhance adherence to treatment by providing opportunities for turning developmental issues into helpful process factors. When adolescents share coping skills during difficult exposure challenges their anxiety is mitigated due to a sense of "being in it together." The earlier example of a young man with gay obsessions showed how important it was to not be judged by his peers when he shared these obsessions. Developmentally, adolescence involves the central psychosocial task of moving emotionally from the family of origin "group" to a peer group. Adolescents who can make this transition and reattach to a positive peer group are better equipped to achieve mature adult functioning, including creating connections to healthy communities (Rachman, 1975). Although a CBGT group for youth OCD does not focus on these developmental issues per se, they are reinforced as important process variables.

Shared humor is another factor that may contribute to the effectiveness of CBGT for youth OCD, and it behooves the facilitators to work with humor. It goes without saying that the facilitators pay attention to when humor may become sarcastic and experienced as diminishing for a group member. Fortunately, the vast amount of humor in these groups is healthy and appropriate. The use of humor may be particularly relevant for people with OCD in that exaggerating fears and worst-case scenarios can promote insight into the "silliness" of obsessions, thereby reducing their power. Humor usually comes easy to adolescents—and it is a helpful reminder to not forget to also work with humor in adult OCD groups. The facilitators can include *warm-up* exercises at the beginning of each youth group to stimulate creative thinking and humor. For example, one game is called *The Big Fat Lie*, where each group member in turn tells a plausible but outrageous story about an object that is passed around the group. Another warm-up game includes working with the alphabet where the first person starts with the letter A saying, "My name is Alison, my partner's name is Adam, we live in Ankara, and sell Anchovies." The next person gives a name, a partner's name, a place, and something to sell starting with B. It is not difficult to picture how these brief warm-ups get the groups off to a good engaged and cohesive start. These warm-ups are another helpful contribution from occupational therapists cofacilitating OCD groups.

Disorders Related to OCD

OCD groups often feel transdiagnostic because of the incredible variation in symptom expression. Each member's unique obsessions and fears whether of not having turned off the stove or of brushing up against a young girl in a crowded area, require a highly individually tailored exposure treatment plan. These differences do, however, not influence treatment outcomes. Part of the education about OCD involves clients' learning that it is the same psychological mechanism that drives the different expressions of obsessions and that the treatment principles are also similar. Efforts to create more pure groups by lumping "washers" or "checkers" or "obsessions only" into distinct groups probably have more to do with lessening the anxiety of the group therapists than the clients. The challenges of working with different subtypes of OCD were reviewed in Chapter 9.

Not only are clinicians encouraged to include all subtypes of OCD in their groups but to further include the OCD-related disorders. For example, a youngster may have both OCD and hair-pulling (trichotillomania) and someone in the group may have body dysmorphic disorder, tics, and only mild OCD (Farrell, Waters, Milliner, & Ollendick, 2012; Himle, Fischer, Van Etten, Janeck, & Hanna, 2003). Our OCD groups for adolescents (and adults) include people with hair-pulling (trichotillomania), skin-picking, and body dysmorphic disorder. All these disorders are now reclassified in DSM-5 as part of *Obsessive–Compulsive and Related Disorders*. Hoarding has also commonly been included in most CBT groups for OCD, but it presents a particular challenge and is best treated in separate compulsive hoarding groups. Hence, consistent with the new DSM-5 diagnosis of hoarding disorder, I have added a separate chapter devoted to hoarding, Chapter 15.

The OCD-Related Disorders involve repetitive behaviors—such as pulling one's hair out, picking at one's skin, or biting nails—that are similar to features of OCD in that they involve a strong urge to engage in a behavior that will bring about a sense of release and relief from pent-up tension. For example, hair pulling (trichotillomania) involves repetitive pulling out of one's hair from scalp, eyebrows, eyelashes, or anywhere on the body, including pubic area. Onset is usually during the teen years and before age 17. Body dysmorphic disorder involves an intense preoccupation with a defect in appearance. The defect is either imagined, or if a slight defect is present, the individual's concern is markedly excessive (e.g., believing one's hair hangs asymmetrically and one's eyes are too far apart or too close together). Like hair-pulling disorder, onset is usually during adolescence, but help is often not sought until early or middle adulthood.

CBT for both disorders involves a number of components, including self-monitoring, relaxation training, cognitive restructuring with primary focus on perfectionism, ERP, and habit reversal training. Habit reversal training involves encouraging the client to engage in a behavior that is incompatible with the habit (an agonist action). For example, a woman who in addition to OCD has a vocal tic in the form of uncontrollable loud grunts may be trained to engage in deep breathing as soon as she notices the slightest urge to "grunt." For a full description of the CBT approach for tics, see O'Connor's treatment manual *Cognitive-Behavioral Management of Tic Disorders* (2005). For body dysmorphic clients, cognitive restructuring in the form of positive self-affirmations and acceptance is included as well as exposure. In a CBT group for OCD, people with these two disorders benefit from the same psychoeducation about how a thought, image, or urge leads to behavior that neutralizes intense anxiety or other negative feelings. So, in addition to working with examples from the OCD people, the facilitators may say to a group member, 16-year-old Ken, with hair-pulling disorder:

THERAPIST: And for you, Ken, the issue is not so much a thought about contamination or inappropriate behavior, but rather an overwhelming urge to reach for your scalp and pull. In fact, you're not even fully aware of this strong urge until after the fact, in a sense. Just like Winnie said she felt better after washing her hands, you feel better after having pulled and find it near impossible to not pull. Did we get that right?

KEN: Absolutely. It's hard to explain, but I feel this sense of peace and calm. However it doesn't last long, because I get angry with myself and I'm ashamed of having no eyebrows, and I really want them to grow out.

COTHERAPIST: For your exposure today, Ken, we wondered if you would be OK with slowing down the movements and process that brings your hand to your eyebrow and then, instead of pulling, you'll bring your hands to some clay and make whatever kind of sculpture you feel like [example of *competing behavior* or *habit reversal*]. Our student therapist, Brian, will support you all the way through and we encourage you to express your feelings, including not giving into your pulling *but doing something else* instead with your hands.

KEN: Sounds good. I also brought some of that silly putty that Jessica suggested I could fiddle with instead of pulling, and it actually helped, especially when on the bus. When my hands are squeezing the putty, they obviously cannot also be in my hair at the same time.

COTHERAPISTS: Good to hear that was helpful. In our homework go-round today, other people may have additional suggestions for how you can more meaningfully occupy your hands over the next week.

For a client with body dysmorphic disorder, exposure to asymmetry is often helpful. This can be as simple as allowing another group member to mark dots on one cheek but not the other, walking in a public place with one pant leg rolled up, and allowing another group member to paint some fingernails, but not others. Positive affirmations aimed at personal acceptance can involve the group writing anonymous compliments on pieces of paper placed in a box. Clients with body dysmorphia can read the compliments out loud, keep them, and begin to broaden their fixed beliefs about what others do or do not fixate on or care about when they look at them. Clinicians agree that a group format is optimal for people with body dysmorphic disorder because of all the explicit and implicit social exposures and strong messages about how other people truly do not see—or care about—the slight flaws in appearance that so concern the afflicted group member. This member's ability to have a positive impact on others, show genuine interest in them, and form social connections become wholesome alternatives to their preoccupation with personal physical imperfections.

Common Challenges in CBGT for Youth OCD

Preventing dropouts and managing the role of parents are two key challenges in creating successful CBT groups for youth with OCD. The majority of this chapter has discussed various ways to make these groups interesting and engaging for youths. But the issue of the role of parents is equally important. Unlike CBT for OCD in younger children, it does not always work to insist that parents partake in treatment—as many youth object to this and are legally able to consent to treatment without parental knowledge and consent. On the other hand, we also know that the home environment is critical in terms of how it accommodates or therapeutically helps people cope with their OCD. Clinicians working with youth must actively work with these ethical issues.

One solution is to offer a parallel parental support group, which meets two or more times during the CBGT youth group. All the youth are informed about this and told that the facilitators will not speak about any one member's treatment in the group but rather inform the parents about general issues in OCD and its treatment. Obtaining this trust from the youth is critical, and in our groups, there has not been an instance where a youth felt betrayed. There is usually a good turnout for such parent information evenings. Some youth have four or more parents, stepparents, grandparents, or other adults who care about them show up. After a general introduction to OCD, issues regarding what is *normal* invariably come up and generate stimulating discussions. For example, a parent may ask if it is normal that the hot water tank gets depleted twice a day, or if other teenage parents rewash the same load of laundry four times, or if other teenage children throw a complete temper tantrum if anybody enters their room and "contaminates" it. The facilitators lead a discussion of what constitutes more normal manifestations of a healthy separation–individuation process and then distinguish which youth behaviors are likely driven by OCD as opposed to more ordinary parent–youth power struggles. It becomes clear that the parents who themselves struggle with anxiety or OCD have an especially tough time staying calm and distinguishing between OCD-enabling and OCD-coping behaviors. Sometimes, information about where the parents can seek treatment themselves is given out. Handouts, such as *Expert Consensus Guidelines for Obsessive–Compulsive Disorder: A Guide for Patients and Families*, can be downloaded from www.psychguides.com/oche.html and given to parents.

Summary

This chapter shows how OCD for youth—similar to OCD for adults—is best treated in a separate CBT group and not in a group with other anxiety disorders. However, consistent with changes to the diagnostic classification system reflected in the DSM-5, people with OCD can be treated in the same group as those with OCD-related disorders such as hair pulling, skin picking, and body dysmorphic. A group format is highly effective for youth with OCD. In addition to the usual benefits of CBGT, a group format for youth includes advantages related to the particular developmental stage of adolescents. Peer validation and sharing are hugely important during adolescence and likely even more so for those youth with OCD who feel, and are, different from the majority. But for these groups to be successful in terms of attracting and keeping youth, therapists may need to consider variations on more traditional CBT techniques. Some examples of this are described and illustrated.

Note

1. The Y-BOCS (Goodman et al., 1989) is considered the gold-standard measure of OCD symptoms. Scores of 0–7 suggests subclinical OCD, 8–15 mild, 16–23 moderate, and above 23 severe.

Recommended Readings for Clinicians

Abramowitz, J. S. (2006). The psychological treatment of Obsessive-Compulsive Disorder. *Canadian Journal of Psychiatry, 51(7)*, 407–416.

Barrett, P. M., Farrell, L., Pina, A. A., Peris, T. S., & Piacentini, J. (2008a). Evidence-based psychosocial treatments for child and adolescent obsessive-compulsive disorder. *Journal of Clinical Child and Adolescent Psychology, 37(1)*, 131–155.

Foa, E., & Franklin, M. E. (2001). Obsessive-compulsive disorder. In D. H. Barlow (Ed.), *Clinical handbook of psychological disorders* (3rd ed., pp. 209–263). New York: Guilford Press.

Foa, E., & Wilson, R. (2001). *Stop obsessing: How to overcome your obsessions and compulsions* (Rev. ed.). New York: Bantam Books.

March, J. S., & Mulle, K. (1998). *OCD in children and adolescents: A cognitive behavioral treatment manual.* New York: Guilford Press.

O'Connor, K. P. (2005). *Cognitive-behavioral management of tic disorders.* West Sussex, UK: John Wiley & Sons.

References

American Psychiatric Association (APA). (2000). *Diagnostic and statistical manual of mental disorders, DSM* (4th ed.). Washington, DC: Author.

APA. (2013). *Diagnostic and statistical manual of mental disorders, DSM* (5th ed.). Washington, DC: Author.

Asbahr, F. R., Castillo, A. R., Ito, L. M., Latorre, M. D. R. D. D. O., Moreira, M. N., & Lotufo-Neto, F. (2005). Group cognitive-behavioural therapy versus Sertraline for the treatment of children and adolescent with obsessive-compulsive disorder. *Journal of the American Academy for Child and Adolescent Psychiatry, 44(11)*, 1128–1136.

Barrett, P., Healy-Farrell, L., & March, J. (2004). Cognitive behavioral family treatment of childhood obsessive-compulsive disorder: A controlled trial. *Journal of the American Academy of Child & Adolescent Psychiatry, 43(1)*, 46–62.

Barrett, P. M, Farrell, L., Pina, A. A., Peris, T. S., & Piacentini, J. (2008b). Evidence-based psychosocial treatments for child and adolescent obsessive-compulsive disorder. *Journal of Clinical Child and Adolescent Psychology, 37(1)*, 131–155.

Barrett, P. M., Shortt, A. L., Fox, T. L., & Wescombe, K. (2001). Examining the social validity of the FRIENDS treatment program for anxious children. *Behaviour Change, 18(2)*, 63–77.

Chowdhury, U., Caulfield, C., & Heyman, I. (2003). A group for children and adolescents with obsessive compulsive disorder. *Psychiatric Bulleting, 27*, 187–189.

Farrell, L., Waters, A., Milliner, E., & Ollendick, T. (2012). Comorbidity and treatment response in pediatric obsessive-compulsive disorder: A pilot study of group cognitive-behavioral treatment. *Psychiatry Research, 199*, 115–123.

Fisher, D. J., Himle, J. A., & Hanna, G. L. (1998). Group behavioral therapy for adolescents with obsessive-compulsive disorder: Preliminary outcomes. *Research and Social Work Practice, 8*, 629–636.

Goodman, W. K., Price, L. H., Rasmussen, S. A., Mazure, C., Fleischmann, R. L., Hill, C. L., et al. (1989). The Yale-Brown Obsessive-Compulsive Scale: Development, use, and reliability. *Archives of General Psychiatry, 46*, 1006–1011.

Hanson, R. (2009). *Buddha's brain: The practical neuroscience of happiness, love and wisdom.* Oakland, CA: New Harbinger Publications.

Himle, J. A., Fischer, D. J., Van Etten, M. L., Janeck, A. S., & Hanna, G. L. (2003). Group behavioral therapy for adolescents with tic-related and non-tic-related obsessive-compulsive disorder. *Depression and Anxiety, 17*, 73–77.

Kessler, R. C., Chiu, W. T., Demler, O., & Walters, E. E. (2005). Prevalence, severity, and comorbidity at 12-month DSM-IV disorder in the national comorbidity survey replication. *Archives of General Psychiatry, 62*, 617–627.

March, J. S., Biederman, J., Wolkow, R., Safferman, A., Mardekian, J., & Cook, E. H. (1998). Sertraline in children and adolescents with obsessive-compulsive disorder: A multi-center randomized controlled trial. *Journal of the American Medical Association, 280*, 1752–1756.

March, J. S., Mulle, K., & Herbel, B. (1994). Behavioral psychotherapy for children and adolescents with obsessive-compulsive disorder: An open trial of a new protocol-driven treatment package. *Journal of the American Academy of Child and Adolescent Psychiatry, 33*, 333–341.

McLean, P. D., Whittal, M. L., Thordarson, D., Taylor, S., Söchting, I., Koch, W. J., et al. (2001). Cognitive versus behavior therapy in the group treatment of obsessive-compulsive disorder. *Journal of Consulting and Clinical Psychology, 69*, 205–214.

Obsessive-Compulsive Cognitions Working Group. (1997). Cognitive assessment of obsessive-compulsive disorder. *Behaviour Research and Therapy, 35*, 667–681.

Obsessive-Compulsive Cognitions Working Group. (2001). Development and initial validation of the Obsessive-beliefs Questionnaire and the Interpretation of Intrusions Inventory. *Behaviour Research and Therapy, 39*, 987–1006.

O'Leary, E. M. M., Barrett, P., & Fjermestad, K. W. (2009). Cognitive-behavioral family treatment for childhood obsessive-compulsive disorder: A 7-year follow-up study. *Journal of Anxiety Disorders, 23(7)*, 973–978.

Rachman, A. (1975). *Identity group psychotherapy with adolescents.* Northvale, NJ: Jason Aronson.

Reynolds, S. A., Bowers, G., Norton, E., Clark, S., Smith, H., Langdon, E., et al. 2013. Randomized controlled trial of parent-enhanced CBT compared with individual CBT for obsessive-compulsive disorder in young people. *Journal of Consulting and Clinical Psychology, 81*, 1021–1026.

Salkovskis, P. M. (1996). *Cognitive-behavioral approaches to the understanding of obsessional problems.* In R. Rapee (Ed.), *Current controversies in the anxiety disorders* (pp. 103–133). New York: Guilford Press.

Schwartz, J. (1996) *Brain lock.* New York: Harper Collins.

Schwartz, J. K., Martin, K. M., & Baxter, L. R. (1992). Neuroimaging and cognitive-behavioral self-treatment for obsessive-compulsive disorder: Practical and philosophical considerations. In I. Hand, W. K., Goodman, & U. Evers (Eds.), *Obsessive-compulsive disorders: New research* (pp. 82–101). Berlin: Springer Verlag.

Söchting, I., & March, J. (2002). Cognitive aspects of obsessive-compulsive disorder in children. In. R. O. Frost & G. Steketee (Eds.), *Cognitive approaches to obsessions and compulsions: Theory, assessment, and treatment* (pp. 299–314). Oxford, UK: Elsevier.

Söchting, I., & Third, B. (2011). Behavioral group treatment for obsessive-compulsive disorder in adolescence: A pilot study. *International Journal of Group Psychotherapy, 61(1)*, 84–97.

Söchting, I., Whittal, M. L., & McLean, P. (1997). *Group cognitive behaviour therapy (GCBT) treatment manual for obsessive-compulsive disorder (OCD).* Vancouver, BC: The University of British Columbia.

Swedo, S. E., Rapoport, J. L., Leonard, H., Lenane, M., & Cheslow, D. (1989). Obsessive-compulsive disorder in children and adolescents: Clinical phenomenology of 70 consecutive cases. *Archives of General psychiatry, 46*, 335–341.

Taylor, S., Thordarson, D. S., Spring, T., Yeh, A. H., Corcoran, K. M., Eugster, K., et al. (2003). Telephone-administered cognitive behavior therapy for obsessive-compulsive disorder. *Cognitive Behaviour Therapy, 32(1)*, 13–25.

Thienemann, M., Martin, J., Cregger, B., Thompson, H.B., & Dyer-Friedman, J. (2001). Manual-driven group cognitive-behavioural therapy for adolescents with obsessive-compulsive disorder: A pilot study. *Journal of the American Academy of Child and Adolescent Psychiatry, 40*, 1254–1260.

Thomsen, P. H., & Mikkelsen, H. U. (1993). Development of personality disorders in children and adolescents with obsessive-compulsive disorder: A 6- 22-year follow-up study. *Acta Psychiatrica Scandinavia, 87*, 456–462.

Valleni-Basile, L. A., Garrison, C. Z., Jackson, K. L., Waller, J. L., McKeown, R. E., Addy C. L., et al. (1994). Frequency of obsessive-compulsive disorder in a community sample of young adolescents. *Journal of American Academy for Child and Adolescent Psychiatry, 33*, 782–791.

Whitaker, A., Johnson, J., Shaffer, D., Rapoport, J. L., Kalikow, K., Walsh, B. T., et al. (1990). Uncommon troubles in young people: Prevalence estimates of selected psychiatric disorders in a non-referred adolescent population. *Archives of General Psychiatry, 47*, 487–496.

Wilhelm, S., & Steketee, G. S. (2006). *Cognitive therapy for obsessive-compulsive disorder: A guide for professionals.* Oakland, CA: New Harbinger Publications.

14

Language, Culture, and Immigration

This chapter discusses how CBT and CBGT in particular have emerged as strong candidates for meeting some of the mental health needs of non-English-speaking immigrants and members of minority ethnic groups. Depression is the most common mental health problem of North American immigrants and minority ethnic groups, especially among women. We will explore how standard CBGT protocols for depression can be made appropriate and effective for different cultures. The practical, here and now focus of CBT helps immigrants cope with barriers to successful integration. The group process supports members in realizing their struggles are shared by other immigrants. Cultural adaptations include an explicit and expanded CBT focus on family and interpersonal issues. This chapter shows how CBGT for depression has been adapted to Chinese and Spanish languages and cultures, as well as African American.

CBT clinicians working in multicultural cities are responding in thoughtful and creative ways to the challenge of balancing fidelity to CBT principles with cultural competence and sensitivity. The potential for offering CBT to a larger global arena is attractive to many CBT therapists, who are painfully aware of how psychotherapy has traditionally been a luxury for the more privileged and affluent members of society. Given that some governments, nongovernmental organizations, and humanitarian groups, such as *Doctors Without Borders*, recognize the serious problems of untreated depression and anxiety (including posttraumatic stress disorder [PTSD]) opportunities exist for disseminating CBGT to people with fewer personal resources, whether within Western countries or in developing countries.

In what follows, I first share a CBGT program I was part of developing for Chinese-speaking immigrants to Canada. The second example describes a CBGT

Cognitive Behavioral Group Therapy: Challenges and Opportunities, First Edition. Ingrid Söchting.

program for Spanish-speaking immigrants to the United States. Although these two examples cover highly different populations, they illustrate similar considerations for clinicians interested in creating CBGT that is culturally appropriate and competent. The examples may inspire clinicians and serve as a template for other types of culturally adapted CBGT.

A Chinese Cognitive Behavioral Treatment Program for Chinese Immigrants

A substantial number of immigrants to North America (Canada and the United States) have Asian origins (6.4%; 22.4 million). There are 5.1 million Asian Canadians (14.5% of Canada's total population; Census, 2011) and 17.3 million Asian Americans (5.8% of the total U.S. population; Pew Research Centre, 2012). With the projected increase in this population, there is a need to develop and evaluate culturally appropriate treatments for Asian North Americans. In our efforts to meet some of these needs by developing a Cantonese-language and a Mandarin-language CBGT program to treat depression in Chinese immigrants to North America, we identified a number of culture-related differences in how participants responded to this program compared to their English-language counterparts. Although a program evaluation for the Cantonese groups using a treatment-as-usual design (mainly management by family doctor) showed that the CBGT intervention was overall highly effective in reducing symptoms of depression, we noted a number of culture-related differences in how Cantonese- and Mandarin-speaking clients respond to this CBGT program (Shen, Alden, Söchting, & Tsang, 2006). Of particular importance are issues related to referral and assessment procedures, conversion of Chinese terms for dysphoric affect into English, and cognitive restructuring for challenging negative automatic thoughts and biases in thinking.

Chinese CBGT Program Rationale

The Chinese CBGT programs were developed in response to a community need, given that individuals of Chinese heritage were underrepresented in our local mental health outpatient clinics. While the total ethnic Chinese population of Canada is presently 1.48 million (4.2%; Census, 2011), the suburb for which these programs were designed has a 47% ethnic Chinese population. Yet, rarely do Chinese people present for outpatient mental health treatment. This is, in part, of course due to language and culture barriers. Consistent with these clinical facts, research indicates that, in general, Asians in North America tend to underutilize mainstream mental health services relative to their population size (Bui & Takeuchi, 1992; Fugita, 1990; Snowden & Cheung, 1990), although they have as many, and as serious, mental health problems as their European-heritage counterparts (Li & Browne, 2000; Sue & Morishima, 1982).

There are various explanations for why Chinese people are reluctant to seek mental health treatment. Some writers propose that Chinese cultural values inhibit participation in mental health programs, especially group therapy. Concerns about bringing shame upon the family by disclosing that "all is not well" are prevalent in Asian collectivistic cultures where loyalty to the family often overrides individuals' well-beings (Lin & Cheung, 1999). Also, a cultural emphasis on emotional restraint and inhibition may not mesh with some types of Western psychotherapy, which generally involve discussion of personal topics, exploration of intrapsychic phenomena (dreams, fantasies, wishes), and a focus on the individual's needs and wants (Leong & Lau, 2001). Chinese people are also influenced by the teachings of Confucius who warned that excessive emotions are dangerous and can create social disharmony (Wong, 2011). People of Asian heritage are therefore generally less willing to disclose their personal problems to a mental health professional, let alone speak to an entire group of strangers.

Another explanation for ethnic Chinese people's reluctance to seek mental health treatment pertains to pragmatic factors involved in accessing appropriate services. Even for nonimmigrants, it can be a challenge to navigate entry into effective mental health care. For Chinese immigrants to North America, there are a number of additional barriers. These include a lack of awareness of available mental health services, language problems that interfere with communication with mental health professionals, and concerns about the credibility of the treatment provider, especially if this person is perceived as a "Western" therapist (Iwamasa, 1997; Leong & Lau, 2001; Shin, 2002). Research on the importance of matching client–therapist language and ethnicity underscores how Chinese clients engage better with therapy if it is delivered by an ethnic Chinese therapist speaking Cantonese or Mandarin (Lin, 1994; Okazaki, 2000; Sue, Fujino, Hu, Takeuchi, & Zane, 1991). Consequently, the development of culture- and language-specific programs appears essential to provide effective psychological services to Asian immigrant populations. The programs discussed in this chapter all involve client–therapist ethnic and language matching, that is, the CBGT leaders spoke Cantonese, Mandarin, or Spanish. For immigrants who speak English, there is evidence that ethnic matching may not be crucial so long as clients and therapists speak the same language.

Despite some literature pointing to the importance of client–therapist ethnic match, this is not necessarily associated with better treatment outcomes. Therapists' personal characteristics, such as their cultural sensitivity and empathy, are also highly valued by Chinese immigrant clients, often more than ethnic status alone (see Karlsson, 2005, for a review). Clinicians working in multicultural settings offer insightful perspectives on a potential double standard if they apply the belief in ethnic matching to a reverse scenario, perhaps one of a graduate clinical psychology student from China. Would he not be considered capable of offering CBT for depression to people of European descent? I have supervised several psychiatry residents whose first degrees were from Mainland China or Hong Kong. Their Caucasian clients indicated feeling both understood and helped by the various CBT they received. A match in language is obviously important, but to say that only personal and intimate familiarity with a certain culture equips a therapist to treat clients from that culture could potentially lead to deprivation of opportunities to strengthen our social fabric and to an endorsement of exaggerated cultural stereotypes as opposed to an acceptance of commonalities among people in emotional distress. Fears of coming across as culturally insensitive may be unfounded—so long as the therapist offers genuine interest in and empathy for their clients, along with demonstrating cultural competence.

Clinicians involved with developing CBGT programs for Chinese people agree that many aspects of CBT appear to mesh well with Chinese cultural values. Several studies show CBT to be helpful for depressed Chinese people (Dai et al., 1999; Wong, 2007). And clinician researchers agree that CBT is highly compatible with Chinese culture. Chinese people have less tolerance for ambiguity and prefer a structured therapy that offers practical and immediate solutions to their problems (Leong, 1986). CBT does not require in-depth discussion or analysis of developmental experiences or intrapsychic conflicts and therefore may be better suited to cultures that value emotional restraint. Along those lines of clinical reasoning, we presented our Chinese CBGT programs to the community as a course on mood management and self-change, rather than therapy. A literal translation of the program title was *A Course on Diligent Practice of New Thoughts*.

The program runs for 10 weeks with 2-hour weekly group sessions. Each group of 8 to 10 members is led by one or two either Cantonese- or Mandarin-speaking group therapists. The therapists are bilingual and, depending on level of training, are supervised by non-Chinese-speaking senior CBT therapists. Even if direct supervision is not needed, we prefer that both the English- and Chinese-speaking CBT group therapists meet regularly for peer supervision. This allows for an opportunity to discuss general issues related to delivering CBT in groups but also for dealing with specific cultural issues. Similar to CBGT for depression for English-speaking clients, the Chinese CBGT consists of a combination of didactic presentations by the therapist regarding strategies for mood management, and group discussion focused on applying those strategies to clients' lives. The protocol incorporates standard CBT interventions for depression, such as mood monitoring, behavioral activation, goal setting that includes strategies for increasing social contacts, and the identification and challenge of unhelpful thoughts and beliefs using Thought Records. Each session also includes homework assignment.

Referral Issues

One challenge facing programs for ethnic minorities is reaching clients to inform them about mental health services and how to enroll in them. Our program sends informational material to Chinese health-care professionals and makes presentations on Chinese radio shows. These kinds of community outreach initiatives are similar to other immigrant CBGT programs. Our primary referral source is Chinese family physicians and psychiatrists, and their willingness to refer patients to the program is essential to treatment delivery. The majority of clients in our program say they have difficulty negotiating the referral process. This seems due either to lack of assertiveness with their physicians, physician reluctance, or problems understanding how the health-care system bureaucracy works in North America. When the referral process itself is a barrier, it does not help to reduce the stigma many immigrants feel with accessing mental health services. Fortunately, many referring Chinese physicians are well aware of the co-occurrence of somatic symptoms along with other indications of depression. Understanding this co-occurrence of somatic symptoms may make it easier for physicians to make appropriate referrals. It also provides an opportunity to educate physicians less familiar with various cultural expressions of depression.

Approximately one-third of our clients self-initiate their referrals. Moreover, nearly all express eagerness to attend the program and seem highly motivated. They look forward to their group treatment and are happy to find a service in their own language. Dropout rates are within a reasonable range at around 18%. We thus do not have much evidence suggesting that Chinese clients feel ashamed or concerned about stigmatization when coming to an outpatient psychotherapy program. The extent to which the program is presented as an *educational course* versus a *mental health* program may help ethnic Chinese people feel more comfortable with seeking help. We suspect it is one of the reasons for the high suitability of CBT to this cultural adaptation.

Assessment

While our Chinese clients have sufficient literacy to fill out the forms and questionnaires in Cantonese or Mandarin, some are less accustomed to filling out such documents than their North American counterparts. Considering how North American public health services tend to include numerous documents advising clients of the rights to confidentiality, how their personal data will be protected, limits to that protection, etc., clinicians working with clients not accustomed to this process may want to think about ways to reduce this barrier. Indeed, in Hong Kong, many people solicit the help of professional "form fillers" when handling formal documents.

Similar to English-speaking clients in a general mental health CBGT service, Chinese-speaking clients also attend an hour-long structured clinical assessment interview in their own language. Again, similar to English-speaking clients, they welcome the interview and are generally at ease during it. Many report that they feel better even after the assessment interview, stressing how they treasure the opportunity to speak with a mental health professional in their own language. Some of the findings gathered from the structured interview nevertheless have important implications for our understanding of culturally competent mental health services.

When asked about their mood, most clients report a dysphoric, or sad, affect. But a substantial majority denies being depressed. The term *depressed* is an uncommon word in the lexicon of everyday conversation in Chinese. It was translated into *you-yu* in Mandarin and *yau-wat* in Cantonese, probably during the days when Western psychiatry was introduced into China. *You-yu* and *yau-wat* both imply a somewhat different emotional construct than the English term *depression*. The problem with the word depression is not unique to the Chinese culture, but to many other non-Western cultures as well. Instead, *sadness* seems to be a concept common to many cultures (Brandt & Boucher, 1986). Our Chinese clients prefer words such as "sad" and "unhappy" instead of "depressed" when talking about their feeling states. In structured clinical interviews, Chinese clients endorse fewer symptoms of depression when asked directly and often fail to meet formal criteria for a mood disorder. This contrasts with how they talk about their problems. Their descriptions of day-to-day functioning suggest they do have significant problems with depression and especially with using helpful coping skills.

In Cantonese, the phrase denoting sadness is *ng hoi sum*, literally meaning "the heart is not open." In Chinese culture, the heart is considered the seat of the psyche and the master of all emotions. It is therefore not surprising that psychology is translated as "the study of the logic of the heart" (*sum lei hok*). Our depressed Chinese clients do make repeated reference to their heart as either open or closed. It is important to recognize this as a metaphor for feelings because expressions of this kind can be mistaken as somatic complaints.

Another difficulty in assessing symptoms of depression in Chinese people involves inquiring about bodily symptoms related to sexual functioning. In general, Chinese people find it hard to distinguish between sexual interest and sexual behavior. When asked about their sexual interest, the majority interpret the question to be about their sexual behavior. They will therefore have difficulty saying they have sexual feelings if they are not actually in a relationship involving sexual connections. For example, several women reported their spouse being away for months working in Asia and they felt the question irrelevant. In contrast, non-Chinese clients are more likely to say they have sexual interests or feelings even when not having opportunities to engage in sexual behaviors with a partner. Or they will express difficulty with sexual arousal, as is common in depression, even if engaging in regular sexual activities with a partner. Questions tapping into sexual interest, which are common in many self-report questionnaires on depression, may not be useful when applied to Chinese clients. Further probing into this area during an interview could be considered too intrusive and voyeuristic according to Chinese standards.

Other difficulties in assessing depression revolve around the concepts of helplessness and hopelessness. The distinction between the two has been accorded clinical significance in the Western literature, especially when considering the risk for suicide. Unlike English-speaking clients, our Chinese clients have difficulty responding to questions about hopelessness. While they find helplessness (*mo jor*) easy to understand, many fail to see how hopelessness (*mo mong*) is any different from helplessness. It appears to them that both terms connote little control over their current and future problems. While many depressed Chinese clients volunteer feelings of helplessness, few talk about hopelessness. Some even look bewildered when asked about it. It is unclear whether this may relate to most Chinese subscribing to spiritual beliefs about not interfering with fate. Although the *Beck Hopelessness Scale* has been successfully translated into the

Chinese Hopelessness Scale (Shek, 1993), this does not necessarily mean that hopelessness is a concept that Chinese clients are used to working with in daily living.

CBGT Treatment Issues for Depressed Chinese People

The vast majority of Chinese clients enrolling in CBGT for depression easily understand the treatment rationale for CBT. They are motivated to learn and apply the various presented interventions. There are, however, some unique challenges in applying CBT to this population—and some valuable insights and suggestions for protocol revisions continue to emerge.

Challenging unhelpful thinking

The most important challenge facing group therapists working with depressed Chinese people is a certain resistance to the idea of unhelpful beliefs displayed by nearly all of the group members (Wong, 2011). Although most easily grasp the concept of the interrelatedness between mood, thoughts, and behavior, they display minimal insight into how their own maladaptive thinking patterns are interfering with their functioning. This is in some contrast to English-speaking clients—or those of European heritage—who more readily acknowledge how their "negative" thinking contributes to their low mood. We have noted that our Chinese clients hold on to several assumptions commonly referred to as *irrational* or *dysfunctional beliefs* in the depression treatment literature, especially beliefs including the following: "Anger is bad," "I must take care of others before myself," and "If I say no, I am a selfish person." Initial attempts by the group therapists to gently challenge these beliefs and frame them as, for example, *black-and-white thinking*, often reveal that group members treat these beliefs as a kind of universal truth intimately linked to their Chinese heritage. They reason, therefore, that any questioning of their beliefs would feel like a betrayal of their culture and, in some cases, a sense of having been corrupted by Western values.

Personally, I admit to disliking even more the original CBT term *irrational* and even *dysfunctional* after my experience of offering CBT to cultures other than the one I was raised in. Although values such as "I must first take care of others before myself" can be highly problematic for people suffering from depression no matter what culture, I hesitate to label it irrational. Someone from a non-Western culture could similarly suggest that a not uncommon Western, individualistic value such as "I have a right to get what I want" is equally irrational. Along with many CBT therapists, I much prefer terms such as *unhelpful* thinking. Group therapists are obviously faced with a unique challenge as no existing manual on CBT for depression addresses these kinds of culture-specific *core beliefs*.

As for references to universal truths about Chinese cultural values, the Chinese-speaking group therapists tread carefully but do address this head-on. A helpful intervention is for the group therapists to generate—with the group—a list of maladaptive beliefs that depressed people in both Western and Asian cultures hold including the belief "My elderly parents' needs are always more important than my own." We see many examples of how cultural expectations for reverence and obedience to older generations can become problematic for a depressed adult child. Therapists thus both educate about the universality of beliefs that can lead to depression and validate the cultural underpinning of strong beliefs. They emphasize the importance of a continuum and that all beliefs—if taken to an extreme—can become implicated in depression. Clients are encouraged to adopt a certain "open stance" to new possibilities coupled with an *experimental attitude*, much like experimenting with a new way of preparing certain foods to bring out maximum flavor. Wong (2011) offers a helpful continuation of this discussion of the challenges in cognitive restructuring. In his CBT groups for depressed Chinese people in Hong Kong, he explicitly refers to the many *rules* about family and interpersonal relationships in Chinese culture. In his groups, he encourages direct questions, such as "How have these rules been affecting you and the people around you?" and "Is it worth holding onto your rules and values?" (Wong, 2011). After some group discussions on these cognitive priming exercises, the group therapists proceed to the full 7-column Thought Records (Greenberger & Padesky, 1995). Similar to CBGT for depressed English-speaking clients as reviewed in Chapter 5, individual examples are used in-turn, and therapists encourage modeling and support between group members.

How to improve homework compliance?

Another challenge is homework. Even though the CBGT program is advertised as a course and the self-help concept is continually reinforced by the therapists, most Chinese clients express strong negative opposition to the requirement of doing homework. (As we will see later, Latino immigrants also struggle with homework completion.) While Chinese clients support the idea of homework in principle, the compliance rate runs only about 60%. Homework assignment is an integral part of any CBT protocol, and while compliance is often an issue in non-Chinese clients, it is rare to encounter the kind of strong opposition shown by Chinese clients. This negative reaction is further surprising given the strong value typically placed on education and achievement in the Chinese community.

A culturally sensitive analysis of homework noncompliance suggests a couple of reasons. One is the possibility that deference to authority figures plays a more important role in this population. Indeed, clients often express a belief that simply coming to the sessions led by an expert should be sufficient and that they do not see any extra gains from struggling on their own outside of sessions. This points to the importance of examining beliefs about homework and about an expert versus a self-help approach. Another, and more subtle, reason may relate to anticipatory shame in the event that one is not able to complete the homework correctly and therefore seen as "failing" the assigned task. From group discussions, it is clear that homework is often experienced as leading to either success or failure, demonstrating a dichotomous black-and-white thinking style.

The group therapists attempt to encourage clients to detach from the idea of success versus failure and instead adopt a more *experimental* attitude. Therapists emphasize that the important issue is not whether clients complete all the homework, but rather what clients learn about themselves, and what makes it easier or more difficult for them to engage in their chosen homework. Another motivational strategy focuses on the economy of time. The therapist reminds the group members, in each group session, that close to a full hour will be allotted to reviewing and assigning homework. Those who do not engage in some homework may, therefore, not feel as engaged with the group—and feel it is a waste of their time—as those who do practice between sessions. This approach sometimes works.

Capitalizing on the group for Chinese immigrants

Although Chinese clients appreciate the more structured CBT approach, with its lower emphasis on personal sharing and stress on education and learning skills, they also consistently express a desire for a more explicit focus on social and interpersonal issues. The majority of the clients in the groups enjoy talking about their immigration experiences, how to adapt and adjust to another culture, and, for many of the women, how to maintain a harmonious family life when their husbands may be in Hong Kong or Mainland China or elsewhere working for months at a time. The social support provided by the group seems especially helpful, and for this reason, clinicians may want to consider extending the group time beyond 10 weeks—or arrange for the continuation of community support beyond the formal group treatment time. Although research shows that CBGT is effective for depressed Chinese people, we do not know the extent to which it is the CBT techniques per se or the mere provision of support to often isolated people coping with a new culture.

Indeed, many group members value opportunities to disclose more personal issues. But many often express a fear of becoming flooded and unable to regulate their emotions. Concerns about being judged and lack of confidentiality are salient. Confidentiality in a group therapy setting does not carry the same meaning among Chinese people as among English speaking. So this issue is repeatedly revisited throughout the group. On the one hand, these clients are eager to address topics like parenting and family struggles, but they tend to be highly reluctant about disclosing issues related to intimate adult/spousal relations until they are certain they can trust the group. Incidentally, the most frequent reason given for seeking help with depression in these Chinese groups is problems with family relations. While CBT may provide the necessary strategies for coping with the depression, the relationship issues that the clients perceive as causing their depression may be better addressed by including an interpersonal focus. Wong draws the same conclusion after years of juggling how to allocate group time to both didactic CBT skills and the hunger for personal disclosures about relationship problems (Wong, 2011).

In our groups, the desire to talk and connect over common issues such as immigration and family concerns is so strong that it goes above and beyond normal group processing. For example, a common theme is worrying about children doing well in school, since a main reason for immigration is often to offer a better future for one's children. These conflicts can be overwhelming for parents who are vulnerable to depression and anxiety. Hence, clinicians working with Chinese immigrants may consider adding a formal family and relationship component to the CBT protocol. In the following text, we will see that this has been done in a CBGT protocol for Spanish-speaking immigrants.

Despite room for improvement in offering culturally sensitive CBGT, we can nevertheless conclude that so long as the CBGT is delivered by a competent, Chinese-speaking therapist who exudes trust and adherence to several ethical standards, including confidentiality, depressed Chinese people are more than willing to seek help for their problems even in a group format. Whether an interpreter would work if no Chinese-speaking therapists are available is a good question. I am not aware of any such groups, but imagine they exist.

We will turn to another example of a validated CBGT protocol for a large immigrant group, that of Latinos, or Spanish-speaking Mexicans, in the United States. We will see that some of the adaptations are similar to those needed for the Chinese protocol. The challenges with implementation also overlap.

A Spanish-Language Cognitive Behavioral Treatment Program for Latino Immigrants

The Latino population is the largest (15%, 45 million) and fastest-growing minority group in the United States, with a projected population of 133 million (29%) by 2050 (Aguilera, Garza, & Muñoz, 2010). Similar to other immigrant populations, including the Chinese discussed previously, disparities in access to effective depression treatment are well documented (Alegría et al., 2008). Latinos in the United States experience higher rates of depression than Caucasians and African Americans but receive fewer mental health services. The need for an innovative and evidence-based intervention has been met by a group of clinician researchers who have all participated since 1985 in creating an evolving CBGT protocol for Spanish-speaking immigrants with depression. As we will see in the following discussion, the initial 16-week protocol has been applied with some flexibility at different sites, and a shortened, 8-session version is also available.

Referral and Access Issues

Similar to the Chinese clients, the Spanish speaking Latinos are primarily referred by their family physicians. For the protocol involving the expanded health module, most referrals come from primary care physicians who refer for behavioral management of a chronic disease such as hypertension and who consider the depression to be secondary. Physically accessing the group treatment is a more serious obstacle for the Spanish-speaking population compared to the Chinese, where the barriers were more psychological in nature. For those who do not own cars or do not live close to convenient public transit, transportation needs to be arranged. Childcare may also need to be coordinated with bilingual volunteer childcare workers on the site where the group takes place. Lastly, legal issues and fear of deportation can also be barriers, and potential clients need reassurance about confidentiality (Shattell, Quinlan-Colwell, Willalba, Ivers, & Mails, 2010).

Assessment

As is the case with Chinese-speaking people and many other cultures, the concept of depression may not be the same among Latinos as it is for English-speaking Americans. This may be an issue when using measures to assess depressions that were originally developed for Western culture and English-speaking people. Although the Spanish-translated measures of depression scales such as the Center for Epidemiologic Studies Depression (CES-D) scale (Radloff, 1977) and the Beck Depression Inventory (BDI; Bonilla, Bernal, Santos, & Santos, 2004) may be adequate, it is possible that some cultural expressions and understanding of depression still get missed. At this time, however, clinician researchers prefer the translated CES-D and BDI over other measures due to their better reliability and validity (Shattell et al., 2010).

Latino CBGT Program Rationale

The *Group Therapy Manual for Cognitive-Behavioral Treatment of Depression* was initially developed to meet the needs of low-income minority individuals with depression who live in densely populated urban Latino communities. This original Spanish CBGT protocol included 12 sessions each lasting 1.5 hours divided into three modules. The *thought* module focuses on standard cognitive interventions aimed at identifying and replacing unhelpful thinking. The *activity* module focuses on the importance of behavioral activation. The *people* module focuses on the impact of positive social relationships on mood and symptoms. This 12-session protocol was later shortened by Muñoz and Miranda (1996) to an 8-session protocol that retains the original three modules of (1) depression and thinking, (2) goal setting and increase in activities, and (3) family and community relationships. The main difference in this shorter protocol is that more time is devoted to the connection between thinking and symptoms of depression and thus reduced time on the other two modules. The 8-session intervention, the *Muñoz and Miranda Group Therapy Manual for Cognitive-Behavioral Treatment of Depression, Spanish version* (Muñoz & Miranda, 1996), can be downloaded for free (www.rand.org/pubs/monograph_reports/MR1198).

The Muñoz and Miranda manual has also been expanded to 16 weekly 1.5 hour sessions in the *Group Cognitive-Behavioral Therapy for Depression in Spanish: Culture-Sensitive*

Manualized Treatment in Practice (Muñoz, Ghosh Ippen, Rao, Le, & Dwyer, 2000). The 16 sessions are divided into four modules each including four sessions. The first three modules are similar to the 8-session manual described earlier with an emphasis on (1) *thought*, (2) *activity*, and (3) *people*. The fourth and new module is *health*, which focuses on the high levels of comorbid physical health problems in the Spanish-speaking immigrant population, such as diabetes.

The separate modules allow for an open intake, where group members enter at different times and for different modules. For example, new members may enter for module 2, which lasts three sessions, and after modules 3 and 4, they will cycle back to module 1 to complete all the modules of the group.

CBGT Treatment Issues

The people module

The formal inclusion of the *people* module in CBGT for Spanish-speaking immigrants is somewhat rare for any CBT protocol, although the CBGT protocol for elderly depressed clients described in Chapter 11 included one session on the *Role of Your Social Life*. The rationale for the *people* module in the Spanish protocol entails awareness of the importance of social cohesion in Latino cultures. The Spanish word for it is *simpatía* (Aguilera et al., 2010). Aguilera and colleagues argue that depression makes individuals less likely to engage in behaviors that promote social interactions or *simpatía* with others; therefore, social disconnection may be particularly distressing among members of this group. The *people* module highlights how our social world influences our well-being. Not only do the group facilitators educate clients about the importance of social connections and keeping up skills for social interactions, but group members also experience it in the group environment in the here and now. Group members get opportunities to practice social skills when new group members arrive at the beginning of new modules by introducing themselves. During these introductions, members are encouraged to share personal information about their family of origin, birthplace, and personal interests. This explicit integration of *simpatía* into the group treatment strengthens the group climate by increasing everyone's sense of belonging. A similar ritual is offered for members' leaving of the group, and phone numbers are often exchanged. Thus, the modular approach is a deliberate attempt to work with important group process factors specific to the Latino culture.

How to improve homework compliance?

Similar to Chinese-speaking clients in CBGT, homework compliance seems to be a particular challenge for Spanish-speaking clients. It remains a problem despite leaders of Spanish groups consistently referring to homework as *personal project* (proyecto personal), with the intention of avoiding any negative connotation associated with completion of homework in a school setting (Aguilera et al., 2010).[1] It is not uncommon for only two of eight members to complete homework.

To improve this problem with homework completion, some therapists running the Spanish CBGT program have started to include technological adjuncts in the form of an *audio coach* and text messaging. The audio coach is especially helpful for clients with limited education and literacy. The *audio coach* involves brief 2–5 minute summaries recorded by the group facilitators of each CBGT module. They remind clients of the key messages from the session, the rationale for certain interventions, and how to apply them. Clients can listen to these audio recordings between sessions and almost anywhere, since audio MP3 recordings are highly portable. The text messaging adjunct (Txt4Mood) sends automated daily text messages to clients inquiring about mood ratings and additional daily messages corresponding to the previous treatment theme. The messages are meant to reinforce skills and provide feedback on progress and any problems encountered. If clients text the word STRESS, they will receive a message suggesting cognitive and behavioral tips to counteract stressors and low moods. Fortunately, Latinos show particularly high use of mobile phones and text messaging, suggesting that these technological adjuncts may increase the effectiveness of CBGT for this population (Aguilera et al., 2010). It is hard to imagine this technological device to not also be incredibly helpful for the Chinese clients—and all clients for that matter—who struggle with keeping up practice between sessions. Indeed, clinicians are increasingly finding technological aids such as text messaging to be valuable adjuncts in their CBT practice (Shapiro & Bauer, 2010). Shapiro and Bauer offer a useful discussion of the positive aspects of automated messages, including some potential downsides.

Capitalizing on the group in CBGT for Latino immigrants

Clinicians offering CBGT for depressed Latino people consistently find that the opportunities for support in the group seem just as important as the actual CBT interventions—but that the combination of both is most effective. Latino immigrants are often eager to tell their stories, feel understood, and learn from each other. The experiences of validation and normalization are tremendously helpful. Learning how to solve problems to decrease social isolation in their new country is well received. For example, some group therapists describe how group members during the behavioral activation module often set goals to email or call their families in Mexico on a more regular basis (Shattell et al., 2010). This is similar to our experience with other immigrants who are able to participate in English CBGT. Their sense of isolation from their families of origin is a common theme. Various beliefs about not wanting to burden their families with their unhappiness or feeling some guilt for not being able to bring the whole family to their new country can get in the way of initiating more regular contact. These barriers are usually best treated as unhelpful beliefs, and once clients begin to initiate more contact, it usually has a positive effect on their depression.

Another salient interpersonal theme for depressed Latino women is their feelings about themselves as mothers. This is in contrast to the Chinese immigrant women, whose more common theme was how they felt about themselves as wives with absent husbands. Considering that for Latinos, the maternal role is culturally imbued with possibly more significance and meaning than in, for example, the United States, feelings of inadequacy become part of the depression for female immigrants feeling isolated from their own mothers and female role models (Shattell et al., 2010). One suspects that Latinos—and other immigrants—who are able to choose communities that could be considered ethnic enclaves feel less isolated compared to those who end up in more ethnically diverse neighborhoods.

A CBGT Program for African American Women

A further adaptation of the Muñoz and Miranda CBGT protocol for Spanish-speaking depressed people, the *Group Therapy Manual for Cognitive-Behavioral Treatment of Depression*, has been offered with some success to depressed, low-income African American women (Kohn, Oden, Muñoz, Robinson, & Leavitt, 2002). The adaptation was similar to that for Latino immigrants in its focus on family issues but different in also highlighting an awareness of the historical and political context of African women living in the United States. Similar to the Latino immigrant protocol described earlier, the African American CBGT protocol consists of three 4-session CBT modules. For the African women, a total of 16 sessions were offered (with one module, one on the relationship between thoughts and moods, being repeated.) The adaptations were both structural and didactic. Examples of structural changes included, for example, making the group closed instead of open. In this closed group, the women all started and ended together.

It is interesting for CBGT therapists to reflect on the advantages and disadvantages of closed versus open groups. The efficiency of the open group is obvious in terms of reducing wait lists. The opportunities for increased group practice of social skills may be especially important in some cultures, as we saw in the Latino example. The downside is a possible impact on cohesion. This was precisely the reason for keeping the African group closed. The therapists felt that the women would be less likely to experience feelings of safety and belonging if the group was open.

Another change involved the ubiquitous CBT problem of homework! The group members agreed that the term "homework" did not resonate for them and opted for calling their homework between sessions "therapeutic exercises." Other changes involved using African American anecdotes and literary examples as much as possible. Chapter 9 included a broader discussion of alternative names for homework that may be especially helpful for clinicians working with immigrant populations.

There were substantial changes to the CBGT manual to address issues relevant to African American women in treatment for depression. The modules were adapted by including the following: (a) *healthy relationships*, with the purpose of combating social isolation of African American women; (b) *spirituality–religiosity*, with the purpose of exploring faith-based coping strategies; (c) *African American family* issues, with the purpose of identifying generational patterns of behavior and reinforce Black families' history of strength; and (d) *African American female identity*, with the purpose of discussing and combating negative images and affirming Black women.

The African American protocol was compared in an open trial to the Muñoz and Miranda Spanish CBGT protocol, which retains a more traditional CBT focus. Although both groups of women obtained improvements in their depression symptoms as measured by the BDI, the African American protocol had greater improvements with BDI average score of 21.8 versus 24.4 after treatment. It is noteworthy that these posttreatment scores for both groups are still in the *moderate* range, but higher than outcomes from CBT for depression among White people, where BDI scores are around 12 in the *mild* range of depression. It also seems noteworthy that therapists offering CBGT to the African American women observed that irritability, as opposed to sadness, seemed to be the most common emotional expression. The authors sensibly conclude that we need more systematic investigations into the effectiveness of culturally adapted CBT interventions.

Common Challenges in Culturally Sensitive CBGT

The barriers to accessing and completing CBGT are unquestionably greater for immigrant populations. It seems as if every issue in standard CBGT delivery becomes magnified for the culturally adapted protocol. Flexible problem-solving strategies are thus needed to prevent therapists and clients from becoming demoralized. The barriers to successful treatment completion are further compounded for immigrants who struggle with poverty. While many immigrants to Western countries such as Canada do not have financial challenges, in the United States, statistically, immigration is often associated with poverty; 50% of Americans from racial or ethnic minority groups are poor, compared to 20% of White Americans (Lamison-White, 1997). Additional steps may need to be taken to ensure that people who seek CBGT are able to bring themselves to and from the sessions, to arrange for day care, to complete home practice, and to finish the entire program.

Dropouts seem to be an especially huge problem for the Spanish-speaking groups, with up to 50% doing so (Miranda, Azocar, Organista, Dwyer, & Areane, 2003). Examples of enhancing CBGT by offering additional case management between group sessions are promising. Miranda and colleagues (2003) found that when Latino immigrants enrolling in CBGT were also offered individual case management, the dropout rate from the groups was only 17%, compared to 50% of those who only attended their CBT group but did not have additional case management. Those with enhanced care also achieved better improvements in their depression. The case managers were trained in CBT, and within this model, they offered help (telephone or home visits) with housing, employment, recreation, physical health problems management, and family relationships.

Another challenge relates to whether immigrants with mental health problems prefer counseling from their peers as opposed to trained professionals. The literature seems fairly consistent in refuting notions that minority people or immigrants, whether Asian or Latino, prefer peers or lay health workers from their community (Leung, 1996; Shatell, Villalba, & Stokes, 2009; Sue & Sue, 2013). In Chinese communities, professional counselors are preferred and may reflect many Chinese people's respect for authority, for a directive rather than nondirective approach, and for reassurance about confidentiality (Leung, 1996). According to Leung, when Chinese people self-disclose, they draw a sharp distinction between those who are considered insiders, and can be trusted, and those who are outsiders. This of course makes the group format particularly challenging. But when group leaders emphasize and model appropriate boundaries and professionalism, Chinese people welcome the group format, finding it a safe refuge to open up to others, with whom they feel understood and accepted. It is not uncommon for Chinese CBGT group members to continue to meet after their groups are over (Wong, 2011).

The preference for an expert group leader is not without possible complications. Although flattering, clinicians need to pay attention to their possibly elevated expert status. Compared to nonimmigrants in countries such as the United States and Canada, many immigrant clients show a high level of deference and appreciation toward their therapists. While it improves compliance with the treatment and the therapists enjoy being less "challenged," there are downsides. Clients may not speak up about something that is not clear to them or that they may even disagree on. They may also have beliefs about the expert "fixing" their problems, which can lead to them becoming complacent about their own role in taking charge of their health. This may be an important factor in the problem with homework completion.

The role of family unequivocally figures prominently in the lives of immigrant populations. Most clinicians agree that any delivery of mental health services ought to be consistent with the beliefs, values, and social conditions of those being served. Thus, clinicians offering CBGT to immigrants must take this into account explicitly by weaving it into all aspects of their CBGT protocols. Clinicians know of the double-edged sword of clients' families, which can be both a source of support and stress. When the immigrant's original family is experienced as supportive, the removal from this through immigration can be a extremely stressful. Younger women, who are severed from regular contact with their mothers, especially when they start their own families, may become more vulnerable to depression. Or even more distressing, depressed Chinese immigrants sometimes leave their young children in China to be raised by grandparents. This allows them to work long hours in their new country and more quickly become financially comfortable. This "satellite baby" phenomenon is increasingly a concern for child mental health professionals because these children, left behind in their country of origin, may consider their grandparents to be their primary attachment figures. If this is the case, it can cause emotional distress for all family members when the parents feel ready to have the child come and live with them in North America.

Lastly, clinicians must be aware that large countries such as China are not homogeneous but comprise subcultures. In the case of China, over 20 significant subcultural groups have been identified, each having their own unique cultural characteristics (Iwamasa, 1997). Although the CBGT protocol is the same for our Mandarin and Cantonese groups, the group therapists are aware of cultural differences and tailor their interventions accordingly. Cantonese people from Hong Kong have been exposed to Western influences much more than Mandarin-speaking people from Mainland China. Clinicians working with various larger cultures must therefore be attentive to subcultures within the more dominant culture.

Summary

This chapter shows how immigrants who are not fluent in their new country's language and who struggle with depression and anxiety can benefit from effective treatments such as CBGT—as long as the groups are run by skilled therapists who share the language of the group members and are familiar with their cultural values. The various CBGT cultural adaptations allow clinicians to reflect on how culturally adapted protocols to Asian, Latino, Black American, and other non-White populations may, in turn, inform their more standard CBGT protocols. For example, poverty is not restricted to immigrants. If CBGT programs offered better opportunities for childcare, transportation, and increased availability of case management, more low-income people may be able to access and benefit from it.

This chapter seeks to increase the confidence of CBGT therapists who practice in areas of high immigration and are interested in adapting their protocols. Although therapists may not always be able to run the groups themselves due to not speaking the same language as their group clients, they can play a role in designing, implementing, and actively advising on culturally competent CBGT interventions.

Note

1. Clever euphemisms do not seem to work. People across cultures know homework when they see it! Chapter 9 offers strategies for improving homework compliance.

Recommended Readings for Clinicians

Aguilera, A., Garza, M. J., & Muñoz, R. F. (2010). Group cognitive-behavioral therapy for depression in Spanish: Culture-sensitive manualized treatment in practice. *Journal of Clinical Psychology, 66(8)*, 857–867.

Atkinson, D. R., Morten, G., & Sue, D. W. (1998). *Counseling American minorities: A cross-cultural perspective* (5th ed.). New York: McGraw-Hill Companies.

Miranda, J., Azocar, F., Organista, K. C., Dwyer, E., & Areane, P. (2003). Treatment of depression among impoverished primary care patients from ethnic minority groups. *Psychiatric Services, 54*, 219–225.

Sue, S., & Morishima, J. (1982). *The mental health of Asian-Americans.* San Francisco, CA: Jossey-Bass.

Wong, F. K. D. (2011). Cognitive behavioral group treatment for Chinese people with depressive symptoms in Hong Kong: Participants' Perspectives. *International Journal of Group Psychotherapy, 61(3),* 439–459.

References

Alegría. M., Chatterji, P., Wells, K., Cao, Z., Chen, C., Takeuchi, D., et al. (2008). Disparity in depression treatment among racial and ethnic minority populations in the United States. *Psychiatric Services, 59(11),* 1264–1272.

Bonilla, J., Bernal, G., Santos, A., & Santos, D. (2004). A revised Spanish version of the Beck Depression Inventory: Psychometric properties with a Puerto Rican sample of college students. *Journal of Clinical Psychology, 60(1),* 119–130.

Brandt, M. E., & Boucher, J. D. (1986). Concepts of depression in emotion lexicons of eight cultures. *International Journal of Intercultural Relations, 10,* 321–246.

Bui, K. V., & Takeuchi, D. T. (1992). Ethnic minority adolescents and the use of community mental health care services. *American Journal of Community Psychology, 20,* 403–417.

Census Statistics Canada. (2011). National Household Survey, Statistics Canada Catalogue no. 99-010-X2011028. Retrieved from http://www12.statcan.gc.ca/nhs-enm/2011 [accessed on March 9, 2014].

Dai, Y., Zhang, S. J., Yamamoto, J., Ao, M., Belin, T. R., Cheung, F., et al. (1999). Cognitive behavioral therapy of minor depressive symptoms in elderly Chinese Americans: A pilot study. *Community Mental Health Journal, 35(6),* 537–542.

Fugita, S. S. (1990). Asian/Pacific-American mental health: Some needed research in epidemiology and service utilization. In F. C. Serafica, A. I. Schwebel, R. K. Russell, P. D. Isaac, & L. B. Myers (Eds.), *Mental health of ethnic minorities* (pp. 66–83). New York: Praeger Publishers.

Greenberger, D., & Padesky, C. A. (1995). *Mind over mood: Change how you feel by changing the way you think.* New York: Guilford Press.

Iwamasa, G. Y. (1997). Asian Americans. In S. Friedman (Ed.), *Cultural issues in the treatment of anxiety* (pp. 99–129). New York: Guilford Press.

Karlsson, R. (2005). Ethnic matching between therapist and patient in psychotherapy: An overview of finding together with methodological and conceptual issues. *Cultural Diversity & Ethnic Minority Psychology, 11,* 113–129.

Kohn, L. P., Oden, T., Muñoz, R. F., Robinson, A., & Leavitt, D. (2002). Adapted cognitive behavioral group therapy for depressed low-income African American women. *Community Mental Health Journal, 38(6),* 497–504.

Lamison-White, L. (1997). *US current population reports: Series P60-198.* Washington, DC: US Bureau of the Census.

Leong, F. T. L. (1986). Counseling and psychotherapy with Asian-Americans: Review of the literature. *Journal of Counseling Psychology, 33,* 196–206.

Leong, F. T. L., & Lau, A. S. L. (2001). Barriers to providing effective mental health services to Asian Americans. *Mental Health Services Research, 3,* 201–214.

Leung, K. (1996). The role of beliefs in Chinese culture. In M. H. Bond (Ed.), *The handbook of Chinese psychology* (pp. 247–262). Hong Kong: Oxford University Press.

Li, H. Z., & Browne, A. J. (2000). Defining mental illness and accessing mental health services: Perspectives of Asian Canadians. *Canadian Journal of Community Mental Health, 19*, 143–159.

Lin, J. C. H. (1994). How long do Chinese Americans stay in psychotherapy? *Journal of Counseling Psychology, 41*, 288–291.

Lin, K. M., & Cheung, F. (1999). Mental health issues for Asian Americans. *Psychiatric Services, 50*, 774–780.

Muñoz, R. F., & Miranda, J. (1996). *Group therapy manual for cognitive-behavioral treatment of depression*. San Francisco, CA: RAND.

Muñoz, R.F., Ghosh Ippen, C., Rao, S., Le, H.-L., & Dwyer, E.V. (2000). *Manual for Group Cognitive-Behavioral Therapy of Major Depression: A Reality Management Approach.* San Francisco: San Francisco General Hospital, University of California.

Okazaki, S. (2000). Treatment delay among Asian-American patients with severe mental illness. *American Journal of Orthopsychiatry, 70*, 58–64.

Pew Research Centre. (2012). *Asian-American Survey*. Washington, DC: U.S. State Department. Retrieved from http://www.pewsocialtrends.org/asianamericans-graphics [accessed on March 9, 2014].

Radloff, L. S. (1977). The CES-D Scale: A self-report depression scale for research in the general population. *Applied Psychological Measures, 1(3)*, 385–401.

Shapiro, J. R., & Bauer, S. (2010). Use of short message service (SMS)-based interventions to enhance low intensity CBT. In J. Bennett-Levy, D. A. Richards, P. Farrand, H. Christensen, K. M. Griffiths, D. J. Kavanagh, et al. (Eds.), *Oxford guide to low intensity CBT interventions* (pp. 281–286). Oxford, UK: Oxford University Press.

Shattell, M.M., Quinlan-Colwell, A., Willalba, J., Ivers, N.N., & Mails, M. (2010). A cognitive-behavioral group therapy intervention with depressed Spanish-speaking Mexican women living in an immerging immigrant community in the United States. *Advances in Nursing Science, 33(2)*, 158–169.

Shatell, M., Villalba, J., & Stokes, N. (2009). Depression in Latinas residing in emerging Latino immigrant communities in the United States. *Hispanic Health Care international, 7(4)*, 190–202.

Shek, D. T. I. (1993). Measurement of pessimism in Chinese adolescents: the Chinese Hopelessness Scale. *Social Behavior and Personality, 21*, 107–119.

Shen, E. K., Alden, L. E., Söchting, I., & Tsang, P. (2006). Clinical observations of a Cantonese cognitive-behavioral treatment program for Chinese immigrants. *Psychotherapy, 43(4)*, 518–530.

Shin, J. K. (2002). Help-seeking behaviors by Korean immigrants for depression. *Issues in Mental Health Nursing, 23*, 461–476.

Snowden, L. R., & Cheung, F. K. (1990). Use of inpatient mental health services by members of ethnic minority groups. *American Psychologist, 45*, 347–355.

Sue, D. W., & Sue, D. (2013). *Counseling the culturally different* (6th ed.). New York: John Wiley & Sons.

Sue, S., Fujino, D. C., Hu, L., Takeuchi, D. T., & Zane, N. W. S. (1991). Community mental health services for ethnic minority groups: A test of the cultural responsiveness hypothesis. *Journal of Consulting & Clinical Psychology, 59*, 533–540.

Wong, F. K. D. (2007). Cognitive behavioral treatment groups for people with chronic depression in Hong Kong: A randomized wait-list control design. *Depression and Anxiety, 25(2)*, 142–148.

15
Hoarding

We are all more or less attached to things. Consumer culture exploits our human propensity to acquire new things and our vulnerability to seeing ourselves reflected in our possessions. But people with compulsive hoarding, who account for about 2–6% of the population of the United States and Europe (American Psychiatric Association [APA], 2013), are off the scale when it comes to their relationship to possessions. They are extremely attached to things. They cannot resist urges to bring new things into their homes however useless they may seem to others. Nor can they bring themselves to throw out or recycle things for which they no longer have any practical or even sentimental need.

People with compulsive hoarding seem to lack the mental ability to sort through their possessions in an ongoing manner, stay task focused, and get the job done, something that is fairly easy for most of us. As a result, their accumulation of stuff often prevents them from using the rooms in their homes for their designed purpose. In milder cases, people with compulsive hoarding cannot have anybody over for dinner because all table surfaces are packed with stuff that would require hours to clear. In extreme cases, people with compulsive hoarding sleep on a tiny space on the floor because their beds are filled with items. Tragically, their attachment to inanimate objects is often stronger than their relationship to people. It is not uncommon for them to lose connection to their adult children or have younger children removed by social services. They are often lonely people living on the margins of society.

When people with compulsive hoarding present to general mental health programs—usually following pressure from a concerned family member—many clinicians feel at a loss for how to best help them. This in part has to do with therapists' lack of specialized knowledge of this problem and what a best practice approach

Cognitive Behavioral Group Therapy: Challenges and Opportunities, First Edition. Ingrid Söchting.

looks like. The other part involves the clients themselves. People with compulsive hoarding often lack insight into their behavior. One client stated she had a problem with "sorting paper" and seemed genuinely unaware of the extent to which her clutter prevented her from moving around freely in her home. One study found that only 15% acknowledged the irrationality of their behavior (Kim, Steketee, & Frost, 2001). It fairly quickly becomes apparent that the client is ambivalent about seeking help, that they feel some pressure from other people in their lives to make changes, and that they do not see much point in coming to a therapist's office when their only problem is at home. For some, though, the problems go beyond their homes and cause significant impairment at work. If working, their general disorganization can make it difficult to manage projects at work, sort through emails, files, or whatever else their work may involve. They obviously also struggle with keeping their work spaces and shared offices tidy. Regardless of whether the hoarding problem is confined to their homes or spills into other areas of life, people with compulsive hoarding are difficult to engage in therapy, often miss sessions, and more often than not drop out of any treatment that is not highly hoarding specific.

When people with compulsive hoarding present to mental health programs that offer specific treatment for OCD, the scenario is usually brighter but still far from optimal. Hoarding has until 2013 been considered a diagnostic subtype of OCD and therefore been treated with the same CBT approach. In programs where group CBT is available, therapists naturally feel compelled to accept people with compulsive hoarding into their CBT groups for OCD. Commonly, we have about one or two members with compulsive hoarding in CBGT for OCD. But, although they share features with other types of OCD, they are quite distinct. Most noticeably, they are not as distressed—compared to the other OCD members in the group—about their compulsions. They do not "buy in" to the CBT treatment rationale as readily as the rest of the group, their progress is painfully slow, they stand out as "very different" in a number of ways from the rest of the group, and they often do not gel. They also tend to be older, usually above age 50, compared to the rest of the group. They have thus lived longer with their hoarding behavior, which makes it more challenging to reverse. The group therapists feel bewildered about what "to do" in terms of exposures, particularly in the absence of being able to offer home visits or other more specific hoarding support. As we shall see in the following text, the unfeasibility of home visits may not be as big of a barrier to effective hoarding treatment as clinicians assume. This growing frustration among clinicians, along with helpful research into the cognitive and psychological processes of the minds of people with compulsive hoarding, has finally resulted in hoarding being removed from the OCD diagnostic category.

With the arrival of DSM-5 (APA, 2013), hoarding now has its own distinct disorder status along with formal diagnostic criteria. CBGT therapists for OCD welcome this. The pressure to include people with compulsive hoarding into our groups has lessened, but we feel a corresponding responsibility to offer helpful and appropriate treatment to alleviate their suffering as living conditions worsen. Risks of evictions from apartments because of fire hazards and reality-based fears of homelessness loom large. I hope this chapter on CBGT for hoarding will encourage mental health services to develop separate group programs for people with compulsive hoarding. There is solid research literature on the benefits of a modified CBT approach for hoarding-specific CBT and CBGT.

This chapter first reviews the new diagnosis of hoarding disorder and associated features and then the literature on CBT and CBGT for hoarding. I will present an example of what hoarding-specific CBGT typically involves. Indeed, it is a different kind of CBGT group and probably requires a different kind of therapist too. If transportation is a problem—as it often is because hoarding is associated with poverty and disability—therapists may have to travel from their familiar therapy rooms and find a community hall in which to conduct the groups. Sometimes, groups are also held in the homes of people with compulsive hoarding. Therapists may need to be prepared to do home visits or supervise them, which can include wearing masks or other protective gear in cases where unsanitary conditions are likely to exceed anything clinicians have previously encountered. The safety of the home may need to be inspected before inviting students or other clients to enter. Tall stacks of items could fall or fires ignite with flammable materials that are placed on propane tanks, stoves, or heaters.

The Diagnosis and Features of Hoarding Disorder

According to DSM-5 (APA, 2013), hoarding now belongs to the class of disorders called *Obsessive–Compulsive and Related Disorders. Hoarding disorder* is characterized by a persistent difficulty parting with possessions, regardless of their actual value (Criterion A). This difficulty is due to a perceived need to save items and to the distress associated with discarding them (Criterion B). People with hoarding compulsions accumulate possessions that congest and clutter their active living areas and substantially compromise their intended use (Criterion C). The hoarding causes clinically significant distress or impairment in social, occupational, or other important areas of functioning (including maintenance of a safe environment for self and others; Criterion D). The hoarding is not attributable to another medical condition (Criterion E) and is not better explained by the symptoms of another mental disorder (e.g., obsessions in OCD, decreased energy in major depressive disorder, delusions in schizophrenia or another psychotic disorder, cognitive deficits in major neurocognitive disorder, restricted interest in autism spectrum disorders; Criterion F). Clinicians diagnosing hoarding have the option of specifying if the problems come with *excessive acquisition*, *good or fair insight*, *poor insight*, or *absent insight/delusional beliefs*.

Approximately 75% of individuals with hoarding disorder have a comorbid mood or anxiety disorder with the most common being major depressive disorder (57%) followed by social anxiety disorder (SAD; 29%), generalized anxiety disorder (GAD; 28%), and obsessive–compulsive disorder (OCD; 17%) (APA, 2013; Frost, Steketee, Tolin, & Brown, 2006). When the client is also depressed and struggling with low motivation and energy, it requires an even more enormous effort to start a declutter treatment program. Therapists may need to start with some of the basic behavioral activation strategies used in depression (see Chapter 4). Daily walks could include trips to the local recycling station or to a place accepting donations. When social anxiety, avoidant, or schizoid personality disorder traits are present, it often prevents the person with compulsive hoarding from seeking treatment or attending regularly. Hoarding symptoms usually begin early in life, around ages 11–15 years, and cause clinically significant impairment by the mid-30s. The symptoms are three times more prevalent in older adults ages 55–94 compared with younger adults ages 34–44 (APA, 2013).

Hoarding can be secondary to a range of neurological and psychiatric conditions, such as brain damage, dementia, schizophrenia, attention deficit hyperactivity disorder (ADHD), and autism. When hoarding begins shortly after brain damage, or onset of dementia, it is referred to as organic hoarding. CBT may not be as effective for organic hoarding as it is for stand-alone hoarding disorder (Mataix-Cols, Pertusa, & Snowdon, 2011). Although far from conclusive, available neuropsychological studies point to possible cognitive information processing deficits in hoarders, deficits linked to abnormalities in the ventromedial frontal lobe area (Mataix-Cols et al., 2011). Specifically, people with compulsive hoarding seem to have greater difficulties with problem solving, planning, procrastination, indecisiveness, and organizing themselves to follow through with their goals. They tend to get easily distracted and unable to stay task focused until completion. This may explain why a task considered simple to most people, such as putting all bills to be paid in a certain place or folder, can be overwhelming for someone with compulsive hoarding. They have difficulty with categorization and grouping similar items together. Bills to be paid may be mixed in with grocery store flyers and other junk mail. They seem to get lost in details and unable to focus on the "bigger picture."

Financial and social burdens

In addition to public health threats such as fire hazards and unsanitary conditions, hoarding comes with other significant economic and social costs. Large surveys of self-identified hoarders suggest that they have difficulty keeping a job and have high rates of chronic and serious medical problems, such as obesity. They are also vulnerable to homelessness, with up to 12% being evicted from their homes (Frost, 2010). If people with compulsive hoarding are unable to pay for cleanouts in order to prevent eviction, this is financially taxing to those municipalities that are willing to help out.

Why do people hoard?

In addition to the information processing deficits mentioned earlier, people with compulsive hoarding seem to attribute greater meaning to their possessions compared to most people. Possessions may have a *sentimental* value (e.g., "Although

I have no idea who the people in the photos are because they are not labeled or dated, my grandfather kept all these boxes and it would feel like a betrayal of him to throw them out"), or an *instrumental* value (e.g., "I may need a recipe at some point in future from one of these magazines"), or an *intrinsic* value (e.g., "This vase is just so beautiful and even though I already have 20 vases, I want this one because it's so unique").

The attachments to possessions involve strong emotional reactions, positive and negative, which become powerfully reinforcing (Frost, 2010). The pleasure and often ecstatic high from acquiring a good deal, as in "I got five toothbrushes for the price of one," is positively reinforcing. The positive feelings associated with purchasing are of course not unique to people with compulsive hoarding. We all get them but with lesser intensity and frequency. An emotion that would be negatively reinforcing is the anticipation of sadness associated with discarding. For example, someone may be reluctant to part with a collection of old books, fearing being flooded with regret and grief at the permanent loss. This mix of emotional positive and negative reinforcement is often the crux of why it seems so hard for people with compulsive hoarding to break out of their hoarding behaviors. Like all other human beings, people with compulsive hoarding seek emotional pleasure and avoidance of pain.

CBT for Compulsive Hoarding

Based on recent literature reviews, clinicians can feel confident that a multicomponent CBT designed specifically for hoarding has shown promising results—with up to 70% of clients reporting substantial improvement in symptoms. Before describing this protocol, it is worth noting that CBT for hoarding is more intense and long term compared to most other forms of CBT, with up to 16–20 group sessions or 26 individual sessions. This approach is setting a standard for evidence-based treatment for hoarding (Muroff, Bratiotis, & Steketee, 2011). Although individual CBT with periodic home visits has been the most common intervention, the Muroff 2011 review article highlights how group CBT is emerging as equally effective. But the high dropout rates from hoarding groups (about 30%) cannot be overlooked. Ways to improve this will be discussed throughout the rest of this chapter.

CBT model of compulsive hoarding

Based on the work of leading hoarding researchers and clinicians, we now have a generally accepted CBT model of hoarding (Frost & Hartl, 1996; Frost & Steketee, 1998; Hartl & Frost, 1999) (Figure 15.1).

The CBT model of compulsive hoarding presumes that problems with acquiring, saving, and building up clutter result from (a) personal vulnerabilities that include early life experiences and cognitive information processing deficits, which contribute to (b) cognitive appraisals about possessions, which in turn result in (c) positive and

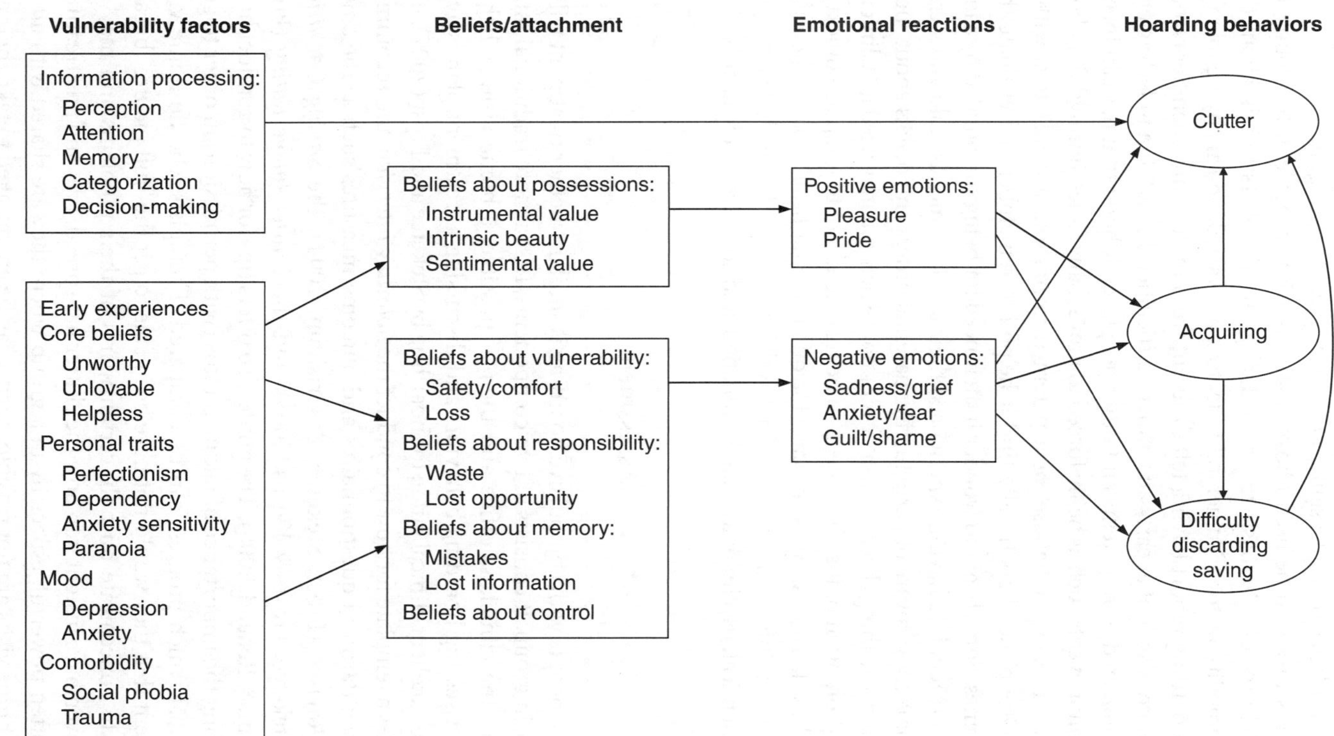

Figure 15.1 Model of compulsive hoarding. Source: From Steketee and Frost (2007). Reproduced with permission of Oxford University Press, USA.

negative emotional responses that trigger (d) hoarding behaviors of clutter, acquiring, and difficulty discarding/saving. These behaviors are reinforced either positively through the pleasure gained from saving and acquiring or negatively through the avoidance of unpleasant emotions of grief, fear, or guilt.

The model is meant to be used idiosyncratically with each client. In groups, this general model provides the basis for individual group members to talk about their unique vulnerability factors. Vulnerability factors are varied, and many people with compulsive hoarding report having felt different from their family members from a young age. Many also hint at early attachment difficulties. In addition to feeling emotionally disconnected from parents and other people, childhood traumas can include major and minor events such as being forced to move many times, immigration, home robbery, house fires, sexual abuse, or a parent throwing out a child's toys without permission. Group members usually find it helpful to remember and evaluate their childhood homes. Some begin to wonder if their need for being surrounded by a lot of stuff may be a reaction to having experienced their family homes as "cold and sterile." Or they become more aware of perpetuating parental orders and beliefs about "never throw away or waste things because you never know when you may need it." Clinicians support this promotion of insight while also being careful not to jump too quickly to simple causal explanations. As is the case for other mental health issues, the causes of hoarding are multifaceted, and as yet not well understood, but include a range of genetic, biochemical, psychological, environmental, and socioeconomic factors.

Assessment

Assessment of people with compulsive hoarding is similar whether treatment will be individual or in group. It consists of two components, first a more traditional intake assessment in the clinician's office and then, if possible, a home visit. A helpful approach to assessing hoarding behaviors and discussing a treatment plan is available from the excellent clinical guide for hoarding by Steketee and Frost (2007). This guide includes a template for how to conduct the *hoarding interview* and recommendations for standardized questionnaires and outcome measures such as the *Saving Inventory—Revised* (Frost, Steketee, & Grisham, 2004), the *Saving Cognitions Inventory* (Steketee, Frost, & Kyrios, 2003), and the *Clutter Image Rating* (Frost, Steketee, Tolin, & Renaud, 2008). The guide also offers tips for how to conduct home visits, including the importance of taking photos (with permission) in order to get a baseline against which progress can be compared. Therapists who do home visits often comment that they would not have been able to get the "full picture" because clients tend to concentrate on only certain parts of their problems and may not themselves even have insight into how the clutter has spread. Pre- and posttreatment photos are often powerful, especially in a group where they are shared with all the members. If home visits are not feasible, clients can be encouraged to take their own photos. In pregroup assessments, preparation for group treatment is also discussed, and this follows one of the formats described in Chapter 6 in this book.

Hoarding-specific CBT

The *Compulsive Hoarding and Acquiring: Therapist Guide* (Steketee & Frost, 2007) describes the treatment components in hoarding-specific CBT whether for individual or group. These include treatment planning, enhancing motivation, skills training for organizing and problem solving, exposure methods, cognitive strategies, strategies for reducing acquiring, and relapse prevention. They will be further described in their applicability to CBGT in the following text.

CBGT for Compulsive Hoarding

We now have evidence for successful adaptations of the individual hoarding-specific CBT manuals (Hartl & Frost, 1999; Steketee & Frost, 2007) to a group setting (Muroff et al., 2009; Steketee, Frost, Wincze, Greene, & Douglass, 2000). CBGT for hoarding usually involves a minimum of 16 weekly 2-hour group sessions and at least two individual 90-minute home sessions. As with other CBT groups, clinicians underline the importance of home practice between sessions. The therapeutic benefit of adding individual home visits to the group treatment is, however, debatable. Muroff and colleagues compared a 20-week CBGT with four home visits to a 20-week CBGT with eight home visits (Muroff, Steketee, Bratiotis, & Ross, 2012). Home visits included an initial tour of the home by the primary clinician with the purpose of collaborating with the client on specific goals for treatment. Subsequent home visits were done by undergraduate assistants who helped clients with sorting and discarding tasks as agreed upon during the CBGT sessions. The control group included people with compulsive hoarding who read a self-help book on hoarding over a 20-week period, *Buried in Treasures* (Tolin, Frost, & Steketee, 2007). Both CBGT groups achieved statistically significant reductions in hoarding symptoms, whereas the self-help study participants only achieved minimal improvements. Interestingly, the additional four home visits added only minimal improvements—suggesting that, somewhat counter to clinical intuition, more home visits may not always be better.

Home visits obviously incur significant additional cost, given their clinician labor intensity. New research questions the added therapeutic benefit of home visits. Gilliam and colleagues reported that a CBGT program for hoarders in an outpatient community clinic that did not include home visits still had outcomes comparable to those studies that did include home visits (Gilliam et al., 2011). Despite the limitations to this study, such as lack of randomization, the clinician researchers are in a position to question the often assumed necessity of adding home visits for successful treatment of compulsive hoarding. Considering that it is precisely that component—with all its problems related to liability and costly travel time for clinicians—which can deter community programs for offering CBGT for hoarders, these results have much clinical programming relevance.

CBGT Protocol for Compulsive Hoarding

Session Themes (Adapted from Steketee & Frost, 2007, and Shuer & Frost, 2011)
Session 1: Psychoeducation: Review Treatment Goals and Baselines
Session 2: Psychoeducation: Review the CBT Model of Hoarding
Session 3: Motivation, Goal Setting, and Readiness to Begin Decluttering
Session 4: Skills Training for Organizing and Problem Solving
Session 5: Skills Training for Organizing and Problem Solving
Session 6: Cognitive Strategies: Challenging unhelpful thinking
Session 7: Cognitive Strategies: Challenging unhelpful thinking
Sessions 8–15: Exposure to Nonacquiring and Letting Go
Session 16: Preventing Relapse

If the CBGT for hoarding program includes home visits, those are usually done at a minimum with one in the beginning and one toward the end of the group. Additional visits may be interspersed and used as a way of supporting clients with their homework.

Psychoeducation

The CBT model is discussed and group members are invited to speak about how it relates to them specifically. Similar to CBGT for depression, as discussed in Chapter 4, group members are invited to insert personal examples into the model. For example, a group member may say that his childhood involved multiple evictions due to his mother, a single parent, being unable to pay the rent. He never lived in one place long enough to develop friendships but managed to bring his favorite toys, including a collection of tin soldiers, with him in a duffle bag. These toys became his steady companions. Although some people with compulsive hoarding do not feel their childhoods were lacking, most voice themes about loneliness and mistrust of others.

This exploration of past histories easily resembles a process psychotherapy group, but, similar to other CBGT, the group facilitators ensure that the personal stories are connected back to the model as much as possible. The aim is to provide education about what makes someone vulnerable to acquiring things and fearful of discarding them and what factors maintain this behavior. The group facilitators create an atmosphere of curiosity by asking questions such as "How might your behavior of bringing home 10 soap bars on sale relate to how you felt before you left your home?" The whole group becomes trained in asking themselves and each other questions designed to promote insight into connections between feelings, appraisals, and behaviors.

Motivation and goal setting

Similar to individual CBT for people with compulsive hoarding, we encourage group members to begin with one room or area. We do a go-round and each client states where they prefer to start. This creates an opportunity for feedback in terms of how realistic the initial chosen area is. One man announced he wanted to clean his entire living room within the first 3 weeks but was able to listen to the group and instead selected one sofa. Sometimes, clients will prefer to pick a type of clutter, as opposed to a room. For example, someone may choose to organize their bills and other paper work. It is interesting to note that these otherwise bright and talented people who hoard have hardly any systematic approach to filing their paper work. Ideas such as creating a file folder for "rent and utilities" and "correspondence with social services" and "income tax" are novel. The sense of universality, that one is not alone, strengthens the group process.

Lack of motivation is an issue that must be confronted. One way to do so is through a group discussion of the pros and cons of hoarding where the facilitators use a board for filling in both columns. Here is an example of how to address motivation enhancement in the group.

THERAPIST: We've talked a lot about how many of you enjoy going to flea markets and garage sales because you often get some good things for hardly any money. Oscar you began to question what is really so bad about that, given that you're not broke.

OSCAR: Yeah, it's going to be hard for me to not go to the flea market because there are some really good ones in this city. The other day I brought this doll to my niece and the whole family was amazed that I'd only paid $2 for it.

THERAPIST: So, I'm going to challenge the group with the question of: What's so bad about flea markets? [writes this question on the board and then a "for" and "against" column]. I'll start by writing "You can get really good deals and nice gifts."

TRUDY: I also like flea markets. I know many of the vendors and they're always so friendly to me.

THERAPIST: We have another argument in the "for" column: "People at flea markets are friendly."

MYRNA: I agree with all that, but my problem is that I don't know where to put new things and I don't have anybody in my life to give them to other than strangers or kids on the playground.

THERAPIST: You OK, Myrna, with us putting in the "against" column that "no free space in my home to put new purchases?"

This "for" and "against" exercise invariably promotes discussion of the downsides to acquiring if one does not begin to discard. It is helpful for motivation because it validates the many benefits to "having an eye" for good deals. In that sense, it shows respect for people with compulsive hoarding and ensures they do not feel stigmatized as "crazy" people. But it challenges them to step back from their lives and engage in a rational weighing of the value of keeping the status quo versus committing to personal change.

Another helpful motivation enhancement exercise, especially in the beginning of the group, is to ask clients to draw a picture or make a collage from cutting and pasting magazine images of where they see themselves 5 years from now. This generates interesting discussion as clients point to clean couches, tables, and people coming over to visit in their homes. This is in some ways similar to the *unclutter visualization* exercise described by Steketee and Frost (2007) where clients imagine a decluttered room in which "everything they wanted to keep is still there, but organized and put in its place." In the final go-round of the group, the clients talk about their drawing and may engage in a vivid discussion when they say, for example: "Here is my couch and this is my friend Miranda and her husband and they are over for a drink. You can see I put some snacks on the table. They are admiring my living room, saying how nice it is to visit me again." These imaginary exposure exercises serve as powerful motivators. If possible, the pictures and collages can be put up on the wall in the group room and serve as constant reminders of why group members are *choosing* to embark on the hard work of decluttering their living spaces.

Skills training for organizing and problem solving

In these sessions the therapists teach how to get started with personal organizing plans for various areas in the homes of the group members. Clients pick their spots and the therapists show how to group items in categories and determine their final location. An example of such a plan is found in *Compulsive Hoarding and Acquiring: Therapist Guide* (Steketee & Frost, 2007). For example, an artist who could not be creative because he was too depressed and overwhelmed with his lack of space decided to pick his home studio as his target area. He created the item category "oil paints." He picked the "final location" to be the shelf in his studio. His action plan involved moving all tubes of oil paint scattered around his apartment to this shelf, from which he removed the books and magazines. This of course created a problem with the books. Those became a new target after the paint was organized and were sorted into categories of "keeping" or "donate to thrift store."

Generating organizing rules with the group is usually an engaging and lively exercise. Group members ask questions such as: "For how long do people keep clothes?" and "How often should I take the garbage out or do the dishes?" Helpful answers to people with compulsive hoarding would be that clothes not worn over the past 2 years should be recycled unless they have obvious sentimental value, such as a wedding dress, or only occasional utility such as a suit for funerals or weddings. Dishes should be done daily and trash taken out twice a week or more depending on the amount. It may be reasonable to keep a sweater a family member knitted even though one doesn't wear it that often. People with compulsive hoarding are often at a complete loss for which practical rules of thumbs to follow. Another idea is to take a photo of an item one is ready to part with but would like to remember. It is helpful to have a list of these organization questions and answers posted on the group room wall for all to see and discuss.

Challenging unhelpful thinking

Similar to other mental health issues, unhelpful thinking maintains problematic behaviors and emotions. People with compulsive hoarding have *negative automatic thoughts*, such as "I need this," "I may never get this buying opportunity again," or "I will most likely need this at some time in the future." In addition to these ongoing automatic thoughts, we also see that people with compulsive hoarding subscribe to the same list of *Biases in Thinking* as we reviewed for depressed people in Chapter 5. Thoughts such as "If I throw it away, I'll regret it for the rest of my life" are examples of *catastrophizing*. Using the list of Biases in Thinking from Appendix F generates helpful group discussions. Specific hoarder-promoting thinking can be challenged and replaced with more adaptive thinking. For example, a person may be able to counter a belief of "this sweater is so pretty I must have it" with "I enjoyed looking at and feeling that sweater, and although it would make me feel good to own it, I know I don't really need it and it would add to the clutter in my home, which I don't want." The cognitive challenging exercises also stimulate group discussions of wants versus needs. They arm group members with another weapon as they practice exposures, such as throwing out or refraining from purchasing. This latter point is the reason some clinicians prefer to ensure the cognitive exercises are covered before the exposures begin.

Exposures and behavioral experiments

Exposures for people with compulsive hoarding come in two forms: exposure to not acquiring something and exposure to getting rid of something. As for other problems involving facing one's fears, we recommend the use of hierarchies. An example of a nonacquiring hierarchy may have the following items:

Feared situation	*SUDS*
Walking around a yard sale	80
Passing up free stuff at curb side	60
Going into the hospital gift store before my group	50
Going into the dollar store	30
Going to a two-for-one sale and only picking one item	25

Hoarding exposure exercises are designed to increase tolerance for the urge to acquire. These urges are triggered in the presence of, or while physically handling, a desired object. Indeed, people with compulsive hoarding often talk about being in a kind of trance state as they pick up or purchase items. Although the majority of high-risk situations are outside of the group sessions, there are opportunities for effective in-session exposures. For example, a therapist may accompany one or more members of the group to the hospital gift store or a nearby mall. Clients are encouraged to pick up and handle items, express their positive feelings and thoughts, and then return the item. They keep track every 10 minutes of their anxiety ratings during the exercise and for 30–60 minutes after. A psychiatry resident who was preparing to move to another city brought a large box of items no longer needed from his household. This box included several treasures, such as intact three-hole binders, wrapping paper, CDs, and local touring books. During in-session exposures, group members search the box but are told they cannot keep anything. We also encourage group members to bring boxes of stuff from their homes. Sometimes, this involves sorting paper work and deciding what needs to be kept and what recycled. Other times, bags of clothes or boxes of kitchenware are brought in. Working with the principle of graded exposures, we agree to keep their items until they decide they are ready to part with them.

Exposure to throwing out can take place in the group if members bring items. This obviously involves only a fraction of what needs to be done in their homes. Working with a *discarding hierarchy*, homework exercises are planned in the group. These often take the form of a *behavioral experiment* where the group asks the client to predict how they will feel during and after a certain discarding task. This is all written down on the *Behavioral Experiment Form* (Steketee & Frost, 2007). In the subsequent group session, the client describes what actually happened, if their predictions came true, and what they learned from the experiment.

Homework

Homework takes on an entirely different level of meaning for people with compulsive hoarding disorder compared to people with anxiety and depression. Indeed, it can be hard for clinicians at times to fully grasp the extent and enormity of the challenges facing our clients in their own homes. In the weekly treatment group, members often present as pleasant, attractive, and helpful people who share moving life stories and positive personal interests. Intellectually, they understand the reasons for committing to new coping strategies for de-cluttering. But when they return home from their group session, they are understandably easily overwhelmed and discouraged. In the absence of home visits, it is crucial to not collude in any denial of the massive amount of homework needing to be done. Coaches and assistants are usually needed for homework to be effective. Some clients agree to arrange for all-day cleanouts and to hire professional assistance if they can afford it. All this can be planned during the group as part of the homework. It is critical that the client feels in control of their homework. Asking family members to help can be problematic because of the family frustration with the hoarder in the family.

As also pointed out by Steketee and Frost (2007), it is best to avoid family members as coaches even though they may be more than willing. Long-standing patterns of criticism and "taking control" can be difficult to break, including the temptation to secretly get rid of the family member's stuff. An extreme example of this is shown in the documentary movie *My Mother's Garden* (2008), directed by Cynthia Lester, where the adult children take over and "trick" their mother into going on a vacation as they essentially gut her house. Not surprisingly, she becomes suicidal upon returning. I will not give the ending of the movie away, but I encourage clinicians to watch it. We have some examples of high school students who volunteer to be a buddy. A fresh, young, and uncritical face can be a good match for a someone with compulsive hoarding filled with self-criticism. Clients appreciate these youngsters—and they in turn get credit for their community service. For example, a couple of high school football players were able to carry away a lot of stuff. Many CBGT programs do not have those resources for training buddies or coaches, but may be able to link with volunteer programs, which may or may not provide training and supervision of the volunteers. Some volunteer organizations require training, whereas others do not.

Group members find it helpful to share their weekly and longer-term goals in the group. The group becomes a witness to their intention. They say they often bring the group to mind as they find themselves in a vulnerable situation, flooded with strong feelings. The recognition and applause by the group creates momentum. Rewards are often talked about in the group, and we have found that groups are creative in terms of avoiding material rewards other than food (e.g., a special coffee or meal). After goals have been accomplished, self-rewards can include going to dinner with a friend, a walk in a park, a movie, a museum, or a concert. This reinforces the pleasure of collecting experiences as opposed to things.

Relapse prevention

Despite substantial progress, people with compulsive hoarding rarely complete all their goals and achieve their ideal home look during a 16–20-week CBGT program. Booster sessions spaced one or more months apart can be helpful and so can clinician check-ins by phone. If available, clients benefit from being connected with local or Internet support groups. As with other CBGT, the last sessions involve supporting clients in becoming their own therapists and setting realistic goals for continued self-help. Chapter 9 offered further suggestion for how to prepare clients for the end of their group. Similar to other CBGT, members of a hoarding group often offer to support each other outside of the group sessions. This may not be encouraged while the group is happening, but after the formal group is over, facilitators support the group members in exchanging phone numbers or email addresses. Group therapists glimpse the longer-term benefits of new friendships for people who do not easily make friends.

Capitalizing on the Group for Compulsive Hoarding

People with compulsive hoarding are notoriously "hard to treat" for all the reasons discussed earlier, including poor insight and lack of motivation. Whenever feasible, I strongly believe that a group format must be offered because it will mitigate some of these treatment-interfering problems and behaviors. People with compulsive hoarding are often lonely people with intense fears of being criticized. They know their behaviors and living situations are highly socially unacceptable. They also know that the therapist most likely does not have significant problems with hoarding. In fact, most clinician offices and group rooms tend to have a sterile feel. Therefore, being in a group with other people who also suffer from compulsive hoarding increases the likelihood of individual group members feeling understood. As with other types of groups, some members in hoarding groups immediately feel validated, while others take longer to warm up and feel comfortable. Similar to other forms of CBGT, powerful group processes are felt in CBGT for hoarding. Perhaps even more so, considering that people with compulsive hoarding tend to be more socially isolated compared to people with OCD, anxiety, and mood disorders. Therapists in such groups can take steps to deepen the sense of connection and belonging by encouraging group members to directly relate to and learn from each other. This spontaneously happens when someone inevitably offers information about a cleanout or personal-assistant service or is aware of an Internet support group.

We have found the process factor of *catharsis* (discussed in Chapter 2) noticeably more prominent in hoarding groups compared to other kinds of CBT groups. During the group sessions in which we explore factors that may have created a vulnerability to attach to things, group members express—often for the first time—the hurts and loneliness they have felt in childhood where it was not safe to attach emotionally to adults. The group becomes an empathic witness, a kind of "fellow sufferer who understands." So long as the facilitators can contain the outpouring of affect and tears, and gently keep moving forward to focus on the here and now tasks, our experience shows that allowing catharsis pays off in terms of increased motivation to commit to a clutter-attack plan.

A specific attention to group process factors is still rare in academic journal articles on CBGT. I felt a pleasant rush of clinician *universality* when reading the article by Schmalisch, Bratiotis, and Muroff (2010) in which they discuss how specific process factors such as altruism, peer modeling, and installation of hope enhance CBGT for hoarding. And I agree with these clinicians that it is necessary to watch out for how the cohesion among people with compulsive hoarding can become counter-therapeutic. This happens when resistance to change becomes greater than the courage to challenge beliefs and behaviors. Group members can be intense in their collective celebration of "good deals," "needed items," and "I'm too old to change."

The opportunity to focus on other people and their stories seems helpful as people with compulsive hoarding easily get overwhelmed in individual therapy when the focus inevitably is on their clutter. Progress is at best slow and steady, and the group keeps people hanging in during the ebbs and flows of treatment. In other words, it is easier for a person with compulsive hoarding, who has not done her homework, to still come to group because she will not be the main focus as she would be in individual therapy.

Group home-based treatment is another possible way to strengthen CBGT for hoarding. Home-based CBT is effective for treatment refractory OCD patients (Rosqvist, Thomas, & Egan, 2002). But no study to date has evaluated clinician-run CBT groups for people with compulsive hoarding in their homes. Given that home visits may not add much benefit to treatment, it is a good question whether running entire groups in members' private homes will be more helpful compared to a mental health center. Still, the home-based option seems a worthwhile possibility so long as liability and insurance issues are surmountable. This option includes the advantage of an incentive to clean up to some degree if it all possible. At minimum, the group member host may create a space for the group to sit on chairs or on couches. People with compulsive hoarding tend not to benefit as much from the "visitor effect," which is helpful to other people because the thought of entertaining guests forces us to sort through our piles and clutter at fairly regular intervals. Interestingly, in an OCD group, one member with compulsive hoarding felt shame about having no place for a visitor to sit, whereas another with ordering obsessions described her home as always "company ready." The contrast between the two group members' homes stimulated an interesting discussion about how to reach the desirable "golden mean."

Electronic CBGT (E-CBGT) for people with compulsive hoarding is another possible version of this group. Online groups using CBT interventions have been in existence for the past decade. Muroff and colleagues have also tested the effectiveness of ongoing private online self-help intervention for hoarding. They found a strong correlation between improvement in hoarding and length of group membership in a study comparing recent group members (less than 3 months) to long-term ones (more than 3 months) and to those waiting to join the online group (Muroff, Steketee, Himle, & Frost, 2010). The study offered compelling evidence that many people with compulsive hoarding have proficient computer and Internet skills, which allow them to access treatment on the web. This offers exciting opportunities for helping people with compulsive hoarding who for geographical and other reasons do not have access to clinician-led CBGT for hoarding.

Common Challenges in CBGT for Hoarding

Attendance is a perennial problem and may be exacerbated by comorbid problems, such as depression and traits of a schizoid or paranoid personality, as well as issues related to functioning, such as managing transportation and rent payments. Clients with significant challenges may need to receive concurrent treatment from another clinician, case manager, or social service agency, which would allow the group facilitators to primarily focus on the hoarding problems. A broader multidisciplinary team is often needed.

The majority of people with compulsive hoarding have great difficulty making progress on their own. The presence of another person can make a big difference as they take steps to buy less and reorganize and declutter their homes. Although the presence of coaches in the actual hoarding group can be helpful, it raises issues about confidentiality for other group members. It is best if members meet with their coaches outside of the group. Clinicians model the role of the coach, which is to stay task focused, provide emotional support, facilitate decision making (by asking open-ended questions), and avoid telling clients how they should feel and what they should do (Steketee & Frost, 2007).

Treating people with compulsive hoarding disorder often becomes a broad public matter beyond the privacy of the therapy room. Group therapists may have to prepare themselves for working with health authorities, government ministries for children and families, landlords, and social service agencies. It may at times be necessary to assume the role of advocate. This poses challenges for balancing respect for the client's dignity and self-determination with a concern for the welfare of others who may be dependent on someone with a hoarding problem.

Summary

This chapter highlights and welcomes hoarding disorder as a distinct mental health problem separate from OCD. The chapter lists renewed possibilities for even more effective treatments. Although CBGT for hoarding has existed for about a decade, it will be easier for clinicians to influence mental health program development to include separate groups for hoarding. The chapter offers guidance on how to implement a hoarding-specific CBGT protocol and describes the challenges involved with getting group members engaged. In addition to the delivery of CBGT, hoarding-specific groups sometimes require more intensive clinical approaches—as partnerships with volunteer coaches and other mental health or social services are introduced. CBGT developers who engage in the complicated treatment of compulsive hoarding can draw on excellent treatment manuals and feel supported by a growing research literature. Many possibilities for innovative and effective CBGT thus exist to serve this group of people who are in the lonely stranglehold of their possessions, unable to shake free through their own efforts.

Recommended Readings and Viewing for Clinicians

Frost, R. O., & Steketee, G. (2011). *Compulsive hoarding and the meaning of things*. New York: Houghton Mifflin Harcourt.

Lester, C. (2007). *Buried in treasures: Help for compulsive acquiring, savings, and hoarding* (A documentary movie). New York: MSNBC Films.

Schmalisch, C. S., Bratiotis, C., & Muroff, J. (2010). Processes in group cognitive and behavioral treatment for hoarding. *Cognitive and Behavioral Practice, 17*, 414–425.

Shuer, L., & Frost, R. O. (2011). *Leading the buried in treasures workshop: A facilitator's manual.* Northampton, MA: Smith College/International OCD Foundation.

Steketee, G., & Frost, R. O. (2007). *Compulsive hoarding and acquiring: Therapist guide.* New York: Oxford University Press.

Steketee, G., Frost, R. O., Wincze, J., Greene, K., & Douglass, H. (2000). Group and individual treatment of compulsive hoarding: A pilot study. *Behavioural and Cognitive Psychotherapy, 28*, 259–268.

Tolin, D., Frost, R. O., &, Steketee, G. (2007). *Buried in treasures: Help for compulsive acquiring, savings, and hoarding.* New York: Oxford University Press.

References

American Psychiatric Association (APA). (2013). *Diagnostic and statistical manual of mental disorders, DSM* (5th ed.). Washington, DC: Author.

Frost, R. O. (2010). Treatment of hoarding. *Expert Review of Neurotherapeutics, 10*(2), 251–261.

Frost, R. O., & Hartl, T. (1996). A cognitive-behavioral model of compulsive hoarding. *Behaviour Research and Therapy, 34*, 342–350.

Frost, R. O., & Steketee, G. (1998). Hoarding: Clinical aspects and treatment strategies. In M. Jenike, L. Baer, & J. Minichiello (Eds.), *Obsessive compulsive disorder: Practical management* (3rd ed., pp. 289–317). St. Louis, MO: Mosby Year Book.

Frost, R. O., Steketee, G., & Grisham, J. (2004). Measurement of compulsive hoarding: Saving Inventory—Revised. *Behaviour Research and Therapy, 42*, 1163–1182.

Frost, R. O., Steketee, G., Tolin, D., & Brown, T. (March 23–26, 2006). *Co-morbidity and diagnostic issues in compulsive hoarding.* Paper Presented at the Annual Meeting of Anxiety Disorders Association of America, Miami, FL.

Frost, R. O., Steketee, G., Tolin, D., & Renaud, S. (2008). Development of an observational measure of hoarding: The clutter image rating. *Journal of Psychopathology and Behavioral Assessment, 30*, 193–203.

Gilliam, C. M., Norberg, M. M., Villavicencio, A., Morrison, S., Hannan, S. E., & Tolin, D. F. (2011). Group cognitive-behavioral therapy for hoarding disorder: An open trial. *Behaviour Research and Therapy, 49*, 802–807.

Hartl, T. L., & Frost, R. O. (1999). Cognitive-behavioral treatment of compulsive hoarding: A multiple baseline experimental case study. *Behaviour Research and Therapy, 37*, 451–461.

Kim, H. J., Steketee, G., & Frost, R. O. (2001). Hoarding by elderly people. *Health and Social Work, 26*, 176–184.

Mataix-Cols, D., Pertusa, A., & Snowdon, J. (2011). Neuropsychological and neural correlates of hoarding: A practice-friendly review. *Journal of Clinical Psychology, 67(5)*, 467–476.

Muroff, J., Bratiotis, C., & Steketee, G. (2011). Treatment for hoarding behaviors: A review of evidence. *Clinical Social Work Journal, 39(4)*, 406–423.

Muroff, J., Steketee, G., & Bratiotis, C., & Ross, A. (2012). Group cognitive and behavioral therapy and bibliotherapy for hoarding: A pilot trial. *Depression and Anxiety, 29*, 597–604.

Muroff, J., Steketee, G., Himle, J., & Frost, R. O. (2010). Delivery of internet treatment for compulsive hoarding (D.I.T.C.H.). *Behaviour Research and Therapy, 48*, 79–85.

Muroff, J., Steketee, G., Rasmussen, J., Gibson, A., Bratiotis, C., & Sorrentino, C. (2009). Group cognitive and behavioral treatment for compulsive hoarding: A preliminary trial. *Depression and Anxiety, 26*, 634–640.

Rosqvist, J., Thomas, J. C., & Egan, D. (2002). Home-based cognitive-behavioral treatment of chronic, refractory obsessive-compulsive disorder can be effective: Single cases analysis of four patients. *Behavior Modification, 26*, 205–222.

Steketee, G., Frost, R. O., & Kyrios, M. (2003). Beliefs about possessions among compulsive hoarders. *Cognitive Therapy & Research, 27*, 463–479.

16

Psychosis

People with psychosis have throughout the centuries attracted the public's simultaneous fascination and fear. Tragically, the media feeds on extremely rare events where someone diagnosed with a psychotic disorder commit murder or other atrocities. But, similar to other mental health issues, problems with psychosis fall on a continuum. Although generally considered to be one of the more severe mental illnesses, lay persons and students in mental health training are often surprised to learn that many people with a bona fide diagnosis of a psychotic disorder are able to enjoy fulfilling lives and hold professional jobs. These positive outcomes are more likely when people remain constantly attentive to managing their illness, usually through a combination of medication and coping skills aimed at minimizing becoming overwhelmed and stressed.

Although CBT was not developed as a form of psychotherapy for ameliorating the distress experienced by people with psychosis, CBT has for decades been recognized as helpful for the so-called *positive* symptoms of psychosis, that is, hallucinations and delusions. More recently, the *negative* symptoms of psychosis, which include social withdrawal, poor social skills, low energy, and lack of goal-oriented behaviors, are responding in equally encouraging ways to CBT. These unintended benefits of CBT likely have to do with its structured, practical, transparent, collaborative, and here and now reality-focused approach, qualities which people with psychotic illnesses appreciate and need. In a user survey, clients receiving CBT for their psychotic problems report they especially value learning how to normalize their symptoms (i.e., learning that their symptoms are experienced by most people, just to a lesser degree) and how to practice specific coping skills (Kilbride, Byrne, & Price, 2012). Less structured therapy approaches with a focus on explorations of the past can be emotionally overwhelming and unhelpful—and even contraindicated for psychosis (Silverstein, 2007).

Cognitive Behavioral Group Therapy: Challenges and Opportunities, First Edition. Ingrid Söchting.

A key message in this chapter is that, despite mixed research and clinician reports on the effectiveness of CBT for psychosis, CBT remains a responsible therapy of choice. But the shrewd clinician will do well in staying open to the present mini-bombardment of new forms of CBT for psychosis: *compassion-focused, narrative enhancement, metacognitive*, and *person-based* CBT, just to name a few. CBT clinicians with expertise in treating psychosis agree that a positive evolution is taking place in CBT for psychosis, driven by the dynamic interplay between theory, research, and practice. The newer treatment approaches seem to be logical, and theoretically consistent, extensions of classic CBT for psychosis (Tai & Turkington, 2009). More research is, however, needed before clinicians can draw firmer conclusions about the additional effectiveness of the newer approaches and how they compare both to classic CBT and to each other. Some clinicians admit to finding it a challenge to keep up with these developments and not the least to discern just how different they are (or are not) from offering "good old CBT" in a context of warmth, empathy, and unconditional regard for our clients.

The chapter reviews efforts to improve the helpfulness of group CBT for psychosis. Although the evidence for CBGT has mostly focused on improvements in positive symptoms of psychosis, many clinicians opine that CBGT may be especially well suited to improved ways of working with the negative symptoms. Still, most mental health therapists supporting people with psychosis are aware of limits to their helpfulness. We see how social isolation and marginalization can have a devastating impact on the fragile self-esteem and identity of people with psychotic illnesses. The chapter reviews the main developments in CBGT for psychosis, with the hope that therapists will regain confidence in the group format. Many therapists admit their confidence has dwindled as their CBT groups fail to bring about changes in positive symptoms, fall apart due to poor attendance, or never really get off the ground with this population, despite excellent manuals and handouts for the group. The presence of negative symptoms is undeniably associated with less successful outcomes of CBT group therapy, with up to 45% dropout rates (Fanning et al., 2012). As this chapter discusses, a better understanding of how to shift therapeutic attention from the positive to the negative symptoms may lead to more effective CBGT for psychosis. The group format has potential to foster increased social comfort and self-acceptance. For these reasons, it seems worthwhile—and ethically responsible—to further concentrate efforts on delivering CBT for psychosis in a group format.

The Diagnoses of Schizophrenia Spectrum and Other Psychotic Disorders

According to the DSM-5, the psychotic disorders are defined by abnormalities in one or more of five domains: delusions (fixed beliefs not amenable to change despite contradictory evidence), hallucinations (perception-like experiences without an external stimulus), disorganized thinking or speech (loose or tangential answers to questions that substantially impair effective communication), grossly disorganized or abnormal motor behavior (can range from childlike "silliness" to unpredictable agitation as well as catatonic behavior marked by a lack of reactivity to the environment), and negative symptoms (diminished emotional expression and lack of self-initiated purposeful behavior). In psychosis, positive symptoms refer to a "presence of" and negative symptoms to a "lack of." Thus, delusions and hallucinations are positive symptoms, whereas poor hygiene and social withdrawal are negative symptoms. The DSM-5 lists six main psychotic disorders, and they include *schizotypal personality disorder* (long-standing pattern of milder psychotic-like symptoms), *delusional disorder* (central themes of, for example, being conspired against that last for at least 1 month), *brief psychotic disorder* (lasting at least 1 day but not longer than 1 month), *schizophreniform disorder* (symptoms last less than 6 months), *schizophrenia* (symptoms last for at least 6 months), and *schizoaffective disorder* (depression or mania coexists with positive symptoms). Prevalence rates for the various psychotic disorders are less than 1% except for brief psychotic disorder with a 9% prevalence (American Psychiatric Association, 2013).

Although CBGT for people with a psychotic disorder is the focus of this chapter, some of the research cited on CBGT for psychosis includes persons with bipolar disorder. Bipolar disorders are, according to the DSM-5, the modern understanding of the classic *manic–depressive disorder* or *affective psychosis* described in the nineteenth century. Although a psychotic episode is not part of the bipolar illness expression, the manic symptoms of inflated self-esteem, grandiosity, racing thoughts, and unpredictable behaviors can be sufficiently severe so as to resemble psychotic symptoms. In addition, psychotic symptoms, including both mood congruent and incongruent delusions and hallucinations, are commonly seen in patients with bipolar disorder.[1] Hence, bipolar disorders are often lumped in with psychotic disorders and referred to as *severe and persistent mental illnesses*.

I use the term psychotic disorders as an umbrella term encompassing some or all of the distinct DSM-5 diagnostic categories of the schizophrenia spectrum and other psychotic disorders. Bipolar disorders are included as well in some of the research I refer to.

Vulnerability to Psychotic Disorders

Similar to other mental health issues, problems with psychosis are best understood as a complex interaction of genetic and environment factors by which some individuals become susceptible to the development of negative symptoms during youth and adolescence. The negative symptoms seem to develop first and may be genetically determined (Rector, Beck, & Stolar, 2005).

Damage to certain brain structures or other structural abnormalities (e.g., enlarged ventricles in the brain) may be involved in a poorer integrative function of the brain and lead to limited resources for processing stimuli whether external to oneself (e.g., noticing unknown people laughing as they walk by) or from within one's own mind and body (e.g., sensation of intense pressure building behind one's temples). Some clients with psychosis talk about a sense of being unable to filter what to pay attention to and what to ignore (e.g., a quick decision to ignore passersby who laugh as opposed to personalizing it by assuming they are "laughing at me"). It is as if the filter mesh is not tight enough and one therefore "takes in too much" and easily becomes overwhelmed. These processing deficits seem to render people with psychosis more vulnerable to a number of cognitive biases (e.g., a reasoning bias where one jumps too quickly to a conclusion of "people are laughing at me" without engaging in a process of more careful review of evidence).

Contemporary research in cognitive neuroscience reviewed by van der Gaag, Nieman and van den Berg (2013) consistently find decreased prefrontal cortex activity and increased amygdala activity in people with psychosis. Whereas the amygdala is the brain structure associated with emotional arousal, the prefrontal cortex regulates emotion by engaging in higher-level cognitive abilities, such as the ability to look or plan ahead and put a present moment of distress into a larger context. Medication and CBT alike is hypothesized to work by strengthening the cortical projections from the prefrontal cortex to the amygdala in an attempt to allow reason to override the automatic fear response (van der Gaag et al., 2013).

As for environmental factors, people with a brain vulnerability predisposing them to overarousal and stimuli overload naturally do better in supportive, calm, and predictable environments. Environmental experiences of any form of abuse, including verbal, can have catastrophic consequences for an already vulnerable brain. Research on environmental factors suggests that patients with psychosis have had more traumatic experiences—including coercive treatment interventions—compared to the general population and thus often also experience posttraumatic stress symptoms and show a greater sensitivity to a variety of triggers and stressors (Lu et al., 2011; Mueser, Lu, Rosenberg, & Wolfe, 2010). Environmental factors can thus play a role in both the cause and maintenance of psychotic illnesses.

CBT for Psychosis

The first 5 years after onset of a psychotic episode are a critical time for preventing further deterioration. While a number of interventions including supportive therapy, case management, social skills training, and family psychoeducation are helpful immediately following a first episode, CBT may be uniquely beneficial for those with prodromal symptoms. These are people who are *at risk for a first episode* of psychosis (van der Gaag et al., 2013) and who continue to experience residual symptoms after their first episode, that is, those with *recent onset*, as opposed to those who are deemed chronically ill (Erickson, 2010; Zimmermann, Favrod, Trieu, & Pomini, 2005).

CBT seems moderately well supported even for those with chronic psychosis (Saksa, Cohen, Srihari, & Woods, 2009). Although CBT initially targeted the positive symptoms of psychosis, it is now also recognized as an effective treatment for the negative symptoms of psychosis (Rector, Seeman, & Segal, 2003). CBT can further be of benefit to those who refuse medication (Christodoulides, Dudley, Brown, Turkington, & Beck, 2008) or have comorbid conditions (Barrowclough et al., 2009). Mostly, CBT has been used as an adjunct to antipsychotic medication therapy for various forms and levels of severity of psychotic disorders, especially if there are no comorbid problems of addiction or other mental health issues (Wykes, Steel, Everitt, & Tarrier, 2008).

As a result of the consistent evidence on the effectiveness of CBT for psychosis as either a stand-alone or adjunctive treatment, government-approved clinical expert panels in both the United Kingdom (National Institute of Clinical Excellence, 2009) and the United States (Lehman et al., 2004) recommend that CBT be offered to people diagnosed with a psychotic disorder to promote recovery. This applies to those with persisting positive and negative symptoms and to those whose symptoms are in remission. Clinicians welcome these recommendations but are left with questions about what symptoms to target, which components of CBT are especially helpful for what type of psychosis, how to alter the delivery of CBT interventions to people whose insight is different from those with depression and anxiety, and how to maximize efficiency and cost-effectiveness by using a group format.

Standard cognitive and behavioral strategies used for depression and anxiety took longer to become applied to psychosis. This was a result of clinicians and researchers (erroneously) assuming that the positive symptoms of psychotic illnesses, such as hearing voices (e.g., a voice that suggests one should kill oneself) or having delusions (e.g., believing that one's neighbor has planted a camera in one's apartment), were encapsulated, or calcified, by the illness and therefore not responsive to any psychological intervention. When clinicians discovered that psychotic symptoms are not best understood as petrified phenomena of the mind but rather as *malleable* to varying degrees depending on the afflicted individual's level of insight, clinicians began applying and researching CBT principles and practices, and the evidence for the helpfulness of CBT mounted rapidly. When clinicians help clients notice links between momentary feelings of anxiety and distress accompanied by an increase in psychotic experiences, they are highlighting the flexibility of psychotic symptoms. As clients become increasingly aware of these connections, CBT therapists proceed to explore whether certain thoughts, or thinking biases, may support and escalate the strong (delusional) beliefs (van der Gaag et al., 2013; Tai & Turkington, 2009).

Initially, CBT for psychosis focused on improving coping and life skills as well as increasing behavioral activity. This behavioral focus on improving functioning, especially social withdrawal and apathy, was in part based on assumptions about the impossibility of accessing the belief system of people with psychotic symptoms. Clinicians now recognize the additional importance of beliefs and of addressing them therapeutically. The cognitive theory of psychosis suggests that in addition to any neurobiological vulnerability, specific cognitive beliefs and appraisals play a prominent role. Most often, people with, or vulnerable to, psychosis have extremely low expectations for deriving pleasure or success from social interaction and goal-oriented pursuits. Although people who experience psychosis may have a lower capacity for sustaining concentration, they may also exaggerate their limitations because of their defeatist thinking style (Rector et al., 2005). For example, a woman who has given up on working with an employment agency may tell herself that there is no point in carrying on as she does not believe she could manage showing up 3 days a week for part-time work. In the absence of any opportunity to gently challenge this belief, she will only become increasingly convinced of her ineptitude.

CBT for psychosis typically includes cognitive and behavioral interventions targeting both positive and negative symptoms, using some or all of the following components: (a) the establishment of a solid psychotherapeutic alliance; (b) psychoeducation with discussion of how biological, social, and psychological factors all play a role; (c) reduction of stigma by normalizing as much as possible symptoms of psychosis; (d) delivery of cognitive and behavioral skills; (e) attention to reducing any comorbid symptoms of anxiety and depression; and (f) relapse prevention education (Rector, 2005). Books such as *Cognitive Behaviour Therapy for Psychosis* (Fowler, Garety, & Kuipers, 1995) guide clinicians through all these interventions. Similar to many CBT clinicians, I was mainly trained in CBT for anxiety and depression and recall feeling buttressed by, and slavishly following, Fowler and colleagues' guide with some of my first clients with psychosis.

One was a 69-year-old woman with chronic waxing and waning symptoms of paranoia. She had become convinced that her upstairs neighbor had rigged a tiny camera in her apartment and got some special thrill out of spying on and mirroring her every move. My client would tell me that if she got up to go to the bathroom at 3:00 a.m., so would her neighbor. If she started listening to the radio at noon, so would her neighbor. My client was impressed with how devious this neighbor was by acting as if nothing was going on when she would invite her up for tea or offer a ride to the shopping mall. Using classic cognitive interventions of gathering evidence for and against the possibility that the neighbor was spying, self-monitoring with careful recordings of neighbor coincidences, reviewing cognitive biases such as *jumping to conclusions*, and discussing the neighbor's motivations, my client slowly became more accepting of the possibility that *maybe* she was not that fascinating to follow (her rediscovered sense of humor was further helpful and relieving) and perhaps she and her neighbor were just two elderly people doing some of the same things some of the time at the same time. When applied to psychosis, CBT engages clients in collaboratively challenging their interpretations of events and experiences and assists them in developing more realistic alternatives to delusions or paranoid thinking.

As previously mentioned, the earlier CBT focus was on the positive symptoms, but ongoing research and clinical practice have uncovered the possibility that many factors in addition to the content and style of a person's thinking may play a role in the development and expression of psychotic disorders. It may be just as therapeutic and helpful to target clients' often negative expectations of themselves and others rather than zooming in on hallucinations or delusions too quickly (Rector, 2005). Encouraging outcomes from CBT research suggest that people with psychosis can identify and pursue life goals *in the face of* residual psychotic symptoms (Cather, 2005) or symptoms suggesting a risk for a psychotic episode (van der Gaag et al., 2013).

CBT that focuses on the negative symptoms pays attention to a number of factors, including people's level of interpersonal adjustment and comfort, their self-esteem and self-acceptance, and their ability to recognize, identify, and regulate their feelings. Unrecognized feelings of threat seem to especially worsen symptoms. The newer CBT-based therapies for psychotic disorder address these by, for example, adding a *narrative enhancement* module to the traditional CBT or a *self-compassion* component. These newer approaches will be described in the following text in the context of group CBT for psychosis. The CBT group for psychosis seems especially well equipped to target negative symptoms, and with this in mind, we may see a renewed clinical interest in and success with CBGT for psychosis. For people with psychotic problems, interactions with other human beings are often their main source of stress and the reason many withdraw from human gatherings as much as possible. Before we turn to the literature on emerging trends in CBGT for psychosis, I offer some comments on the assessment for group readiness for people with psychosis.

Assessment

Unlike the standard clinical intake assessment, the psychosis group intake clinician keeps the focus on present functioning and does not attempt to follow a case formulation approach where predisposing, precipitating, perpetuating, and protective factors are summarized and reviewed with the client. People with psychotic problems are not expected to have this level of interest or insight, although they may develop it over the course of successful therapy. Given that CBGT for psychosis also works with the here and now, it is possible for people with limited insight into their illness to participate in and benefit from groups.

Clients with psychosis who are interested in a group usually already have a small team of caretakers supporting them. This team should at minimum include a psychiatrist who is responsible for monitoring medication and a case manager who assists the client with their needs for housing, income assistance, working, and transportation. Thus, there is usually ample material and sources of information making the group assessment less onerous. However, if the chart information about the client is limited, the *Client's Assessment of Strengths, Interests and Goals* (CASIG-SR; Lecomte, Wallace, Caron, Perreault, & Lecomte, 2004; Wallace, Lecomte, Wilde, & Liberman, 2001) is a helpful template for conducting an assessment of the client's level of functioning and motivation for making changes. The CASIG-SR comes in both a clinician-administered and a client self-report format that covers many areas, including goals for physical health (e.g., *Would you like to improve your physical health in the next year*?) and satisfaction with several areas such as money (e.g., *In the past 3 months, did you keep your money in a safe place?*), medication (e.g., *Do you feel good about your current medications and their dosages?*), and care of personal possessions (e.g., *In the past 3 months, did you wash your clothes at least once in the past 2 weeks?*).

A more specific symptom measure often used as a treatment outcome measure is the *Positive and Negative Syndrome Scale* (PANSS; Kay, Fiszbein, & Opler, 1987). The PANSS includes seven positive items (e.g., delusions), seven negative (e.g., blunted affect), and 16 general psychopathology items (e.g., anxiety, guilt, tension). Each item is rated by a clinician on a scale from 1 to 7 with a score of 1 indicating the symptom is "absent," a score of 5 indicating "moderate–severe" symptoms, and a score of 7 indicating "extreme" symptoms. The PANSS has been successfully used as an outcome measure in CBT trials for psychosis for both individual (Leucht et al., 2005) and group treatment (Klingberg et al., 2010). Another commonly used clinician-administered assessment tool in CBT trials is the *Psychosis Rating Scale* (PSYRATS; Haddock, McCarron, Tarrier, & Faragher, 1999). The PSYRATS focuses on different dimensions of delusions and hallucinations and is therefore useful in therapy trials.

The group intake clinician explains what the group is about. If the intake clinician is not one of the group therapists, it is critical that the intake clinician who does the assessment has detailed and accurate information about the group so that this can be shared with the client. Ideally, a brief written description of the group will be given to the client. It is important that this individual pregroup orientation mirrors the upcoming group in terms of frankness and directness in explanation and answering questions. It is a good idea to reinforce the team approach to the client's care and get permission, if not already in place, for the group leaders to connect with the client's case manager and psychiatrist. In order for these caregivers to optimally support their client in attending the group, they will need to know the content and approach of the group. Once the group has started, it is helpful if the case manager or psychiatrist continues to show an interest in the group and willingness to review group materials with the client.

Increasing Evidence Supports CBGT for Psychosis

The first CBT groups were specifically designed for targeting the positive symptoms of auditory hallucinations, *Hearing Voices* groups (Chadwick, Sambrooke, Rasch, & Davies, 2000; Wykes, Parr, & Landau, 1999).[2] In contrast to research on individual CBT, the initial empirical support for a group format was weaker (Johns & Wykes, 2010). But the past 5 years have produced research challenging the notion that individual CBT is, as a rule, superior to group CBT for psychosis. For example, Saksa and colleagues (2009) reviewed eight studies on individual CBT and five on group CBT for early psychosis. Their results suggest that the group format may be more effective and preferable—although the results need to be replicated given that some of the studies lacked in methodological rigor. The authors speculate about the positive effects of various group process factors. Specifically, group members with psychosis may be more receptive to CBT concepts when they are reinforced by peers and a sense of learning and modeling new coping strategies together. The authors further suggest the group setting may be experienced as less intense—and less threatening—compared to directly facing one therapist, as is the nature of individual CBT. In a group, it is easier for members to vary their level of engagement, and even though some members are more passive and only listen, they may still benefit.

Other studies have also found a group CBT format effective for both positive and negative symptoms when compared to standard psychiatrist and case management care for people with early onset of psychosis. But group CBT was not as effective for those who had a psychotic illness for longer periods (Barrowclough et al., 2006; Lawrence, Bradshaw, & Mairs, 2006). To test the possibility that CBGT may be more effective if the stage of psychosis (i.e., early, late, chronic) perspective is considered, Gaynor and colleagues compared CBGT for 25 people with early onset to 40 clients with stable psychosis (Gaynor, Dooley, Lawlor, Lawoyin, & O'Callaghan, 2011). People with bipolar disorder were included in this study. Gaynor and colleagues reported significant improvement in positive symptoms and depression as well as anxiety in first-episode psychosis, *as well as* among those with ongoing, stable psychosis. But only first-episode clients experienced an improvement in negative symptoms.

Most recently, Chung, Yoon, Park, Yang, and Oh (2013) treated 24 patients with first-episode psychosis in 12 weekly group sessions. They followed a manual that includes four components: (1) enhancing emotional flexibility, (2) enhancing thought flexibility, (3) enhancing personality flexibility, and (4) finding a positive meaning in the illness. Results showed significant improvements in positive and negative symptoms according to self-reports, as well as improvements in emotional functioning. There was a special emphasis on targeting positive symptoms related to ideas of reference by using humorous, didactic cartoons and video clips. The authors suggest that group members with psychosis may derive more benefits from group-related factors (e.g., the experience of helping others) than manual-based treatment factors (e.g., CBT psychoeducation about the connection between thoughts, feelings, and behaviors). This study did not include a control group, and one must thus be careful drawing conclusions about the unique effectiveness of CBGT.

The reviewed research suggests that CBGT may be especially helpful for people who are in the early stage of their psychotic illness. But is CBGT superior to other forms of group therapy for psychosis?

Some of the first clinical outcome studies on group CBT for early psychosis were conducted in Canada by Tania Lacomte and colleagues. They include a protocol consisting of 24-session CBGT with a focus on goal setting, thought challenging, and self-esteem. Although some have questioned the research methodology for relying too heavily on small samples and qualitative methods, and others have questioned whether the interventions are truly CBT because the modules also include a focus on self-esteem, the outcomes consistently support this group format (Lecomte, Leclerc, Wykes, & Lecomte, 2003). When this CBGT approach has been compared directly to another group approach focusing on social skills training, the two were equal in decreasing positive symptoms. But the members of the CBT groups did better with their use of active coping strategies during stressful times and enjoyed an improvement in negative symptoms due to better self-esteem (Lecomte et al., 2008). At 1-year follow-up, there were further gains in negative symptoms, including social support and insight, but no further improvement in positive symptoms (Lecomte, Leclerc, & Wykes, 2012). The 1-year follow-up study was hampered by dropouts and thus a small final sample size, which makes it difficult to draw firm conclusions.

Another study comparing CBGT directly to a "goal-focused supportive contact" group intervention was not able to conclude that CBGT was superior (Granholm, Ben-Zeev, & Link, 2009). Both groups achieved improvements in beliefs about social competence, which were associated with enhanced functioning. These results lead the authors to wonder if the nonspecific social interactions during group therapy lead to increased beliefs about competence, regardless of whether these beliefs are specifically targeted, as in CBT, or indirectly addressed in supportive-type group therapy. I wonder if the lack of difference could also be a result of the goal-focused comparison group including strong elements of CBT, given that CBGT is both a goal-focused and supportive treatment approach.

The Granholm studies suggested that the social support felt in the groups helped members to develop skills and confidence to reach out, ask for help, and surround themselves with caring and understanding family and friends. Other clinical researchers have similarly found social support to be helpful for warding off self-stigmatizing. Klingberg and colleagues (2010) concluded that CBGT was effective in delaying relapse due to improvement in negative symptoms. That is, the CBGT clients had more helpful social contacts compared to those who received standard psychiatric care. The CBGT in this study consisted of psychoeducation, social–emotional skills training, social interaction addressing leisure, living situation, and employment, family education sessions, and stress management.

Integrating evolving trends in CBGT for psychosis

From the aforementioned research, clinicians can conclude that any improvements in reducing the negative symptoms of social withdrawal and self-stigma bode well for the prognosis of psychotic disorders. The stress of living with psychosis is complicated and uniquely experienced by each person, but broader issues such as judging oneself harshly (e.g., "I'm incompetent") or internal stigmatization (e.g., "I'm shameful") make social interactions enormously challenging. People with psychosis desire human connections as much as the rest of us, but fears of not measuring up, or of being rejected outright, hold them back from approaching relationships. The group can help counter the push into social isolation by fostering group members' resources for engaging with their own stories (narratives) and those of others.

Narrative enhancement and cognitive therapy

An explicit approach to becoming accepting of one's unique life story is group-based *narrative enhancement and cognitive therapy* (NECT; Yanos, Roe, & Lysaker, 2011). This program runs for 18–20 weeks, with each session lasting 90 minutes. The treatment manual includes three sessions of psychoeducation with an emphasis on recovery and the inaccuracy of stigmatizing views of severe mental illness. The next eight group sessions focus on standard cognitive restructuring, which supports group members in challenging dysfunctional cognitions about themselves and their illness (e.g., "I have a mental illness and don't expect to ever recover"). The last eight group sessions support group members in constructing a personally useful and meaningful narrative of themselves, their illness, and their relationship to their illness. These narratives may be verbally shared, written down, or both. The stories can be about past or recent events; they focus on bringing together clients' previously fragmented and isolated aspects of their experiences through the telling of a coherent story. For example, a group member shared a story about how his brother "freaked out" and refused to let his children, the group member's nieces and nephews, visit him alone after learning about his diagnosis. The rest of the group offered reflections and feedback, and in this case, helped the member to not buy into stereotypical and often erroneous beliefs about psychosis. The group also supported the member in moving from a passive stance to becoming more assertive both in his treatment and in interactions with family members. The latter involved telling family members more about his treatment and about situations that are especially anxiety provoking for him. The ultimate goal in the NECT group is thus to offer group members opportunities to practice their skills at negotiating and rewriting their personal stories. This practice helps to internalize the confidence-boosting role of the narrator. Some pilot studies, which included people with both psychotic and bipolar disorders, have yielded good outcomes (Yanos et al., 2011). The NECT approach is intended for people who are in a stable phase of their illness and not for early or acute stages of psychotic illness.

Compassion-focused therapy

The aforementioned example included a person experiencing a number of *threat emotions*, such as anxiety and anger, associated with a fear that his brother perceived him as potentially harmful to children. Based on evidence that people with psychosis struggle with processing and regulating perceived threats, the *compassion-focused* therapy (CFT) approach was developed (Braehler et al., 2012). This approach supports people with psychosis in expanding their capacity for self-calming—including reaching out to others, because supportive social relationships can also be calming. CFT recognizes that some people with psychosis who easily experience shame and self-criticalness also have the hardest time using supportive relationships as a means for calming. The group CFT protocol consists of 16 group sessions and integrates aspects of mindfulness and group processes in psychosis (Braehler, Harper, & Gilbert, 2013). The first third, called the formation phase (sessions 1–5), explores the impact the psychosis has on group members' lives and focuses on reducing shame, stigma, and increasing skills for self- and other compassion. The middle phase (sessions 6–13) include a gradual development of compassion by exploring the nature of compassion and how that might be expressed in the group and used for oneself. Compassion skills such as mindfulness, appreciation, imagery, attention, positive behaviors, and reframing are practiced and applied in relation to the internal and external threats and related difficulties members bring up. These difficulties typically include shame, social anxiety, paranoia, self-attacking, hostile voices, and poor motivation. The ending phase (sessions 14–16) involves expressive writing tasks to help members reflect on and integrate changes in their recovery from a compassionate stance. The developers of this protocol emphasize that throughout the group facilitators foster a caregiving mentality by developing a *compassionate group mind*. A compassionate group mind involves supporting members' interactions and capacity to relate to one another. A large part of the CFT group involves helping members to become aware and accepting of their own needs and to respond to themselves with warmth and compassion. Any self-attacking, or inner bullying, is seen as a psychological vulnerability factor that can increase the potential for relapse. After practicing being more forgiving of oneself, people with a vulnerability to a psychotic episode may become more confident in expressing their needs to those around them. The following exchange illustrates how the group can help a member, Sebastian, become more forgiving of and compassionate toward himself:

THERAPISTS: In our last session we talked a lot about how hard it can be to tell family members that you cannot always participate in family events as much as they want you to. We are curious to hear if you have noticed any change in the way you show care for yourselves when you sometimes have to disappoint others.

SEBASTIAN: Everyone is very upset because I refused to come out from my room to have Thanksgiving dinner with the family. They said I had promised to make an effort for Uncle Bob and Aunt Miriam.

SUZANNE: So did they make you feel guilty for breaking a promise?

SEBASTIAN: Yep.

IGOR: That is not fair. They know about your illness and how you cannot always predict how you will feel from one day, or even 1 hour, to the next. Makes me angry to hear [Igor clenches his fists and gets up from his chair].

SEBASTIAN: Well, interestingly, Uncle Bob and Aunt Miriam slipped a note under my door saying they missed me but understand, and wish me good luck with my new volunteer job.

THERAPIST: I imagine that note made you feel a bit better. Did it help you to understand that your aunt and uncle are right in the sense that you're not trying to deliberately upset your family?

SEBASTIAN: Yes it did.

SUZANNE: Well your aunt and uncle get it, and I just want to say that I think you should really try not to feel bad. I too do not always know if I am able to be with the whole family. This group is helping me understand that I am not doing it to be mean but that it is part of my illness.

SEBASTIAN: I know that too. I will try to tell my parents that the need to stay in my room sometimes feels beyond my control, and that I too feel sad about not seeing everyone.

THERAPIST: Sounds like a fine plan to try and get your parents to not put pressure on you. You're already too hard on yourself. Let's just review again that you're all struggling with an illness, and it's the illness that sometimes makes you feel super uncomfortable around other people.

A first randomized controlled trial of group CFT suggests this group approach to psychosis is safe, acceptable, and helpful. A significantly greater proportion of the participants in the group (65%) were rated as having improved compared to 5% of the participants in the treatment-as-usual group (case management and medication). Improvements involved increases in compassion and decreases in negative beliefs about psychosis, symptoms of depression, and fear of relapse. Moreover, the dropout rate of 18% is unusually low compared to other groups for people with psychosis (Braehler et al., 2012).

Person-based cognitive therapy

Person-based cognitive therapy (PBCT) integrates traditional cognitive therapy with a mindfulness-and acceptance-based approach (Chadwick, 2006). According to Strauss and Hayward (2013), the group person-based cognitive therapy (G-PBCT) for psychosis includes four components. The first two components involve traditional CBT and cover (1) *symptomatic meaning* (e.g., psychoeducation with emphasis on identifying and evaluating beliefs about psychotic experiences) and (2) *schema* (e.g., to recognize and strengthen a positive understanding and evaluation of oneself). The final two components are termed (3) *relationship with internal experience* (e.g., mindfulness practice is used to develop a different way of relating to psychotic experiences), and (4) *symbolic self* (e.g., emphasis on the self as complex, at times contradictory, and always changing). Strauss and Hayward underscore the importance of the therapeutic relationship and argue that the CBT model of client-centered collaboration is of utmost importance. In fact, they call this ingredient in PBCT *radical collaboration*. In the group context, they draw attention to eight specific therapeutic factors as identified by Yalom and Leszcz (2005), the same factors discussed in Chapter 2 in this book.

The PBCT group usually runs for 12 weeks with each session being 90 minutes. All sessions follow a consistent structure, recognizing that structure is paramount in groups for psychosis. Sessions begin with a 10-minute mindfulness practice (see Chapter 5 for a description of using mindfulness relapse prevention in depression or

Chapter 8 for mindfulness in groups for GAD) and then move onto specific CBT exercises such as A–B–C work sheets. "A" refers to an antecedent event (e.g., a voice comment), "B" to beliefs (e.g., beliefs about voice power and control), and "C" to consequences of A and B (e.g., feelings and behaviors in relation to voices or other symptoms). Detailed questioning encourages participants to increase self-awareness. The group learns to ask questions of each other, such as "What did you feel when the voice told you not to go out?," "What did you notice in your body?," and "What did you do?" Other specific standard CBT exercises throughout the group program include individual identification and rating of unhelpful beliefs. These exercises are followed by group discussions of evidence that supports and does not support unhelpful beliefs about voices or other symptoms, identification and strengthening of positive self-schemas, and weekly beliefs about the self in relation to voices. Strengthening of positive self-schemas involves exercises similar to the challenging of core beliefs for the depression group described in Chapter 5. The PCBT group helps members develop positive core belief statements such as "I'm OK as I am" or "I am capable" (Strauss & Hayward, 2013). Each session ends with assignment of a home task, which could be mindfulness practice, monitoring of beliefs, and gathering evidence that may not support a particular belief.

It is apparent that the relatively short-term PCBT group is ambitious in its attempt to integrate standard CBT approaches, mindfulness practice, and group process. Evidence for the effectiveness of the specific use of mindfulness in psychosis and for the general integrative approach of PCBT is still being gathered, and although promising, we await firmer conclusions (Chadwick, Newman-Taylor, & Abba, 2005; Strauss & Hayward, 2013).

Metacognitive training

Metacognitive training (MTC) focuses on the many cognitive biases to which people with psychosis are vulnerable (Moritz & Woodward, 2007a). The metacognitive approach especially targets cognitive biases such as *jumping to conclusions* (e.g., being convinced that crackling on a telephone line is evidence of surveillance), bias against *disconfirmatory evidence* (e.g., failure to integrate evidence that may disconfirm a belief), and a *self-serving attributional style* (e.g., blaming someone else for being untrustworthy or blaming oneself for being "bad"). Research continues to reveal the strong presence of these cognitive biases in people with psychosis and how they operate largely outside of conscious awareness. This treatment approach thus seeks to relieve the stress associated with cognitive biases as well as to act prophylactically against relapse (Moritz & Woodward, 2007a). Clients are offered specific skills to better challenge their biases in thinking. Some of these involve the standard cognitive techniques of reviewing evidence for and against an idea, which could be a conviction that a television commercial offers messages aimed directly at the individual. Other skills are unique to the MCT approach and are briefly reviewed in the following text.

A group intervention has been developed for MCT for people with psychosis. The group protocol is available in English and 29 other languages free of charge via the Internet http://www.uke.de/kliniken/psychiatrie/index_17380.php (Moritz & Woodward, 2007a). The facilitators of metacognitive groups review a number of cognitive biases and discuss how all human beings are vulnerable to them, but that people with psychotic problems are especially vulnerable. Group participants are invited to talk about their personal biases. The facilitators present exercises that help to counter the biases, or "cognitive traps," as they are also called. It is important to create a group atmosphere that feels safe, supportive, and even fun and thus "lecture style" teaching is avoided.

The metacognitive group program runs for 16 sessions and involves two parallel groups with 8 sessions each. Clients attend both groups at two separate times during the week. The two parallel groups target the same content but use different examples. Groups include 3–10 members. Each group session lasts from 45 to 60 minutes and targets a particular bias. For example, an exercise aimed at challenging a *bias against disconfirmatory evidence* involves showing the group a cartoon sequence in a "scrambled" order that makes it hard to grasp the sequence of events and what exactly is going on in a particular scenario. After each new picture, clients are asked to (re)rate the plausibility of four interpretations. Although on some pictures the initial most likely interpretation prevails, on others, group members are "led up the garden path," that is, they are challenged to reconsider their initial interpretation given new and perhaps surprising information. Thus, members learn to withhold strong judgment until sufficient evidence has been collected, and they are encouraged to maintain an open attitude toward counterarguments and alternative views (Moritz & Woodward, 2007a).[3]

Similar to other forms of psychotherapy for psychosis, MCT works in conjunction with medication. A handful of pilot studies have suggested MCT groups do better compared to treatment as usual and are well received by participants. Group members evaluate their groups with words such as "fun," "less boring," and "useful in daily life" (Moritz & Woodward, 2007b). A recent multicentered double-blind randomized controlled trial found that MCT significantly reduced delusions (measured by the PANSS and PSYRATS) at the end of the study and at 6 months follow-up (Moritz et al., 2013). A large randomized controlled study funded by the Canadian Institutes of Health Research on the benefits of metacognitive group therapy has just begun in Vancouver, BC, with Todd Woodward, Steffen Moritz, and Mahesh Menon as principal investigators. Metacognitive group therapy will be compared to control groups. The outcomes will be most valuable to group therapists with a special interest and expertise in psychosis as well as to mental health facilities invested in improving their care for people with psychosis. An attractive feature of MCT is its firm origin in clinical research documenting how people with psychosis have certain rigid thinking styles, but that they are fully capable of responding to their thoughts being challenged so long as this is done in a collaborative and safe therapeutic environment. The MCT approach broadens the cognitive strategy repertoire available to clinicians offering CBGT for psychosis.

Capitalizing on the Group for Psychosis

The stigma associated with psychosis is perhaps stronger than for any other mental health problem. People in groups for psychosis are often for the first time meeting others who also hear voices and who feel highly suspicious of other people. The group helps everyone in dealing with the external and internal stigma. If the CBT group is experienced as safe and benign, *simply being* in the group offers the person with psychosis a powerful disconfirming experience of previous beliefs about threats inherent from interactions with unfamiliar people.

Social support following a first episode of psychosis can have long-term positive effects for participants, especially in off-setting their self-stigmatizing behavior (Mueller et al., 2006). A group format facilitates socialization, the practice of reaching out, and of connecting. The opportunity to tell one's story, the narrative, and be fully listened to and validated can be powerful for people who have come to fear social connections. When feelings of threat become diminished, the group provides opportunities to modify (restructure) fearful beliefs about social interactions and make them more manageable. People with psychosis are especially helped by experiencing that rewarding social relationships are possible and helpful for achieving improvements in functioning and quality of life. Supportive interactions with others can provide stress-buffering information about how one is perceived by others, which in turn challenges beliefs about self-worth and biases about the negative intentions of others.

Common Challenges in CBGT for Psychosis

Although the very nature of a group format holds ideal possibilities for healing, the reality of course is that the group also has the potential for being damaging. Considering how easily the threat system is activated for people with psychosis, the inevitable problems associated with all types of CBT groups can become magnified in a psychosis group.

Clinicians must first remind themselves that CBT for psychosis rarely produces outcomes as excellent, whether in individual or group format, as CBT for other mental health problems. This is largely due to the difficulty with engaging clients with psychosis in mental health services. Our clients often have transient lifestyles and are more likely to have additional mental health problems such as substance abuse or socioeconomic problems including, inadequate or no housing. If they live with family members, some can be overprotective and obstruct access to group therapy worrying that it may be too stressful for their loved one (Lecomte et al., 2012).

Dropout rates are a problem. To begin with, groups for psychosis tend to be smaller, with four to six clients. This does not offer much room for dropouts and groups too often become reduced to one or two members before dissolving. In addition to the aforementioned problems with engagement, clinicians identify other barriers to successful groups. These include large discrepancies in intellectual functioning and insight, as well as medication compliance. The more similar group members are, the more likely the group is to be helpful. One option is to stratify groups on those variables so that members are more or less at the same level, but this requires a fairly large client pool from which individual group programs can select. People with psychosis struggle with feeling marginalized, and sensitivity to being different and "not fitting in" can therefore be especially hurtful and harmful in terms of setbacks.

The newer trends in group CBT for psychosis were developed as attempts to make groups more successful, and the lower dropout rates reported in the CFT are encouraging and leave clinicians feeling more optimistic about improving CBGT for psychosis. Still, at times, an individual treatment component may be needed in addition to a group. This allows group members to process their experience of the group with an individual therapist or case manager. This of course compromises the cost-effectiveness of the group format.

Careful screening will identify those clients who may especially need individual therapy in addition to their group. People with early life abuse or trauma have been identified as benefiting from individual treatment in addition to the group (Braehler et al., 2012). Warman, Grant, Sullivan, Caroff, and Beck (2005) found that a mix of group and individual CBT resulted in impressive gains maintained over an 11 months follow-up period. Delusions became less distressing and less credible, and symptoms of anxiety and depression, including hopelessness, were also reduced to mild levels.

Similar to other CBT groups, the CBT group for psychosis can only be efficient and cost-effective if the therapists are adequately skilled in both CBT and group facilitation. With the newer treatment approaches, this places an additional challenge on therapists to obtain continuing education and skill development. Although mental health programs will incur costs for training their staff, the investment is likely to pay off in terms of reduced needs for intensive hospital care for people with psychosis. Clinicians are thus faced with deciding which infusion into the traditional CBT group works best for them, given their level of training and their interests. A commitment to stay abreast of the literature on CBGT for psychosis over the next few years should help clinicians make evidence-informed decisions.

Summary

This chapter reviews a number of studies showing the potential for CBGT to mediate between neurocognitive vulnerabilities and functioning, in particular social functioning. The group format offers unique opportunities for supporting people with psychosis in developing more satisfying social relations. New research tentatively points to the effectiveness of group CBT for both positive and negative symptoms, but especially the negative. CBGT for psychosis offers its members opportunities for coping better with external and internal stigmatization and beliefs about threats related to social interactions. The chapter encourages clinicians to stay open to emerging trends in group CBT for psychosis—and other severe mental illness such as bipolar disorder—potentially increasing the effectiveness of CBGT for psychosis. The reviewed trends are *narrative enhancement and cognitive therapy* (NECT), *compassion-focused therapy* (CFT), *person-based cognitive therapy* (PBCT), *and metacognitive training* (MCT).

Notes

1. As noted in Chapter 4, mood congruent delusions and hallucinations are also seen a small subgroup of patients with severe unipolar depression.
2. These initial Hearing Voices groups were treatment based, whereas presently, many peer-led support groups for psychosis use the same name.
3. Cognitive remediation (CR) is another form of cognitive training aimed at improving cognitive performance related to attention and memory. Using computers or paper-and-pencil work sheets, clients are taught techniques. The intervention is time limited, about two training sessions per week for 3–6 months. CR produces only modest effects, however, with small reductions in overall symptoms of psychosis (Wykes, Huddy, Cellard, McGurk, & Czobar, 2011).

Recommended Readings for Clinicians

Fowler, D., Garety, P., & Kuipers, E. (1995). *Cognitive behavior therapy for psychosis: Theory and practice*. West Sussex, UK: Wiley & Sons.

van der Gaag, M., Niemna, D., & van den Berg, D. (2013). *CBT for those at risk of a first episode psychosis: Evidence-based psychotherapy for people with an "at risk mental state."*. East Sussex, UK: Routledge.

Strauss, C., & Hayward, M. (2013). Group person-based cognitive therapy for distressing psychosis. In E. M. J. Morris, L. C. Johns, & J. E. Oliver (Eds.), *Acceptance and commitment therapy and mindfulness for psychosis* (pp. 240–255). West Sussex, UK: Wiley-Blackwell.

Tai, S., & Turkington, D. (2009). The evolution of cognitive behavior therapy for schizophrenia: Current practice and recent development. *Schizophrenia Bulletin, 35(5)*, 865–873.

References

American Psychiatric Association. (2013). *Diagnostic and statistical manual of mental disorders, DSM* (5th ed.). Washington, DC: Author.

Barrowclough, C., Haddock, G., Beardmore, R., Conrod, P., Craig, T., Davies, L. et al. (2009). Evaluating integrated MI and CBT for people with psychosis and substance misuse: Recruitment, retention, and sample characteristics of the MIDAS trial. *Addictive Behaviors, 34*, 859–866.

Barrowclough, C., Haddock, G., Lobban, F., Jones, S., Siddel, R., & Roberts, C., et al. (2006). Group cognitive-behavioural therapy for schizophrenia: randomized controlled trial. *British Journal of Psychiatry, 189*, 527–532.

Braehler, C., Gumley, A., Harper, J., Wallace, S., Norrie, J., & Gilbert, P. (2012). Exploring change processes in compassion focused therapy in psychosis: Results of a feasibility randomized controlled trial. *British Journal of Clinical Psychology, 52(2)*, 199–214.

Braehler, C., Harper, J., & Gilbert, P. (2013). Compassion focused group therapy for recovery after psychosis. In C. Steel (Ed.), *Cognitive behavior therapy for schizophrenia: Evidence based interventions and future directions* (pp. 236–266). West Sussex, UK: Wiley-Blackwell.

Cather, C. (2005). Functional cognitive behavioral therapy: A brief, individual treatment for functional impairments resulting from psychotic symptoms in schizophrenia. *Canadian Journal of Psychiatry, 50*, 258–263.

Chadwick, P. (2006). *Person-based cognitive therapy for distressing psychosis*. West Sussex, UK: Wiley-Blackwell.

Chadwick, P., Newman-Taylor, K., & Abba, N. (2005). Mindfulness groups for people with psychosis. *Behavioural and Cognitive Psychotherapy, 33*, 351–359.

Chadwick, P., Sambrooke, S., Rasch, S., & Davies, S. (2000). Challenging the omnipotence of voices: Group cognitive behavior therapy for voices. *Behaviour Research and Therapy, 38*, 993–1003.

Christodoulides, T., Dudley, R., Brown, S., Turkington, D., & Beck, A. T. (2008). Cognitive behavior therapy in patients with schizophrenia who are not prescribed antipsychotic medication: A case series. *Psychology and Psychotherapy: Theory, Research and Practice, 81*, 199–207.

Chung, Y.-C., Yoon, K.-S., Park, T.-W., Yang, J.-C., & Oh, K.-Y. (2013). Group cognitive-behavioral therapy for early psychosis. *Cognitive Therapy and Research, 37*, 403–411.

Erickson, D. (2010). Cognitive-behaviour therapy for medication-resistant positive symptoms in early psychosis: A case series. *Early Intervention in Psychiatry, 4*, 251–256.

Fanning, F., Foley, S., Lawlor, E., McWilliams, S., Jackson, D., Renwick, L., et al. (2012). Group cognitive behavioural therapy for first episode psychosis: Who's referred, who attends and who completes it? *Early Intervention in Psychiatry, 6*, 432–441.

Gaynor, K., Dooley, B., Lawlor, E., Lawoyin, R., & O'Callaghan, E. (2011). Group cognitive behavioural therapy as a treatment for negative symptoms in first-episode psychosis. *Early Intervention in Psychiatry, 5*, 168–173.

Granholm, E., Ben-Zeev, D., & Link, P. C. (2009). Social disinterest attitudes and group cognitive-behavioral social skills training for functional disability in schizophrenia. *Schizophrenia Bulletin, 35*, 874–883.

Haddock, G., McCarron, J., Tarrier, N., & Faragher, E. B. (1999). Scales to measure dimensions of hallucinations and delusions: The psychotic symptom rating scales (PSYRATS). *Psychological Medicine, 29(4)*, 879–889.

Johns, L., & Wykes, T. (2010). Group Cognitive Behaviour Therapy for psychosis. In F. Larø & A. Aleman (Eds.), *Hallucinations: A guide to treatment and management* (pp. 61–80). New York: Oxford University Press.

Kay, S. R., Fiszbein, A., & Opler, I. A. (1987). The positive and negative syndrome scale (PANNS) for schizophrenia. *Schizophrenia Bulletin, 13*, 261–276.

Kilbride, M., Byrne, R., & Price, J. (2012). Exploring service users' perceptions of cognitive behavioural therapy for psychosis. *Behavioural and Cognitive Psychotherapy, 41*, 89–102.

Klingberg, S., Wittorf, A., Fishers, A., Jakob-Deters, K., Buchkremer, G., & Wiedemann, G. (2010). Evaluation of a cognitive behaviourally oriented service for relapse prevention in schizophrenia. *Acta Psychiatrica Scandinavica, 121*, 340–350.

Lawrence, R., Bradshaw, T., & Mairs, H. (2006). *Journal of Psychiatric and Mental Health Nursing, 13*, 673–681.

Lecomte, T., Leclerc, C., Corbière, C., Wykes, T., Wallace, C. J., & Spidel, A. (2008). Group cognitive behavior therapy or social skills training for individuals with a first episode of psychosis. *Journal of Nervous and Mental Diseases, 196*, 866–875.

Lecomte, T., Leclerc, C., & Wykes, T. (2012). Group CBT for early psychosis—a re there still benefits one year later? *International Journal of Group Psychotherapy, 62(2)*, 309–321.

Lecomte, T., Leclerc, C., Wykes, T., & Lecomte, J. (2003). Group CBT for clients with a first episode of psychosis. *Journal of Cognitive Psychotherapy, 17*, 375–384.

Lecomte, T., Wallace, C. J., Caron, J., Perreault, M., & Lecomte, J. (2004). Further validation of the client assessment of strengths interests and goals. *Schizophrenia Research, 66*, 59–70.

Lehman, A. F., Kreyenbuhl, J., Buchanan, R. W., Dickerson, F. B., Dixon, L. N., Goldberg, R., et al. (2004). The schizophrenia patient outcomes research team (PORT): Updated treatment recommendations *Schizophrenia Bulletin, 30(2)*, 193–217.

Leucht, S., Kane, J. M., Kissling, W., Hamann, J., Etschel, E., & Engel, R. R., 2005 What does the PANNS mean? *Schizophrenia Research, 79*, 231–238.

Lu, W., Mueser, K. T., Shami, A., Siglag, M., Petrides, G., Schoepp, E., et al. (2011). Post-traumatic reactions to psychosis in people with multiple psychotic episodes. *Schizophrenia Research, 127(1–3)*, 66–75.

Moritz, S., Veckenstedt, R., Bohn, F., Hottenrott, B., Scheu, F., Randjbar, S., et al. 2013. Complementary group Metacognitive Training (MCT) reduces delusional ideation in schizophrenia. *Schizophrenia Research, 151*, 61–69.

Moritz, S., & Woodward, T. (2007a). Metacognitive training in schizophrenia: From basic research to knowledge translation and intervention. *Current Opinion in Psychiatry, 20(6)*, 619–625.

Moritz, S., & Woodward, T. (2007b). Metacognitive training for schizophrenia patients (MCT): A pilot study on feasibility, treatment adherence, and subjective efficacy. *German Journal of Psychiatry, 10*, 69–78.

Mueller, B., Nordt, C., Lauber, C., Rueesch, P., Meyer, P. C., & Roessler, W. (2006). Social support modifies perceived stigmatization in the first years of mental illness: A longitudinal approach. *Social Science and Medicine, 62*, 39–49.

Mueser, K. T., Lu, W., Rosenberg, S. D., & Wolfe, R. (2010). The trauma of psychosis: Posttraumatic stress disorder and recent onset psychosis. *Schizophrenia Research, 116(2–3)*, 217–227.

National Institute of Clinical Excellence. (2009). *Schizophrenia: Core interventions in the treatment and management of schizophrenia in primary and secondary care (update)*. London: National Institute of Clinical Excellence.

Rector, N. A. (2005). Cognitive-behavioural therapy for severe mental disorders. *Canadian Journal of Psychiatry, 50*, 245–246.

Rector, N. A., Beck, A. T., & Stolar, N. (2005). The negative symptoms of schizophrenia: A cognitive perspective. *Canadian Journal of Psychiatry, 5*, 247–257.

Rector, N. A., Seeman, M. V., & Segal, Z. V. (2003). Cognitive therapy for schizophrenia: A preliminary randomized controlled trial. *Schizophrenia Research, 63*, 1–11.

Saksa, J. R., Cohen, S., Srihari, V. H., & Woods, S. W. (2009). Cognitive behavior therapy for early psychosis: A comprehensive review of individual vs. group treatment studies. *International Journal of Group Psychotherapy, 59(3)*, 357–383.

Silverstein, A. R. (2007). Integrating Jungian and self-psychological perspectives within cognitive-behavior therapy for a young man with a fixed religious delusion. *Clinical Case Studies, 6*, 263–276.

Wallace, C. J., Lecomte, T., Wilde, J., & Liberman, R. P. (2001). CASIG: A consumer-centered assessment for planning individualized treatment and evaluating program outcomes. *Schizophrenia Research, 50*, 105–119.

Warman, D. M., Grant, P., Sullivan, K., Caroff S., & Beck, A. T. (2005). Individual and group cognitive-behavioural therapy for psychotic disorders: A pilot investigation. *Journal of Psychiatric Practice, 11*, 27–34.

Wykes, T., Huddy, V., Cellard, C., McCurk, S. R., & Czobar, P. (2011). A meta-analysis of cognitive remediation for schizophrenia: Methodology and effect sizes. *American Journal of Psychiatry, 168*, 472–485.

Wykes, T., Parr, A., & Landau, S. (1999). Group treatment of auditory hallucinations: Exploratory study of effectiveness. *British Journal of Psychiatry, 175*, 180–185.

Wykes, T., Steel, C., Everitt, B., & Tarrier, N. (2008). Cognitive behavior therapy for schizophrenia: Effect sizes, clinical models, and methodological rigor. *Schizophrenia Bulletin, 34*, 523–537.

Yanos, P. T., Roe, D., & Lysaker, P. (2011). Narrative enhancement and cognitive therapy: A new group-based treatment for internalized stigma among persons with severe mental illness. *International Journal of Group Psychotherapy, 61(4)*, 578–595.

Yalom, I. D., & Leszcz, M. (2005). *The theory and practice of group psychotherapy* (5th ed.). New York: Basic Books.

Zimmermann, G., Favrod, J., Trieu, V. H., & Pomini, V. (2005). The effects of cognitive behavioral treatment of the positive symptoms of schizophrenia spectrum disorders: A meta-analysis. *Schizophrenia Research, 77*, 1–9.

17

Addictions

Addiction to substances affects millions of people and is, according to the World Health Organization (2010), the third leading risk factor for early death and disabilities. Mental health clinicians sometimes wonder why the problem of addiction, which so clearly is a candidate for CBT, is often the least likely to be paired with this treatment in community mental health services. Research shows CBT can bring about significant improvement in addictions, lasting at least 1 year after treatment. CBT is especially effective in treating addictions because of its emphasis on behavioral conditioning (e.g., "I need alcohol to relax") and cognitive expectancies (e.g., "alcohol will make me feel better about myself and other people"). Fortunately, this situation seems to be slowly reversing.

Numerous studies support the use of integrated CBT delivered individually or in groups for the full range of substance use, including alcohol, nicotine, cocaine, marijuana, etc. Integrated CBT requires basic CBT interventions to be expanded to address clients' *motivation* and *readiness* to alter their substance use behaviors. The integrated CBT approach to addiction will be elaborated throughout this chapter. Two separate reviews of an impressively large number (one review included 34 and the other 54) of randomized controlled trials conclusively point to an integrated CBT approach as being superior to general drug counseling or management by family doctors (Magill & Ray, 2009; McHugh, Hearon, & Otto, 2010). These studies did not include direct comparisons of individual versus group CBT. Direct comparisons were part of Sobell and Sobell's CBT *Guided Self-Change Approach* (2011), which demonstrated that group is at least as effective as individual CBT and obviously more cost-effective (Nyamathi et al., 2011; Sobell, Sobell, & Agrawal, 2009).

Cognitive Behavioral Group Therapy: Challenges and Opportunities, First Edition. Ingrid Söchting.

If so helpful, why is CBT for addictions not more easily accessible in public mental health care? One reason may be the ubiquitous problem of the dearth of therapists trained in comprehensive CBT for addictions. Another reason may be found in the remnants of the long-standing debate over whether addiction is a moral failure or a disease with no cure, making total abstinence imperative. The opposing argument, consistent with the more recent *controlled* drinking or *harm reduction* approach (Inciardi & Harrisons, 2000), posits that any addiction is a complex mental health issue, rather than a disease one either has or does not have. Further, addiction is best understood as occurring on a continuum where relapse is expected but recovery possible. For some types of addiction, such as eating or shopping, abstinence is not even possible.[1] The harm reduction reasoning thus stands in contrast to the philosophy of Alcoholics Anonymous (AA), which advocates lifelong abstinence.

AA is the largest of several *mutual help groups*. These groups differ noticeably from professional-led treatment groups. AA groups rely primarily on the model of those who have recovered from an addiction helping others. AA supports the 12-step approach (the first step acknowledges one's powerlessness over the addiction; subsequent steps focus on developing a relationship with a higher power and committing to the fellowship of helping others recover). Developed before the harm reduction paradigm, the 12-step AA program has for decades been the go-to place and authority, to the point of some communities offering no alternative. Perhaps this situation alleviated community mental health programs of the pressure to develop services for addictions. Senior psychologists today share my graduate school training experience where we were encouraged to simply refer any client with an addiction problem to the local AA group.

Unquestionably, AA, along with Gamblers Anonymous, Sexaholics Anonymous, Overeaters Anonymous, and Shopaholics Anonymous, and similar 12-step programs continue to help people with addictions around the world. The possible limitations of 12-step programs are, however, increasingly noticed. Most importantly, peer counselors in 12-step are not trained in mental health, which may be one of the reasons why several additional problems facing those with addictions go unrecognized and untreated. Many, if not most, people with addictions have additional psychiatric issues such as anxiety, depression, psychosis, and personality disorders (Swendsen et al., 2010). The addiction to substances or other activities, such as gambling or pornography, thus *co-occurs* with another mental health problem. Without attention to co-occurring problems, recovery from the addiction can be problematic. For example, people with anxiety disorders often use alcohol as a way of calming themselves before going into situations that are likely to trigger their anxiety. Because taking alcohol as a form of self-medication works to a point, it will be challenging to overcome an addiction without also being offered specialized help for anxiety.

Despite endorsing the effectiveness of CBT as a best practice approach to addictions, there is a persistent problem with high relapse rates past the first year of treatment. In a review article on understanding and preventing relapse, relapse rates for a range of addictions including substances, food, and smoking ranged from 50% to 90% (Brownell, Marlatt, Lichtenstein, & Wilson, 1986). However, there is a lack of agreement on what defines a relapse versus a lapse for various addictions. Moreover, relapse rates depend on characteristics of the addiction, individual variables related to a person's environment, culture, and physiology, and the type of treatment (e.g., emphasizing coping skills and motivation especially help to prevent relapse). The authors caution that the percentages for relapse may be inflated given that the majority of people with an addiction recover through their own efforts (and we don't know much about their relapse rates) with only the more severe cases receiving formal treatment.

Despite lack of exact knowledge about relapse rates, the need for improved treatment and relapse prevention remains. The end of the chapter will return to literature on ways to augment the more problem-focused CBT group for addiction with a paramount focus on strengthening the addicted person's identity and self-definition. Mindfulness-based and spiritually oriented approaches to relapse prevention will be discussed as ways to support people in developing a new understanding of their addiction and a larger sense of life purpose.

Although this chapter is focused on adults, it is important to note that systematic reviews on the effectiveness of CBT and CBGT for adolescent substance use, including marijuana, indicate this as a well-established and responsible choice, although not superior to other treatment models including family therapy (Diamond et al., 2002; Waldron & Turner, 2008).

The Diagnoses of Substance-Related and Addictive Disorders

In the DSM-5 (American Psychiatric Association [APA], 2013), the *Substance-Related Disorders* encompass 10 separate classes of drugs, including alcohol, caffeine, cannabis, hallucinogens, inhalants, opioids, sedatives, hypnotics, and anxiolytics, as well as stimulants such as cocaine, tobacco, and other substances. All drugs taken in excess have in common direct activation of the brain reward system, which is involved in the reinforcement of addictive behaviors. Although the mechanisms work differently, all drugs produce feelings of pleasure, often referred to as "a high." Individuals with lower levels of self-control may be especially predisposed to develop substance-related disorders.

In addition to *Substance-Related Disorders*, the DSM-5 has added *Addictive Disorders*. The nonsubstance-related disorders, or *Addictive Disorders*, are presently limited to *Gambling Disorder*, which has a distinct set of diagnostic criteria and activates reward systems similar to drugs. The DSM-5 recognizes other kinds of behavioral addictions such as *Internet gaming*, *sex addiction*, *exercise*, *overeating*, and *shopping addictions*, although these are not yet formal diagnoses given a lack of evidence to establish diagnostic criteria. *Substance-Related Disorders* are further divided into *Substance Use Disorders* or *Substance-Induced Disorders*. For example, the alcohol-related disorders include separate diagnoses for *Alcohol Use Disorder*,

Alcohol Intoxication, and *Other Alcohol-Induced Disorders*. The latter captures how an anxiety or mood disorder can be induced by excessive alcohol use.

The essential feature of all *Substance Use Disorders* (I will not review the *Substance-Induced Disorders* but refer the reader to the DSM-5) is a cluster of cognitive, behavioral, and physiological symptoms indicating that the individual continues using the substance despite significant substance-related problems. The DSM-5 *Substance Use Disorder* diagnosis focuses on an unhealthy pattern of use where the individual takes the substance in larger amounts or over a longer period than was originally intended (Criterion 1); expresses a desire to cut down or reports many unsuccessful attempts to decrease (Criterion 2); spends a great deal of time obtaining the substance, using it, or recovering from its effects (Criterion 3); and craves the substance (Criterion 4). The second group of criteria (Criteria 5–7) includes *social impairment*, such as failing to fulfill major role obligations at work, at school, or at home; continuing to use despite recurrent social or interpersonal problems; or withdrawing from friends, family, and interest and hobbies. The third group of criteria (Criteria 8–9) involves the risks associated with continued use, such as compromised physical safety and physical and psychological problems. Lastly, the final group of DSM-5 criteria (Criteria 10–11) is pharmacological and involves problems with building *tolerance* to the substance or problems with *withdrawal*. Substance use disorders can be specified as *mild* (two to three symptoms), *moderate* (four to five symptoms), or *severe* (six or more symptoms), and neither tolerance nor withdrawal is required for a diagnosis.[2] Other specifiers such as *in early remission* or *on maintenance therapy* are also available.

Prevalence rates for *Alcohol Use Disorder* in the United States is 4.6% among 12–17-year-olds and 8.5% among adults aged 18 and older. Rates are greater among men (12.4%) than women (4.9%). For *Cannabis Use Disorder*, the 12-month prevalence is 3.4% for 12- to 17-year-olds and 1.5% among adults aged 18 and older. Prevalence rates for other substances can be found in the DSM-5 (APA, 2013).

Why do people become addicted?

Similar to other mental health problems, the reasons people become addicted are multiple and complex. Genetics, brain chemistry, temperament, adverse early life experiences, and vulnerability to other mental health issues all play a role. Addiction is a process in which people initially use drugs for coping (e.g., decreasing pain or feeling more relaxed in social situations) or for just wanting to enhance their mood (e.g., feeling deserving of a treat or enjoying being in the company of friends). For some people, over time, the addiction takes over and increasingly controls their lives. Advances in brain research are shedding light on why some people may be more vulnerable to becoming addicted. Some of us are neurochemically at risk.

Simply stated, intake of substances or immersion in other "pleasures," such as gambling or shopping, affects the dopaminergic pathways by increasing the amount of this substance in the brain. Dopamine is associated with sensations of well-being and pleasure, and people differ in how much their brains produce this "naturally." Thus, with continued use, this neurochemical pleasure circuitry in a sense becomes "hijacked" with people no longer deriving the same level of pleasure from a lower level of activity; their dopamine circuitry becomes underresponsive requiring more and more in order to achieve the desired feeling of pleasure (Bien & Bien, 2002). In other words, two glasses of wine, two new pairs of shoes, a $50 limit in a card game, or one sexual partner is no longer enough to produce a sensation of satisfying pleasure.

In addition to biochemical factors, behavioral habits and beliefs about oneself play a prominent role in pulling people into addictions as a way of feeling better. In the next sections, I elaborate on these powerful behavioral and cognitive determinants of addictions and how CBT therapists directly target them in their therapy. I first discuss general CBT for addictions, then assessment, and lastly CBGT for addictions. Although issues pertaining to assessment are usually discussed before treatment, I believe that the treatment section in the following text will make the subsequent assessment section—with its focus on motivation—more relevant.

CBT for Addictions

The behavioral and cognitive parts of CBT have each, separately, contributed to the larger framework within which the majority of clinicians offer their integrated CBT for addictions. Behavioral approaches are influenced by both classical conditioning (Pavlovian) and operant conditioning (Skinnerian; O'Brien, Childress, McLellan, & Ehrman, 1992). Classical behavioral theory operates under the assumption that learned behaviors can become unlearned. One example of a behavioral technique for the treatment of substance abuse is *counterconditioning*, sometimes referred to as aversive conditioning. For example, someone who has become *conditioned* to reach for the whiskey bottle and pour into a glass upon returning home from work can engage in a counterconditioning behavioral program. This could involve taking a medication such as Antabuse (disulfiram), which induces vomiting at the first sip of whiskey. Over time, the taste, or even smell of, whiskey no longer becomes paired with feelings of pleasure and relaxation but instead with unpleasant feelings of nausea and vomiting.[3]

Operant conditioning involves promoting behaviors that lead to lesser drug abuse or abstinence. Such behaviors can be positively reinforced and strengthened. For example, a voucher program for purchase of goods was used in the treatment of cocaine users (Silverman et al., 1998). The value of the voucher increased as the number of consecutive cocaine-free urine samples increased. Other forms of *contingency management* include extensions of employment contracts, offers of subsidized housing, and any form of reward that is meaningful to the person. *Behavioral contracts* with family members can be helpful in influencing behaviors (e.g., "If I attend my treatment sessions regularly, my husband and I will celebrate by going on a weekend trip; if I miss more than 25% of sessions, my husband has the right to delay any talks about a weekend trip for another 6 months").

Other behavioral techniques focus on self-control by developing new *coping skills*. These include how to assertively refuse offers of drinks, how to slow down rate of drinking, or how to develop an engaging interest to immediately turn to when the craving is strong. Not that any of this is easy, but clients in groups inspire each other to consider new ways of coping so as not to give in to their cravings. A 65-year-old woman in our depression group who had a co-occurring serious gambling addiction became able to call her daughter, or grandchild, as a way of countering her urge to get in her car and head for the local casino. The group supported her with how to disclose her gambling problem to her daughter. Fortunately, the daughter took it well and became more than willing to help.

Cognitive approaches to substance use and other addictions assume that, similar to depression, unhelpful, untrue beliefs play a significant role in both the onset and maintenance of an addiction (Beck, Wright, Newman, & Liese, 1993). Our understanding and treatment of addiction is greatly enhanced by awareness of the many cognitive variables mediating between the stimulus (opportunity to engage in the addiction) and the behavior (actual engagement with the addiction).

Cognitive theory emphasizes three main types of thoughts that increase the likelihood of choosing to engage with an addiction: *outcome expectancies*, *negative automatic thoughts*, and *facilitating thoughts* (Wenzel, Liese, Beck, & Friedman-Wheeler, 2012). Outcome expectancies are highly related to relapse and involve positive anticipatory and relief-oriented expectancies. *Positive anticipatory expectancies* involve expecting an increase in well-being (e.g., "I can't wait to have some drinks and have fun after a tough week at work" or "My new clothes will make it easier to feel confident in all the meetings coming up next week"). *Relief-oriented expectancies* involve expecting reduced discomfort and distress by engaging in the addiction (e.g., "With a few drinks, I'll get through this family event better" or "Playing a few rounds of Black Jack at the casino will be a nice break from my ex-wife harassing me again for financial support"). The more traditional *negative automatic thoughts*, which are common in depression, also figure prominently in people with addictions who experience them as an ongoing "commentary" exerting a powerful influence on the likelihood of giving in to an addiction behavior. Examples may be "I deserve a drink," "It's Friday, time to relax and party," or "I see a sale sign in my favorite clothing store." Lastly, *facilitating thoughts* play a powerful role in giving permission to engage with the addiction and are characterized by minimizing the harmful effects and denying the extent of one's problem. Examples may be "After my divorce is finalized, I'll not need to gamble anymore" or "Everybody will be drinking at the wedding, so what's the big deal if I, too, enjoy myself?"

Although the ultimate outcome measure for addiction treatment is the degree to which people are able to reduce their addictive behaviors measures of the thoughts that promote an addiction are also helpful indicators. Chapter 6 recommended such specific outcome measures for addiction, the Drinking Expectancy Questionnaire (DEQ; Young, Oei, & Crook, 1991).

Assessment

In addition to the standard clinical intake assessment, an intake clinician for a client with addiction usually develops a cognitive case conceptualization (Wenzel et al., 2012). This follows a standard CBT approach to case formulation where predisposing, precipitating, perpetuating, and protective factors (the four Ps) are summarized and reviewed with the client at the end of the assessment. To get a good picture of what factors may be involved in maintaining an addiction, the clinician conducts a Functional Analysis focusing on a recent trigger situation and what kinds of thoughts followed, including any anticipatory or relief-oriented thoughts as well as positive and negative consequences of engaging in the addiction. I will return to the use of the Functional Analysis when discussing CBGT for addiction.

Motivation and readiness to change are also assessed, and as will be described later, CBGT for addictions usually welcome clients at various stages of readiness. Clinicians validate and explore ambivalence using motivational interviewing (MI; Miller & Rollnick, 2002). Inquiring about thoughts and beliefs that may maintain the addiction is helpful for a better understanding of the client's ambivalence. The assessor makes notes about which type of cognitions especially need to be addressed in treatment. Readiness for change is assessed by reviewing the different stages of motivation as suggested by the transtheoretical model of behavioral change (TTM; Prochaska & DiClemente, 1984): precontemplation, contemplation, preparation, action, and maintenance. The assessor talks to the client about how the group will include people who are at different levels of motivation and readiness.

It is also helpful to review any religious or spiritual beliefs the client may have and how they relate to their addiction in a helpful or hurtful way. Religion and spirituality can be important factors either precipitating the addiction (e.g., feeling closer to God by engaging in the addiction) or protecting against it (e.g., feeling a transcendent sense of purpose that the addiction risks undermining). Some people come to CBT groups because they cannot tolerate the AA approach, whereas others find it puzzling why CBT group therapists do not pay more attention to religious or spiritual beliefs and practice. Practically, it makes sense for clinicians in their assessment of addictions (or any other mental health issue for that matter) to make spiritual inquiries along the line of "Many people experience a sense of the sacred, or something larger than themselves, that provides their lives with a sense of purpose and meaning. What are your thoughts and feelings about this?" It may become apparent that clients' addictions are interfering with their ability to discover and connect with what may be sacred in their lives. Or they may experience a particular closeness to the sacred only when engaging with their addictions (Johnson, 2013). This is indeed relevant information with implications for treatment and relapse prevention.

Although the idea of doing a *spiritual history* as part of a standard psychological assessment seems foreign to many secularly trained mental health practitioners, pressure to do so—and to get the necessary training—is mounting. The lead accreditation body for health care in the Unites States, the Joint Commission, now requires that clinicians in public health organizations providing addiction services are able to administer a spiritual assessment (Hodge, 2011).

CBGT for Addictions

CBGT for addictions comes in various flexible forms. There are groups targeting primarily the addiction and groups targeting both the addiction and co-occurring mental health issues. We will first look at the latter before reviewing the components comprising CBGT primarily for addictions.

Co-occurring CBGT

As mentioned earlier, people with addictions often have other mental health problems. A better integration of treatment programs targeting both the addiction and other mental health concerns is increasingly mandated by governments funding mental health programs. Of particular interest for CBGT therapists is new clinical research showing that CBGT for co-occurring substance use and other mental health problems, such as depression and anxiety, produces improvements in both depression and substance use. For example, Watkins and colleagues (2011) found that offering CBGT for depression to clients with persistent depressive symptoms who were also receiving residential substance abuse treatment produces improved outcomes for both problems. Substance use was reduced by 50% and depression status went, on average, from severe to mild as measured by the Beck Depression Inventory (BDI; Beck, Steer, & Brown, 1996). The CBGT protocol for this study was an adapted version of the 16 2-hour group sessions' *Manual for Group Cognitive-Behavioral Therapy of Major Depression: A Reality Management Approach* (Muῆoz, Ippen, Rao, Le, & Dwyer, 2000). A version of this manual was discussed in Chapter 12. The Watkins study adapted this CBGT manual by integrating examples specifically about substance use and its connection to mood, thoughts, and behavior as well as by adding a 45-minute individual orientation session aimed at increasing motivation prior to the group. Encouragingly, our community clinicians have been able to reproduce these outcomes—using the BDI—in groups for depression and substance abuse.

Social anxiety and substance use are other examples of how two disorders usually treated separately can be successfully integrated. In typical outpatient CBT groups for anxiety, it is often stipulated that the client must first control their substance use before being eligible for the social anxiety group. There are now inspiring outcomes suggesting that a protocol specifically for social anxiety (Heimberger & Becker, 2002) can be adapted to groups for social anxiety and substance use (Courbasson & Nishikawa, 2010). The main adaptation consists of making explicit connections to substance use during all treatment components. Although not all outcome measures improved to the extent of being in the nonclinical range in the Courbasson and Nishikawa study, the improvements were sufficient to allow the clinician researchers to recommend an integrated CBGT model focusing on the interrelationship between social anxiety and substance use. Unfortunately, the dropout rate for this group targeting both substance use and social anxiety was very high at 56%. The study did not mention how the group facilitators worked with group process factors. If those were neglected, there may be room for improvement for group therapists wishing to offer this kind of CBGT.

As for integrating treatment for substance use with posttraumatic stress disorder (PTSD), the *Seeking Safety* group treatment protocol has yielded promising but not unequivocal results. The *Seeking Safety* group was developed for women by Lisa Najavits (2002). *Seeking Safety* is a structured CBT group addressing topics such as safe versus unsafe coping behaviors, detaching from emotional pain, setting boundaries in relationships, and other self-care strategies. The *Seeking Safety* group does not involve explicit exposure to traumatic memories (Chapter 7 reviewed a CBGT protocol which does include active exposure). This group is designed to run for 25 2-hour sessions. Various outcome studies, including homeless female veterans and low-income adult and adolescent women, consistently show positive results in terms of improved scores on PTSD and substance use measures—as long as the full length of the program is delivered (Najavits, 2002). A shortened version of 12 sessions was not more effective than an active control condition involving health education for women (Hien et al., 2009). These studies support clinicians in developing new CBGT models for integrated care. Although developed for women only, clinicians report that the protocol works just as well for men, and that, in all male groups it is preferable to have the group therapists also be men. A full description of this program for men is available (Najavits et al., 2009).

CBGT protocols for addictions

A number of core components comprise the protocols clinicians use in their CBT groups for substance use. There seems, however, to be only a few protocols specifically developed for a group setting. The group protocol by Monti, Kadden, Rohsenow, Cooney, and Abrams (2002) is often used as a basic framework with its emphasis on identification of high-risk situations, coping skills, challenging unhelpful thinking, problem solving, and relapse prevention. A recent CBGT

Early Experiences
Difficult family, social, cultural, and/or economic circumstances

Formation of Core Beliefs
"I'm worthless"
"My situation will never improve"
"I can't cope with painful feelings"

Exposure to and Experimentation with Addictive Behaviors
Friends who engage in and encourage addictive behaviors
Family members who engage in addictive behaviors
Community glamorization of addictive behaviors

Development of Addictions-Related Beliefs
Drugs and alcohol make me feel better about myself
My friends and I have more fun when I use drugs
I'm more accepted by my group of friends and family

Beliefs Become Pervasive with Continued Use

Exposure to Activating Stimuli and Activation of Anticipatory and Relief-Oriented Expectancies

Figure 17.1 Cognitive Model of Addiction. Adapted from Liese and Franz, 1996. Reproduced with permission of Guilford Press.

manual, *Group Cognitive Therapy for Addictions*, for different kinds of addiction emphasizes psychoeducation, coping skills, and cognitive restructuring. In this protocol, each session begins with a review of the *Cognitive Model of Addiction* as a springboard for discussion about situational triggers, thoughts, and lapses (Wenzel et al., 2012) (Figure 17.1). This manual is based on an open group where new members enter and leave on a continuous basis.

Following is an outline of a standard CBGT group for addiction. It includes the common CBT practice of devoting the last session(s) to reviewing learned skills and planning for ongoing practice, but does not include a specific relapse prevention component. It is assumed that most clients graduating from this group will need to transition into a specific relapse prevention program, which I discuss later in this chapter. Although I separate relapse prevention skills from the active CBT treatment in this proposed treatment outline, this is not necessarily the norm in CBT for addictions. There seems to be a range of what we as clinicians mean when we talk about CBT for addictions. To some, it includes ongoing practice of relapse prevention and other coping skills including challenging thoughts and beliefs. For others, it means primarily offering behavioral coping skills. What is offered here is a comprehensive CBT protocol with behavioral, cognitive interventions, and limited relapse prevention components. Additional, and more extensive, relapse programs are discussed later in this chapter.

Group sessions are 90 minutes in length, usually once a week for 12 weeks. The CBGT for addiction group follows the same basic format outlined in Chapter 1 as other forms of CBGT and includes go-rounds, homework review and assignment. CBT approaches to addiction are consistent with a harm reduction approach, and are also compatible with the 12-step model. Following is a proposed outline of a treatment protocol for CBGT for addictions.

Session Themes (Adapted from Monti et al., 2002; Sobell & Sobell, 2011; Wenzel et al., 2012)

Session 1: Psychoeducation: Review the CBT Model of Addiction and Individual Goals
Session 2: Psychoeducation: Review the CBT Model of Addiction
Session 3: Motivation and Readiness
Session 4: Functional Analysis: Identification of High-Risk Situations
Session 5: Functional Analysis: Identification of High-Risk Situations
Session 6: Cognitive Strategies
Session 7: Cognitive Strategies
Session 8: Coping Skills: Assertiveness Training—Refusal Skills
Session 9: Coping Skills: Assertiveness Training—Refusal Skills
Session 10: Coping Skills: Anger Management
Session 11: Coping Skills: Problem Solving
Session 12: Relapse Prevention and Preparing for the Future: Pleasurable Activities, Repairing Damaged Relationships, and Developing Activities and Interests Incompatible with the Addiction

This outline is in practice not as fixed as it seems and can be used for both open and closed groups. CBGT clinicians for addiction show flexibility in adapting the general protocol to the particular needs of their populations. Depending on the needs of the members in the group, facilitators may pay more attention to some components over others. Facilitators may also vary the length of the sessions. For example, in residential settings where group members have more severe addictions, some clinicians find that the group cannot sustain concentration for more than 1 hour. Thus, they split sessions into two shorter sessions per week. They also offer an ongoing repetition of session 3, the Motivation and Readiness module, for 30 minutes each week. This allows clients to "try out" what it feels like to be in a group, and whether they feel ready to make a change, before fully committing. Some groups also repeat certain sessions more than others (e.g., Coping Skills: Anger Management), or work with the Functional Analysis in every session as part of the go-round when reviewing how everyone's week went.

Psychoeducation

This part is similar to the psychoeducation about the cognitive model for depression reviewed in Chapter 5. Therapists leading addiction groups offer the same mini-lecture as illustrated in that chapter while inserting addiction examples.

We suggest sketching a version of the *Cognitive Model of Addiction* on a board for every session and ensure several blank copies, that is, copies where clients can insert their own examples. In open groups, it is important that facilitators bring these for every session for the new members. Group members who are willing to discuss the development of their addiction in their lives are encouraged to do so. Because all members reviewed this at their intake assessment, it is usually not difficult for them to engage with the material. The exercise presents a rich opportunity for group members to bond by showing empathy as they listen, by supporting each other in promoting awareness and insight, and by collectively buying into the cognitive rationale that underpins subsequent coping skills and interventions.

Motivation and stages of change

In addition to the intake interview prior to the group, the group itself is a helpful place to further validate and explore some members' ambivalence about decreasing or giving up their addictions. Similar to the motivation component in CBGT for hoarding reviewed in Chapter 15, the addiction group members support each other in talking about the advantages and disadvantages of engaging with their addictions. Readiness for change is addressed directly—by inviting group members to reflect on it. The ideal client is in the action stage and engaged in active coping with clear results. However, the reality is that many clients are in the contemplation stage, where they recognize they have a problem but are not committed to giving it up or not sure what giving it up "would be like." The group becomes a unique source of support and validation for clients at all levels of readiness. Those who are "ahead" inspire and model what change can look like.

Functional analysis

The Functional Analysis is a tool that helps clients understand what keeps certain behaviors going by identifying the *function* of the behavior and what positive consequences reinforce the behavior. The Functional Analysis is not unique to CBT for addiction, but a general strategy for better understanding what maintains all sorts of problematic behaviors. However, the Functional Analysis is an especially relevant skill in the broad repertoire of support for those with addictions. After the underlying function of the behavior has been identified, clients can then consider alternative and healthier behaviors (Sobell & Sobell, 2011). The Functional Analysis consists of reviewing what situation triggered addiction-supportive thoughts, feelings, and behaviors and which coping strategies were used. The

Functional Analysis asks: Did the client engage with their addiction or not, and what were the positive and negative consequences? See Appendix I for a Functional Analysis work sheet.

During Functional Analysis review, a group member, George, may share that he "fell off the wagon" and was brought home intoxicated by a friend. His wife was upset and he is feeling ashamed. The group facilitators help George complete the sheet. He identified the trigger situation as being turned down for a promotion. He felt angry and hopeless and thought: "I give up. This is my third attempt to become foreman. Screw this company, and screw trying to stay clean and sober and be a good husband and dad." His coping behavior involved giving into his addiction by leaving work early and stopping at a bar on his way home—a place where his buddies are likely to also show up after work. At first, George denied that anything positive came of his becoming drunk, but as the group continued to challenge him, he admitted that he did enjoy the first beer, especially because his friend also had a beer and they talked about some recent local event. He almost forgot about the failed promotion. The negative consequences for George, however, included upsetting his wife and feeling embarrassed and ashamed. As for alternative coping behaviors, with the aid of the group, George vowed to next time call, or text, his wife immediately after feeling upset at work or anywhere else. He acknowledged that she is very understanding and supports him in his work frustrations and in looking for another job.

Addiction group therapists prepare themselves for how challenging the Functional Analysis work can be. They recognize that the words *Functional Analysis* are a bit of a mouthful and awfully clinical sounding. One nickname for this exercise is the "slow motion" or "slow mo" exercise referring to the benefits of reviewing slowly, step by step, all the links in the chain of an addiction episode. Somewhat surprisingly to nonaddiction therapists, clients often struggle the most with acknowledging the positive consequences of their addictions to the point of becoming angry with the group for suggesting there is anything whatsoever that could be positive about falling into their addictions. For more severely addicted people, it is as if any reminder of, or exposure to, their addiction is misunderstood as not supporting avoidance of triggers. One therapist sadly shared that this issue, of being asked about the positive consequences of addiction, had led to two people "storming out" of their groups during the same week. This brings up an important point about the extent to which therapists support their group members in avoidance or exposing themselves to addiction cues. CBT therapists are aware of possibly colluding with clients' avoidance if we do not encourage them to face their triggers or fears. On the other hand, dominant approaches to addiction involve attempts by the individual and those around them to remove all triggers and cues. Skilled CBT therapists relax into working with this dynamic tension and do not attempt to push any individuals or groups faster than they are ready for. Full exposures to addiction cues, as will be demonstrated later, typically do not begin until a client is well into a relapse prevention program.

Challenging unhelpful thinking

Similar to the depression group, the addiction group helps members to identify, evaluate, and modify thoughts and beliefs that promote their addiction. Therapists can create their own approaches and Thought Records as long as they are aimed at identifying an addiction-facilitating thought (e.g., "I deserve to relax and have fun") and replace it with an alternative response (e.g., "I realize I can work on becoming relaxed by practicing deep breathing or yoga"). The manual, *Group Cognitive Therapy for Addictions* (Wenzel et al. 2012), has a helpful example of a 6-column Thought Record for addiction. In this book, Chapter 5 offers suggestions for how to engage the entire group when supporting one member at a time in completing their Thought Records. The same suggestions are helpful for the addiction CBT group.

Most addiction therapists will recognize a certain cognitive style exhibited by people who have attended 12-step programs for years. These clients may refer to themselves as "powerless addicts." For some clients, this means "I'm taking steps in my recovery with the support of a force beyond my own self," whereas others are quick to label themselves as "disgusting and hopeless." Group therapists must discern the potential for group members' self-understanding to either promote healthy self-esteem or to undermine it. For example, Doug had been sober for 20 years but continued to refer to himself in highly self-loathing ways. It took several sessions of intense cognitive work as the group supported him in replacing negative automatic thoughts and core beliefs. One of his core beliefs was "I'm a disgusting nobody who has harmed many innocent people." Slowly, Doug became more comfortable with also reminding himself of "I'm a strong person who daily commits to keep healthy relationships with the people who love me." Considering that core beliefs are often especially self-critical in people with addictions, therapists may want to repeat this cognitive work over several sessions using the approach outlined in Chapter 5.

Coping skills training

A number of coping skills including but not limited to assertiveness, anger, counterconditioning, and problem solving are helpful for people with addictions. For example, assertiveness training is valuable for learning how to communicate a refusal to engage with an addiction. Problem-solving skills follow the same format as described in Chapter 7 for the generalized anxiety group. For counterconditioning skills aimed at helping clients engage in healthier, constructive behaviors and interests that are incompatible with the addiction, therapists can use the Leisure Skills Inventory introduced in Chapter 13.[4] The group can become a helpful source of inspiration, suggestions, and support as clients try to develop counterconditioning skills. One woman with an addiction to alcohol eventually became able to pursue a childhood interest in lace work. After 2 years of stable recovery, she completed a laced baptism dress for her grandchild. This activity is indeed incompatible with alcohol abuse, since lace work requires steady hands, clear head, stamina, and hours of concentration. The *Cognitive-Behavioural Coping Skills Therapy Manual* from the project MATCH (National Institute of Health, 2003) offers suggestions for a range of constructive coping skills.

Homework

Perhaps more than other groups, CBT therapists reiterate the need to make the addiction group a low-barrier group that welcomes as many as possible. For some group members, simply arriving for the group and committing to another session are more than enough "homework" in a given week. For those who are further along the change continuum, homework usually includes weekly challenges related to practicing coping skills. Again, it is crucial that therapists do not support thinking related to success and failure in homework, but rather to what lessons can be learned from homework that did not work out as planned. The opportunity to learn from lapses is always present, and the Functional Analysis comes in handy as an aid in what one client called the "ongoing personal change project."

Relapse prevention

The traditional CBT approach involves preparing for the future by becoming more aware of high-risk situations. It thus involves continued practice of the learned coping skills. Therapists encourage people who graduate from CBT groups for addiction to connect with local mutual aid groups. In residential settings for substance use and addictions, members of these groups are sometimes invited to make connections with people before they leave the facility. In addition to the 12-step groups (e.g., AA, Narcotics Anonymous, etc.), there are alternative support groups that do not follow the 12-step approach. Self-Management and Recovery Training (SMART), LifeRing, and Women for Sobriety are just some examples of addiction-specific mutual aid groups with chapters throughout the world.

Given that the ultimate test of any addiction program's effectiveness is how well people manage once they leave their treatment and return to their previous life, it is somewhat puzzling that our treatment programs do not focus more on life beyond "the four-walled treatment box," the life that initially "spawned and maintained the person's substance use and misuse." This is an apt phrase Barry Brown used in an expert dialogue on addiction and religion (Borras et al., 2010). Brown warns that failing to support our clients in creating healthier and more meaningful lives in their home communities can make the "chronic relapsing patient" a self-fulfilling prophecy (Borras et al., 2010).

In the following text I present two approaches to relapse prevention. One is the mindfulness-based approach, for which there is quite substantial research evidence. The other is the spiritually oriented approach, for which the research is scant but worth considering given that we are in the early days of gathering evidence for spiritually oriented CBT.

Mindfulness-based relapse prevention

Mindfulness for addiction relapse prevention targets craving. Research studies over the past 5 years conclude—based on carefully designed experiments—that mindfulness training after active CBT treatment for substance use substantially lowers people's cravings and therefore their vulnerability to relapse, at least 4 months after ending treatment (Bowen et al., 2009; Witkiewitz, Bown, Douglas, & Hsu, 2013). The ultimate, longer-term effectiveness of mindfulness for substance abuse and addiction has yet to be determined (Appel & Kim-Appel, 2009). Similar to mindfulness-based relapse prevention (MBRP) for depression reviewed in Chapter 5, this approach for addictions focuses on helping clients (a) sustain attention on the immediate experience of craving and (b) adopt an open, curious, accepting attitude toward that experience. Clients are encouraged to "stay with" the experience of craving without attempting to alter it by either giving into it or suppressing it.

A complete manual on a group approach to integrating mindfulness into a relapse prevention model is now available (Bowen, Chawla, & Marlatt, 2011). This group approach consists of eight 2-hour sessions with 6–10 participants. Sessions include guided meditations, experiential exercises, and discussions. Experiential exercises specifically focus on craving and involve increasing exposure to, and intensity of, the craving response (a dialogue in the following text illustrates an example). This can consist of imaginal exposure to substance use triggers, where group members learn how to stay in contact with their internal reactions to the triggers, how to bring forth a competing response (such as approaching the experience with curious awareness), and how to de-escalate the process by refraining from engaging in habitual thoughts and behaviors that intensify the craving. Similar to other forms of exposure therapy, group members learn to tolerate the affective and physical discomfort without reacting in ways that may temporarily relieve distress but perpetuate the longer-term cycle of giving into cravings. Outcomes show that mindfulness components such as acceptance, awareness, and nonjudgmental attitude toward experiences of cravings decreased the cravings. Clients receiving MBRP have significantly lower levels of self-reported cravings compared to those who received more standard relapse prevention skills. This manualized mindfulness approach to relapse prevention has also produced good outcomes for people with binge eating who learn to slow down and savor the full meal experience of flavors, colors, and conversations (Kristeller, Baer, & Quillian-Wolever, 2006).

In addition to group discussions, the group also provides the opportunity for subgroup exercises. Following is a demonstration of how two group members take turns encouraging verbalizations of the experience of craving. The following exchange may take place during an experiential group exercise involving imaginal exposure. In this exercise, group members work in pairs:

MARIA: Daphne, I am here to listen to you describe a high-risk situation for you involving going to your parents' house for dinner where there's always lots of red wine and not a lot of understanding, you said, about your struggles with alcohol.

DAPHNE: For sure. I think my mother is an alcoholic too but she gets very upset when I suggest we skip the wine and have sparkling water instead. She just tells me that we're all adults here who have a right to drink as much or as little as we feel like.

MARIA: It must be tough for you. OK, how about you closing your eyes and describing what happens when you sit down at the table with your parents?

DAPHNE: [Eyes closed, relaxed pose in her chair] I am at the table and placing food on my plate. My father reaches toward me with the bottle of wine. I want to say "no thanks" but I can already taste the delicious first sip of wine and that fantastic buzz it gives me. It's sometimes uncomfortable to be with my parents and it's easier if I join them in their love of red wine. Then they seem to like me better. I am thinking of all this as my father begins to pour. I then hear myself say: "No thanks Dad. I am not drinking wine these days but please go ahead and enjoy yours." I look firmly into his eyes and know I speak directly, clearly, and assertively. He pulls back, makes a bit of a face, but does not say anything. I immediately feel proud and am thinking of how all of you in my group will be pleased to hear about my success.

MARIA: Daphne, I am so proud of you. You have come so far since you first talked about being afraid of standing up to your father. Believe me I too know how hard it is to be seen as the "party-pooper." Amazing how hard it is for some people to understand that one glass is too much.

The success of a mindfulness-based approach to relapse prevention has led some to wonder if part of the attraction and effectiveness may be a spiritual component. Mindfulness is influenced by Buddhist religion, even though the Western version presented in psychology treatment centers tries to rid mindfulness of any religious connotations. This begs the question of whether it is the more spiritual component or the more experiential component that drives the positive response to MBRP for addiction.

Spirituality is commonly understood and defined as a person's private and existential relationship with God or the Transcendent (Gallup & Jones, 2000)—with an acceptance of specific spiritual beliefs related to meaning and purpose in one's life, beliefs that can, but do not need to, include a mindful approach to life experiences. In this sense, spirituality can be understood as an adoption of a set of philosophical beliefs, whereas mindfulness may be a way of approaching experiences. Either perspective could theoretically include the other, but does not necessarily do so (Leigh, Bowen, & Marlatt, 2005).

Interestingly, Leigh and colleagues found that people who scored high on mindfulness (Freiburg Mindfulness Inventory, FMI) also had higher self-reported substance use. In contrast, people who scored high on spirituality (Spiritual Transcendence Index, STI) had lower substance use reports. The researchers speculate that some people who are drawn to pleasurable physical and emotional experiences may also be attracted to mindfulness training because of its emphasis on paying attention to one's body sensations (Leigh et al., 2005). Can heightened sensitivity to bodily experiences be a risk factor for misuse of substances? More research is needed to answer this question, including well-researched and meaningful measures of spirituality and religion. But the finding that high spirituality scores were associated with less substance use supports other research and is not a new idea.

The literature shows that the higher people score themselves on measures of religion and spirituality, the less likely they are to be controlled by their addictions (Longshore, Anglin, & Conner, 2008). Perhaps those with high spirituality scores have a higher internal sense of self-control. This is of course what has informed groups such as 12-step. And it is an unusual clinician who does not support his or her clients in turning to a higher power if this offers them support during challenging times, when the pull to give in to their addiction is overwhelming. The question is why we clinicians have relegated any mention of spirituality and the sacred to peer groups when surveys consistently show that clients—over 80%—want more emphasis on spirituality in their secular CBT and other forms of addiction treatment (Hodge, 2011). Research, including randomized controlled trials, also suggests that spiritually based treatments are effective for a number of mental health issues for clients who welcome this approach (Rosmarin, Pargament, Pirutinsky, & Mahoney, 2010; Rosmarin, Pargament, & Robb, 2010; Tan & Johnson, 2005).

Spiritually oriented relapse prevention

In a keynote address at a conference I attended in Seattle in 2009, Alan Marlatt, the substance abuse relapse prevention pioneer, offered a phrase that resonated with many clinicians treating addictions. Dr. Marlatt credited Carl Jung when he referred to many people with addictions as *frustrated mystics*. Addiction therapists and recovered people alike often point to the role of religion or spirituality in both onset and recovery from addiction. Unfortunately, academic psychology, which leads research on treatment outcome studies, including for addiction, has up until very recently not seen itself as competent to actually address spiritual issues in addiction. In the aforementioned discussion, we touched on these empirical questions: Do people turn to addictions because of a lack of meaning and purpose in life? How can clinicians in secular settings integrate issues of meaning and purpose into their relapse prevention programs? How do we ourselves understand the difference between religion and spirituality and become competent to "work with" both?

Spirituality was defined earlier as a person's existential relationship with what feels transcendent and sacred in their lives. Religion is often viewed as expressions of spirituality following particular and standard forms, beliefs, and ritualized practices that have been developed in a community with others who share similar experiences. Simply put, spirituality has more to do with the personal and private and religion with the communal and institutional (Hodge, 2011; Todd, 2009).

CBT has for some time been recognized as a therapy approach that lends itself well to a spiritual augmentation. CBT concepts such as beliefs, schemas, and expectations can be mapped in regard to a particular faith. Spiritually modified CBT is being developed for various mental health issues as they relate to a number of religions, including Christianity, Islam, Buddhism, and Taoism—with results similar to or superior to traditional CBT (Hodge, 2011). We also have a highly promising CBGT approach, likely the first of its kind, in the *Spirituality & CBT* group at Boston's McLean Hospital inpatient psychiatry unit (Rosmarin, Auerbach, Bigda-Peyton, Björgvinsson, & Levendusky, 2011). This 50-minute, open group follows a specific protocol, which includes looking at how spiritual references can increase the effectiveness of cognitive and behavioral exercises. It also provides instructions for practicing and monitoring spiritual exercises, such as gratitude, remembering miracles, and setting aside time for silence and deeper conversations. The group presumes a basic familiarity with CBT. Clients must first participate in a prerequisite CBT group before being invited to the Spirituality & CBT group. The developers of this group use generic, nonreligious terminology, but encourage discussions about particular faith traditions as desired by the group members. Based on client satisfaction ratings, the group is extremely well received by its members from a range of religious backgrounds, including nonreligious.

Spiritual self-schema therapy, or 3-S therapy, is perhaps the best attempt to integrate CBGT with a spiritual approach specifically for relapse prevention in addictions (Avants, Beitel, & Margolin, 2005). Similar to the Spirituality & CBT group, spiritual self-schema therapy is suitable for people of all faiths and is based on CBT principles. In contrast to the Spirituality & CBT group, however, it chooses a specific religion, Buddhism, as a framework. Group and individual manuals exist for this 8-session program and are available from the Spiritual Self-Schema Development Program website: http://info.med.yale.edu/psych/3s/training.html.[5] This therapy is based on assumptions central to Beck's cognitive therapy (as reviewed in Chapter 5) that people's beliefs, or schemas, about themselves will influence how they process and filter information. For example, if someone has a schema of "I'm a hopeless addict," they are less likely to pay attention to instructions about how to engage in safer needle use, sex, or alcohol intake. Each of the eight sessions includes a specific focus aimed at moving the schema of "addict self" to one of "spiritual self." Naturalistic studies conducted by the developers of this program using a number of outcomes, including urine samples, suggest 3-S therapy is helpful in reducing substance use, lowering impulsive behaviors, and increasing spiritual practice (Avants et al., 2005), but more sophisticated outcome studies are needed (Johnson, 2013).

Based on the preceding text, there is room for improving efforts in strengthening relapse prevention for addictions. We can conclude that mindfulness-based approaches are promising, especially for those who have improved to the point of being able to tolerate exposure to addiction cues. However, the experiential aspect of mindfulness may be problematic for some people whose heightened sensitivity to bodily experiences may be a risk factor for relapse into substance abuse. Addiction clinicians also caution that mindfulness concepts can be quite abstract and difficult to grasp, especially for clients who have co-occurring cognitive impairment from a brain injury. For those clients, addiction therapists suggest that they engage in wholesome distractions as a way of coping with cravings. Physical exercise is often recommended and so is having conversations with a supportive person. The Leisure Skills Inventory in Appendix H is, again, a helpful tool to broaden a person's options for meaningful activities. Finally, we can also conclude that most clients are hungry for support with strengthening a personal life philosophy, whether this involves a particular religious orientation or a more private spiritual one (including a secular humanist worldview).

Addiction clinicians may enjoy contemplating what a spiritual, purpose-oriented relapse prevention group could include. They may become inspired by the 8-week group model used in mindfulness-based relapse prevention, or the spiritual self-schema-based relapse prevention, or the McLean Hospital Spirituality & CBT group. Why not consider extending relapse prevention to include an additional focus on a larger meaning and purpose framework? In CBGT for relapse prevention, the following questions can provide springboards for rich discussions: "Where do you find peace?" "For what are you deeply grateful?" "What are you striving for in life?" and "When have you felt most deeply and fully alive?" (Pargament, 2007). Through structured group discussions, as exemplified in the Spirituality & CBT group, CBGT therapists can help group members create a personal life philosophy with a sense of purpose that helps them organize their daily living, goals, and priorities. For groups run in public settings, there will be a wide range of interest, or lack of interest, among members in religious and spiritual matters, which must be respected. However, the preliminary good outcomes from the McLean Hospital group suggest that the public system can meet our clients' needs for wrestling with larger meaning-of-life issues and that a CBT framework is especially well suited for this. Therapists must naturally be realistic about how much can be accomplished in any short-term relapse prevention program. The best results will likely be for those clients who have already had an interest in thinking about their life values and purpose but lost sight of that when their addiction took over.

Capitalizing on the Group for Addictions

Perhaps more than any other mental health issue, the problem of addiction has a strong group therapy tradition, mostly stemming from the mutual aid approach of AA. Some people even wonder if the success of AA especially has to do with the group format and the openness to discussing spiritual matters. Still, dropout rates are high in AA (40–80%) and secular CBT addictions groups alike (40–70%; Malat et al., 2008; Tonigan, Toscova, & Miller, 1996). Group therapists running CBGT for addiction thus feel the challenge of creating a safe, welcoming, and helpful yet effective group treatment experience.

Critical group process factors revolve around members feeling understood and met with empathy. In the addiction group more than any other, people are often moved to tears as they speak about feeling accepted, understood, and validated. Many have been rejected by their home communities or family members. Although the client often understands and accepts this rejection, their need to belong is strong, and the group can become a healthy temporary surrogate family or community. The therapists must convey empathy and can do so by making references to how we all engage in some things too much, and that addictions, along with other human problems, exist on a continuum. Sometimes clinicians are challenged by group members who buy into a belief that *one must have an addiction in order to effectively treat one.* This is a false belief. When therapists come across as genuinely empathic and competent in their interventions, this kind of challenging usually abates.

Interactions among group members are important, both the positive and negative. The therapists ensure that any conflicts between members are worked through and provide a practice environment for also using improved interpersonal skills outside of the group. Many people with addictions experience simply belonging to a CBT group with all its inherent social support as a powerful feeling of *being in community.* If more meaning or spiritually oriented components are introduced, the group may further unite in positive emotions of gratitude and joy, which are all powerfully reinforcing in successful reintegration with home communities.

Common Challenges in CBGT for Addictions

Addiction clinicians agree that the specific CBT part may be the least complicated aspect of running CBGT for addiction. Other client-specific issues such as motivation, readiness, and attendance are the main challenges. With dropout rates being high, I support running open groups as much as possible, as demonstrated in the *Group Cognitive Therapy for Addictions* (Wenzel et al., 2012). Not only does this prevent long wait lists, but most importantly, it prevents a situation of a 10-member group diminishing to one of three and thus "wasting" empty seats. The Wenzel guide is particularly helpful with its flexible approach to group members' readiness and ability to commit to the group, and I hope we will see a wide implementation of this particular CBGT for addiction.

Any CBT approach to addiction works best if clients have intact levels of cognitive functioning and some ability at abstract reasoning (Maude-Griffin et al., 1998). Various levels of brain damage as a result of substance abuse are a common presentation. Therapists work with this by reducing the complexity of the cognitive exercises and by using many graphic illustrations—and fewer words—to make key points. Ideas to simplify CBT interventions were outlined in Chapters 11 and 12 and may be helpful for adults with brain damage.

In addition to dealing with varying levels of cognitive ability, it is a huge challenge for therapists running addiction groups to respond to different levels of readiness to change. This gets further complicated when readiness to change varies for different substances. For example, a group member may be ready to quit using heroin but remain adamant that cannabis is not an issue. Lastly, therapists struggle with how much exposure to addiction cues is tolerable. For groups to be successful, the lowest level of tolerance will likely need to determine the pace—unless it is possible to run parallel groups with lower and higher levels of readiness to change.

Summary

This chapter reviews a substantial body of research supporting various innovative CBGT models both for when an addiction co-occurs with another mental health problem and when it is the main focus of treatment. The delivery of specific CBT techniques is often the least problematic task. The challenges lie in working with groups where members are at different levels of readiness to make changes, subscribe to different beliefs about abstinence versus controlled drinking, and are at high risk for relapse due to factors in their environment outside of the group room. The excellent new manual *Group Cognitive Therapy for Addictions* (Wenzel et al., 2012) helps clinicians with all of these issues for a range of addictions not limited to substance use disorders.

Although considered important to many people struggling with addictions, issues of religion and spirituality have up until recently been relatively neglected in academic addiction research, and therefore, clinicians have been deprived of evidence for best practice guidelines. The CBGT format lends itself well to augmentations, including a focus on issues related to life purpose, meaning, and individual experiences of the sacred. Similar to the success of MBRP training for addiction, I suspect several CBGT addiction therapists await opportunities for training in how to better integrate spiritual approaches into traditional CBT relapse prevention. This chapter encourages group therapists to experiment with creating flexible approaches to both the active CBGT treatment phase of addictions as well as to the relapse prevention.

Notes

1. There is controversy among addiction experts about whether some addictions such as those involving, for example, eating or pornography are true addictions or not better understood as an eating disorder or impulse control disorder, respectively. However, a prominent group therapy approach, the CGT for addictions, which will be described later, is successful for a wide range of addictions.
2. Whereas the previous diagnostic system, the DSM-IV (APA, 2000), distinguished between *substance abuse* and *substance dependence*, the new DSM-5 collapsed this distinction, placing substance use on a continuum where the level of use is rated as mild, moderate, or severe depending on the number of symptoms met, including the symptoms of *tolerance* and/or *withdrawal.*

3. Clinical impressions suggest that one of the problems with Antabuse is that people who want to drink will stop taking it. To be effective, people need to take it regularly. This is one of the reasons for the lack of more widespread use of Antabuse.
4. Chapter 13 discussed how to support people with OCD who wish to engage in something more constructive and wholesome than their senseless rituals.
5. In their article, Avants and colleagues (2005) encourage readers to go to this website.

Recommended Readings for Clinicians

Inciardi, J. A., & Harrisons, L. (2000). *Harm reduction: National & international perspectives*. Thousand Oaks, CA: Sage Publications.

Johnson, T. J. (2013). Addiction and the search for the sacred: Religion, spirituality, and the origins and treatment of substance use disorders. In K. I. Pargament (Ed.), *APA handbook of psychology, Religion, and Spirituality: Vol. 2. An applied Psychology of religion and spirituality*. Washington, DC: American Psychological Association.

Monti, P. M., Kadden, R., Rohsenow, D. J., Cooney, N., & Abrams, D. (2002). *Treating alcohol dependence: A coping skills training guide* (2nd ed.). New York: Guilford Press.

Najavits, L. M., Schmitz, M., Johnson, K. M., Smith, C., North, T., Hamilton, N., et al. (2009). *Seeking safety* therapy for men: Clinical & Research Experiences. In L. Katlin (Ed.), *Men and addictions: New research* (pp.37–58). Hauppage, NY: Nova Science Publishers.

Sobell, L. C., & Sobell, M. B. (2011). *Group therapy for substance use disorders: A motivational cognitive-behavioural approach*. New York: Guilford Press.

Wenzel, A., Liese, B. S., Beck, A. T., & Friedman-Wheeler, D. G. (2012). *Group cognitive therapy for addictions*. New York: Guilford Press.

References

American Psychiatric Association (APA). (2000). *Diagnostic and statistical manual of mental disorders, DSM* (4th ed.). Washington, DC: Author.

APA. (2013). *Diagnostic and statistical manual of mental disorders, DSM* (5th ed.). Washington, DC: Author.

Appel, J., & Kim-Appel, D. (2009). Mindfulness: Implications for substance abuse and addiction. *International Journal of Mental health and Addictions, 7*, 506–512.

Avants, S. K., Beitel, M., & Margolin, A. (2005). Making the shift from 'addict self' to 'spiritual self': results from a stage I study of Spiritual Self-Schema (3-S) therapy for the treatment of addiction and HIV risk behavior. *Mental Health, Religion & Culture, 8(3)*, 167–177.

Beck, A. T., Steer, R. A., & Brown, G. K. (1996). *Manual for the beck depression inventory–II*. San Antonio, TX: Psychological Corporation.

Beck, A. T., Wright, F. D., Newman, C. F., & Liese, B. S. (1993). Cognitive therapy of substance abuse. New York: Guilford Press.

Bien, T., & Bien, B. (2002). *Mindful recovery: A spiritual path to healing from addiction*. New York: John Wiley & Sons.

Borras, L., Khazaal, Y., Khan, R., Mohr, S., Kaufmann, Y.-A., Zullino, D., et al. (2010). The relationship between addiction and religion and its possible implication for care. *Substance Use & Misuse, 45*, 2357–2410.

Bowen, S., Chawla, N., Collins, S. E., Witkiewitz, K., Hsu, S., Grow, J., et al. (2009). Mindfulness-based relapse prevention for substance use disorders: a pilot efficacy trial. *Substance Abuse, 30*, 295–305.

Bowen, S., Chawla, N., & Marlatt, G. A. (2011). *Mindfulness-based relapse prevention for addictive behaviours: A clinician's guide*. New York: Guilford Press.

Brownell, K. D., Marlatt, G. A., Lichtenstein, E., & Wilson, G. T. (1986). Understanding and preventing relapse. *American Psychologist, 41*, 765–782.

Courbasson, C. M., & Nishikawa, Y. (2010). Cognitive behavioral group therapy for patients with co-existing social anxiety disorder and substance use disorders: A pilot study. *Cognitive Therapy and Research, 34*, 82–91.

Diamond, G., Godley, S. H., Liddle, H. A., Sampl, S., Webb, C., Tims, F. M., et al. (2002). Five outpatient treatment models for adolescent marijuana use: A description of the Cannabis Youth Treatment Interventions. *Addiction, 97(1)*, 70–83.

Gallup, G. J., & Jones, T. (2000). *The next American spirituality: Finding God in the twenty-first century*. Colorado Springs, CO: Victor.

Heimberg, R. G., & Becker, R. E. (2002). *Cognitive-behavioural group therapy for social phobia: Basic mechanisms and clinical strategies*. New York: Guilford Press.

Hien, D. A., Wells, E. A., Jian, H., Suarez-Morales, L., Campbell, A. N. C., Cohen, L. R., et al. (2009). Multisite randomized trial of behavioral interventions for women with co-occurring PTSD and substance use disorders. *Journal of Consulting and Clinical Psychology, 77*, 607–619.

Hodge, D. (2011). Alcohol treatment and cognitive-behavioral therapy: Enhancing effectiveness by incorporating spirituality and religion. *Social Work, 56(1)*, 21–31.

Kristeller, J. L., Baer, R. A., & Quillian-Wolever, R. (2006). Mindfulness based approaches to eating disorders. In R. A. Baer (Ed.), *Mindfulness-based treatment approaches: Clinician's guide to evidence base and applications* (pp. 75–91). San Diego, CA: Elsevier.

Leigh, J., Bowen, S., & Marlatt, A. (2005). Spirituality, mindfulness and substance abuse. *Addictive Behaviors, 30*, 1335–1341.

Liese, B. S., & Franz, R. A. (1996). Treating substance use disorder with cognitive therapy: Lessons learned and implications for the future. In P. Salkovskis (Ed.), *Frontiers of cognitive therapy* (pp. 470–508). New York: Guilford Press.

Longshore, D., Anglin, M. D., & Conner, B. T. (2008). Are religiosity and spirituality useful constructs in drug treatment research? *Journal of Behavioral Health Services & Research, 36(2)*, 177–188.

Magill, M., & Ray, L. A. (2009). Cognitive-behavioral treatment with adult alcohol and illicit drug users: A meta-analysis of randomized controlled trials. *Journal of Studies on Alcohol and Drugs, 70*, 516–527.

Malat, J., Leszcz, M., Negrete, J., Collins, J., Liu, E., & Toneatto, T. (2008). Interpersonal group psychotherapy for comorbid alcohol dependence and non-psychotic psychiatric disorders. *American Journal on Addictions, 17*, 402–407.

Maude-Griffin, P. M., Hohenstein, J. M., Humfleet, G. L., Reilly, P. M., Tusel, D. J., & Hall, S. M. (1998). Superior efficacy of cognitive-behavioral therapy for urban crack cocaine users: Main and matching effects. *Journal of Consulting and Clinical Psychology, 66*, 832–837.

McHugh, R. K., Hearon, B. A., & Otto, M. W. (2010). Cognitive behavioral therapy for substance use disorders. *Psychiatric Clinics of North America, 33*, 511–525.

Miller, W. R., & Rollnick, S. J. (2002). *Motivational interviewing: Preparing people for change*. New York: Guilford Press.

Muñoz, R., Ippen, C., Rao, S., Le, H., & Dwyer, E. (2000). *Manual for Group Cognitive-behavioral therapy of major depression: A reality management approach.* San Francisco, CA: San Francisco General Hospital, University of California.

Najavits, L. M. (2002). *Seeking safety: A treatment manual for PTSD and substance abuse.* New York: Guilford Press.

National Institute of Health. (2003). *Cognitive-behavioural coping skills therapy manual: A clinical research guide for therapists treating individuals with alcohol abuse and dependence* (Project Match Monograph Series, Vol. 3. Publication No. 94-3774). Washington, DC: Author.

Nyamathi, A., Nandy, K., Greengold, B., Khalilifard, F., Cohen, A., & Leake, B. (2011). Effectiveness of intervention on improvement of drug use among methadone maintained adults. *Journal of Addictive Diseases, 30,* 6–16.

O'Brien, C., Childress, R., McLellan, A. T., & Ehrman, R. (1992). Classical conditioning in drug-dependent humans. *Annals of the New York Academy of Sciences, 654,* 400–415.

Pargament, K. I. (2007). *Spiritually integrated psychotherapy: Understanding and addressing the sacred.* New York: Guilford Press.

Prochaska, J. O., & DiClemente, C. C. (1984). *The transtheoretical approach: Crossing the traditional boundaries of therapy.* Malabar, FL: Krieger.

Rosmarin, D. H., Pargament, K. I., Pirutinsky, S., & Mahoney, A. (2010). A randomized controlled evaluation of a spiritually integrated treatment for subclinical anxiety in the Jewish community, delivered via the internet. *Journal of Anxiety Disorders, 24(7),* 799–808.

Rosmarin, D. H., Pargament, K. I., & Robb, H. B. (2010). Introduction to special series: Spiritual and religious issues in behavior change. *Cognitive and Behavioral Practice, 17(4),* 343–347.

Rosmarin, D. H., Auerbach, R. P., Bigda-Peyton, J. S., Björgvinsson, T., & Levendusky, P. G. (2011). Integrating spirituality into cognitive behavioral therapy in an acute psychiatric setting: A pilot study. *Journal of Cognitive Psychotherapy: An International Quarterly, 25(4),* 287–303.

Silverman, K., Wong, C. J., Umbricht-Schneiter, A., Montoya, I. D., Schuster, C. R., & Preston, K. L. (1998). Broad beneficial effects of cocaine abstinence reinforcement among methadone patients. *Journal of Consulting and Clinical Psychology, 66(5),* 811–824.

Sobell, L. C., Sobell, M. B., & Agrawal, S. (2009). Randomized controlled trial of a cognitive-behavioural motivational intervention in a group versus individual format for substance use disorders. *Psychology of Addictive Behaviors, 23,* 672–683.

Swendsen, J., Conway, K. P., Degenhardt, L., Glantz, M., Jin, R., Merikangas, K. R., et al. (2010). Mental disorders as risk factors for substance use, abuse and dependence: Results from the 10-year follow-up of the National Comorbidity Survey, *Addiction, 105,* 1117–1128.

Tan, S.-Y., & Johnson, W. B. (2005). Spiritually oriented cognitive-behavioral therapy. In L. Sperry & E. P. Shafranske (Eds.), *Spiritually oriented psychotherapy* (pp. 77–103). Washington, DC: American Psychological Association.

Todd, D. (2009, September 5). Ending the war between "religion" and "spirituality"; at their best, both are a means to reaching the same goal. *The Vancouver Sun*, p. C5.

Tonigan, J. S., Toscova, W. R., & Miller, W. R. (1996). Meta-analysis of the literature on Alcoholics Anonymous: Sample and study characteristic moderate findings. *Journal of Studies on Alcohol, 57,* 65–72.

Waldron, H. B., & Turner, C. W. (2008). Evidence-based psychosocial treatments for adolescent substance abuse. *Journal of Clinical Child & Adolescent Psychology, 37(1),* 238–261.

Watkins, K., Hunter, S. B, Hepner, K. A., Paddock. S. M., de la Cruz, E., Zhou, A. J., et al. (2011). An effectiveness trial of group cognitive behavioral therapy for patients with persistent depressive symptoms in substance abuse treatment. *Archives of General Psychiatry, 68(6),* 577–584.

Witkiewitz, K., Bowen, S., Douglas, H., & Hsu, S. H. (2013). Mindfulness-based relapse prevention for substance craving. *Addictive Behaviors, 38,* 1563–1571.

World Health Organization. (2010). *Global strategy to reduce the harmful use of alcohol.* Geneva, Switzerland: Author. www.who.int/substance_abuse/msbalcstrategy.pdf [accessed on February 26, 2014].

Young, R. M., Oei, T. P. S., & Crook, G. M. (1991). Development of a drinking self-efficacy questionnaire. *Journal of Psychopathology and Behavioral Assessment, 13,* 1–15.

Appendix A

CBGT depression protocol outline

Session	*Topic*	*Handouts*
1	Education about depression	
2	The cognitive model of depression	Appendix B
3	Self-monitoring of mastery and pleasure	
4	Goal setting	Appendix C
5	Goal setting and identification of moods	Appendix D
6	Identifying negative automatic thoughts	
7	Alternative and balanced thinking: Thought Records	Appendix E
8	Alternative and balanced thinking: Thought Records	Appendix E
9	Alternative and balanced thinking: Thought Records and assumptions	Appendices E and F
10	Alternative and balanced thinking: Thought Records and core beliefs	Appendices E and F
11	Relapse prevention and preparing for the future	Appendix G
12	Relapse prevention and preparing for the future	

Appendix B

Cognitive Model of Depression

EARLY EXPERIENCES

Unfavorable comparison with twin sister
Father (and main supporter) dies

FORMATION OF DYSFUNCTIONAL ASSUMPTIONS

I am inferior as a person
My worth depends on what other people think of me
Unless I do what other people want, they will reject me

CRITICAL INCIDENT(S)

Marriage breaks down

ASSUMPTIONS ACTIVATED

NEGATIVE AUTOMATIC THOUGHTS

It's all my fault—I've made a mess of everything
I can't handle my life
I'll be alone forever—it's going to be dreadful

SYMPTOMS OF DEPRESSION

Behavioral—low activity level, staying mostly home
Motivational—loss of interest and pleasure, everything is a huge effort
Emotional—sadness, guilt, anxiety, shame
Cognitive—indecisiveness, poor concentration, rumination about past perceived mistakes, self-criticism
Body function—loss of sleep, or sleeping too much, loss of appetite, loss of sexual interest

Cognitive Behavioral Group Therapy: Challenges and Opportunities, First Edition. Ingrid Söchting.

My Cognitive Model of Depression

EARLY EXPERIENCES

FORMATION OF DYSFUNCTIONAL ASSUMPTIONS

CRITICAL INCIDENT(S)

ASSUMPTIONS ACTIVATED

NEGATIVE AUTOMATIC THOUGHTS

SYMPTOMS OF DEPRESSION

Behavioral:

Motivational:

Emotional:

Cognitive:

Body function:

Appendix C

Name ______________________________ Date__________

Ten Things I Like to Do (Or Used to Like to Do)

Activity	*Can do it alone*	*Need to be accompanied by one or more people*	*Barriers including financial*
1.			
2.			
3.			
4.			
5.			
6.			
7.			
8.			
9.			
10.			

Appendix D

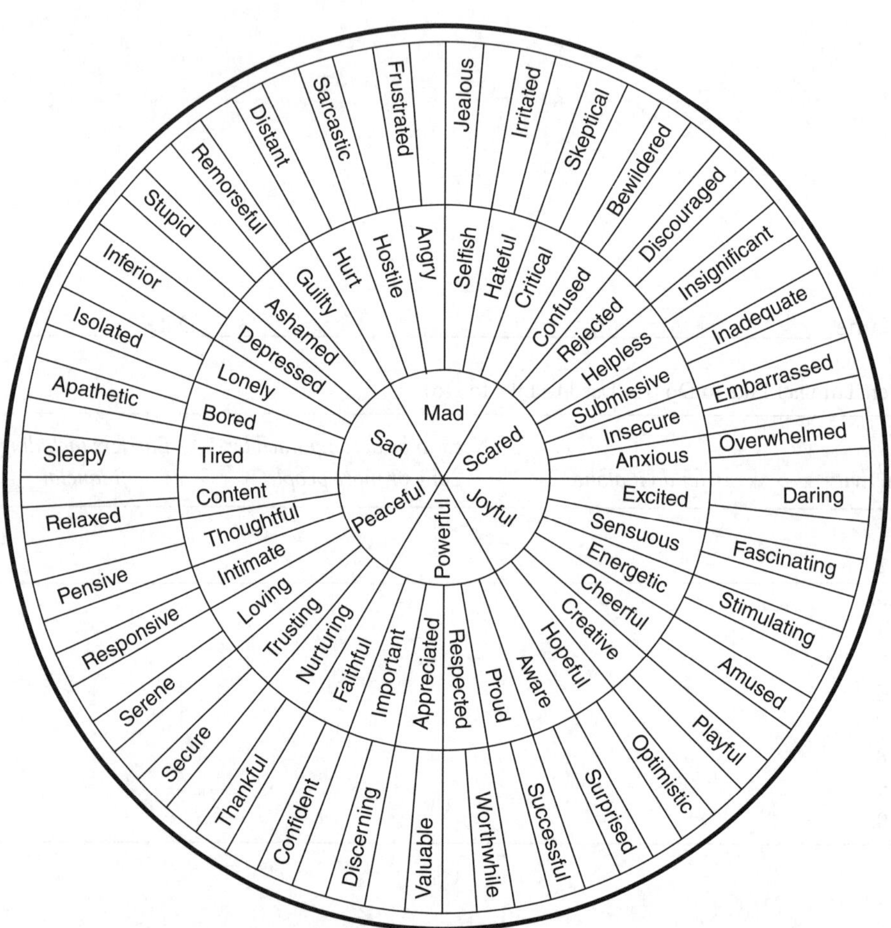

The Feeling Wheel. Developed by Dr. Gloria Willcox

Cognitive Behavioral Group Therapy: Challenges and Opportunities, First Edition. Ingrid Söchting.

Appendix E
Juanita's Thought Record

Juanita's completed thought record

Situation	*Moods*	*Automatic thoughts (images)*	*Evidence that supports the hot thought*	*Evidence that does not support the hot thought*	*Alternative/balanced thoughts*	*Rate moods now*
At home by myself Saturday night talking to my mother on the telephone	Scared—90%	I'm a selfish person	Yes, I have faltered on my debt payment plan for a second time	I'm in therapy and working on my issues	I, Juanita, am aware I have a problem with spending more than I and my husband can afford at this time	Scared—40%
	Angry—70%	I'm behaving like a child	I'm also keeping this debt a secret from my husband	I listen and am open to advice	I'm taking full responsibility and am working with a financial advisor and my therapy group	Angry—30%
	Helpless—90%	**I'm a financial failure**	It's about not living within my means at this present time	I'm certainly far from bankruptcy		Helpless—20%
		I can't stand up to my mother		I have a history of managing my money well		
		I don't trust myself		The reality of less income makes it harder but does not mean failure		
		What if I go broke? *Answer some of the following questions:*				

		What was going through my mind just before I started to feel this way? *What does this say about me?* *What does this mean about me? My life? My future?* *What am I afraid might happen?* *What is the worst thing that could happen if this is true?*				
Who were you with?		*What does this mean about how the other person(s) feel(s) think(s) about me?*	*Circle hot thought in previous column for which you are looking for evidence*			
What were you doing?		*What does this mean about the other person(s) or people in general?*	*Write factual evidence to support this conclusion*		*Write an alternative or balanced thought*	*Copy the feelings from Column 2*
When was it? Where were you?	*Describe each mood in one word. Rate intensity of mood (0–100%)*	*What images or memories do I have in this situation?*	*(Try to avoid mind reading and interpretation of facts)*		*Rate how much you believe in each alternative or balanced thought (0–100%)*	*Rerate the intensity of each feeling from 0% to 100% as well as any new records*

Padesky and Greenberger, 1995. Reproduced with permission of Guilford Publications, Inc.

Reference

Padesky, C. A., & Greenberger, D. (1995). *Clinician's guide to mind over mood.* New York: Guilford Press.

Appendix F

Biases in Thinking or Faulty Assumptions

Faulty assumptions aren't the only problems in thinking. It is possible to start out with accurate assumptions and still reach wrong conclusions if your thinking is biased in some way. The following list describes each of these biases in turn. Place a check mark by those that seem to affect you. After each description there is a reminder that you could repeat to yourself when you find that bias influencing your thinking.

All-or-nothing thinking

With all-or-nothing thinking you see things as being either black or white, never as shades of gray. You are either fat or thin, on the diet or off the diet, smart enough or completely stupid, depressed or happy, competent or incompetent, and so on. The same can apply to others. A relationship can be either perfect or horrible, and someone can be considerate or completely self-centered. All-or-nothing thinking relates to perfectionism, because the "good" category is usually defined absolutely. You have to conform to the letter of the diet, otherwise you are in the other category: off the diet (and since you are off the diet you might as well eat everything in the fridge). A partner has to be perfect in every way; otherwise he or she slides into the "monster" category.

Cognitive Behavioral Group Therapy: Challenges and Opportunities, First Edition. Ingrid Söchting.

Overgeneralization

You see a single negative event as a never-ending pattern. Like most people you look for patterns in events, but your patterns tend to be negative and you think you see them before you really have enough evidence. One rainy day means you won't see the sun for the rest of your vacation. One criticism from your new partner is the start of a series. One fall and you think you will *never* learn to ride a horse. One missed question and you are bound to fail your course. Overgeneralization causes people to have restricted lives because of beliefs about what they can't do, don't like, or have to avoid.

Filtering

Every moment of every day, we screen out most of the sights and sounds around us. We have to do this. There is too much information at any one time to understand all at once. The problem comes when you screen out all of the positive and neutral information and only pay attention to the negative things in your life. As a result, your life seems unrelentingly bleak and depressing. It can be tempting to wait until the problems in your life are solved, assuming that you will then feel better. But everyone's life has negative aspects, so you will always be able to find and pay attention to the negative.

Underfocusing

Underfocusing means that you think of too many problems at once. Perhaps you think of a demand that is being made on you, or a project you want to complete, or a dispute that you want to solve. Then that reminds you of another problem or demand, then another, and then another until you feel completely overwhelmed. "I have to clean out the garage, but I also wanted to call about my insurance, and the house is a mess, and the kids are coming home for lunch, and I don't have any food, and I just started the laundry, and I have to get that report done for work …" Sound familiar? This is a big problem for many people with depression or anxiety. Human beings are only able to think *clear* about one thing at a time. The goal is to become able to set aside the main stack of demands and focus on the one thing that you are working on. You may find it helpful to write a list of your problems and projects so that you don't have to keep them all in your head.

Disqualifying the positive

You reject all of the positives in your life by insisting that they "don't count" for some reason or other. In this way, you can hold onto a negative belief about things no matter how many positives there may be. The supportive friend you have doesn't count because she's the only one. The accomplishment you made doesn't count because it came about by pure luck. The step you took the other day doesn't count because "anybody can do that." How can you overcome this tendency? Recognize that the positive things in your life are at least as important and meaningful as the negative things.

Mind reading

You don't have to ask what someone else is feeling or thinking, or why they did something. You know it by mind reading. "He's just in it for the money." "She just said that because she feels sorry for me." "He secretly wants out of this relationship." "She thinks I'm stupid." "He's a bigot—I can tell by the way he looked at me." Mind reading tends to focus on negative possibilities. While the interpretations you make are usually *possible*, other possibilities are often missed. Maybe he's in that business because he enjoys it. Maybe she said that because she respects you. Maybe he looked at you that way because you took the parking space he wanted. Mind reading usually leads you to feel too certain about the negative guesses you make. Try to remind yourself that you don't really know what other people are thinking until they tell you.

The fortune-teller error

In addition to mind reading, you can also tell the future, and the future looks grim. You anticipate that things will always turn out badly and you feel convinced that your predictions are accurate. You've signed up for a course, but you are sure to fail it. You have met someone new, but he or she will dump you soon. One of the problems with fortune telling is that you can make the future you predict come true. If you are going to fail, why study? If your partner will dump you, why put a lot of effort into the relationship? The resulting outcome confirms your belief that you can tell the future, and as a result you make even more negative predictions the next time. Instead, remind yourself that you can't tell the future. Try to deal with events in the present.

Magnification and minimization

You exaggerate your own foul-ups and other people's achievements ("She has her degree—a genius!—and I took the wrong bus the other day—want an idiot I am"). At the same time, you minimize your own achievements and other people's foul-ups ("I landed a good job, but I don't know everything I should about it; she lost her job, but it was probably politics"). This way you almost always come out looking inferior. The problem is that you use completely different standards for yourself than for anyone else—standards that make it difficult for you to feel good about yourself.

If you were to have the same standards for yourself that you have for others you might find it easier to look good in your own eyes.

Catastrophizing

You take a relatively small event (a quarrel, a bad haircut, missing your dental appointment) and imagine extreme and horrible consequences that could happen as a result. A turndown for a date means you will spend your entire life alone. Making a mistake at work means that you will be fired for incompetence and never get another job. Having a brief dip in your mood means that you are on the road to the worst depression yet. Once the problem has been blown up into something huge, you experience an emotional impact as though the entire thing had *really happened* (as though you really had lost your job, for example). Because you focus on the imaginary catastrophe, you are unable to cope with the real event ("Oh, I forgot that meeting. Maybe I should get a datebook …")

Emotional reasoning

You assume that your negative emotions reflect things the way they really are. "I feel it, so it must be true." "I'm afraid of getting more depressed, so I must be on the way to depression." "I feel hopeless, so there must be no hope." But remember: Your emotions depend on what you *think* is going on, not what's *really* going on. If you see the situation the wrong way ("the boss's frown means she hates me"), you will experience the wrong emotion (fear of being fired). Strangely, most people who use emotional reasoning only do it with unpleasant emotions. They never assume that when they feel happy everything must be fine.

Labeling

Labeling means turning a temporary event into a permanent *characteristic*. When you make a mistake, you *could* focus on the error and how to correct it. Instead, with labeling, you quickly attach a negative label to yourself: "I'm a loser." Now you have defined the problem: It's not that you made a mistake, it's that you have an unchangeable personal characteristic that *causes mistakes*. As a result, there is nothing you can do about it and you feel helpless. Labeling, then, is a way to make a problem unsolvable. Oddly, people who do this rarely label themselves when things go well ("I'm a winner"). Labeling can also be used with other people or organizations. When someone's behavior rubs you the wrong way, you attach a negative label to him/her: "He's a pig." If that's true, the person probably can't change and the problem is now unsolvable. To keep the problem solvable, you must focus on what actually happened.

Catching your biases

Most people find that they use more than one of the biases listed in the last few pages. Which one seems to give you the *most* trouble?

___

___

You probably don't use this bias all of the time. Which situations are you *most* likely to distort in this way?

___

___

___

___

___

___

Distortions work best when you're not aware that they are happening. The next time you find yourself in one of the situations you have described above, try to catch the distortion as it happens. Then remind yourself what to do instead (perhaps using the reminder provided). What would be a more reality-based way of thinking in one of the situations you have listed?

___

___

___

___

___

___

Repeat this revised way of thinking over to yourself a number of times. It will probably feel quite artificial at first because you are not used to it. With time it will become more familiar and will begin to feel right.

Paterson, 2002. Reproduced with permission of Randy J. Paterson.

Reference

Paterson, R. J. (2002). *Your depression map: Find the source of your depression and chart your own recovery.* Oakland, CA: New Harbinger Publications, Inc.

Appendix G

Relapse Prevention

People who have suffered a major depressive episode are at risk of further episodes. It is important to use periods of wellness as an opportunity to actively prevent relapse. Depression, like disorder such as diabetes, requires you to "self-monitor," or pay attention to how you are feeling, so you can catch early warnings of a possible relapse and possibly prevent a full depressive episode.

1. *To help prevent a relapse, monitor changes in your mood, develop a list of personal warning signs, and pay attention to activities that have a positive impact on your moods.* When feeling better, pay attention to the variations in your moods. Don't ignore changes, such as sleep disturbances, or negative or hopeless thoughts, that may suggest a potential relapse. Pay attention to activities that help to stabilize or improve how you are feeling, and incorporate these into your everyday activities. For example, if walking your dog or visiting friends is helpful, make sure these are part of your structured routines. If you sense those warning signs coming, you should see your family doctor or, if applicable, your mental health worker right away.
2. *A healthy lifestyle is important: proper nutrition, exercise, and good sleep habits.* It makes sense to pay special attention to these areas if you are struggling with depression. Fatigue is worsened if you eat very little, or eat an unhealthy diet. Research has demonstrated that regular exercise can have a positive effect on mood. If you are struggling with falling asleep, staying asleep, or waking up early in the morning and being unable to get back to sleep, it is important for you to develop good sleep

routines. Repeating these routines each night can help restore better sleep patterns. Try to go to bed at the same time each night. Avoid stimulating activities close to bedtime; plan on paying bills, completing work, or having important discussions earlier in the day or evening. Many people find that relaxation exercises, easy reading, or a warm, noncaffeinated beverage just before retiring are ways to promote a relaxed state of mind. Expect that it will take you some time to fall asleep and try not to anticipate sleep problems, as this will only add to your anxiety. For some people, a sleep medication provides relief and allows them the much-needed rest they have been deprived of due to depression.

3. *You cannot avoid stress, but you may learn to cope better by adopting new strategies.* Many people with depression tend to use only one coping strategy. For example, they hide their worries and avoid dealing with problems. This may work in some cases, but not in others. Where possible, try different strategies. Deal with some problems as they happen. Avoiding them allows stress to build up. Be realistic about your stress-breaking point. Work toward recognizing what aspects of relationships in your life might be unhealthy and, if possible, try to avoid situations that may trigger relapse.
4. *Remember that meaningful relationships and social support are important for your sense of self-worth and happiness.* Spending too much time alone can contribute to depression and relapse, yet the feelings of depression often make people want to isolate themselves. Strong social networks and social support can serve as a buffer against depression. Try to avoid spending too much time alone and work toward both maintaining contact with your social network and expanding it.
5. *Try to develop a well-balanced life with enough time for work, family and friends, and leisure activities.* It might seem easy at first to escape from your depression by focusing entirely on one area, such as work, or a hobby. Eventually, however, this coping strategy may not work, and you will need to develop other aspects of your life. It is important to keep in contact with all the facets of our lives, such as school, work or volunteer activities, family and friends, and hobbies. As you recover, investing energy into several areas will help you develop a more balanced and satisfying lifestyle, which will help you to avoid relapse.
6. *Continue working on your hot thoughts.* Hot thoughts are those very automatic and negative thoughts that pop into your mind as you go through various situations. They are blue-tinted glasses that serve to bring your mood down. Continue practicing looking at the evidence for and against these hot thoughts to arrive at a state of more balanced thinking. It is hard work at first, but with enough practice, it too can become automatic as well.
7. *If your mood drops, don't catastrophize!* It is common for your moods to go up and down over time. Gradually, things may improve, but there can be setbacks along the way. If you notice your mood going slightly down throughout the day, you might worry that these small changes mean that "the problem is coming back," or "it's getting worse." You might picture yourself sinking into a pit of depression. These ideas can be frightening to think about and so your mood actually *does* get worse. Therefore, it is helpful to remember that worrying,

over-interpreting the drop, and resisting the drop all tend to make the problem worse. Instead, try to accept the change in mood as a normal part of the recovery process. Recognize that it is not permanent, and then carry on with the other activities you had planned for the day.

8. *If your mood drops, some people theorize as to why.* Some people respond to the drop in mood by searching for the causes of these emotions. They come up with theory after theory about why they are having the problem. While sometimes this can be useful in preventing the problem from happening again, in general, these theories upon theories are a bad idea. You probably will not find the cause of your emotion because usually there is no single true cause. Even if you did find it, the emotion wouldn't go away. Instead, the main effect of this kind of thinking is to make the dip worse. A better strategy is to focus on action that will take you in a positive direction.
9. *As your mood rises, avoid constant mood checking.* Imagine for weeks you have a sore shoulder. One day you notice that you haven't had any pain for a while. You will probably try to produce the pain by stretching or prodding that part of the body. Your idea is that if the pain comes back, the injury needs more time to heal. If you cannot produce the pain, then you must be cured. You may try the same for depression. You may test yourself by trying to think about the most negative aspects of your life. Sure enough, you will begin to feel worse. Does this mean that you are really still depressed or anxious "underneath it all"? No. Being better won't mean that you *can't* make yourself miserable, only that you don't do so. If depression and anxiety aren't there, don't go looking for it.
10. *As your mood rises, keep your enthusiasm in check.* Mood problems rob you of energy and enthusiasm. Often you don't feel like doing anything. In order to get your enthusiasm back, you needed to reduce your expectations of yourself and set easy, step-by-step goals. Succeeding at these small goals builds your motivation and interest. But then, when your enthusiasm begins to come back, you may fall into a trap. Your eagerness to get better may tempt you to forget all about your easy, step-by-step goals and jump to much bigger goals that are beyond your reach. If you overcommit yourself too early and try to do far too much, you will probably feel overwhelmed and your mood may sink. Remember to scale back your expectations and return to the step-by-step process. Celebrate the return of your enthusiasm, but don't let it get away from you.
11. *Finally, be aware that it is common for patients, once recovered, to silently worry about relapse.* Think about establishing an emergency plan with your family, partner, or a friend just in case you begin to feel unwell again. This plan will include knowing who will notify your doctor and take you to appointments, who will notify your school or work or look after your children, and who will ensure your rent and bills are paid should you need to be hospitalized. You may feel less anxious about the future if you know that a backup plan exists.

Reference

Paterson, R. J. (2002). *Your depression map: Find the source of your depression and chart your own recovery*. Oakland, CA: New Harbinger Publications, Inc.

Appendix H

Leisure Skills Inventory

Activity	*Have done*	*Do now*	*Would like to do*
(A) Sports	☐ Volleyball	☐ Volleyball	☐ Volleyball
	☐ Basketball	☐ Basketball	☐ Basketball
	☐ Tennis	☐ Tennis	☐ Tennis
	☐ Baseball	☐ Baseball	☐ Baseball
	☐ Swimming	☐ Swimming	☐ Swimming
	☐ Hockey	☐ Hockey	☐ Hockey
	☐ Golf	☐ Golf	☐ Golf
	☐ Curling	☐ Curling	☐ Curling
	☐ Skiing—downhill	☐ Skiing—downhill	☐ Skiing—downhill
	☐ Skiing—cross-country	☐ Skiing—cross-country	☐ Skiing—cross-country
	☐ Jogging	☐ Jogging	☐ Jogging
	☐ Bicycling	☐ Bicycling	☐ Bicycling
	☐ Boating, etc.	☐ Boating, etc.	☐ Boating, etc.
	☐ Horseback riding	☐ Horseback riding	☐ Horseback riding
	☐ Football	☐ Football	☐ Football
	☐ Calisthenics	☐ Calisthenics	☐ Calisthenics
	☐ Soccer	☐ Soccer	☐ Soccer
	☐ Archery	☐ Archery	☐ Archery
	☐ Badminton	☐ Badminton	☐ Badminton
	☐ Target, rifle, skeet shooting	☐ Target, Rifle, Skeet Shooting	☐ Target, rifle, skeet shooting

Cognitive Behavioral Group Therapy: Challenges and Opportunities, First Edition. Ingrid Söchting.

(*cont'd*)

Activity	*Have done*	*Do now*	*Would like to do*
	☐ Watching sports	☐ Watching Sports	☐ Watching sports
	☐ Racquetball	☐ Racquetball	☐ Racquetball
	☐ Squash	☐ Squash	☐ Squash
	☐ Weight lifting	☐ Weight lifting	☐ Weight lifting
	☐ Skating	☐ Skating	☐ Skating
List others:			
(B) Nature	☐ Hiking	☐ Hiking	☐ Hiking
	☐ Camping	☐ Camping	☐ Camping
	☐ Walking in parks	☐ Walking in parks	☐ Walking in parks
	☐ Gardening	☐ Gardening	☐ Gardening
	☐ Raising pets	☐ Raising pets	☐ Raising pets
	☐ Indoor plant care	☐ Indoor plant care	☐ Indoor plant care
	☐ Hunting	☐ Hunting	☐ Hunting
	☐ Fishing	☐ Fishing	☐ Fishing
	☐ Trapping	☐ Trapping	☐ Trapping
List others:			
(C) Hobbies and crafts	☐ Sewing	☐ Sewing	☐ Sewing
	☐ Cooking	☐ Cooking	☐ Cooking
	☐ Leather craft	☐ Leather craft	☐ Leather craft
	☐ Macramé	☐ Macramé	☐ Macramé
	☐ Model building	☐ Model building	☐ Model building
	☐ Carpentry/ woodworking	☐ Carpentry/ woodworking	☐ Carpentry/ woodworking
	☐ Knitting	☐ Knitting	☐ Knitting
	☐ Crocheting	☐ Crocheting	☐ Crocheting
	☐ Minor home repairs	☐ Minor home repairs	☐ Minor home repairs
	☐ Interior decorating	☐ Interior decorating	☐ Interior decorating
	☐ Car repairs	☐ Car repairs	☐ Car repairs
	☐ Embroidery/ needlework	☐ Embroidery/ needlework	☐ Embroidery/ needlework
	☐ Weaving	☐ Weaving	☐ Weaving
	☐ Pottery	☐ Pottery	☐ Pottery
	☐ Rug making	☐ Rug making	☐ Rug making
	☐ Furniture refinishing/ upholstery	☐ Furniture refinishing/ upholstery	☐ Furniture refinishing/ upholstery
	☐ Soccer	☐ Soccer	☐ Soccer
	☐ Making candles	☐ Making candles	☐ Making candles
	☐ Metal work	☐ Metal work	☐ Metal work
List others:			
(D) Creative	☐ Painting	☐ Painting	☐ Painting
	☐ Photography	☐ Photography	☐ Photography

(*Continued*)

(cont'd)

Activity	*Have done*	*Do now*	*Would like to do*
	☐ Sculpturing	☐ Sculpturing	☐ Sculpturing
	☐ Creative writing	☐ Creative writing	☐ Creative writing
	☐ Ceramics	☐ Ceramics	☐ Ceramics
	☐ Dancing	☐ Dancing	☐ Dancing
	☐ Stained glass	☐ Stained glass	☐ Stained glass
	☐ Drama	☐ Drama	☐ Drama
	☐ Playing a musical instrument	☐ Playing a musical instrument	☐ Playing a musical instrument
	☐ Writing music	☐ Writing music	☐ Writing music
	☐ Singing	☐ Singing	☐ Singing
	☐ Sketching/drawing	☐ Sketching/drawing	☐ Sketching/drawing
List others:			
(E) Entertainment, social and cultural	☐ Watching TV	☐ Watching TV	☐ Watching TV
	☐ Watching a play or dramatic presentation	☐ Watching a play or dramatic presentation	☐ Watching a play or dramatic presentation
	☐ Going to museums	☐ Going to museums	☐ Going to museums
	☐ Going to art gallery displays	☐ Going to art gallery Displays	☐ Going to art gallery displays
	☐ Shopping for pleasure	☐ Shopping for pleasure	☐ Shopping for pleasure
	☐ Taking an academic course	☐ Taking an academic course	☐ Taking an academic course
	☐ Taking a hobby course	☐ Taking a hobby course	☐ Taking a hobby course
	☐ Visiting friends	☐ Visiting friends	☐ Visiting friends
	☐ Going to a pub	☐ Going to a pub	☐ Going to a pub
	☐ Traveling for pleasure	☐ Traveling for pleasure	☐ Traveling for pleasure
	☐ Reading fiction	☐ Reading fiction	☐ Reading fiction
	☐ Reading non-fiction	☐ Reading non-fiction	☐ Reading non-fiction
	☐ Read newspaper/magazine	☐ Read newspaper/magazine	☐ Read newspaper/magazine
	☐ Attend lectures	☐ Attend lectures	☐ Attend lectures
	☐ Visiting tourist attractions	☐ Visiting tourist attractions	☐ Visiting tourist attractions
	☐ Attending auctions/sales	☐ Attending auctions/sales	☐ Attending auctions/sales
	☐ Going to conservation parks	☐ Going to conservation parks	☐ Going to conservation parks

(cont'd)

Activity	Have done	Do now	Would like to do
	☐ Going to parties	☐ Going to parties	☐ Going to parties
	☐ Dancing at social gatherings	☐ Dancing at social gatherings	☐ Dancing at social gatherings
	☐ Dining out	☐ Dining out	☐ Dining out
	☐ Taking self-improvement course	☐ Taking self-improvement course	☐ Taking self-improvement course
	☐ Attending religious functions	☐ Attending religious functions	☐ Attending religious functions
	☐ Going to movies	☐ Going to movies	☐ Going to movies
	☐ Attending concerts	☐ Attending concerts	☐ Attending concerts
	☐ Listen to radio	☐ Listen to radio	☐ Listen to radio
	☐ Listening to music	☐ Listening to music	☐ Listening to music
List others:			
(F) Clubs and groups	☐ Religious	☐ Religious	☐ Religious
	☐ Sport	☐ Sport	☐ Sport
	☐ Educational	☐ Educational	☐ Educational
	☐ Social	☐ Social	☐ Social
	☐ Ethnic	☐ Ethnic	☐ Ethnic
	☐ Community	☐ Community	☐ Community
	☐ Youth or senior citizens	☐ Youth or senior citizens	☐ Youth or senior citizens
	☐ Political	☐ Political	☐ Political
	☐ Volunteer or service	☐ Volunteer or service	☐ Volunteer or service
	☐ Hobby	☐ Hobby	☐ Hobby
	☐ Cultural	☐ Cultural	☐ Cultural
List others:			
(G) Games	☐ Chess	☐ Chess	☐ Chess
	☐ Checkers	☐ Checkers	☐ Checkers
	☐ Bridge	☐ Bridge	☐ Bridge
	☐ Euchre	☐ Euchre	☐ Euchre
	☐ Other card games	☐ Other card games	☐ Other card games
	☐ Pool	☐ Pool	☐ Pool
	☐ Ping Pong (table tennis)	☐ Ping Pong (table tennis)	☐ Ping Pong (table tennis)
	☐ Horseshoes	☐ Horseshoes	☐ Horseshoes
	☐ Lawn bowling	☐ Lawn bowling	☐ Lawn bowling
	☐ Croquet	☐ Croquet	☐ Croquet
	☐ Charades	☐ Charades	☐ Charades
	☐ Puzzles	☐ Puzzles	☐ Puzzles
	☐ Shuffleboard	☐ Shuffleboard	☐ Shuffleboard

(Continued)

(cont'd)

Activity	*Have done*	*Do now*	*Would like to do*
	☐ Table games (monopoly) ☐ Scrabble ☐ Darts	☐ Table games (monopoly) ☐ Scrabble ☐ Darts	☐ Table games (monopoly) ☐ Scrabble ☐ Darts
List others:			
(H) Collection	☐ Coins ☐ Stamps ☐ Antiques ☐ Cars ☐ Art ☐ Autographs ☐ Pictures ☐ Stones/Shells ☐ Records/CDs/ Cassettes/DVD	☐ Coins ☐ Stamps ☐ Antiques ☐ Cars ☐ China ☐ Autographs ☐ Pictures ☐ Stones/Shells ☐ Records/CDs/ Cassettes/DVD	☐ Coins ☐ Stamps ☐ Antiques ☐ Cars ☐ China ☐ Autographs ☐ Pictures ☐ Stones/Shells ☐ Records/CDs/ Cassettes/DVD
List others:			
(I) Volunteer services	☐ Hospital/health services ☐ People with disabilities ☐ Service groups (lion's) ☐ Recreation/ entertainment ☐ Clerical/office work ☐ Administrative ☐ Fund raising/ collection ☐ Publicity/ advertisement	☐ Hospital/health services ☐ People with disabilities ☐ Service groups (lion's) ☐ Recreation/ entertainment ☐ Clerical/office work ☐ Administrative ☐ Fund raising/ collection ☐ Publicity/ advertisement	☐ Hospital/health services ☐ People with disabilities ☐ Service groups (lion's) ☐ Recreation/ entertainment ☐ Clerical/office work ☐ Administrative ☐ Fund Raising/ collection ☐ Publicity/ advertisement
List others:			

Appendix I

Functional Analysis

Situation	*Thoughts/feelings/ behaviors*	*How I coped*	*Positive consequences*	*Negative consequences*

Cognitive Behavioral Group Therapy: Challenges and Opportunities, First Edition. Ingrid Söchting.

Appendix J

Screen for CBGT Intake Assessment

Depression

1. During the past 12 months have you had significant problems with feeling lonely, sad, depressed, or hopeless about your future?
2. Changes in sleep—too much, too little?
3. Changes in appetite—eating too much, too little; weight changes?
4. Changes in energy?
5. Changes in interest/motivation?
6. Do you blame yourself for anything or feel guilty?
7. Do you feel worthless?
8. Concentration? Slowed thinking or indecisiveness?
9. Recurrent thoughts of death or of harming yourself? How much do you think about it? Determine attempts, frequency, plan, prior attempts, and recent thoughts?
10. How would you rate your mood from a scale of 1–10?

Manic episodes

1. Have there been times when you have felt unusually energetic and self-confident?
2. Did you have a feeling of being especially connected to other people and the world?
3. Did you sleep very little for more than 3 days?
4. Did you have great ideas for projects or did you find yourself starting projects, or shopping or lot, spending lots of money or taking out a loan?

Cognitive Behavioral Group Therapy: Challenges and Opportunities, First Edition. Ingrid Söchting.

Panic disorder

1. In the past month, have you had times when you felt a sudden rush of intense fear or discomfort?
2. Do you experience palpitations, sweating, trembling, shortness of breath, chest pain, nausea, chills or hot flushes, dizziness, feelings of unreality, fear of dying?
3. How many attacks in the past month?
4. Are you worried about another attack?
5. Have you avoided certain places fearing a panic attack?

Social anxiety

1. In the past month, have you felt anxious when you're the center of attention, or have to perform in front of others?
2. Do you get anxious when you write, read, or do something in front of others?
3. Do you avoid social situations out of a fear of embarrassing or humiliating yourself?

Generalized anxiety disorder

1. In the past month, have you continually worried or been anxious about a number of minor or larger matters in your daily life?
2. What kinds of things do you worry about?
3. Do you feel restless, keyed up or on edge?
4. Are you easily fatigued?
5. Do you have trouble sleeping?

Obsessive compulsive and related disorder

1. In the past month, have you been bothered by thoughts, images, or impulses that keep recurring to you and that seem inappropriate or nonsensical but that you can't stop from coming into your mind?
2. Do you feel driven to repeat some behaviors or to repeat something in your mind over and over again to try to feel less uncomfortable?
3. Do you wash or clean a lot?
4. Are you concerned about things being done in a certain, orderly way?

Body dysmorphic disorder

1. Do you think you have a minor flaw in your physical appearance that is not observable or appear slight to others?
2. Do you do a lot of checking in mirrors, or picking of your skin, or perform certain mental acts such as comparing your appearance with that of others?

Hair-pulling disorder (trichotillomania)

1. Do you pull out hair from you scalp or other places on your body?

Skin-picking disorder (excoriation)

1. Do you pick at your skin so that it causes lesions?

Hoarding disorder

1. Do you have trouble parting with possessions regardless of their actual value?
2. Do you have a lot of stuff that makes it difficult to use the rooms or spaces in your house for their purpose?
3. Do you think this is a problem you would like some help with?

Posttraumatic stress

1. Have you ever experienced or witnessed a traumatic event such as physical or sexual assault, accident, or seeing someone badly injured or killed?
2. Do you avoid thinking and talking about this event?
3. Do you feel emotionally distant from others?
4. Do you feel irritable and have outbursts of anger?

Addictions

1. Have other people commented on your drinking/drug taking or gambling?
2. Do you feel a need to cut down on your drinking/drug taking/gambling?
3. Do you use alcohol/drugs/gambling as ways of coping with some problems in your life such as anxiety or depression?

Psychosis

1. Do you sometimes feel that people are talking about you or taking special notice?
2. Has someone got out of their way to give you a hard time or plot to hurt you?
3. Have you ever received special messages from the TV, radio, or from the way things were arranged around you?
4. Did you ever feel that you were especially important or had the power to do things that other people couldn't do?
5. Have you ever felt that something or someone outside of yourself was controlling your thoughts or actions against your will?
6. Did you ever see, feel, or hear things that other people don't?

Author Index

Cognitive Behavioral Group Therapy: Challenges and Opportunities, First Edition. Ingrid Söchting.

Subject Index

Cognitive Behavioral Group Therapy: Challenges and Opportunities, First Edition. Ingrid Söchting.